TOURISM POLICY AND INTERNATIONAL TOURISM

IN OECD COUNTRIES

1990-1991

LHBEC

ORGANISATION FOR ECONOMIC CO-OPERATION AND DEVELOPMENT

ORGANISATION FOR ECONOMIC CO-OPERATION AND DEVELOPMENT

Pursuant to Article 1 of the Convention signed in Paris on 14th December 1960, and which came into force on 30th September 1961, the Organisation for Economic Co-operation and Development (OECD) shall promote policies designed:

— to achieve the highest sustainable economic growth and employment and a rising standard of living in Member countries, while maintaining financial stability, and thus to contribute to the development of the world economy;

— to contribute to sound economic expansion in Member as well as non-member countries in the process of economic development; and

— to contribute to the expansion of world trade on a multilateral, non-discriminatory basis in accordance with international obligations.

The original Member countries of the OECD are Austria, Belgium, Canada, Denmark, France, Germany, Greece, Iceland, Ireland, Italy, Luxembourg, the Netherlands, Norway, Portugal, Spain, Sweden, Switzerland, Turkey, the United Kingdom and the United States. The following countries became Members subsequently through accession at the dates indicated hereafter: Japan (28th April 1964), Finland (28th January 1969), Australia (7th June 1971) and New Zealand (29th May 1973). The Commission of the European Communities takes part in the work of the OECD (Article 13 of the OECD Convention).

Publié en français sous le titre :

POLITIQUE DU TOURISME
ET TOURISME INTERNATIONAL DANS LES PAYS DE L'OCDE
1990-1991

FOREWORD

The Tourism Committee has, for more than thirty years, published information on government policies in the field of tourism. This has been accompanied by statistics on recent trends in the development of international tourism in the OECD area.

Chapter I of this annual report generally examines each Member country's policy and action in the field of tourism and analyses them in a more general economic context. Every two or three years, however, this alternates with a presentation in this chapter of a policy issue which is of common interest to Member countries. Thus, the 1990 issue examined the possible future influence on tourism of the developments in transport policies.

Chapter I of the present issue summarises the discussion held by the Committee at its June 1992 meeting on state involvement in tourism promotion.

The discussion which launches a long term project of the Tourism Committee on a subject of essential interest for tourism policy officials, was based on case studies describing experiences in Austria, Spain, the United States, France, the United Kingdom and Sweden. It provided a number of preliminary insights into the justification for government involvement in this field; it also made it possible to outline various aspects deserving a more thorough analysis before a common policy can be developed. Such a common policy is the aim of the Committee's discussions.

Chapters II and III and the Statistical Annex study the evolution of international tourism supply and demand in OECD Member countries and outline the trends observed in 1990 and 1991.

The report was adopted by the Tourism Committee which recommended its derestriction by the Council. The OECD Council decided on 24th February 1993 to make it publicly available.

TABLE OF CONTENTS

Chapter I

GOVERNMENT INVOLVEMENT IN TOURISM PROMOTION

Chapter II

INTERNATIONAL TOURIST FLOWS IN MEMBER COUNTRIES

Chapter III

THE ECONOMIC IMPORTANCE OF INTERNATIONAL TOURISM IN MEMBER COUNTRIES

Introduction

TRENDS IN INTERNATIONAL TOURISM IN THE OECD AREA

MAIN DEVELOPMENTS

Despite an unfavourable situation as a result of the Gulf war, the start of the Yugoslav crisis, upheavals in central and eastern European countries and a rather gloomy economic situation, the trend in international tourism in the OECD area in 1991 was on the positive side, even if all available data points to a slowdown:

-- Arrivals at frontiers: up 2 per cent (compared with a 4 per cent increase in the previous year);
-- Nights spent in various forms of accommodation: down 1 per cent (compared with an increase of 3 per cent);
-- Receipts in real terms: up 1 per cent (compared with 7 per cent);
-- Receipts in current dollars: up 3 per cent to $194 billion in 1991 (against $188 billion in 1990).

In the OECD area, Europe was the hardest hit by the effects of the political and economic difficulties in 1991, despite the efforts of the government and tourist authorities to cushion them. The countries that suffered most were Turkey (down 27 per cent in nights spent in all forms of accommodation), the United Kingdom (down 8 per cent), Greece (down 16 per cent) and Sweden (down 14 per cent); on the other hand, Portugal, Denmark and Spain avoided the worst.

North America saw a marked increase in arrivals (+ 5 per cent), mainly in the United States as a result of the weaker dollar and the diversion of tourists to that country from destinations affected by the Gulf war.

Despite a slowdown in growth, tourist travel to Australasia-Japan again increased due to heavy inter-regional flows and to the Dynamic Asian Economies.

During this period, tourist activity, which had been affected by political tensions and economic difficulties, thus developed (+ 7 per cent in arrivals at frontiers) mainly on the intra-regional front, to the detriment of long-distance air travel, while the question of security remained decisive in the expansion of international tourism.

The countries whose international tourist traffic was in fact most affected were those close to the danger zones such as Greece, Turkey and Italy, plus some traditional destinations for the more security-conscious North American and Japanese travellers, e.g. the United Kingdom, Switzerland, Germany and Finland. In the case of Sweden, the explanation for its poor performance in 1991 is that this latter factor was compounded by the effect of a bleak economic situation its main markets and high prices.

For a number of OECD Member countries, however, 1991 does not seem to have been marked by a general decline in international tourism.

Trend of international tourism in the OECD area

Per cent change over previous year

	Arrivals at frontiers[1]		Nights spent in means of accommodation[2]		Receipts in national currency		Receipts in real terms[3]	
	% 90/89	% 91/90	% 90/89	% 91/90	% 90/89	% 91/90	% 90/89	% 91/90
Austria			−0.2	5.1	7.5	6.9	4.1	3.4
Belgium[4]			5.9		1.8	0.4	−1.6	−2.7
Denmark			8.9	11.7	21.6	8.1	18.3	5.3
Finland			−2.0	−10.8	2.5	7.9	−3.3	3.6
France	6.0	4.4	3.8	2.3	6.1	9.7	2.6	6.3
Germany[6]			3.8	−4.6	6.9	2.4	4.1	−1.0
Greece	9.8	−9.6	6.3	−15.9	25.4	17.9	4.1	−0.8
Iceland	8.2	1.1			15.9	−2.5	0.3	−8.7
Ireland	12.3	−2.3	7.4	−1.2	15.9	7.3	12.2	4.0
Italy[7]	2.9	−1.0	−2.5	3.1	43.9	−3.4	35.6	−9.3
Luxembourg[4]			5.8	−0.4	1.8	0.4	−1.6	−2.7
Netherlands			16.1	4.5	1.7	15.8	−0.8	11.5
Norway			5.4	8.0	4.8	12.7	0.7	9.0
Portugal	12.7	7.9	6.1	13.5	18.4	7.3	4.4	−3.6
Spain	−3.7	2.8	−8.4	3.8	−2.4	6.0	−8.5	0.1
Sweden			−13.3	−13.9	4.9	−3.9	−5.1	−12.1
Switzerland	4.8	−4.5	2.6	0.3	3.5	7.4	−1.8	1.5
Turkey	20.9	2.4	11.8	−26.9	52.3	31.6	−5.0	−20.7
United Kingdom	3.9	−7.5	4.8	−7.9	12.8	−8.5	3.0	−13.6
EUROPE[5]	3.3	0.7	2.5	−0.4			4.7	−1.7
Canada	0.7	−1.8			9.7	3.1	4.7	−2.4
United States	8.1	8.0			18.7	12.3	12.6	7.7
NORTH AMERICA	5.9	5.3					11.8	6.7
Australia	6.5	7.0	16.9	−1.1	17.9	9.8	9.9	6.4
New Zealand	8.3	−1.3	9.5	−6.6	12.0	2.5	6.5	−0.1
Japan	14.2	9.2			19.1	−10.9	15.5	−13.7
AUSTRALASIA-JAPAN[5]	10.5	6.9	15.0	−2.4			11.8	−4.0
OECD[5]	4.0	1.9	3.4	−0.6			7.1	0.8

1. Arrivals of tourists except in Australia, Ireland, Japan, Spain, Turkey and United kingdom where arrivals concern visitors.
2. Nights spent in all means of accommodation except in Finland, Luxembourg and Spain where nights spent concern hotels and similar establishments.
3. After correcting for the effects of inflation. For the regional and OECD totals, the receipts of the individual countries are weighted in proportion to their share in the total expressed in dollars.
4. Receipts apply to both Belgium and Luxembourg.
5. Overall trends for countries with data available from 1989 to 1991.
6. The data relate to the territory of the Federal Republic of Germany prior to 3rd October 1990.
7. Break of series (for payments only) in 1990 due to the liberalisation of capital movements.

In Europe, the trend was definitely positive in five countries: Austria, Denmark, Spain which returned to its growth curve, Norway mainly owing to European demand, and Portugal which recorded a significant upturn in 1991.

Then come the European countries which recorded uneven though generally satisfactory results: France where nights in hotels were down 5 per cent, apparently as a result of a shift on the part of its clientele to other forms of accommodation, since nights spent in all forms of accommodation were up (by 2 per cent), as were tourist arrivals at frontiers (by 4 per cent); the Netherlands also recorded an increase of 5 per cent in nights spent in all forms of accommodation and one of 1 per cent in arrivals in various forms of accommodation, although the number of nights spent in hotels was virtually stationary (down 1 per cent).

In North America, arrivals at frontiers in the United States rose at the same pace (up 8 per cent) as in 1990 in the case of travellers from Mexico (up 6 per cent), Japan (up 3 per cent), the United Kingdom (up 11 per cent), Germany (up 19 per cent) and Canada (up 10 per cent); however, decreases were recorded particularly for travellers from the Scandinavian countries (down 8 per cent).

Canada had a generally disappointing year in 1991 with a downturn in arrivals of tourists at frontiers (2 per cent). Its traditional markets showed a decline (Japan and the United Kingdom, down 4 per cent; Asia/Oceania, down 8 per cent) and this has not yet been offset by the growth in travel from certain European countries (France up 18 per cent and Germany up 8 per cent).

In the Pacific region, Japan has seen a sharp increase in arrivals at frontiers (up by 9 per cent in 1991 after a rise of 14 per cent in 1990), mainly from non-Member countries (up 15 per cent). For its part, Australia set a new record for arrivals at frontiers in 1991 (up 7 per cent), these coming mainly from Japan, New Zealand, the United States and Asia, while the European market was down. In the case of New Zealand, the year 1991 was disappointing with a decrease in both arrivals at frontiers (down 1 per cent) and in nights spent in various forms of accommodation (down 7 per cent), with most of its main markets in the OECD area showing a decline except for Japan (up 8 per cent); only the Asian markets showed an increase.

The picture for the main generating countries is also varied. The highest growth in terms of nights spent was recorded in the case of travel by Germans to almost all the countries in the OECD area (except Turkey, down 18 per cent; Sweden, down 6 per cent and Japan, down 6 per cent in arrivals) and Italians who travelled more to all the OECD Member countries (nights spent in Europe up 15 per cent, with arrivals up 17 per cent in North America and up 1 per cent in Australasia and Japan).

Although Canadians travelled more in 1991, mainly to the United States, their trips overseas were generally fewer, significantly so to Europe (down 49 per cent in arrivals to Turkey, 37 per cent to Greece and 26 per cent to the United Kingdom).

The French travelled less to Turkey (nights spent in the country down 60 per cent), to the United Kingdom (nights spent down 13 per cent) and to Germany (down 5 per cent), but more to Norway (up 22 per cent) and Portugal (up 13 per cent); outside Europe, they also travelled more to Canada and New Zealand but less to Japan (down 2 per cent).

The decreases in travel abroad among the main generating countries included flows from Japan (particularly as a result of government recommendations), the Netherlands (a marked decrease of 10 per cent in nights spent in France), the United Kingdom (mainly travel to Europe, with the exception of Portugal, Norway and Netherlands).

The tourism balance sheet was still in the red in 1991 ($6 billion), even if the deficit was less than the previous year since the increase in receipts exceeded that of expenditure in all the OECD regions.

International tourism receipts expressed in real terms were up 1 per cent in the OECD area as a whole (compared with a 7 per cent rise in the two previous years); growth was fuelled by North America (up 7 per cent) but receipts were down in Australasia-Japan (by 4 per cent) and in Europe (by 2 per cent).

In all, the OECD area spent about $200 billion in 1991 on international tourism, or 1 per cent less than in 1990. Expenditure expressed in current dollars rose only in North America (by 1 per cent) as a result of increased spending by Canadians, while it was down in Australasia-Japan (by 2 per cent) and in Europe (by 1 per cent).

With the uncertainties which affected tourism in 1991, the part played by the authorities in promoting this activity came increasingly under the spotlight; questions as to the justification for this intervention also became more pointed.

Although the importance of tourism in national economies has for a long time been seen as a justification for action by the authorities, the reasons for such action have been challenged for some years now on a number of ideological and budgetary grounds.

With the aim of enlightening the competent authorities in OECD Member countries and helping them to define a line of conduct in this regard, the OECD Tourism Committee has decided to study this question, particularly in the context of national experience.

The Committee debated the issue for the first time in June 1992, on the basis of case studies presented by Austria, France, Spain, Sweden, the United Kingdom and the United States; these studies described government experience in these countries and focused mainly on the various aspects of action by the authorities to promote tourism; they also discussed the economic and social justifications for such action.

A summary of the discussions is presented along with the case studies in Chapter I. It is the start of an analysis which the Committee intends to pursue of this crucial issue concerning the justification for the government's role and the possibility for the tourist industry to take over, within limits still to be defined, government action for the promotion of tourism.

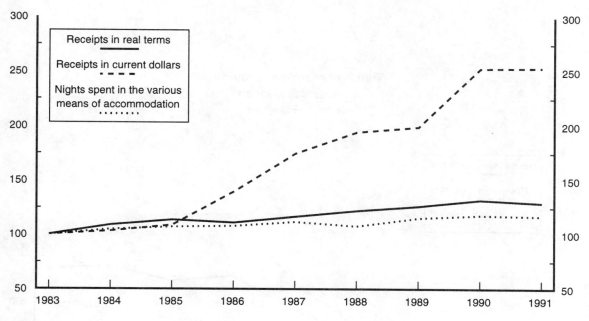

Trends of international tourism
in Europe
(Indices 1983 = 100)

Receipts in real terms

Receipts in current dollars

Nights spent in the various
means of accommodation

Source: OECD

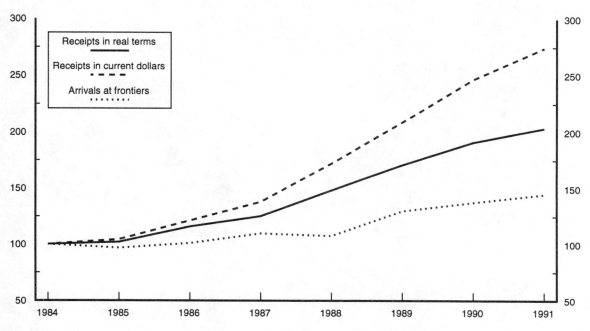

Trends of international tourism
in North America
(Indices 1984 = 100)

Receipts in real terms

Receipts in current dollars

Arrivals at frontiers

Source: OECD

Trends of international tourism
in Australasia-Japan
(Indices 1983 = 100)

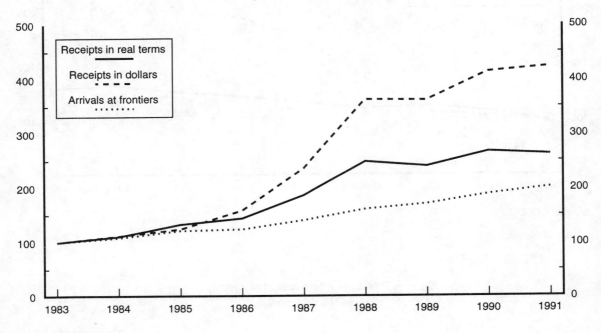

Source: OECD

Chapter I

GOVERNMENT INVOLVEMENT IN TOURISM PROMOTION

I. INTRODUCTION

Whether measured in terms of foreign exchange revenues, capital investment or employment, tourism is a major contributor to national economies. It also helps promote regional development and, more significantly, the development of poorer regions which might not survive economically without tourism.

OECD Member countries have always participated, either directly or indirectly, in the development of their tourism sector. Over the past few years, however, the rationale for their involvement in the promotion of their countries as tourist destinations has been increasingly questioned.

This re-examination has also been in response to political and economic developments, notably the liberalisation of political systems and privatisation, which have encouraged much closer scrutiny of activities traditionally undertaken by the public sector. As a result, many national tourism agencies (NTAs) have been facing growing difficulties in planning, financing and performing the tasks involved in national tourism promotion.

With the growing climate of liberalisation, many governments around the world have recently been questioning the rationale for their continuing involvement in and financing of national tourism promotion. The belief in market forces and privatisation has encouraged governments to reduce and, in one case, even to relinquish their role in tourism promotion. Instead, there appears to be an increasing move towards market responsive and private sector driven national tourism organisations or structures.

This change in thinking is partly motivated by increasing constraints on government budgets and the need to find ways of curbing public expenditure. Can governments continue to justify the use of taxpayers' money to support and promote tourism development when, in most Member countries, there is no such funding and support of other industries? Would it not perhaps be more cost effective to invest funds directly in the smaller, poorer regions of their countries and in small and medium-sized enterprises (SME), rather than through the tourism sector? More importantly, is government involvement in tourism promotion legitimate in the general context of the General Agreement on Tariffs and Trade (GATT), or does it risk being interpreted as a trade distorting activity?

These issues are compounded by the fact that traditional points of reference are no longer valid, whether they be political, sociological or economic. The political developments in Central and Eastern Europe at the end of the 1980s and early 1990s -- from the fall of the Berlin wall to the collapse of the Soviet Union and the centrally planned economies in other East European countries -- heralded a political and economic shift to market driven economies. In addition, with the current trends towards globalisation and concentration of the industry, what were formerly national private sector organisations are increasingly becoming multinational concerns. So government support of the industry is no longer necessarily purely in national interests.

Concern over these issues has also been voiced by other intergovernmental and international organisations and associations, such as the World Tourism Organisation (WTO), and by regional industry bodies such as the European Travel Commission (ETC) and the Pacific Asia Travel Association

(PATA). The OECD Tourism Committee believes it can be a catalyst in addressing the issue of governments' role in the tourism sector.

In an effort to assist governments in their decision-making process, the OECD Tourism Committee therefore decided in 1991 to study the issue more closely. A preliminary discussion on the subject was held during its 61st Session, in November of that year, based on a document prepared by the delegate for Australia. It was decided to address the issue in more depth during its 62nd Session (June 21-23 1992). The ultimate objective of these discussions within the committee, which were open to other interested parties -- such as NTAs and the operating sector of the industry -- was to draw common lines that governments could use in their decision-making process regarding the role of states in tourism promotion and the ways in which it is funded.

As a basis for the planned discussions, case studies were presented by six OECD Member countries, namely Austria, France, Spain, Sweden, the United Kingdom and the United States (see annexes).

These case studies highlighted the experiences of their respective governments, focusing primarily on the policy aspects of government intervention in tourism promotion. Technical details were also covered, including the economic and social rationale for governments' involvement in this field, the priority areas of activity and the role of the private sector.

II. LESSONS TO BE DRAWN FROM MEMBER COUNTRIES' EXPERIENCES

The six case studies (see annexes), together with the open discussions that followed, highlighted the lack of homogeneity in OECD Member countries' policies regarding the public sector role in national tourism promotion. Not only is there widely different legislation in some of the countries surveyed, but responsibility for tourism comes under a variety of different ministries - from employment and trade to national heritage. Not all OECD Member countries have ministers of tourism, either, and Australia is the only OECD Member Country in which tourism enjoys a full portfolio.

The varying importance attributed to the industry in a country's marketing strategy and plan is noticeable. There are a number of lessons to be learned from countries' experiences and they provide a useful basis for future discussions.

1. Countries' objectives in tourism promotion

There are three primary reasons for government involvement in national tourism promotion: to promote the image of the nation as a whole, to maximise potential benefits for the national economy, and to offset market failures.

Image building

A country's image is seen as an integral part of the its overall economic development and tourism is not the only industry to be influenced by the image of the country. It is therefore, the responsibility of a country's government to build an image which matches the aspirations of the citizens of the country. In addition, only the government is able to make the necessary financial investment to build this image.

Thus the UK is not alone in believing that if there were no central, or federal government activity in the area of national tourism promotion, the promotion of the country overall as a tourist destination would simply not occur. It is not in the commercial interests of any single group of firms to invest in promoting the generic image of the country, because the returns from such promotion would be widely and uncertainly spread among direct competitors and other sectors. Left to themselves, local and regional authorities and the private sector would focus on their own interests, promoting specific regions within the country, or specific sectors of the industry.

Maximum benefits for the national economy

There are subtle differences in the roles assumed by respective governments. Some -- like France, the USA and Australia -- are involved in domestic as well as international tourism promotion; others are not. But the end goals are more or less the same for all countries: an optimum balance of payments on the country's travel and tourism account. The prime method of achieving this goal is by maximising international tourist receipts. But Member countries also recognise that by promoting domestic tourism, they are effectively also discouraging expenditure on travel abroad (import substitution).

Japan should be mentioned as an exception to the general rule since, with its trade surplus still a contentious issue in international circles, one of the government's policies is to encourage outbound travel by Japanese to improve international balance of payments.

Offsetting market failures

Market failures -- whether in promotion, product development, or the provision of information -- are exacerbated by the fact that the industry is fragmented. Companies benefiting from tourism are drawn from several sectors, and there is a preponderance of SMEs. This means that the industry has difficulty in taking the kind of cooperative action necessary to exploit market opportunities fully. Thus, NTAs act as regulators, helping to promote fair competition and foster the growth of SMEs and poorer regions of their countries.

2. The role of government

While there appears to be a general consensus of opinion on the broad role of government intervention in tourism, two case studies reflect the extremes in thinking. Most NTAs are funded partly by central government, partly by regional or local authorities, and partly by the private sector. However, Turespaña, the national institute of tourism promotion in Spain, which has been linked to the Department of Industry and Trade since 1991, derives its core funding totally from public sources, except for some revenues generated by its own commercial activities.

Sweden, in contrast, has adopted a new policy regarding tourism since the end of 1991, the basic principle of which is that the tourism sector should be treated as any other branch of industry, and the individual enterprise should be fully responsible for its destiny. The government's role is simply to create general conditions that are favourable to business and interventions in markets should be limited to a minimum. Only in one respect does the Swedish government see justification in involving public sector efforts. This is in the case of more general promotional activities abroad which would benefit tourism and other Swedish industries.

Despite the fact that the Swedish government has disbanded the Swedish Tourist Board, thus sharply reducing its role in national tourism promotion, it has still allocated financial resources of around $15 million for the fiscal year 1992/93 for the professional marketing of Sweden and particularly, the promotion of tourism. This compares with a total budget for the Swedish Tourism Board of about $20 million in 1991/92. The resources are being channelled through a new governmental body, Image Sweden.

However, while this body is responsible for the strategic planning of the promotional activities and market performance evaluations, these governmental efforts must be carried out together with and through private operators, and the latter must assume responsibility for these at the operational level. The country's tourism sector has since formed a joint enterprise called Swedish Travel and Tourism Council Inc. (Swedrac) to take on the private sector role, but the Swedish Trade Council and the

Swedish Institute might also be suppliers of services to Image Sweden. The governmental body will not operate any offices abroad, although Swetrac could well establish this kind of representation if it were deemed necessary.

Between those two extremes, there are other examples of approaches taken by member countries:

-- One of the key functions of the US Travel & Tourism Administration (USTTA) is to educate regional authorities and the private sector in the 50 states of the USA on how to develop good value, sustainable tourism products and how to promote their products and services abroad. It works closely with the regional authorities, despite the fact that the latter have their own individual territorial budgets - of between $4 million to $12 million a year - and act autonomously in terms of deciding their budgets and their promotional activities.

-- The Austrian National Tourist Office (ANTO) believes its role is to support, or act as a service agency for the country's tourism industry.

-- Maison de la France, the promotional arm of the French Ministry of Tourism, refers to itself as a grouping of economic interests - or a partnership linking the interests of the state, local communities and the operating sector, whether totally private or parastatal. It conducts domestic as well as international tourism promotion and marketing and provides information services to the travelling public.

-- In the United Kingdom, the British Tourist Authority (BTA) works alongside the country's twelve regional tourism boards to promote the country as a tourist destination overseas. However it relies heavily on private sector support to fund promotional campaigns and other activities. The British government funds the BTA because it acknowledges that there are market failures in the tourism industry. This rationale, although not expressed in the same terms, is the basis for a number of other countries' support of tourism.

3. Role of the private sector

While other OECD Member countries have also been reassessing their financial contributions to national tourism promotion, none has so far taken such a major step as Sweden. However the level of public sector funding in the sector does vary widely from country to country.

Some NTAs rely on industry contributions mainly for marketing, advertising and the funding of special promotional campaigns. Others, such as the BTA and Maison de la France, count on private sector funding for their core budgets. Consequently, private enterprise has a far greater say in the development of tourism policy and NTA operational strategies, as well as in how the overall budgets are spent.

As an example, Maison de la France groups some 850 different companies in its membership. Since this is up from only 40 in its first year of existence, in 1986, the structure has clearly found favour with the industry. Its General Assembly, headed by France's Minister of Tourism, approves the organisations's budget and its 27-strong Administrative Council, which is elected from the membership every two years - with only nine public sector participants - defines Maison de la France's strategy in the framework of the generally defined French government tourism policy. Some of its services to members are free of charge, others are provided on a user pays basis. These are generally offered through participation in special "clubs", grouping members interested in specific sectors or products.

4. National tourism agency budgets

NTA budgets, according to the case studies presented, appear to bear little relation to the volume of visitor arrivals or receipts registered by their respective countries. However, comparisons are not really meaningful since the structure of tourism budgets varies considerably from country to country. Some include the salaries of staff in the home countries; others do not. Some cover domestic as well as international tourism promotion. Some cover policy and planning staff and activities as well as marketing and promotions, as in the case of Spain and the USA.

The USTTA, which has a total of 94 staff, 50 of whom in regional offices and in nine countries abroad, has one of the lowest annual budgets from central government, especially in view of the fact that it has to cover tourism planning and policy. Its budget has effectively remained static over the past couple of years, passing from $20.6 million in 1991 to $17.4 million in 1992 (including $5 million and $2 million in each respective year allocated as special disaster relief grants), and to a planned $17.4 million in 1993. In addition, however, the USTTA generates up to $15 million or so a year in corporate funding by using seed money to lever funds from the private sector. Depending on the project concerned, this can attract up to 20 times the basic seed money. It also earns some $1.5 million from services to the travel industry, which it tries to ensure is ploughed back into its budget.

The BTA has one of the largest overall national tourism promotion budgets, considering the fact that the twelve regional tourist boards in the UK -- not to mention those of England, Scotland, Wales and Northern Ireland -- operate autonomously, albeit collaborating with the BTA in overseas promotions. BTA maintains a staff of close to 400, 183 of whom are based abroad in 29 overseas offices and seven additional representative agencies. In the fiscal year 1991/92, its total budget was £44.6 million ($84.7 million), up 9.6 per cent over the previous year. A further 9.9 per cent increase was planned for 1992/93. However, government funding accounts for less than two-thirds of the overall budget and the share has fallen from 60 per cent in 1990/91. The balance comes primarily from industry, but it also includes a share of funding from local authorities.

ANTO, the Austrian national tourist office, has 271 staff, 180 of whom are abroad in its own tourist offices or as tourism managers within Austrian trade delegations. Since ANTO is not involved in policy and planning, its budget of Sch 499 million in 1992 ($ 47 356 000) - representing an increase of 3 per cent a year over the previous two years - is exclusively for marketing and promotions. The total includes Sch. 24 million from the interests on its bank balance, sponsorship, the proceeds of barriers agreements, etc. The budget is funded 60 per cent by the Austrian Federal Ministry of Foreign Affairs, 20 per cent by the Federal Chamber of Commerce, and 20 per cent by nine provinces. These shares are, nevertheless, renegotiated every year for each planned budget increase.

Turespaña, which has 183 staff abroad out of a total 595, including 104 civil servants, had a budget of Pta 8 547 million ($89 million) in 1992 - a 17.1 per cent increase over 1991 - with 72 per cent of it coming from central government and the balance from the sale of services and products (Congress Centers and Publications). Spain is one of the few OECD Member states that permits commercial activities by its NTA. In many other countries, the non-profit status of NTAs excludes them from generating revenues from such sources.

Maison de la France currently has a staff of 270, with 200 spread through 38 French government tourist offices abroad. In 1992, its total budget was FF 380 million ($76 million), representing an increase of 0.8 per cent over the previous year. It should be noted, however, that 1991's increase was 24.6 per cent over 1990. The government share of funding has fallen from 63 per cent to 55 per cent over the last three years. Of the 45 per cent non-central government share in 1992, 25 per cent came from regional and local authorities and 20 per cent from the private sector. State participation is not expected to fall any further.

By way of comparison, it is interesting to note that the Australian Tourist Commission (ATC) received A$ 69.4 million in its central government funded budget in the fiscal year 1991/92, supplemented by revenue from industry of $24.8million. An 18 per cent increase in government funding has been approved for 1992/93 to A$76.1million, with a further A$29.4million expected to be generated from alternative sources, such as the ATC's cooperative marketing schemes.

The Norwegian Tourist Board operates with a budget of around $20 million a year, of which 50 per cent is funded by government and 50 per cent by industry contributions.

5.   Breakdown of budget spending

Once again, it is difficult to make comparisons between the different NTA budget spending priorities, since accounting methods are not standard. Fixed costs are usually considered to include administration, overheads, staff and other operational commitments not directly related to promotional activities. In the case of the British Tourist Authority's budget, staff costs in the UK are excluded. The allocation for overseas offices, on the other hand, represents some 24 per cent of the total 1992/93 budget for the organisation.

Staff costs for the USTTA include $1.6 million for staff in the USA, plus $6.5 million for those abroad, thus totalling around 47 per cent of its overall budget of $17.4 million. Some 70 per cent of ANTO's budget goes in fixed costs, with half of this related to staff salaries. In contrast, less than 20 per cent of Turespaña's budget is for fixed costs such as personnel. For Maison de la France, the respective share is just 6 per cent.

Variable costs generally include sales promotions and marketing activities, the production of brochures and other printed and photographic/video material, participation in trade fairs, educational programmes, market research and advertising.

Advertising and marketing account for the highest share of variable costs. For the BTA, the share is over 40 per cent, with 16 per cent for advertising alone. For Maison de la France, advertising accounts for around 30 per cent, for Turespaña 31 per cent, and for ANTO 21 per cent. International advertising may take the form of press, television or radio campaigns promoting the country, but is often carried out in cooperation with commercial partners.

Joint marketing is likely to be focused on a particular type of product, such as country house hotels, winter sports' resorts, or short weekend breaks. BTA's policy is to kick-start the campaign, but to leave it to the industry to take full responsibility for it after a couple of years. Marketing also includes workshops - to put the foreign travel trade in touch with local suppliers - and public relations, including familiarisation trips for the trade and media.

For most of the case studies presented, both advertising and sales promotions are undertaken on a co-operative basis. This means that the national tourism agency puts up seed money and depends on generating the bulk of funding from the industry or from local and regional authorities. The total amount of additional funds generated can be as much as 20 times the original seed money. Co-operative programmes are also carried out for participation in trade and public travel fairs, special promotional campaigns and educational activities. The BTA has a target of 66 per cent industry contribution to joint marketing activities. Some agencies, such as Turespaña, also support individual companies in the private sector in their sales promotions abroad without asking for a financial contribution.

6.   Measuring performance

Responsibility for the use of public funds dictates that government actions meet the criteria of visibility, accountability and control. Government outlays must be open to scrutiny. It is therefore understandable that one of the key concerns among governments with regard to national tourism promotion is whether public expenditure generally provides value for money. The majority of governments are increasingly expecting some kind of formal and quantified performance measurement or evaluation.

Monitoring activities to measure intermediate outputs is fairly widespread. Since many promotional campaigns are conducted with industry partners, it is possible to gain some idea of the effect of the campaign from increases in the partners' business over and above projected levels. The image of an NTA within its own national industry or in international circles, can be ascertained by its success in gaining industry awards. It is also possible to measure the impact of campaigns in terms of the coupon response to advertising, or the telephone enquiries generated. Ongoing, or ad hoc surveys also indicate how many foreign visitors obtained information from the NTA before travelling to the country, and whether it was useful information.

However, measurement of intermediate outputs does not indicate whether the NTA itself is meeting its objectives and providing value for money. While it is much more difficult to isolate the impact of national tourism promotion from other influences on the travel and tourism market - such as currency fluctuations, political and economic developments - most OECD Member country NTAs have at least started to develop evaluation strategies based on their primary objectives, i.e. increasing tourism receipts, increasing geographic and seasonal spread, etc. These strategies invariably depend on close collaboration between the NTA's marketing and research divisions. Attempts have been and are being made to evaluate the impact and cost effectiveness of each marketing and promotional activity. However, there are as yet few concrete results from such initiatives.

The BTA has recently embarked on an evaluation strategy, during which it will look at the effect of a sample of its programmes. It hopes in this way to form a composite picture of its effectiveness as the results become available from the projects, so that it will eventually have enough information about the relative effectiveness of different programmes and the responsiveness of different markets to be able to use them in their planning.

As a result of evaluations and analyses carried out two to three times a year on its programmes and activities, Maison de la France estimates that for every FF1 it invests, an additional FF100 are earned in international tourist receipts. The ATC's experience in Australia points to a more modest return of 1:30. But in both cases, as with other NTAs, it is felt that more experience will be needed before reliable measures can be identified.

Turespaña's policy stands out from the rest of the case studies since, although it does carry out some analysis of campaigns, it makes no attempt to try to justify its tourism investments in terms of returns. The Spanish government believes it cannot afford to reduce investments because of the threat of competition, even if they are not justifiable in revenue terms.

III. SOME COMMON FEATURES

1. Challenges and problems facing governments

There is little doubt in the view of the OECD Tourism Committee as to the relevance of government intervention in the tourism industry - in the context of market failures, or minimising impediments to growth, such as unnecessary regulations and taxes, inefficiencies in the provision of transport services, or distortions in existing tax or regulatory systems which discriminate against the industry. Governments can also facilitate access to capital, land and skilled employees. In summary, they alone can ensure that tourism is developing in the best interests of the community.

There are many challenges facing OECD Member countries and their NTAs. These range from marketing issues such as how to exploit specific markets or, in the case of Spain, diversify its tourism markets by developing and promoting new products to complement its traditional sun and beach tourism. There are also social concerns, such as how to use tourism to contribute to the economic development of rural regions.

Another over-riding concern is financial. Fixed costs and administrative expenses are rising disproportionately compared with funds available. ANTO believes that its annual 3 per cent budget increase over the past couple of years is far too low to keep up with rising costs. It claims it needs at least 10 per cent to maintain the status quo and that without this increase, the impact of its tourism promotion and marketing will continue to dwindle. Moreover, it may have to close offices to reduce fixed costs spending. This is also a prime concern for the Swiss National Tourist Office.

Some NTAs are also faced with the problem of how to co-ordinate and reconcile the interests of the different provinces or regions in their countries. Since it is important for them to have a non-partisan approach, it leaves little room for short term campaigns with individual partners. So the prospects of being able to generate additional contributions from the private sector are slim.

Financial concerns are also apparent in a number of other countries, even in those where the private sector and local authorities already contribute significantly to financing marketing and promotional activities. At the same time though, governments are being encouraged to reduce their own spending and even question the rationale of funding national tourism promotions and marketing at all. NTAs are being asked to prove that they are cost effective, as well as adding value, rather than merely substituting for the industry.

2.   Elements of a rationale for government tourism promotion

In a highly developed, liberal political system, does government tourism promotion still have an important place? If so, should this simply be image promotion? Or can governments justify involvement in marketing activities as well?

The results of the case studies suggest that the majority of governments do feel they have a role and a responsibility to remain involved in national tourism promotion and marketing. The rationale for government funding of tourism promotion in countries which have already studied the issue in depth, such as Australia, is that it provides for the generic promotion of a country or region, which benefits not only the tourism industry, but also the community as a whole. Since tourism, unlike other markets, is not product specific, tourists must be persuaded to purchase a range of goods and services, not just particular products, and this package includes the economy, environment and culture of the country.

Few individual operators are able to influence the fundamental decision of a tourist to visit one particular country as opposed to another. Although the tourism industry benefits collectively from such general, or generic marketing, the benefits are too dispersed to provide sufficient incentive for investment by individual firms or tourism organisations.

However, there are risks involved. If NTAs promote individual regions or sectors, it can lead to a conflict of interests since they often only promote regions which already have tourism potential. This means that other regions continue to suffer. The same argument is valid in the case of specific product marketing.

In some countries, there seems little likelihood of a major shift in government thinking over their role in marketing as well as image promotion. The Austrian government, for example, is committed for economic reasons to a policy of general trade promotions. Tourism receipts account for one-third of the country's export earnings. Spain can also be expected to maintain its very strong commitment to tourism, although in other countries, this may not be the case.

3.   The need to review the mandate of the NTAs

As umbrella organisations, NTAs can play a co-ordinating role pulling together the fragmented tourism industry. At the same time, there are questions as to how far that role should go. Many small players in the industry which do benefit directly from government support are not even aware that they are beneficiaries, and even more make no contributions to promotional campaigns themselves.

There is clearly a need for greater flexibility to adapt to changing market conditions, and much closer synergy with the private sector. To reduce the cost to taxpayers, government should seek increased private sector funding for their promotional activities without compromising their fundamental role. Current trends even suggest that if most governments are to continue funding tourism promotion, there will be a need for strategic reorientation, a complete closing of ranks between the public and private sectors, and cooperation on a regional basis, particularly in the new single European market.

The initiative of Maison de la France in looking outside the tourism sector for funding is interesting. Constraints on government budgets generally mean that NTAs will have to rely more and more heavily on industry funding, and on a case by case basis. So why not involve companies from other industries, such as automobiles or telecommunications? Synergy with other industries and sectors could lead to a better image transfer to potential tourism markets.

4. Measuring the performance

Meanwhile, there are a number of questions confusing governments' decision making. How high do the returns on tourism promotion have to be to justify investment in the first place? How can they assess the added value for poor areas of a country, or where there is strong seasonality?

5. The issue of domestic marketing

Is a common consensus possible on the issue of domestic versus international tourism promotion? Do governments have any interest in promoting tourism within their countries except to stop money going out of the country, thus boosting the balance on their tourism accounts? Would it be more effective to fund regional economic development, or to support SMEs directly, rather than to do it through tourism?

6. The issue of data destination systems

One important issue that needs more careful study is the development of national destination data bases. If theses are to provide reservations' facilities as well as information, might this not conflict with governments' non-commercial status in most countries?

IV. CONCLUSION

The general climate today is towards privatisation, but there are inherent risks in the privatisation of national tourism promotion and marketing. Governments are responsible for national transportation policy and economic policy aimed at maximising tourism's contribution to the nations' economy. It is also government's responsibility to deal with issues related to the workforce, training matters, consumer affairs and public awareness campaigns. The provision of specific public infrastructure and facilities for the tourism industry, as well as local planning and zoning arrangements, land use, environmental protection matters and national parks are other examples - even if some of these functions are delegated to the local or municipal levels of government.

If national tourism promotion and marketing were left entirely to the private sector, this could result in the unbalanced development of infrastructure and market expansion, with the risk of growing congestion and increased pressure on environmental resources.

Annex

SIX CASE STUDIES

AUSTRIA
FRANCE
SPAIN
SWEDEN
UNITED KINGDOM
UNITED STATES

AUSTRIA

1. HISTORICAL BACKGROUND

The first tourism promotion took place in Graz (Styria) in 1884 to promote tourism in the Alpine countries, and the first provincial tourist boards were founded around 1900. There were already information offices throughout the Austro-Hungarian Empire, even in New York and Auckland.

In 1923, the "Österreichische Verkehrswerbung GmbH" was founded as a limited company, comprising the Austrian Federal Railways (ÖBB), the Danube Steamship Company (DDSG) and the Österreichisches Verkehrsbüro (a travel agency). Eleven years later the company was, for the first time, granted government support and re-named the "Werbedienst des Bundesministers für Handel und Verkehr" ("Promotion Agency of the Federal Minister of Commerce and Transport").

All activities of the Agency were dissolved during World War II. Shortly after the war, the Austrian National Tourist Office (Österreich Werbung") was founded in its present form as the main division of the Austrian Verkehrsbüro. It was established as an association 38 years ago and has maintained its legal status up to the present day.

The branch offices in Zurich, New York, London, Brussels and Copenhagen were re-instituted from 1947.

The significance of domestic tourism was not recognized until 1974 when it was included in ANTO's charter. The full bearing of that decision becomes evident today, if one takes into account the fact that Austrian visitors rank second in overnight stays in their own country with a share of 23 per cent, only surpassed by their German counterparts.

1.1. Organisation and Size of the Agency

The Agency comprises 25 branch offices, six tourism managers and 51 honorary representations. In the major tourism generating markets and in several growth markets, ANTO has its own branch offices with an average of six staff members per office charged with this task. Tourism managers, who are closely affiliated to the Austrian Trade Delegation, represent and promote Austria in the major markets targeted for future development. In countries which are of comparatively small tourism interest for Austria, the trade commissioners themselves engage in promotion activities as honorary representatives, with the support of the ANTO head office in Vienna.

The Vienna-based head office has a total staff of 91 in eleven different departments. Some 180 staff are currently employed in all offices abroad (including tourism managers).

This means that the total number of staff engaged in promoting Austria within the framework of ANTO is 271 in 1992.

1.2. The Role and Objectives of ANTO

The Austrian National Tourist Office (ANTO) is the national marketing organisation for all forms of tourism in Austria. ANTO's activities are not directed towards making any profits, but at attaining a maximum benefit for Austria's national economy. The guiding principles that underly ANTO's

24

activities are an orientation towards the market, efficiency and an overall approach which is based on medium- and long-term strategies.

ANTO co-operates closely with all levels of tourism on a partnership basis. Marketing instruments and existing know-how must be carefully matched and used efficiently by a division of labour.

ANTO's primary objective as national marketing organisation has been clearly defined: to influence travel decisions to the benefit of Austria. This involves the following goals:

-- presenting and promoting Austria and its multi-faceted tourism offers as a vacation destination;

-- exploiting Austria's advantages and building a positive image in markets where Austria is already well-known;

-- clearly demonstrating the competitive attractions of Austria.

1.3. Activities of the agency

ANTO's activities cover two major areas:

-- communications: i.e. the creation and enhancement of the label "Austria - a destination for vacations";

-- services: i.e. supporting and acting as a service agency for Austria's tourist industry.

ANTO's marketing includes the following instruments: international marketing ; market research; product development; communications: promotion, information, and public relations; and marketing policies/sales promotion.

The main lines of activity pursued by ANTO's international representations are:

a) Sales promotion: This involves promoting the sale of Austria's tourism product by maintaining close contacts and providing information and support to all multipliers, active involvement in product design/development and supporting sales co-operation. Another priority is assisting Austrian operators and agents with promotional tours, workshops and participation in fairs and exhibitions.

b) Press and public relations; this includes the constant provision of information, handling the media, organising press conferences and coverage trips and mailings of regular press releases.

c) Within the framework of the "URLAUBSINFORMATION" holiday information service, potential clients interested in information on Austria are given information or advice either direct, by phone or mail. Brochures and folders of resorts, regions, provinces or on Austria as a whole are mailed or handed out on specific request.

2. THE BUDGET OF THE AGENCY

Given its size, the economic dimension and its significance for the national economy, an organisation such as ANTO must be able to draw on a secure financial basis, which is guaranteed over the medium term, in order to pursue its activities continuously.

2.1. Budgetary trends

In 1991, ANTO disposed of a budget of Sch 490 488 000 which was 4.3 per cent higher than in the previous year. In 1992, members agreed a further 3 per cent rise, which brought the annual budget for 1992 to a total of Sch 499 400 000. As far as 1993 is concerned, a decision on possible funding increase has not yet been taken.

According to a survey on the development of the budget, which took into account factors such as increase of contributions, cost increases, foreign exchange developments and total income/total expenditure, increases in the funding contributions were not able to offset cost increases and additional burdens. As a consequence, ANTO's performance -- or promotional impact -- is gradually weakening.

To counteract this development, member's contributions would need to be raised by at least 10 per cent annually over the coming four years.

2.2. Sources of Income

The members of the association "Österreich Werbung" (Austrian National Tourist Office) are:

a) the Federal Ministry of Economic Affairs
b) the Federal Chamber of Commerce and Trade
c) the nine provinces (Vorarlberg, Tyrol, Salzburg, Upper Austria, Lower Austria, Vienna, Styria, Carinthia and Burgenland).

The association members contribute the following shares to ANTO's budget:

Federal government	60 per cent
Federal Chamber of Trade	20 per cent
9 provinces	20 per cent

The shares paid by the individual provinces are re-negotiated for every increase.

Some 50 per cent of the amount by which the provinces' contributions are raised are allocated according to a breakdown that goes back to 1985 (Burgenland, 5 per cent, Vorarlberg 7.5 per cent and all other provinces 12.5 per cent each). The remaining 50 per cent are allocated on the basis of respective overnight figures recorded in the previous year.

Income 1992:

Members' contributions	Sch 475 380 431
Other income	Sch 24 019 569
	Sch 499 400 000

"Other income" refers to interest on bank accounts, proceeds from barter agreements, sponsoring funds, reimbursement of mailing fees and miscellaneous contributions.

3.   BUDGET ALLOCATION BY TYPE OF COSTS

3.1. Fixed Costs

Salaries	175 403 541
Social security contributions	34 689 800
Employee benefits and other staff expenditure	6 758 629
Termination pay reserves	5 200 000
Reserves	300 000
Building/maintenance/rent	44 114 630
Office	17 756 170
Travel	10 680 909
Mailing/postage	35 427 343

Other operating expenditure	10 314 159	
Investments	6 400 000	
Reserve	250 000	
	347 295 281 Sch	

3.2 Variable Costs

Marketing budget

Advertising materials	31 790 750	
Market research	2 380 000	
Advertising and fairs	44 949 000	
Film/photo	1 478 000	
Printing/production	3 128 000	
Press/public relations	15 699 000	
Sales promotion	45 163 000	
Reserves (advertising)	7 516 969	
	152 104 719	
	499 400 000 Sch	

4. SUPPLEMENTARY EXPENDITURE

It is very difficult to quantify the total financial contribution made by all institutions involved in tourism in Austria. It is estimated that the provinces, regions, resorts, operators and transport companies as well as incoming agents together invest four times more than the amount ANTO is spending.

5. ASSESSMENT ON ANTO

Since ANTO is run as a non-profit organisation, it is very difficult to assess and quantify economic success or failure. From a business management perspective, overnight statistics and arrivals' figures alone are not valid yardsticks by which to measure the development of tourism in a particular country.

Foreign currency earnings, however, underscore the over-riding significance of tourism for a country's national economy. In 1991, tourism in Austria generated foreign currency earnings of Sch 160 billion, or approx. 8 per cent of GNP (gross national product). Austria leads the international ranking for per capita revenues generated by tourism, with an income of Sch 20 000 per capita generated by travel and tourism. Tourism's 32 per cent share of foreign currency earnings in overall export earnings, means that it is by far the most important industry in Austria in foreign exchange earnings.

More important to a national tourism promotion agency than bare figures are distinctions and awards in international competitions. In recent years ANTO's promotional campaigns have won more than 20 Creative Awards, including the bronze medal at the International Advertising Festival of New York, the Merit Award of the Art Directors Club in New York, the State Award for Industrial Promotion and the 1991 HSMAI Adrian Award.

6. **THE AGENCY IS CURRENTLY FACING TWO MAJOR PROBLEMS:**

-- Given the fact that in Austria tourism comes within the jurisdiction of the federal provinces and that, naturally, the various provinces have different interests, the major problem is how to co-ordinate and reconcile these different interests. Given that its budget comes from public funds, ANTO must take a non-partisan position, which leaves little scope for short-term campaigns with individual partners.

-- Fixed costs and administrative expenses are rising disproportionately compared with the amount of funds available for promotional purposes. It has been anticipated that a budget increase of *no more than 3 per cent* will lead to some branch offices being closed down in the coming years.

7. **ANTO HAS SET ITSELF THE FOLLOWING AIMS AND POLICY GUIDELINES FOR THE NEXT TEN YEARS**

-- Penetration of promising markets in Eastern Europe and overseas
-- New special interests campaigns
-- Further training and development within the framework of the "Tourism Academy"
-- Elaboration of an Austrian EDP-assisted information and reservation system
-- Closer co-operation with industry and the business community in view of growing budgetary constraints. Better image transfer through synergy effects.

ANTO is convinced that national tourist offices as umbrella organisations will have to be accorded even higher priority in the future. What is needed is a strategic reorientation and a closing of ranks and more co-operation between European countries.

FRANCE

I. PRESENTATION OF "MAISON DE LA FRANCE"

1. Background: the Reasons behind the Creation of Maison de la France

In 1987, France's tourism industry was suffering, having lost market share at world level.

The government decided to intervene to arrest that trend:

-- Maison de la France was set up as the single organisation to promote tourism to France in foreign markets. The objective was to co-ordinate and develop schemes operated abroad, and also to give a coherent picture of French tourism products.

-- It also introduced a policy to enhance the quality of French products, in particular by providing those in the tourism sector with better information and alerting them to the expectations of foreign customers.

2. Organisation and Structure of Maison de la France

Maison de la France consists of:

-- a small Paris headquarters with a staff of 70,

-- an international network with 38 offices (Services Français du Tourisme à l'Etranger) in 29 countries, making a total staff of 200.

3. Role and Objectives of Maison de la France

The role of Maison de la France is, first and foremost, to ensure *the promotion of French tourism products*, in France and abroad, in such a way as to enable the professionals to market these products as effectively as possible. The underlying concept is that of a partnership within the framework of a novel legal structure, the GIE or "groupement d'intérêt économique" (grouping of economic interests), bringing together the government, local authorities and private firms.

Herein lies Maison de la France's originality. It *ensures that the government and private or institutional partners work together* (eg: travel agencies, hoteliers, carriers, regional tourism committees, departmental tourism committees and tourism bureaux).

The GIE thus encompasses all the different organisations (numbering around 850) which pay an annual subscription to belong to Maison de la France. Members meet at the General Assembly and on the Board of Directors.

The General Assembly of Maison de la France comprises all members. It is chaired by the Minister of Tourism and has responsibility inter alia for approving the budget.

The Board of Directors is a smaller body, with 27 members, of which government representatives are in the minority. It helps to draw up the broad strategy of Maison de la France, within the framework of the general tourism policy established by the Ministry.

The Director-General, who is appointed by the Minister, administers and manages the GIE.

The objectives of Maison de la France:

-- To increase tourism receipts,
-- To expand tourism flows and control them more effectively,
-- To encourage tourists to stay longer,
-- To increase receipts per tourist, and
-- To enhance customer loyalty,

stem from the need to consolidate and improve earnings from French tourism in 1991 (FF120 billion).

If this goal is to be achieved, supply will have to be expanded and diversified by converting tourism potential into products that match demand, while the techniques for bringing such products on to the market need to be improved and brought up to industrial standards.

The major challenges facing France over the next few years are to strengthen its position in world tourism, develop new sources of tourism (Central European countries), focus on areas where there is scope for growth (United States and Japan), encourage the French to discover their own country.

It is on the basis of these objectives that Maison de la France is outlining a clear strategy covering all the markets in which it has chosen to intervene.

4. Activities of Maison de la France

In addition to providing information for the general public in foreign countries, the task of the GIE is to promote French products on behalf of its members. To this end, it provides them with a whole array of services -- some free of charge, some not. Ranging from individual services to joint schemes, these cover the needs of tourism professionals in their dealings with markets.

The commercial activities of Maison de la France include: participation in trade fairs, shows and exhibitions, workshops, advertising campaigns and specific promotional schemes. It also provides access to strategic information on markets and competition, training (primarily marketing), advice, access to its files, assistance with market prospection, logistical support, etc.

Thanks to the partnership formula, which allows all the promotional budgets to be merged, the impact of the GIE's activities is maximized. At present, 45 per cent of the overall budget comes from members.

The key to the success of Maison de la France lies in its ability to sound out the markets. Its constant vigilance enables it to analyse any shifts in tourism consumption and to detect the smallest changes. Thanks to the finely-tuned nature of its information, Maison de la France has been able to adopt promotional strategies which differ from one market to another.

The prime markets are defined according to their current importance, their estimated potential and their elasticity. Germany, the United Kingdom, the United States and Japan account for more than 50 per cent of earnings from tourism. The Netherlands, Italy and Spain are now rapidly expanding markets.

In all these countries, and in many others which hold out promise in various ways, Maison de la France organises special programmes which are described in detail every year in the "Guide des Opérations en Partenariat" (guide to partnership schemes). These are devised jointly by Maison de la France and its partners, which translate them into products responding to market demand.

Each market has its own characteristics and is the subject of a rational approach. This begins with the collection of information, which also involves cultural and economic parameters, and is followed by analysis, leading to the conception of suitable local strategies; and, lastly the outlining of a specific action programme: advertising campaigns, publications, workshops, familiarisation trips, etc. In the interests of promoting a particular image, all Maison de la France schemes in 1991 and 1992 have come under the heading "Art de Vivre".

In its quest for consistency and efficiency, Maison de la France has divided tourism products into four main groups: business travel, "art de vivre", recreation, leisure activities. This breakdown reflects the main criteria selected as a result of careful market analysis. For each family of products, a promotion strategy is devised which takes account of the specific features of the market being targeted.

Maison de la France's members, both private and institutional, thus also have the opportunity to join 'theme clubs'. While providing ample scope for discussion and analysis, these clubs are primarily intended to be action-oriented. Within the general Maison de la France marketing plan, the clubs carry out their own action programmes on a partnership basis and in conjunction with the Maison de la France network abroad. They use all available means of communication, including brochures, sales promotion campaigns, shows and exhibitions, etc.

Maison de la France has eleven clubs promoting its activities: "Club Français du Tourisme d'Affaires Réceptif"; "Club Français du Tourisme des Jeunes"; "Club Français du Tourisme de Nature et Découverte"; "France Golf International"; "Club Français du Naturisme"; "Club Montagnes"; "Club Français de Pêche et Tourisme"; "Club France Festivals"; "Club France Gastronomie"; "Club Châteaux, Musées, Monuments"; "Club France Mers".

In summary, the activities of Maison de la France can be broken down as follows:

Information (22 per cent of the budget)

-- *General public (public interest):* Most French Tourism Services are open to the public and distribute pamphlets and information on all French tourism products. In 1991, these services abroad provided information to more than 2 million people, representing a total of 6 million tourists, and distributed 650 tons of pamphlets. A network of interactive terminals is being set up in nine European countries.
-- *Members:* Advice, access to files, market surveys are available.
-- *Publications:* Guidebooks, general or specific brochures (some 1.9 million copies).

Advertising (30 per cent of the budget)

-- Advertising campaigns (magazines, posters).

Sales promotion and public relations (34 per cent of the budget)

-- Exhibitions and workshops (14) and seminars (32) have resulted in visits to a total of 24 countries, 105 towns (some several times a year), 1 600 exhibitors and 12 000 visitors.

-- Contacts with the press. This essential component of Maison de la France's promotion policy involves both traditional means of information (bulletins, communiqués, conferences) and also press trips, the effectiveness of which is more apparent every year. These trips today constitute half of Maison de la France's 'welcome' activities.

-- The 'Welcome' Service. In 1991, the Welcome Service of Maison de la France hosted 1 305 tourist industry professionals (newspaper, radio and television journalists; people in the travel business: tour operators, travel agents, 'incentive travel' organisers...). The various travel business partners (carriers, regional tourism committees, departmental tourism committees, hoteliers, receptionists and other providers of services) contributed to these activities to the tune of some FF8.3 million. In the space of five years, Maison de la France has hosted 7 900 travel industry professionals, including 3 900 journalists.

II. MAISON DE LA FRANCE'S BUDGET

The consolidated budget was FF302 million in 1990, FF377 million in 1991 and FF380 million in 1992.

The breakdown between the contribution from government (Ministry for Tourism) and the private sector (including local authorities) has changed from:

-- 63 and 37 per cent in 1990 and
-- 56 and 44 per cent in 1991, to
-- 55 and 45 per cent in 1992 (of which 25 per cent from local authorities and 20 per cent from the private sector).

The 1992 budget breaks down as follows:

-- 8 per cent of appropriations goes to operating costs (salaries and rent in respect solely of administrative services),
-- 22 per cent for information campaigns,
-- 30 per cent for advertising,
-- 34 per cent for sales promotion and public relations,
-- 6 per cent for miscellaneous and reserves.

Non-operating credits include financial contributions by the different partners of Maison de la France (private and public).

Measuring the results achieved by Maison de la France

It is generally estimated that every franc invested yields FF100 in tourism receipts, but this is based on macroeconomic calculations. More specifically, Maison de la France performs an average of two to three performance evaluations per year on selected markets. The best test of the effectiveness of its activities is still whether the partners involved renew their financial contributions. An indirect measure of tourism supply is the increase in earnings from tourism: FF110 billion in 1990 and 120 billion in 1991.

The future of Maison de la France is bound up with the difficulties it may encounter in maintaining and increasing its financial commitments.

Funding must be commensurate with the ambitious nature of its targets, yet government budgets are limited. This means there is an increasing need to fall back on private contributions which, while they can theoretically reverse the trend of the financial breakdown between government and its partners, can also render the financial equilibrium of Maison de la France more fragile. For this reason, the solution now being envisaged involves looking instead for specific partners for given schemes of limited duration.

Usually it is non-tourism partners, who are not members of Maison de la France, who agree to contribute to one or two advertising campaigns with the GIE (eg. Citroën, Renault, Volvic, etc.) because they see them as helping to promote their own products.

III. CONCLUSION

As far as Maison de la France is concerned, the role that the government has played has had the effect of co-ordinating activities in an area -- tourism -- in which there are many players and decision-making is fragmented. This is something a totally private organisation, with no moral authority, could not have achieved. The structure of the GIE is such that the government has been able to take part in promoting tourism. Since tourism is a very individualistic sector this participation would otherwise probably not have been accepted. Although sometimes difficult to manage, the partnership approach has proved successful since Maison de la France was created in 1987.

It should also be emphasized that government appropriations do undoubtedly have a multiplier effect that would not be achieved by private sector credits alone. The limits of government intervention in the specific area of tourism promotion are thus defined by the need to maintain this equilibrium.

SPAIN

1. THE STATE-FUNDED TOURISM PROMOTION AGENCY

1.1 Brief historical background

The Spanish government was directly responsible for tourism promotion until 1985, when a national authority for the promotion of tourism was set up under the name of *Instituto Nacional de Promoción del Turismo* (INPROTUR). This was a body formed under public law and linked to the government through the Office of the Deputy Minister for Tourism and the Department of Transport, Tourism and Communications. The Deputy Minister's Office was the governing body of INPROTUR.

In 1988, INPROTUR was renamed *Instituto de Promoción del Turismo de España* (Institute for the Promotion of Spanish Tourism) or Turespaña, an acronym still in use today.

In 1990 the Institute's full name became *Instituto de Turismo de España*, or Spanish Tourist Authority. Since 1991, it has been linked to the government through the Department of Industry, Commerce and Tourism.

1.2. Organigram of Turespaña

The Secretary General for Tourism, who as Chairman, presides over Turespaña is appointed by the Cabinet on the recommendation of the Minister for Industry, Commerce and Tourism.

The Secretary General's duties comprise:

-- managing and representing Turespaña at the highest level, including the signing of contracts falling within his competence;
-- approving broad operational plans;
-- authorising expenditures.

Two Directorates General share responsibilities. One is responsible for Tourism policy, namely:

-- co-ordination with the country's autonomous commmunities;
-- international co-operation, bilateral and multilateral;
-- commissioning studies, reports or projects concerning the tourism sector and its infrastructure.

The other one is responsible for Turespaña; this implies,

-- managing Turespaña and the Agency's staff;
-- drafting the Agency's budget;
-- implementing the general plans drawn up for Turespaña.

The Director General of Turespaña heads a team of four Deputy Directors General and the managers of the Madrid and Torremolinos Conference Centres. The four Deputy Directors General are in charge of general administration, promotional resources, promotional activities, tourist information.

Turespaña has a staff of 104 tenured civil servants and 308 untenured employees to run its central services. Between them, these two categories of government staff deal not only with promotional activities but also with tourism policy and financial/administrative management. Spanish Tourist Offices abroad employ a total of 43 tenured civil servants and 140 untenured staff.

1.3. Role and objectives of Turespaña

Turespaña's promotional targets are:

-- to establish government policy for the promotion of foreign tourism, following the broad lines laid down by the Deputy Minister for Tourism;
-- to co-ordinate and encourage publicly financed schemes to promote foreign tourism as a complement to private sector promotional initiatives and activities.

Turespaña's promotional activities consist in:

-- setting up the necessary marketing tools, including information, advertising and public relations' activities and campaigns;
-- preparing, producing and publishing a wide range of tourist information for promotional needs;
-- running and managing tourism agencies and facilities;
-- planning, setting up and contributing to Spain's participation in travel exhibitions and tourist fairs:
-- drawing up plans and programmes to promote foreign tourism in association with company representatives;
-- providing public and private enterprises with financial assistance for their activities abroad relating to prospection and the tapping of foreign tourism markets;
-- providing firms with financial support to set up and develop business networks abroad;
-- undertaking whatever is needed to accomplish the tasks with which it has been entrusted by the Agency.

2. PROMOTIONAL BUDGET OF TURESPAÑA

2.1. Promotions -- total annual budget:

1991: Ptas 7 285 million
1992: Ptas 8 547 million

2.2. Source of income (1992)

Central government: Ptas 6 196 million
Sale of services and products (conference centres and publications): Ptas 2 351 million

3. BUDGET ALLOCATION (in million pesetas, 1992)

3.1. Fixed:

Administrative overheads	756	
Staffing	922	
Total		1 678

3.2. Variable

Promotions		6 869

3.3. Cost breakdown

Advertising

Local campaigns	1 700	
International campaign	975	
Total		2 675

Promotional material

Printed matter	550	
Videos	200	
Gifts and giveaways	150	
Others	155	
Total		1 055

Fairs and exhibitions ... 450

Promotional activities (public-relation agencies, educational tours, journalists' visits and entertainment expenses);

Tourist offices in Spain	2 122		
Tourist offices abroad	567		
Total		2 689	
Grand total			6 869

4. CONTRIBUTION TO FUNDING

Ptas 760 million.

5. PERFORMANCE MEASUREMENT

Turespaña is aware that marketing has only a limited impact on consumer behaviour. The number of holidaymakers, like their spending, does not always match the effort invested. Clearly though, any failure to meet obligations is bound to benefit Spain's competitors.

Despite all the resources at Turespaña's disposal, they are never totally adequate. The supply of products that are able to be offered is so great that it is hard to determine what the optimal level of marketing resources would be. However, good use could be made of any new funds allocated from any source, public or otherwise. The ceiling on resources determines how much is undertaken and how the money is apportioned between activities. One exercise is to monitor the results of selected campaigns. Marketing is effective only up to a certain point and its impact takes time. This confirms the findings of studies by tourism promotion agencies in other countries.

Turespaña's concerns are therefore twofold. Firstly, nothing is undertaken unless it can count on the resources needed to secure essential efficiency of performance. Secondly, it implements marketing plans in such a way as to be sure that everything possible has been done to meet the objectives set.

Projects have been highly successful over the past few years, accomplishing even more than was originally planned.

6. THE MAIN PROBLEMS FACING TURESPAÑA

The achievements of Turespaña are undeniable, in particular the highly successful promotion of Spain's beaches -- although this has somewhat changed the image of a country which is essentially mountainous (second only to Switzerland in Europe) and endowed with an immense cultural heritage. This year, 206 beaches and 39 marinas flew the European "blue flag". This means that over 20 per cent of all the blue flags in Europe were awarded to Spain. There is more to Spain however than its beaches. Many other features of the country's heritage remain unknown. Fortunately, products are available and more will be coming on to the market.

The infrastructure and supply already exist. The task now is to inform people and put new products on the market.

Other problems, beyond Turespaña's control, are the current disorders and economic problems in markets close to Spain, as well as the emergence of new competitors.

7. TURESPAÑA's FUTURE

Basically, Turespaña will have to ensure that Spain's tourism products become more competitive. Quality is the motto, which is why central government and the 17 autonomous communities have signed a Master Plan for Competitiveness to be phased in over the next four years.

Turespaña is well aware that competitiveness is as much a factor in Spain's travel market as it is in the private sector, and accordingly, Turespaña's role is to provide more than just assistance and support. The private sector is already working actively with Turespaña -- in fairs, workshops, etc. -- and making a significant financial contribution to the Agency's resources. Turespaña is now trying to develop an even more active policy of collaboration with the private sector by backing corporate initiatives, especially if the following conditions are met:

-- if corporate plans for promoting tourism are comprehensive and sustainable;
-- if they successfully promote specific products and markets by developing trade-name recognition;
-- if they promote high-quality, environment-friendly products;
-- if plans by joint ventures to promote trade names are based on strict management/training/quality criteria and propose uniform, high-prestige services.

Similarly, the goal is to see the private sector play a part in planning Turespaña activities.

Spain is becoming a mature market and the trend is taking hold. Individual travel is growing as package holidays decline, which is the logical outcome of the process of holidaymakers' growing familiarity with a country. While both kinds of tourist are welcome, work methods in Turespaña and Spanish Tourist Offices abroad are being adapted to this changing trend by taking into account not only traditional partners, the tour operators, but also individual tourists with more experience and hence more critical attitudes.

All these factors contribute to Turespaña's desire to develop a promotional policy of diversification and specialisation, with a view to marketing a range of typical products on each source market. Similarly, it is hoped that the promotion of special products will become an integral part of Turespaña's activities.

A NEW APPROACH - MARKETING IN SWEDEN

1. INTRODUCTION

The Swedish government introduced a new policy concerning the tourism sector at the end of 1991. The basic principle is that the tourism sector should be looked upon as any other branch of industry. It is the individual enterprise which should take full of account of its destiny. Government's role is to create general conditions that are favourable to business, and interventions in markets should be limited to a minimum.

It is essential to establish efficient markets, efficient taxation policies and to limit the amount of administrative burden. Of particular interest to the tourism sector are policies concerning small and medium-sized enterprises, since a large part of the sector's output is produced by enterprises belonging to this group.

Private enterprises in the tourism sector should, in principle, take responsibility for their common marketing and promotional activities in the domestic market. They are more suited to carrying out these kind of activities than public sector organisations.

Only in one respect is it justified to involve governmental efforts and that is in the case of more general promotional activities abroad, which will also benefit the tourism sector. For the Swedish government, it is of utmost importance to establish a more general approach to such promotional activities and the promotion of tourism to Sweden has to be integrated with presentations of other kinds, such as presentations of Swedish industry and promotional activities targeted at foreign investors.

2. PARLIAMENTARY DECISION

The new strategy that the government established at the end of 1991 was presented to the Swedish parliament, the Riksdag, in the 1992 Budget Bill. The decision by the Riksdag menat that financial resources of approximately $15 million for the fiscal year 1992/93 are to be allocated to the professional marketing of Sweden and particularly, the promotion of tourism. It was also decided that for the coming years, these resources should be channelled through a governmental body.

3. THE NEW APPROACH

Based on the decision by the Riksdag, the following guidelines have been established.

-- Tourism promotion has to be integrated with other marketing activities.
-- Those most apt to deal with promotional activities are the private operators in the sector. Any governmental efforts must, therefore, be carried out together with or through private operators.
-- The governmental body involved - Image Sweden - should be responsible for the strategic planning of the promotional activities while at the operational level, the private sector should be responsible. Resources should be used in a flexible way and the permanent organisational

structure should be maintained as small as possible. The board - Image Sweden - comprises mainly business and marketing people.

After the decision by parliament, the larger part of the tourism sector has formed a joint enterprise called Swedish Travel and Tourism Council Inc. (Swedtrac), which will be responsible for the sector's joint promotional activities. The government, on the other hand, has formed a small organisation called Image Sweden. Image Sweden will not have any operational activities of its own but will set out the strategy for promotional activities and also carry out regular evaluations. The operations will be carried out by Swedtrac and other private operators on behalf of Image Sweden. The Swedish Trade Council and the Swedish Institute might also be suppliers of services to Image Sweden.

As a result, Image Sweden will not run any offices abroad. However, it might decide to establish this kind of representation if it finds it necessary to be able to achieve its different operational goals. By promoting and selling through tour operators and by using new techniques, it is intended to limit the opening of offices in foreign countries since this is a rather expensive way to operate.

The Swedish Tourist Board will, in accordance with governmental decisions, discontinue its operations by 1 July 1992.

UNITED KINGDOM

1. BACKGROUND

Domestic and overseas tourism are together worth some £25 billion to the UK economy, or around 5 per cent of total UK GDP. Overseas tourism accounts for between one-third and one-half of this, and direct tourism earnings from overseas visitors were £7.1 bn in 1991. The tourism industry in the UK employs some 1.5 million people, or 7 per cent of the country's total workforce. This is higher than for health services or the construction industry.

The UK ranks as the fifth most popular tourism destination in the world, after the USA, France, Spain and Italy. In 1991, foreign visitor arrivals totalled 16.7 million. This represented a decline of 7 per cent over the record results of 1990 -- due to the Gulf war. Nevertheless, visitor arrivals have been rising steadily in the past decade and more, up 34 per cent since 1980.

The major tourist markets for Great Britain, ranked in terms of tourism earnings, are the USA, France, Germany, Ireland, Italy and Canada. The USA is by far the largest, accounting in 1990 for some 17 per cent of visits and 21 per cent of earnings. Japan was seventh in the ranking, but it has the potential to rival Germany and France over the next four to five years.

2. INSTITUTIONAL STRUCTURE FOR TOURISM IN THE UNITED KINGDOM

The British Tourist Authority (BTA) is responsible for overseas promotion. Responsibility for the BTA and the English Tourist Board (ETB), both statutory bodies dating back to 1969, now lies with the newly formed Department of National Heritage, having been transferred from the Department of Employment in April 1992.

The ETB is concerned with the promotion of domestic tourism; it does not operate overseas. Scotland, Wales and Northern Ireland all have their own Boards, concerned with the promotion and development of tourism to those parts of the UK. They also co-operate with the BTA on overseas promotions. These Boards report to their own Ministers with overall responsibility for their respective countries.

BTA Board Members are drawn from the industry and approved by the Secretary. Nearly 400 people work for the BTA, split almost 50:50 between London and overseas. The international marketing director in London has three general managers based abroad -- in the main markets of the Americas, Europe and Pacific Asia. These general managers have devolved responsibility for their markets. They bid for funds and make decisions about where to focus them and what programmes to use. Other parts of the world are covered from desks in London, where there is also an advertising section. There are 29 overseas offices overall, with agents in a further seven countries.

3. BTA's ROLE AND OBJECTIVES

The British Government funds the BTA because it accepts that there are market failures in the tourism industry. Left to itself, it would not carry out sufficient promotion, research and product development.

The main market failure lies in promotion and information -- selling Britain abroad. It is not in the commercial interests of any single firm, or group of firms, to spend enough on marketing the generic image of Britain, because the returns from such promotion would be widely and uncertainly spread among direct competitors and other sectors. The tourism product also needs to develop in line with the fast changing and sophisticated requirements of today's visitor. Once again, the split ownership of the tourism product means the industry needs help to respond.

These market failures in promotion, product development and the provision of information are made more extreme because the industry is fragmented. Firms benefiting from tourism are drawn from several sectors -- and there is a preponderance of small firms. This means that the industry has difficulty in taking the sort of co-operative action necessary to exploit market opportunities fully.

Finally, the industry also tends to take a short term view of the value of an investment. BTA has a crucial role in pioneering new markets for long term benefit.

BTA receives public funds to help it address the market failures in the industry. Its main objectives are to optimise Great Britain's tourism receipts, and to extend the geographical and regional spread of tourism to Britain. The first of these objectives is expressed in terms of tourist expenditure rather than numbers of tourists. Where choices are to be made, BTA will bias its activities towards the higher spending markets.

The second objective recognises two important factors. First, the economic benefits of tourism are greater to less wealthy regions of the country. Secondly, the concentration of tourism in certain key locations at certain times of the year is both counter-productive and costly -- tourists will find the experience unpleasant and not return.

BTA has also certain specific objectives concerned with developing tourist facilities and infrastructure, meeting the information needs of overseas visitors and advising the government on tourism.

4. BTA's MAIN ACTIVITIES

-- International advertising takes the form of press, television, or radio campaigns promoting Britain, but invariably in co-operation with commercial partners.

-- Joint marketing is usually focused closely on a particular type of product, such as country house hotels or English gardens. BTA will typically get the campaign off the ground, but leave it to the industry to take full responsibility for the campaign after two or three years.

-- Other marketing includes workshops -- to put the overseas travel trade in touch with British providers -- public relations -- with BTA arranging trips for foreign journalists to see the British tourism product -- and the work of the business travel department.

-- BTA produces a large amount of printed material, mainly for distribution through its overseas offices and mailing lists.

-- BTA's network of offices and agents provide information about Britain to potential tourists and to the trade. Some of them share premises with commercial partners so that visitors can make reservations as well as getting information. An office based on this model is soon to open in Paris.

-- Finally, BTA has an extensive programme of research, monitoring and evaluation.

5. BUDGETS

The following table shows the BTA budget for the years 1990-93, split between the government grant-in-aid and non-government funding. The non-government element is primarily industry funding, although it does contain some other sources, for example local authorities.

British Tourist Authority
Budget (£ million)

YEARS	GOVERNMENT FUNDING	NON-GOVERNMENT FUNDING	TOTAL	NON-GOVERNMENT FUNDING (%)
1990/91	27.5	13.2	40.7	32
1991/92	29.5	15.1	44.6	34
1992/93 (plan)	30.9	18.1	49.0	37

The proportion of non-government funding has remained roughly constant since 1990, at around one-third of the total. The proportion would be much higher if the share related to the marketing budget alone -- about two-thirds -- because this is how the BTA attracts industry cash, through contributions to marketing and promotions. BTA has a target of a 66 per cent industry contribution to joint marketing initiatives.

The industry contribution to the overseas offices is very low, and confined to those offices where the space is shared by commercial companies.

In the current financial year (1992), over 40 per cent of BTA's budget will be allocated between advertising and marketing, and nearly 25 per cent on the overseas offices. The next biggest consumer of funds is the print programme.

By comparison, it is interesting to note that the Scottish, Welsh and Northern Irish Tourist Boards spend about £5.5 million between them annually, including their industry contribution. Some of the English Regional Tourist Boards and local authorities also spend some money on overseas promotion, although details are unavailable. As far as the industry is concerned, the airlines are the major spenders, but only a fraction of their spending goes on promoting Britain.

6. PERFORMANCE MEASUREMENT

BTA is highly regarded by the travel trade with which it deals and has won a number of awards in overseas markets as the best national tourism organisation operating in those markets. However, the UK government continues to be very concerned with more formal and quantified performance measurement in its pursuit of value for money and hence clear outputs for all public expenditure.

BTA has always monitored its activites. It does this in three ways:

-- First, since many promotions are with industry partners, it is possible to get some idea of the effect of campaigns from increases in the partners' business over and above projected levels.
-- Secondly, it is also possible to measure the effect of campaigns in terms of the coupon response to advertising, or the telephone enquiries generated.
-- Thirdly, BTA also has standing surveys of tourists which tell them how many visitors to Britain have obtained information from them before coming, and whether it was useful. In

1990, for example, 24 per cent of visitors to Britain obtained BTA information before arrival and 87 per cent of these said that it was useful or very useful.

However, monitoring measures mainly intermediate outputs. What is also very important is to assess final outputs -- that is, whether or not BTA is meeting its objectives. Other factors do intrude in this -- such as the US economy, the weakness of the dollar and the Gulf war on the US market in 1991. In most markets, it is very difficult to isolate the effect of BTA's tourism promotions from all these other influences.

BTA has, therefore, recently established an evaluation strategy. This is mainly directed at BTA's two main objectives of increasing tourism receipts and geographical and seasonal spread. It will attempt to establish the responses to three questions:

-- What was the effect of the BTA initiative?
-- Was that effect additional? In other words, if BTA had not participated, would the industry have run the campaign anyway?
-- How cost effective was the activity? What did it cost BTA, and what was its return in terms of tourism receipts?

It is not easy to obtain this type of information. It requires sophisticated inerviewing of consumers about their intentions, before and after contact with BTA -- and, of course, later, to find out whether they actually visited the UK as planned.

It also requires interviews with the commercial partners involved in the promotions and a system of allocating costs very precisely to individual initiatives.

BTA has embarked on a five-year strategy, during which it will look at the effect of a representative sample of its programmes. Results are expected soon from the first pilot study of an overseas office. In this way, it is hoped to form a composite picture of BTA's effectiveness as results become available from the projects. Eventually, there should be enough information about the relative effectiveness of different programmes and the responsiveness of different markets for BTA to use the results in its planning.

UNITED STATES

1. HISTORICAL BACKGROUND

The United States established a national tourism policy in 1961. The United States Travel Service was set up that same year by the International Travel Act to serve as the official US government tourism office which co-ordinates and implements that national policy. The United States Travel Service was renamed the US Travel and Tourism Administration (USTTA) in 1981 by the National Tourism Policy Act and took on similar tasks and responsibilities.

As the official government tourism organisation at the federal level, USTTA chairs an interagency committee formed to co-ordinate policy and works within the federal government on international trade issues which affect US tourism interests. USTTA is also involved in collecting, analysing, and distributing statistics on travel trends and movements.

In the area of marketing, USTTA is responsible for promoting the USA abroad, as well as educating US travel and tourism businesses in how to promote themselves in the international market. USTTA also works with 50 states to stimulate domestic tourism.

While USTTA and its predecessor have been responsible for promotion at the federal level, the 50 states of the USA have generally been responsible for promoting their own territories. Historically, many have had tourism departments or divisions in their commercial or development agencies. They have their own budgets appropriated by their individual legislatures. These range from $4 to $14 million per year depending on state resources and priorities.

With respect to government and private sector co-operative involvement in tourism promotion abroad, USTTA and the industry have worked together in differing degrees over a period of time. USTTA remains entirely governmental, but uses co-operative funding from the private sector for various projects. Acceptance of these funds is strictly regulated by US administrative law. Most recently, beginning during the Gulf War, USTTA and many sectors of the industry have combined efforts in the GO USA Coalition, whose main purpose was to stimulate tourism in the face of the downturn in travel due to those hostilities and economic difficulties in many countries. A crowning joint effort has been the video featuring President Bush inviting people to visit the USA. Funding for this campaign has come from the industry acting in this coalition.

2. ORGANISATION AND SIZE OF USTTA

USTTA is located in the US Department of Commerce. It is under the responsibility of the Secretary of Commerce who is a member of the President's cabinet.

USTTA operates with a full-time staff of 94. Of these, 50 are assigned to regional offices in nine countries and one in the USA. The nine are located in Paris, London, Amsterdam, Milan, Frankfurt, Sydney, Tokyo, Mexico City, and Toronto. The sole office in the USA is in Miami and serves the markets in Latin America. In countries where USTTA does not have regional offices, such as Spain and Argentina, the US Foreign and Commercial Service often serves as promoter for travel to the USA. The remaining 44 staff members are assigned to the main offices in Washington, DC. These offices are staffed as follows:

The Office of the Under Secretary is headed by an Under Secretary and a Deputy Under Secretary, who are appointed by the President and confirmed by the Senate. There are five staff members, and the office has overall responsibility of the marketing, policy, and research activities of the agency. The Office of the Assistant Secretary for Tourism Marketing is headed by an Assistant Secretary and has 14 staff members. This is the office at headquarters responsible for all tourism marketing activities, whether involving the promotion or education of US businesses interested in promoting their locations or services abroad.

The Office of Research has six staff members and is responsible for collecting, analysing, and distributing statistics. The Office of Policy and Planning has eight staff members and is responsible for working with domestic and international policies which affect US tourism interests. The Office of Strategic Planning and Administration also has eight staff and is responsible for budget and other administrative functions.

3. ROLE AND OBJECTIVES OF THE FEDERALLY-FUNDED TOURISM PROMOTION AGENCY

USTTA is charged with promoting travel from abroad and for stimulating travel within the United States. The objectives of the USTTA are to develop US tourism in an effort to spark economic growth and stability, improve international competitiveness, and expand foreign exchange earnings. Some of the elements of the national tourism policy for which USTTA is responsible include encouraging international visitors to visit the USA, stimulating the development of affordable tourism products, and promoting the use of US air carriers.

4. ACTIVITIES OF THE AGENCY

USTTA implements programmes that are designed to:

-- increase awareness of tourism as an export market and of the benefits of tourism in general;
-- stimulate consumer demand for travel to the USA;
-- provide US tourism with better access to international markets;
-- develop co-operative trade development campaigns with the industry;
-- promote tourism development as an economic option for rural and ethnic communities;
-- provide research on international travel markets to the US tourism industry; and
-- co-ordinate tourism trade policies and legislative initiatives, and reduce restrictive barriers to the growth of US tourism services.

5. USTTA BUDGET

The total appropriated budget in the fiscal year 1991 was $20 696 000. In the fiscal year 1992, it is $17 480 000. For 1993, it is expected to be $17 454 000. The annual budgets for the fiscal years 1991 and 1992 include $5 million and $2 million respectively for the Disaster Relief Grants Programme. This programme provides grants to locations which have suffered a natural disaster, such as a hurricane, and will be used to promote their areas internationally where their market share has sagged because of the publicity resulting from the disaster. This programme will not be continued in the fiscal year 1993.

The basic budget for USTTA is provided by the US government in annual appropriations, as outlined above. In addition, co-operative funding from private sector organisations allows USTTA to multiply the effects of appropriated resources. USTTA regularly seeks private sector funding to develop tourism promotion for the USA. Private sector contribution ratios to USTTA contributions vary, but are often higher than 10:1. In the fiscal year 1992, it is estimated that USTTA will participate in partnerships that will generate approximately $18 million in cooperative funding.

USTTA also provides products and services to the travel trade industry for which it receives "user fees", i.e. payment of cost or below for the service or product. In the fiscal year 1992, these efforts are expected to generate approximately $1.5 million in revenue for the US government which, it is hoped, can be put back into tourism promotion.

USTTA's fixed costs are those associated with supporting the central operations of USTTA, such as administrative overheads, staff support and centralised services pertaining to these offices. The total for the fiscal year 1992 is $1 630 000.

USTTA's variable costs are related to the functions of marketing, research, policy, and regional offices abroad to conduct programme-related activities. In the fiscal year 1992, these are targeted in the following manner:

Co-operative advertising	$ 388 000
Promotion material (printing, films and photos, brochures and displays, supplies and equipment)	$ 541 000
Trade shows	$ 56 000
Educational and familiarisation tours	$ 31 000
Informational and promotional activities	$ 3 649 000
Marketing, research, and staff at Headquarters	$ 2 585 000
Remuneration of staff abroad	$ 6 506 000

6. WHAT ARE THE MAIN PROBLEMS FACING USTTA?

In its promotional capacity, USTTA is a relatively small agency with limited financial and staff resources. The main challenge is to utilise and mobilise these resources in the most productive manner in an increasingly competitive world market.

The opening of borders in central and eastern European countries and the Republics of the former Soviet Union represents additional markets for the future. As barriers to travel are reduced through international efforts, such as the General Agreement on Trade in Services (GATS), and expanding air services, more opportunities for travellers are created throughout the world. USTTA will need to serve as an effective catalyst at the federal level for promoting the United States as an international destination.

In this role, USTTA will seek appropriated resources along with substantial contributions from the private sector to develop contemporary, long-term promotional campaigns in all markets of opportunity. This approach will need to be pursued at the federal, state, and regional levels in an effective partnership with the private sector.

7. APPRAISING THE FUTURE OF THE AGENCY

USTTA will continue to promote the USA as a whole in international markets. It will seek additional partnerships with state and regional groups as well as with the private sector, such as the GO USA Coalition.

USTTA will also continue to serve as a catalyst for the creation and development of new products, such as rural tourism and ethnic tourism. Not only do these serve as economic development tools, but they offer new, enticing opportunities for international visitors to the USA who are looking for new experiences after visiting the well-known tourist destinations. USTTA will also work toward educating business entrepreneurs in tourism in the USA as to how they might effectively develop products and services for international visitors and market those products abroad.

Finally, the marketing function of USTTA will continue to be supported by its research, policy, and planning functions. Market research and reduction of barriers are two areas of activity which can support tourism promotion.

8. THE RATIONALE FOR THE US GOVERNMENT INVOLVEMENT IN TOURISM PROMOTION

Developing and maintaining a vibrant tourism industry in the USA, which remains competitive worldwide, also stimulates other business development, community development, and the preservation of historical, cultural, and natural resources. Another important factor is the contribution tourism makes to international understanding. As far as the limitations of its role are concerned, USTTA does not regulate or control the growth of tourism. Rather, it acts as a co-ordinator and a catalyst.

Chapter II

INTERNATIONAL TOURIST FLOWS IN MEMBER COUNTRIES

This Chapter brings together, in the form of summary tables, the most recent data available on international tourist flows to the Member countries of the Organisation for Economic Co-operation and Development (OECD). The statistical tables give regional totals for each of the three geographical areas of the OECD -- Europe, North America and Australasia-Japan -- plus the OECD total.

Annual data by country of origin of foreign tourists or visitors, for 1990 and 1991, are set out in the Statistical Annex.

Section A outlines the general trends noted in 1990 for the OECD area as a whole.

Section B records changes in international tourist flows in individual Member countries in 1991. The data cover:

a) Arrivals at frontiers of tourists (persons spending more than one night in the country being visited or, where such figures are not available, all visitors (tourists plus excursionists). For further details as to how travellers are classified, please refer to Chart A in the Statistical Annex.

b) The number of nights spent by foreign tourists in hotels and similar establishments (generally speaking, hotels, motels, inns and boarding houses).

c) The number of nights spent in all forms of accommodation without distinction.

For further details on the types of accommodation covered by the data for each receiving country, please consult Table C in the Statistical Annex.

Lastly, Section C describes international flows from the OECD's main generating countries: Canada, France, Germany, Italy, Japan, the Netherlands, the United Kingdom and the United States.

A. INTERNATIONAL TOURISM IN THE OECD AREA

The year 1991 was marked particularly by the Gulf war in the first quarter and then by the start of the crisis in Yugoslavia. At the same time a number of major tourist countries in the OECD area were affected by the recession and, in Europe, political upheavals persisted. The transition process in central and eastern European countries continued and the break-up of the former USSR gathered momentum. Similarly, the process of European union was speeded up and strengthened, particularly with the increased involvement of the European Free Trade Association (EFTA) countries, the introduction of harmonised policies in the run-up to the Single Market in 1993 and preparation of the future Maastricht Treaty.

The tourist industry as a whole stood its ground rather well in quite a difficult situation; the various indicators for the OECD area showed changes from 1990 ranging from a decrease of 1 per cent in nights spent in all forms of accommodation (Europe only) and in nights spent in hotels and an increase of 2 per cent in arrivals at frontiers. Although these figures were down from the previous year, tourism remained an essential aspect of the various national economies (see Chapter 3) and, according to recent forecasts by the World Tourism Organisation (WTO), it should see brisk growth in the next ten years and expand by 40 per cent by the year 2000 to a world total of 650 million international tourist arrivals.

According to WTO, international tourism expressed in terms of arrivals remained virtually stationary at world level at 453 million arrivals in 1991, or 0.2 per cent less than in the previous year. This global figure in fact masks quite a varied regional pattern: arrivals were down 10 per cent in the Middle East and 2 per cent in Europe (according to the WTO's geographical breakdown), but up 6 per cent in Africa and 4 per cent in the Americas.

It was again noticeable that tourism is sensitive to political tensions and that crises like those of 1991 not only give a fillip to domestic tourism but, in the case of international tourist flows, also boost the share of intra-regional tourism to the detriment of long-distance air travel. What this means is that a feeling of security, which the tourist needs have, is still a vital factor in the development of international tourism.

The results for the various sectors of the tourist industry differ widely. According to the International Air Transport Association (IATA), air services were particularly hard hit in 1991 and the number of international passengers was down by about 4 per cent. The decrease was 25 per cent in the first few months and it was not until October that traffic started to pick up again.

According to the International Hotel Association (IHA), sharp drops occurred in hotel occupancy rates during the first three months of 1991. The crisis affected high-class hotels in particular. Among the tour operators, it seems that those who were highly specialised (in one destination or one product) suffered the most.

Despite these developments, however, in 1991 the international tourism scene in the OECD area is admittedly varied. Europe, in particular, suffered further consequences of the crisis and showed a decrease in nights whereas Australasia-Japan and North America have progressed slower than in the previous year:

Europe:

--   Arrivals at frontiers: + 1 per cent (against + 3 per cent in 1990);

--   Nights spent in hotels and similar establishments: - 1 per cent (against + 1 per cent);

--   Nights spent in all forms of accommodation: - 1 per cent (against + 3 per cent)

North America:

--   Arrivals at frontiers: + 5 per cent (against + 6 per cent)

Australasia-Japan:

--   Arrivals at frontiers: + 7 per cent (against + 11 per cent).

Arrivals at frontiers (Table 1)

Table 1 sets out the figures for 15 Member countries. Of the European Member countries, only 12 compile statistics on foreign tourist or visitor movements at frontiers. Two of these 12 countries, Austria and Germany, record all traveller arrivals at frontiers, a much broader yardstick than that used for analysing tourist flows, since it includes travellers in transit (for information see Table A of Statistical Annex). These figures have not therefore been included in Table 1, but are shown for information in Table 6 of the Statistical Annex.

In *Europe*, growth in arrivals slowed down considerably for the third year running, amounting to only 1 per cent. Of the various OECD regions, Europe was the hardest hit by the effects of the economic situation and lost a significant number of its long-haul tourists; although the authorities and bodies tried to encourage travel after the Gulf War (especially from North America), European destinations felt the impact of the economic difficulties in the main generating countries and the Yugoslav conflict. This also explains the marked decline in departures from the United Kingdom which affected most of the receiving countries.

The largest decreases in numbers were for the United Kingdom which lost 1.3 million visitors, Greece 0.8 million tourists and Switzerland 0.6 million tourists. These falls were offset by the performance of two major European receiving countries, i.e. France (up 4 per cent) and Spain (up 3 per cent). Portugal recorded for the highest percentage increase (8 per cent).

In *North America*, tourist arrivals rose by more than twice the number in the OECD area as a whole. But although the United States showed continued steady growth (up 8 per cent from 1990), particularly as a result of more tourists from Canada, its main market, the same did not apply to Canada itself (down 2 per cent) owing to the weakness of its major partner, the United States. The US benefited from the weakness of the dollar and the diversion of tourist flows which would have gone to the regions of the world affected by the Gulf war.

Australasia-Japan recorded a slowdown in the rate of growth but was still the most dynamic region with an increase of 7 per cent, despite a drop (of 1 per cent) in the number of visitors to New Zealand. This progress was mainly due to the healthy state of intra-regional tourism and the Dynamic Asian Economies; the impact of some rapidly expanding markets such as Hong Kong, Korea, Singapore and Taiwan is significant.

Nights spent in hotels and similar establishments (Table 2)

Seventeen European countries plus Australia compile data on nights spent in hotels and similar establishments; generally speaking these data concern nights recorded in hotels, motels, boarding houses and inns (see Table C in the Statistical Annex).

In 1991 *Europe* recorded a 1 per cent decrease despite Spain's improved position (+ 4 per cent after two very poor years) and Austria's good results (+ 4 per cent); Portugal recorded the highest growth (14 per cent). The general picture, however, was still quite bleak since two-thirds of the European countries were down, three of them -- Finland, Italy and Sweden -- for the second year running.

Europe's hotels seem to have been particularly hard hit by the collapse of long-haul travel and the unsettled economic climate. A comparison with nights spent in all forms of accommodation shows that, on average, hotels were more vulnerable and that there is a definite trend away from hotels to other types of accommodation.

Australia, which has also compiled data on hotels and similar establishments since 1989, recorded an 8 per cent decline and all its markets were down, except for Japan (+ 5 per cent) and Germany (+ 12 per cent).

Nights spent in all forms of accommodation (Table 3)

Nights spent in all forms of accommodation are available for 18 Member countries; this category includes both hotel and non-hotel accommodation (see Table C in the Statistical Annex).

Europe as a whole recorded a 1 per cent decrease; six countries were down, including the United Kingdom which lost almost 16 million nights (a drop of 8 per cent on the previous year). The other sharp downturns were in Turkey (27 per cent), Greece (16 per cent) and Sweden (14 per cent). In the case of nine countries, the trend was better in terms of nights spent in all forms of accommodation than in terms of nights spent in hotels (the OECD Tourism Committee considers this a more representative indicator than the preceding ones since it gives a better idea of the use of accommodation as a whole).

51

Table 1. Annual growth rates of number of arrivals of foreign tourists at frontiers[1]

	T/V	% 89/88	% 90/89	% 91/90	1991 Millions of arrivals
Austria					
Belgium					
Denmark					
Finland					
France[4]	T	29.4	6.0	4.4	54.8
Germany					
Greece	T	3.9	9.8	−9.6	8.0
Iceland	T	−0.4	8.2	1.1	0.1
Ireland	V	16.5	12.3	−2.3	3.0
Italy	T	−0.8	2.9	−1.0	26.4
Luxembourg					
Netherlands					
Norway					
Portugal	T	7.4	12.7	7.9	8.7
Spain	V	−0.2	−3.7	2.8	53.5
Sweden					
Switzerland[2]	T	7.7	4.8	−4.5	12.6
Turkey[3]	V	6.9	20.9	2.4	5.5
United Kingdom	V	9.7	3.9	−7.5	16.7
EUROPE[1]		8.9	3.3	0.7	
Canada	T	−2.1	0.7	−1.8	15.0
United States[5]	T	33.5	8.1	8.0	42.7
NORTH AMERICA		20.7	5.9	5.3	
Australia	V	−7.5	6.5	7.0	2.4
New Zealand	T	4.2	8.3	−1.3	1.0
Japan	V	20.4	14.2	9.2	3.5
AUSTRALASIA-JAPAN[1]		6.3	10.5	6.9	
OECD[1]		11.2	4.0	1.9	

V Visitors.
T Tourists.
Note: Canada, Italy and Portugal dispose of both series (V and T); see annex.
1. Overall trend for all countries with data available from 1988 to 1991.
2. Estimates.
3. Travellers.
4. Change of series in 1989: new frontiers' survey.
5. New series from 1989.

Table 2. Annual growth rates of nights spent by foreign tourists in hotels and similar establishments[1]

	% 89/88	% 90/89	% 91/90	1991 Millions of beds-nights
Austria	9.0	0.8	3.7	64.2
Belgium	21.2	4.5		
Denmark	11.6	11.1	9.8	6.0
Finland	9.5	−2.0	−10.8	2.2
France	24.4	8.2	−5.2	53.0
Germany[3]	12.5	4.9	−6.7	27.8
Greece	−1.2	6.3	−14.7	29.9
Iceland	1.8			
Ireland	23.4	8.5	11.4	9.2
Italy	−3.2	−3.1	−0.5	65.7
Luxembourg	5.0	5.8	−0.4	1.1
Netherlands	6.2	12.9	−1.3	8.0
Norway	2.2	3.1	10.7	3.9
Portugal	3.1	8.0	14.2	19.1
Spain	−11.4	−8.4	3.8	74.4
Sweden	5.5	−5.2	−11.5	2.8
Switzerland	7.3	2.7	−3.2	20.4
Turkey	3.3	5.7	−21.1	8.1
United Kingdom				
EUROPE[1]	2.8	1.0	−1.2	
Canada				
United States				
NORTH AMERICA				
Australia[2]	−25.5	19.0	−8.3	11.5
New Zealand				
Japan				
AUSTRALASIA-JAPAN				
OECD[1]	1.8	1.4	−1.4	

1. Overall trend for all countries with data available from 1988 to 1991.
2. New series from 1989.
3. The data relate to the territory of the Federal Republic of Germany prior to 3rd October 1990.

Table 3. Annual growth rates of nights spent by foreign tourists in all means of accommodation[1]

	% 89/88	% 90/89	% 91/90	1991 Millions of beds-nights
Austria	8.4	−0.2	5.1	99.6
Belgium	15.0	5.9		
Denmark	5.6	8.9	11.7	10.4
Finland				
France[4]	14.8	3.8	2.3	372.2
Germany[3]	11.5	3.8	−4.6	33.2
Greece	−1.8	6.3	−15.9	30.5
Iceland				
Ireland	19.7	7.4	−1.2	33.3
Italy	−5.9	−2.5	3.1	87.4
Luxembourg			5.9	2.6
Netherlands	12.1	16.1	4.5	17.2
Norway	2.8	5.4	8.0	6.3
Portugal	2.5	6.1	13.5	22.0
Spain				
Sweden	6.6	−13.3	−13.9	5.7
Switzerland	4.4	2.6	0.3	37.0
Turkey	1.8	11.8	−26.9	9.7
United Kingdom	8.4	4.8	−7.9	180.8
EUROPE[1]	8.8	3.4	−0.7	
Canada	−2.0			
United States				
NORTH AMERICA[1]				
Australia[2]		16.9	−1.1	64.6
New Zealand	1.8	9.5	−6.6	19.3
Japan				
AUSTRALASIA-JAPAN				
OECD[1]	8.6	3.5	−0.9	

1. Overall trend for all countries with data available from 1988 to 1991.
2. New series from 1989.
3. The data relate to the territory of the Federal Republic of Germany prior to 3rd October 1990.
4. Change of series in 1989: new frontiers' survey.

Outside Europe, the figures were down for Australia (by 1 per cent) and New Zealand (by 7 per cent).

B. INTERNATIONAL TOURISM IN INDIVIDUAL MEMBER COUNTRIES

Australia. After a very good year in 1990, nights spent in all forms of accommodation were down by 1 per cent in 1991, with a decrease of 8 per cent in hotels and similar establishments. This fall was largely attributable to a drop of 27 per cent in nights spent by Japanese tourists and one of 3 per cent for UK tourists (two of Australia's major markets).

On the other hand, foreign visitor arrivals were up 7 per cent to 2.4 million, which was a new record for tourist travel to Australia, despite the combined effects of a weak world economy and the Gulf war. The preceding record was set in 1988, the year of the bicentenary celebration. Japan, which has been Australia's top market since 1990, kept its place in 1991 with a 10 per cent increase and accounted for 22 per cent of the total number of visitor arrivals.

The conflicting trends changes in the case of the Japanese market as expressed in the number of visitors (up 10 per cent) and the number of nights (down 27 per cent) are due to a significant decrease in the average length of stay by Japanese tourists from 13 nights in 1990 to 8 nights in 1991.

New Zealand and the United States accounted for respectively 20 per cent and 11 per cent of all visitors. Arrivals from Asia (excluding Japan) were up considerably (by 13 per cent), with an increase of 67 per cent from the Korean market, 37 per cent from Taiwan, 26 per cent from Thailand and 15 per cent from Singapore, Hong Kong and the Philippines; Asia now accounts for 16 per cent of arrivals.

On the negative side, the European market was down 3 per cent particularly owing to the weakness of its top-ranking European market, the UK (down 5 per cent).

Austria. In 1991 foreign tourists spent almost 100 million nights in all forms of accommodation, or 5 per cent more than in 1990. Most of the main markets were up, in particular Germany which accounted for 65 per cent of all nights (+ 13 per cent); German unification seems to have contributed greatly to the development of flows between the two countries. The other main European markets were also up.

However, the UK (- 15 per cent) and the United States (- 44 per cent) were down considerably. In the case of the United States, it seems that the drop is due to a number of factors such as the country's economic   recession and the crisis in Yugoslavia; the same reasons also apply to the United Kingdom.

Belgium. No 1991 data were available for Belgium at the time of writing.

Canada. The number of foreign tourist and visitor arrivals at frontiers in 1991 declined by respectively 2 per cent and 3 per cent. In particular, the number of Americans spending one night or more in Canada (a total of 12 million tourists) was down by 2 per cent in 1991. The number of tourists from overseas countries dropped (by 2 per cent for the first time since 1985; of the major markets, Japan and the UK (- 4 per cent) and Asia-Oceania (- 8 per cent) were down. However, the European market as a whole expanded with notable increases in the case of France (up 18 per cent) and Germany (up 8 per cent).

The most buoyant growth in visitor numbers during the decade was in those from the Asia-Pacific and Oceania region; in 1991, however, the number of tourists from this area fell by 5 per cent.

At the time of writing, the 1990 and 1991 data for nights in all forms of accommodation, broken down by country of origin, were not available.

Denmark. Denmark noted an increase of 12 per cent in the number of nights spent in all forms of accommodation, bringing the figure for 1991 to over 10 million. Growth was mainly due to its three major markets -- Germany (+ 18 per cent), Sweden (+ 20 per cent) and Norway (+ 4 per cent). By contrast, its North American and Japanese markets were down by respectively 20 and 14 per cent. In the case of its European markets, the drop 7 per cent for the UK should also be noted.

The trend was similar in hotel nights which rose in total by 10 per cent.

Finland. In 1991, the number of nights spent in hotels fell sharply by 11 per cent, following what had been a slight downturn in 1990. One of the main reasons for this trend was the Gulf war which in particular affected travel from distant markets, such as the United States (- 27 per cent), and Japan (- 10 per cent) to Europe. The economic recession in a number of major generating countries also had a negative impact.

The sharpest decline concerned the former USSR, Finland's third-ranking market (down 38 per cent) from which tours stopped being operated in 1991.

There were, however, some happier notes with slight increases for the two main markets, Sweden (+ 1 per cent) and Germany (+ 4 per cent).

France. An analysis of tourist flows in 1991 reveals differing trends that were generally positive but slightly less so than in the previous year, particularly in the case of hotels. Nights spent in all forms of accommodation rose by 2 per cent and tourist arrivals at frontiers by 4 per cent, while nights in hotels were down by 5 per cent.

Taking the number of nights spent in all forms of accommodation, which is the most accurate indication of the trend in occupancy, this shows that the downturn in long-haul travellers' nights was offset by an upturn in intra-regional tourism, particularly from Germany (+ 10 per cent), Italy (+ 20 per cent) and Belgium (+ 7 per cent). Germans easily led the field with 85 million nights, followed by the British with 50 million. Substantial falls were recorded in the number of nights for visitors from the United Kingdom (- 3 per cent), the Netherlands (- 10 per cent) and Spain (- 7 per cent). In addition, nights spent by Japanese tourists were down 25 per cent and in the case of North American tourists by 16 per cent.

The decrease in nights spent in hotels can be attributed mainly to a structural trend, with the clientele shifting to other forms of accommodation and/or a shorter duration of stay in hotels.

The year 1991 will always be associated with the massive advent of tourists from the central and eastern European countries, particularly from the Czech and Slovak Federal Republic.

Germany. Following the substantial increases that occurred in 1990, the 1991 figures for nights spent in all forms of accommodation (5 per cent down on 1990) and in hotels (7 per cent down) show a marked decline. The major non-European markets were down considerably: the United States by 28 per cent and Japan by 16 per cent. In Europe (67 per cent of the total market), the trend was more varied with decreases for the United Kingdom (- 9 per cent) and France (- 5 per cent), coupled with what were to some extent offset increases for the Netherlands (+ 5 per cent) and Sweden (+ 3 per cent). All in all, the OECD market (Europe) remained stable.

The case of the Central and Eastern European countries should be stressed as they accounted for 7 per cent of the market and recorded growth of 18 per cent over 1990. The Czech and Slovak Federal Republic and the former USSR were up respectively by 33 and 22 per cent.

Greece. With 8 million arrivals in 1991, Greece accounted for 10 per cent fewer tourists than in the previous year and thus went back down to the 1989 level. Fewer Germans (- 20 per cent), Italians (- 9 per cent) and French (- 17 per cent) travelled to Greece, while the United Kingdom, its main market, remained relatively stable. As far as tourists from Europe are concerned, however, the tremendous growth for the central and eastern European countries must be noted (up 58 per cent to 9 per cent of total arrivals).

The sharpest downturns were recorded outside Europe with North America down 35 per cent and Australasia-Japan 40 per cent. These poor results can be attributed both to the proximity of Yugoslavia and also to the impact of the Gulf war.

The 1991 data for nights spent in hotels and similar establishments, broken down by country of origin, were not available at the time of writing.

Iceland. The year 1991 was subdued (+ 1 per cent) following a very good year in 1990 (+ 8 per cent). There was a particularly sharp decrease in the case of Scandinavian markets (down 11 per cent to 24 per cent of total tourist arrivals at frontiers), but this was offset particularly in Europe by the performance of its second market, Germany (+ 9 per cent), and its fourth market, the United Kingdom (+ 7 per cent). Arrivals from North America slipped by 1 per cent, mainly owing to the situation in the United States.

Ireland. In terms of the most representative data, i.e. nights in all forms of accommodation, international tourism was down by 1 per cent in 1991, although nights spent in hotels rose by 11 per cent over the same period. This contrasting trend was largely due to the UK market which was up 35 per cent for nights spent in hotels (3.6 million nights in 1991) but down 6 per cent for nights in all forms of accommodation (14.7 million, or 44 per cent of the total). The other European markets as a whole were up 9 per cent, thus continuing the pattern of growth for previous years.

Decreases were reported in the case of France (3 per cent), the United States (13 per cent) and Belgium-Luxembourg (52 per cent). The large decrease in the Belgium-Luxembourg market occured because of the abnormal increase in traffic from this market in the first half of 1990 due to Ireland's presidency of the Economic Community. All the other OECD markets were on an uptrend, in particular the Canadian market (+ 12 per cent) and the Australia/New Zealand market (+ 34 per cent).

Italy. Visitor arrivals at frontiers were down 15 per cent in 1991, representing a drop of 9 million tourists compared with the previous year. This decrease concerned all OECD Member and non-member countries; it was more pronounced outside Europe, particularly in the case of North America (- 22 per cent) and Australasia-Japan (- 17 per cent). In Europe, Italy suffered particularly from the Yugoslav crisis, with arrivals from Yugoslavia, its fifth-ranking market, down by 51 per cent.

Only the central and eastern European countries were still an expanding market in 1991 (up 11 per cent to 4 per cent of arrivals).

The 1991 data for nights spent in hotels and similar establishments and those spent in all forms of accommodation, broken down by country of origin, were not available at the time of writing.

Japan. International tourist travel continued to expand in terms of visitor arrivals at frontiers (by 9 per cent in 1991 as against 14 per cent in 1990). However, all the OECD regions either were at a standstill or showed a decline in 1991. The decline was relatively small in the case of Europe (0.3 per cent) because of a slight improvement in Japan's main market, the United Kingdom (+ 2 per cent) and was 2 per cent in the case of North America.

The overall increase was due mainly to non-Member countries which accounted for 67 per cent of the market and were up by 15 per cent in 1991 (compared with 18 per cent in 1990). The regions showing the largest increases included Latin America (+ 33 per cent) and Asia-Oceania (+ 14 per cent). Korea and Taiwan, which accounted for 43 per cent of arrivals, were up by 16 and 8 per cent respectively.

Netherlands. In 1991 the number of arrivals in all forms of accommodation rose by 1 per cent to 5.8 million. The fall in inter-continental demand as a result of the Gulf crisis and unfavourable economic trends was offset by an increase in arrivals from Europe, particularly from Central and Eastern Europe.

The number of nights spent in all forms of accommodation was up by 5 per cent, while nights spent in hotels were down by 1 per cent. This increase can be attributed not only to longer stays but also to the breakdown of nights between hotels and other types of accommodation, with a continual swing in favour of camping sites, residential leisure parks, etc. Thus, in terms of nights, the share of hotels and similar establishments fell from 51 per cent in 1989 to 46 per cent in 1991. Moreover, a stay in hotels and similar establishments is always shorter than in other forms of accommodation.

Germany, the country's main market with 49 per cent of total nights, was up 12 per cent from 1990. Increases were also recorded for the United Kingdom (+ 1 per cent) and Austria (+ 7 per cent). On the other hand, the United States and France, its fourth and fifth markets, were down by 18 per cent and 4 per cent respectively. Italy was also down (- 10 per cent). These three countries had surged ahead in 1990 (with increases ranging from 13 to 44 per cent), which was partly due to the impact of the Van Gogh exhibition.

New Zealand. Tourist arrivals at frontiers (down 1 per cent) and nights spent in all forms of accommodation (down 7 per cent), meant that 1991 was a disappointing year for New Zealand. In terms of arrivals at frontiers (the most complete statistical series), the fall was particularly sharp in January and April. Of the four main markets (Australia, United States, Japan and United Kingdom) which accounted for 70 per cent of total arrivals, only Japan was up (by 6 per cent); the United Kingdom was more or less stationary. North America (- 6 per cent) was down, with a decrease of 5 per cent for the United States and 11 per cent for Canada.

Among the other main markets, worth noting is the 14 per cent increase in the number of German tourists.

Of the non-Member countries (17 per cent of total arrivals), Asia remained particularly dynamic and especially South Korea (+ 52 per cent), Hong Kong (+ 20 per cent), Taiwan (+ 15 per cent), Thailand (+ 24 per cent), Singapore (+ 14 per cent) and Indonesia (+ 14 per cent).

Norway. International tourist demand rose by 11 per cent in 1991 to almost 4 million nights in hotels. All the European markets were up, in particular the four leading countries which accounted for about 60 per cent of the market: Germany (+ 23 per cent), Sweden (+ 20 per cent), Denmark (+ 23 per cent) and the United Kingdom (+2 per cent). Other European markets showed a sharp increase: Italy (+ 52 per cent); Spain (+ 23 per cent); France (+ 22 per cent) and the Netherlands (+ 19 per cent). However, for countries outside Europe, the number of United States visitors was down sharply (by 23 per cent).

According to the national authorities, success in controlling inflation and therefore increased competitiveness, an energetic marketing policy based on the "green tourism" concept and greater effort behind the policy to develop tourist products are the main explanations for Norway's flourishing tourism industry.

Portugal. All the indicators for international tourism demand showed significant growth in 1991 over the previous year. Tourist arrivals were up 8 per cent, while nights spent in hotels and in all forms of accommodation rose by 14 per cent. Taking this latter figure, which is considered the more meaningful, the five top markets in terms of volume were still buoyant and expanding considerably: the United Kingdom (+ 7 per cent), Germany (+ 34 per cent), Spain (+ 5 per cent), the Netherlands (+ 16 per cent) and France (+ 13 per cent). The other major changes concerned Finland (+ 68 per cent), Italy (+ 32 per cent), Sweden (+ 26 per cent) and Ireland (+ 37 per cent).

The other non-European OECD countries were all down, except for Australia (+ 3 per cent).

The duration of stay rose in 1991 (7.6 days as against 7.4 days in 1990), which explains the higher growth in terms of nights than in arrivals. At regional level, the Algarve benefited most from international tourism (nights spent up 25 per cent) followed by the autonomous region of Madeira (up 11 per cent).

The number of Spanish visitors (up 6 per cent to 74 per cent of the total) rose faster than the number of tourists (up 5 per cent to 48 per cent of the total), contrary to the general trend. Excursions thus continue to be the predominant form of travel in the case of Spaniards, accounting for about 55 per cent of visitor arrivals in the country.

Spain. After a few difficult years, foreign tourist travel to Spain recovered in 1991 with a 4 per cent increase in nights spent in hotels and a rise of 3 per cent in visitor arrivals at frontiers. In terms of nights, Europe which accounted for 91 per cent of the market, rose by 6 per cent. Its top market,

Germany, went up considerably (+ 14 per cent). The good shape of the German market was partly balanced by the decrease of British nights (- 3 per cent) which still represent a quarter of the total market. On the other hand, sharp decreases were posted for all the regions outside Europe: North America (- 26 per cent) and Japan (- 30 per cent).

The increase in the number of visitors (+ 3 per cent) was similar. Europe was up slightly by 4 per cent since its main markets did well, except, however, for the United Kingdom (- 2 per cent). Arrivals from the other OECD regions declined considerably: North America (- 21 per cent) and Australasia-Japan (- 19 per cent). The same applied to arrivals from non-Member countries (- 10 per cent).

Sweden. For the second year running, nights spent in all forms of accommodation were down by about 14 per cent and nights in hotels by 12 per cent. This situation was partly due to the poor economic situation on the main markets together with Sweden's relatively high prices. Value-added tax payable by hotels and restaurants was reduced to 18 per cent in January 1992, which should increase the competitiveness of this sector of the tourist industry.

An 18 per cent decrease in nights spent in all forms of accommodation was recorded in the the case of tourists from the other Scandinavian countries who account for 40 per cent of the market. In particular, Norway was down by 30 per cent and thus lost its place as Sweden's number one market to Germany, which accounted for 23 per cent of total nights despite a drop of 6 per cent. Even higher decreases were recorded in the case of North America (- 27 per cent).

Switzerland. Results were uneven in Switzerland with nights spent in all forms of accommodation stationary and a 3 per cent decrease in those spent in hotels. The number of nights spent by Europeans in all forms of accommodation rose by 5 per cent while the figure for non-Europeans fell by over 20 per cent. A very sharp upturn was recorded in the number of Germans (+ 10 per cent from 1990) who accounted for 44 per cent of the Swiss market. The increased influx of German tourists was mainly due to those coming from the new Länder. Switzerland's other main European markets were up considerably. To be noted among those showing a decrease, however, were the United Kingdom (- 9 per cent), plus the weakness of the Scandinavian market as well as some Mediterranean countries (Greece, Portugal and especially Turkey). The very sharp rise for Central and Eastern Europe is also worth noting.

Outside Europe, marked decreases were recorded in the case of North America (- 35 per cent) and Australasia-Japan (- 17 per cent), and other non-Member countries.

Turkey. After several years of expansion, international tourism demand slowed down considerably in 1991 with a falls in the number of nights in all forms of accommodation (- 27 per cent) and in hotels (- 21 per cent). The only positive result was the figure for arrivals at frontiers (+ 2 per cent) owing to the massive inflow of travellers from the central and eastern European countries (Yugoslavia excluded) (up 143 per cent from 1990 and 50 per cent of total arrivals in 1991).

In terms of nights spent in all forms of accommodation, the European market accounted for almost 4 million fewer (down by 33 per cent). The sharpest downturns were for France (- 60 per cent), Greece (- 60 per cent), Austria (- 58 per cent) and the United Kingdom (- 38 per cent). However, the central and eastern European countries were up 85 per cent and, with 7 per cent of nights, are now a major market. The figures given concern only the accommodation establishments registered by the Ministry; according to a survey, these tourists stay more frequently in establishments registered by the municipalities where they probably account for 44 per cent of total demand.

United Kingdom. In 1991, the number of nights spent in all forms of accommodation and the number of visitor arrivals at frontiers dropped by 8 per cent. This decline in the number of international travellers, partly due to the Gulf crisis, resulted mainly from the 17 per cent drop in the number of nights spent by travellers from North America and the 11 per cent drop in those from Australasia-Japan.

The European market remained stable on the whole but in fact the trends differed widely from country to country. Of the leading countries, Germany and Spain (+ 9 per cent) were up, while considerably fewer French citizens (- 13 per cent) and Irish citizens (- 11 per cent) visited the United Kingdom. The largest percentage decreases (from 20 to 29 per cent) concerned travellers from Luxembourg, Greece, Denmark, Belgium and Austria.

United States. Tourist arrivals (43 million in all) rose by by over 8 per cent in 1991 after similar progress in 1990. Despite the Gulf war at the start of 1991, during which arrivals from most of the major European markets were down significantly, the end of the year was very satisfactory.

The Canadian market, which accounted for 45 per cent of arrivals, was again up (+ 10 per cent); it must be noted, however, that Canada's share of total arrivals has declined from 86 per cent in 1960 to 73 per cent in 1970 and 51 per cent in 1980.

Mexico was still the second market of the United States with almost 8 million arrivals. The 6 per cent increase in 1991 followed two years of decline. Since 1984 the number of Mexican travellers within the 40 kilometre frontier strip has decreased considerably (by 41 per cent), whereas over the same period arrivals by air (+ 89 per cent) and at points beyond the 40 km area (+ 49 per cent) have increased greatly.

The other three leading markets in terms of volume were all up: Japan (+ 3 per cent), the United Kingdom (+ 11 per cent) and Germany (+ 19 per cent). In terms of growth, Argentina was in the lead with an increase of 52 per cent, followed by Korea (+ 32 per cent), with about 280 000 visitors in each case. Then came Italy and Spain with growth of over 20 per cent.

Downturns were recorded in the case of some regions such as Oceania (- 3 per cent as against + 9 per cent in 1990), the Scandinavian countries (- 8 per cent) and the Middle East (- 2 per cent).

C. MAIN GENERATING COUNTRIES

This part sets out recent developments in the main international tourism generating countries in the OECD area (Tables 4, 5, 6 and 7), namely Canada, France, Germany, Italy, Japan, the Netherlands, the United Kingdom and the United States. In the Annex, summary tables covering the period 1980-1991 give an historical overview of the trends in these main generating countries.

These countries have been selected on the basis of their contribution to the development of international tourism as expressed in terms of dollar expenditures, the standard unit of account for the "Travel" item in the balance of payments. These eight countries together accounted for 78 per cent of total expenditure by the 24 OECD Member-countries in 1990. Of these eight countries, the United States, Germany, Japan and the United Kingdom accounted for 55 per cent of total expenditure.

The data in the summary tables were compiled by adding up the totals for arrivals or nights spent in the various receiving countries. Although gross national statistics are not always comparable with one another, they do give an order of magnitude and an idea of recent trends.

Canadians travelled more to other countries in 1991 (up 7 per cent on 1990 according to Tourism Canada and up 9 per cent in terms of dollar expenditures). In terms of arrivals at frontiers, for which data are available for all the OECD regions, the 1991 increase was entirely due to travel to the United States (+ 10 per cent); Canadians showed a preference for car travel (+ 18 per cent), while the other means of transport were down.

Overseas travel by Canadians decreased for the first time in five years. Their trips to Europe were down by 21 per cent (- 18 per cent in terms of nights). The decrease was particularly marked for Turkey (- 49 per cent), Greece (- 37 per cent), Italy, the United Kingdom and Portugal (down by about 25 per cent). Their arrivals in the Australasia-Japan region were also down (by 4 per cent) and by more in the case of New Zealand (11 per cent).

The decrease in travel by Canadians to Europe was partly due to the impact of the Gulf war, but probably still more to the economic recession affecting this market, the effort to promote domestic tourism and competition from new destinations.

Nights spent by *French* travellers in Europe were down 7 per cent. In the other OECD regions, arrivals at frontiers of French tourists were up 10 per cent in North America and 3 per cent in Australasia-Japan. Expenditures in dollar terms on international tourism in the OECD area decreased by 1 per cent. In Europe, a number of countries recorded a decrease in the case of the French market: nights spent by French travellers were down 60 per cent in Turkey, 13 per cent in the United Kingdom and 5 per cent in Germany. However, the French travelled more to Norway (+ 22 per cent) and to Portugal (+ 13 per cent). Outside Europe, the increase in travel by the French to Canada (+ 18 per cent) and New Zealand (+ 35 per cent) and the decrease in trips to Japan (- 2 per cent) should be noted.

In Europe, the dominant **German** market returned to its pattern of high growth in 1991 (+ 11 per cent in terms of nights and + 4 per cent in dollar expenditure on international tourism) after more or less marking time in the previous year, that of German unification. Germans from the new Länder probably contributed to this increase in outbound tourism. The number of German travellers rose by over 20 per cent in Portugal, Norway and Luxembourg. Two destinations showed a drop: Turkey (- 18 per cent) and Sweden (- 6 per cent). Outside Europe, arrivals of German tourists at frontiers rose by 17 per cent in North America and 2 per cent in Australasia-Japan, although this latter figure marks a 6 per cent drop in the numbers travelling to Japan.

Italians travelled more in 1991 in all the OECD regions: in Europe (nights spent up 15 per cent), North America (arrivals up 17 per cent) and in Australasia-Japan (arrivals up 1 per cent). The most popular European destinations for Italians were Norway (+ 52 per cent), Portugal (+ 32 per cent), Ireland (+ 26 per cent) and France (+ 20 per cent) where they accounted for 10 per cent of nights spent. However, they travelled less to Turkey (- 31 per cent), the Netherlands (- 10 per cent following a rise of 43 per cent in 1990) and Sweden (- 5 per cent). Outside Europe, the United States attracted 21 per cent more Italian tourists and New Zealand 14 per cent more.

The trend for *Japanese* tourist travel abroad was sluggish in 1991, particularly in Europe where nights spent were down 14 per cent, and growth was at a slower pace in the other regions: in North America (+ 2 per cent) and Australasia-Japan (+ 9 per cent). The Japanese heeded the government's advice to stay at home, particularly because of the Gulf war; nonetheless, over 10 million Japanese travelled abroad in 1991 -- twice as many as in 1986. This total marked the end of the so-called 10-million programme, and the government has launched a new plan to increase international tourist flows to and from Japan. Despite this slowdown, studies carried out by the Japanese tourism industry forecast that Japanese outbound tourist travel should again double by the year 2000.

In 1991, the Japanese spent 2 per cent less in dollar terms on international tourism, which was the first time since 1980 that Japanese tourists, expenditure abroad was down.

In Europe, the sharpest downturns were in Turkey (- 33 per cent in nights spent), Spain (- 30 per cent), France (- 25 per cent) and Germany (- 16 per cent). There were, however, a few slight increases: in the United Kingdom (+ 2 per cent) and in Norway (+ 1 per cent). In North America, the number of Japanese tourists rose by 3 per cent in the United States, where they were the third-ranking market, and declined by 4 per cent in Canada. Arrivals were up substantially in Australia (+ 10 per cent) and New Zealand (+ 6 per cent).

The number of nights spent by *Netherlands* tourists in Europe was down 3 per cent, particularly as a result of a 10 per cent decrease in France which is one of the principal destinations. Nights spent by Netherlands travellers were also down for Finland (- 4 per cent) and for Sweden (- 16 per cent).

Table 4. Annual growth rates of number of arrivals at frontiers from main generating countries

	T/V	Total Variation % 91/90	From France		From Germany		From United Kingdom		From United States	
			Relative share % 90	Variation % 91/90	Relative share % 90	Variation % 91/90	Relative share % 90	Variation % 91/90	Relative share % 90	Variation % 91/90
Austria										
Belgium										
Denmark										
Finland										
France (R)	T	4.4			23.1	12.9	13.3	−2.0	3.9	−17.5
Germany										
Greece (N)	T	−9.6	6.4	−16.7	21.7	−18.8	18.6	1.7	3.1	−34.1
Iceland (N)	T	1.1	7.2	0.5	14.9	8.9	9.9	6.7	16.3	−0.5
Ireland (R)	V	−2.3	6.4	11.7	5.6	12.8	58.2	−3.2	12.9	−21.0
Italy (N)	V	−14.9	15.3	−1.1	17.7	−13.8	3.4	−16.4	2.4	−19.9
Luxembourg										
Netherlands										
Norway										
Portugal (N)	T	7.9	7.7	8.0	7.7	26.6	13.2	9.5	2.3	−22.0
Spain (N)	V	2.8	22.3	3.7	13.2	11.4	12.1	−2.2	1.6	−22.0
Sweden										
Switzerland										
Turkey (N)	V	2.4	5.8	−62.3	18.1	−19.9	6.5	−42.9	3.8	−61.5
United Kingdom (R)	V	−7.5	12.8	−0.7	10.4	10.7			16.9	−26.2
EUROPE		−3.2	11.9	0.4	16.9	2.0	9.7	−3.4	4.1	−23.3
Canada (R)	T	−1.8	1.7	18.3	1.7	7.6	3.7	−4.0	80.4	−1.8
United States (R)	T	8.0	1.8	7.6	3.0	18.9	5.7	11.2		
NORTH AMERICA		5.3	1.8	10.4	2.7	16.9	5.1	8.2	22.4	−1.8
Australia (R)	V	7.0	1.0	7.6	3.4	4.7	12.5	−5.1	11.3	8.4
New Zealand (R)	T	−1.3	0.4	35.4	3.1	14.4	8.9	0.8	14.3	−5.0
Japan (N)	V	9.2	1.6	−1.8	2.0	−6.1	6.6	2.3	17.1	−2.1
AUSTRALASIA-JAPAN		6.9	1.2	2.5	2.6	2.3	9.0	−1.4	14.7	0.3
OECD		−1.3	9.6	0.8	13.7	2.6	8.7	−2.0	8.0	−10.1

V Visitors.
T Tourists.
(R) Tourist count by country of residence.
(N) Tourist count by country of nationality.

Their numbers rose sharply in the case of other destinations, particularly Denmark (+ 24 per cent), Norway (+ 19 per cent), Ireland (+ 23 per cent), Portugal (+ 16 per cent) and Spain (+ 17 per cent). Outside Europe, the figures for arrivals, which are the only ones available so far, show a continued sharp increase for North America (+ 9 per cent) but somewhat slower growth in Australasia-Japan (+ 1 per cent). Dollar expenditures were up by 8 per cent on 1990.

The *United Kingdom*, which was still one of the major OECD generating countries, made less of an impact in 1991 at most European destinations. Nights spent by the British in Europe were down by 4 per cent on 1990. The steepest falls were in Turkey (- 38 per cent), Sweden (- 18 per cent), Austria (- 15 per cent), Germany and Switzerland (- 9 per cent). However the British spent more nights in Portugal (+ 7 per cent), Norway (+ 2 per cent) and Netherlands (+ 1 per cent) in 1991.

Outside Europe, arrivals by the British at frontiers rose in the United States by 11 per cent and to a lesser extent in New Zealand (+ 1 per cent) and Japan (+ 2 per cent). On the other hand, the number of British tourists in Canada declined by 4 per cent and in Australia by 5 per cent.

Expenditure by the British abroad declined by 2 per cent in 1991. The economic recession in the United Kingdom was one of the main reasons for the weakness of this market in that year.

Foreign travel by *United States* citizens was down substantially in 1991 (by about 10 per cent in the OECD area and by 1 per cent in dollar terms). This decrease was very marked in Europe but also affected countries like Canada (a 2 per cent drop in arrivals from the United States) where the US accounted for 81 per cent of tourists. The economic situation in the United States, the Yugoslav crisis in Europe and the Gulf war, as well as a dollar which remained stable against most Member country currencies (after having fallen sharply in 1990) did nothing to encourage Americans to travel abroad more.

Nights spent in Europe were down by 19 per cent on average; the decrease was general but very sharp in Austria (- 44 per cent), Switzerland (- 36 per cent), Germany (- 28 per cent) and Finland (- 27 per cent). The number of arrivals in Australasia-Japan was virtually unchanged. Although Australia attracted 8 per cent more Americans, Japan (- 2 per cent) and New Zealand (- 5 per cent) reported fewer US travellers.

Table 5. Annual growth rates of number of arrivals at frontiers from main generating countries

	T/V	Total Variation % 91/90	From Japan		From Netherlands		From Canada		From Italy	
			Relative share % 90	Variation % 91/90	Relative share % 90	Variation % 91/90	Relative share % 90	Variation % 91/90	Relative share % 90	Variation % 91/90
Austria										
Belgium										
Denmark										
Finland										
France (R)	T	4.4	1.2	−25.9	7.6	−10.7	1.2	−9.5	10.8	20.8
Germany										
Greece (N)	T	−9.6	1.2	−46.2	5.6	−9.2	0.8	−36.5	7.0	−16.7
Iceland (N)	T	1.1	0.8	7.7	2.2	−1.4	0.8	−17.3	2.6	33.0
Ireland (R)	V	−2.3					1.2	−21.1		
Italy (N)	V	−14.9	1.1	−12.1	3.5	−27.7	0.8	−26.3		
Luxembourg										
Netherlands										
Norway										
Portugal (N)	T	7.9	0.4	−18.6	3.7	8.9	1.0	−24.5	2.4	32.3
Spain (N)	V	2.8	0.5	−23.5	3.8	10.4	0.3	−12.6	3.2	6.7
Sweden										
Switzerland										
Turkey (N)	V	2.4	0.7	−47.7	2.8	−28.8	0.6	−48.9	2.9	−59.0
United Kingdom (R)	V	−7.5	3.2	−23.1	5.5	8.0	3.9	−25.8	4.0	0.0
EUROPE		−3.2	1.1	−22.2	4.9	−8.0	1.0	−21.0	4.4	12.8
Canada (R)	T	−1.8	2.7	−3.6	0.6	2.4			0.6	−2.0
United States (R)	T	8.0	8.2	2.8	0.7	11.5	43.6	9.6	1.0	20.9
NORTH AMERICA		5.3	6.6	2.0	0.7	9.4	31.5	9.6	0.9	16.6
Australia (R)	V	7.0	21.7	10.1	1.0	1.4	2.4	−0.6	1.1	−0.4
New Zealand (R)	T	−1.3	11.0	6.4	0.8	−2.5	3.5	−10.9	0.3	13.6
Japan (N)	V	9.2			0.5	2.7	2.0	−2.4	0.9	1.3
AUSTRALASIA-JAPAN		6.9	9.1	9.4	0.7	1.2	2.4	−3.7	0.9	1.3
OECD		−1.2	2.4	−5.7	3.9	−7.3	7.3	6.2	3.6	13.0

V Visitors.
T Tourists.
(R) Tourist count by country of residence.
(N) Tourist count by country of nationality.

	H/A	Total Variation % 91/90	From France		From Germany		From the United Kingdom		From the United-States	
			Relative share % 90	Variation % 91/90	Relative share % 90	Variation % 91/90	Relative share % 90	Variation % 91/90	Relative share % 90	Variation % 91/90
Austria (R)	A	5.1	3.2	3.0	59.9	13.1	5.2	−14.7	2.3	−44.3
Belgium (R)	A		9.8		15.1		10.5		4.9	
Denmark (N)	A	11.7	1.6	2.6	35.9	17.1	4.2	−7.2	4.5	−26.2
Finland (R)	H	−10.8	3.4	−3.4	13.7	3.8	5.8	−7.3	8.0	−27.0
France (R)	A	2.3			21.1	10.4	14.2	−2.8	4.7	−17.3
Germany (R)	A	−4.6	5.0	−4.6			9.4	−8.6	13.5	−28.3
Greece (N)										
Iceland										
Ireland (R)	A	−1.2	9.3	−2.9	8.2	15.9	46.3	−5.5	13.2	−12.6
Italy (N)	A	3.1	7.3		38.7		7.1		6.3	
Luxembourg (R)	A	5.9	5.5	−1.8	6.9	23.4	3.7	−3.1	2.8	−21.3
Netherlands (R)	A	4.5	4.8	−4.0	45.2	12.4	11.7	0.7	6.2	−17.5
Norway (N)	H	10.7	4.8	22.1	16.4	23.0	9.6	1.9	10.3	−23.1
Portugal (N)	A	13.5	6.8	12.7	15.3	33.8	28.0	6.6	3.6	−27.3
Spain (N)	H	3.8	9.1	2.7	31.7	14.3	27.3	−2.7	2.4	−26.2
Sweden (N)	A	−13.9	2.8	−9.7	21.3	−5.9	5.1	−18.2	5.2	−26.2
Switzerland (R)	A	0.3	6.6	2.8	39.9	9.5	7.6	−9.2	7.6	−36.4
Turkey (N)	A	−26.9	12.0	−60.2	40.9	−18.0	5.1	−37.9	2.7	−19.5
United Kingdom (R)	A	−7.9	8.7	−12.5	8.9	9.0			14.6	−15.6
EUROPE		−0.1	4.2	−7.2	23.5	11.2	11.8	−3.8	7.2	−19.3
Canada (R)										
United States										
NORTH AMERICA										
Australia	A	−1.1			4.9	−4.1	23.9	−3.4	8.9	14.8
New Zealand	A	−6.6			4.3	28.1	15.5	−1.7	10.3	−10.5
Japan										
AUSTRALASIA-JAPAN										
OECD		−0.1	4.2	−7.2	23.5	11.2	11.8	−3.8	7.2	−19.3

H Hotels and similar establishments.
A All means of accommodation.
(R) Tourist count by country of residence.
(N) Tourist count by country of nationality.

Table 7. **Annual growth rates of nights spent in the various means of accommodation from main generating countries**

	H/A	Total Variation % 91/90	From Japan		From Netherlands		From Canada		From Italy	
			Relative share % 90	Variation % 91/90	Relative share % 90	Variation % 91/90	Relative share % 90	Variation % 91/90	Relative share % 90	Variation % 91/90
Austria (R)	A	5.1	0.5	−11.9	9.6	1.4	0.3	−21.1	3.3	7.0
Belgium (R)	A		1.3		37.3		0.9		3.0	
Denmark (N)	A	11.7	1.2	−13.5	5.5	23.5			2.0	16.7
Finland (R)	H	−10.8	2.6	−10.1	2.2	−4.2	1.3	−22.3	3.2	3.2
France (R)	A	2.3	1.3	−24.7	9.3	−10.1	1.7	−11.1	9.7	19.7
Germany (R)	A	−4.6	4.0	−16.2	16.5	4.6	1.2	−21.7	5.1	2.9
Greece (N)										
Iceland										
Ireland (R)	A	−1.2			2.4	23.4	1.2	11.6	3.1	25.9
Italy (N)	A	3.1	1.9		3.6		0.9			
Luxembourg (R)										
Netherlands (R)	A	4.5	1.2	−7.1			1.3	−25.2	4.7	−9.9
Norway (N)	H	10.7	2.4	0.6	3.6	19.3			2.9	52.1
Portugal (N)	A	13.5	0.4	−6.6	9.6	16.4	2.0	−25.8	2.8	32.4
Spain (N)	H	3.8	1.2	−29.7	2.9	16.5	0.2	−26.1	6.0	8.2
Sweden (N)	A	−13.9	1.5	−7.5	5.8	−15.6	0.4	−37.0	2.1	−4.8
Switzerland (R)	A	0.3	2.3	−11.1	9.1	1.1	0.8	−22.2	5.2	4.9
Turkey (N)	A	−26.9	1.0	−32.6			0.2	−31.0	4.0	−31.2
United Kingdom (R)	A	−7.9	2.0	2.2	2.8	10.3	4.8	−21.4	4.3	7.5
EUROPE		0.1	1.5	−13.7	7.4	−3.0	2.1	−17.9	6.7	14.9
Canada (R)										
United States										
NORTH AMERICA										
Australia	A	−1.1	8.9	−27.0			4.1	−14.4		
New Zealand	A	−6.6	5.8	7.7	1.6	−0.6	3.7	−13.5		
Japan										
AUSTRALASIA-JAPAN										
OECD		0.1	1.5	−13.7	7.4	−3.0	2.1	−17.9	6.7	14.9

H Hotels and similar establishments.
A All means of accommodation.
(R) Tourist count by country of residence.
(N) Tourist count by country of nationality.

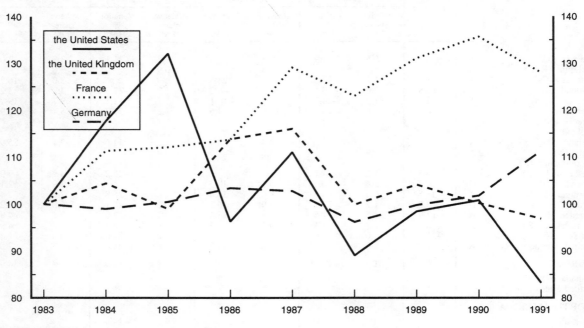

**Trends of international tourism
in Europe, from:**
(Overnights in accommodation, indices 1983=100)

Source: OECD

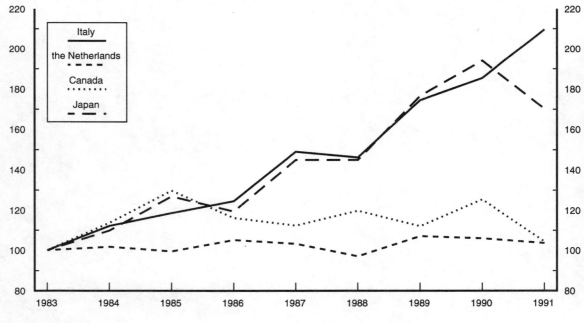

**Trends of international tourism
in Europe, from:**
(Overnights in accommodation, indices 1983=100)

Source: OECD

Trends of international tourism
in North America, from:
(Arrivals at frontiers, indices 1983 = 100)

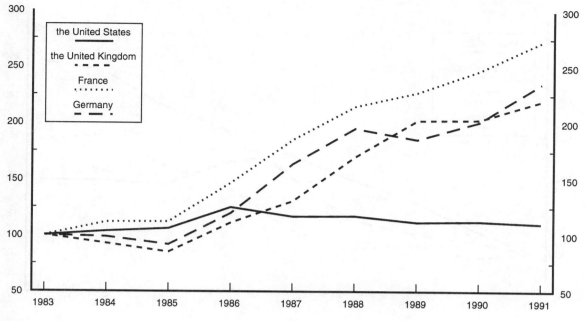

Source: OECD

Trends of international tourism
in North America, from:
(Arrivals at frontiers, indices 1983 = 100)

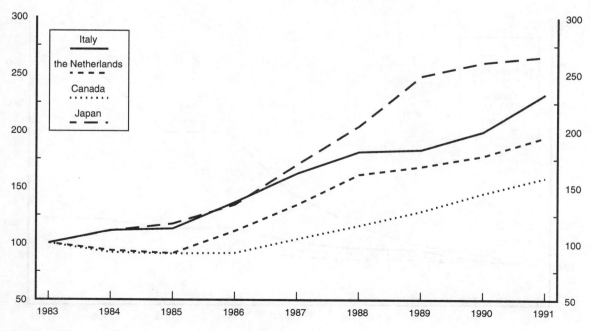

Source: OECD

Trends of international tourism
in Australasia-Japan, from:
(Arrivals at frontiers, indices 1983 = 100)

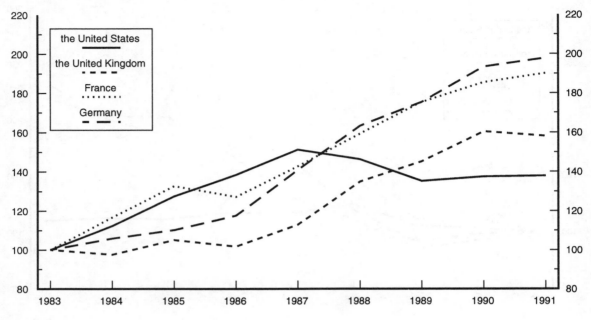

Source: OECD

Trends of international tourism
in Australasia-Japan, from:
(Arrivals at frontiers, indices 1983 = 100)

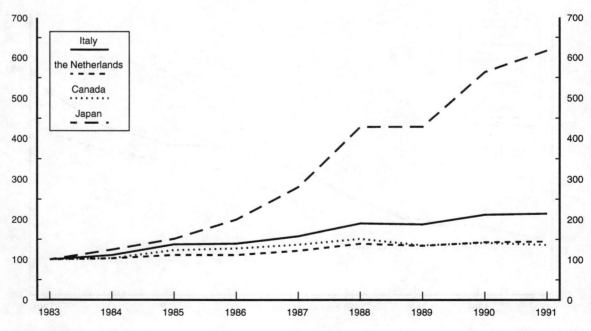

Source: OECD

Chapter III

THE ECONOMIC IMPORTANCE OF INTERNATIONAL
TOURISM IN MEMBER COUNTRIES

This Chapter brings together the most recent data available on international tourism receipts and expenditure in 1991 for the 24 OECD Member countries. The figures do not include international fare payments, except where explicitly stated (see Table 18 in the Statistical Annex).

The first part of the Chapter (Section A) considers:

-- receipts expressed in both national currencies and US dollars, first in current terms and then in real terms, i.e. adjusted for the effects of inflation and for changes in parities between the dollar and national currencies;

-- expenditure, again in both national currencies and US dollars, in current terms;

-- the tourism balance sheet for the OECD area and its three constituent regions.

The dollar was used as the common unit of account to evaluate trends for a range of countries. However, when considering the tables which give figures in "current dollars", the reader must take into account the marked fluctuations that have taken place in recent years in most OECD currencies against the dollar. Great care must therefore be taken when drawing any conclusions from these figures. The dollar remained relatively stable compared with most OECD currencies in 1991, following a year during which the dollar fell against the currencies of most (17) Member countries.

In 1991, the currencies of 20 of the 24 OECD Member countries fluctuated little against the US dollar (see Table 17 of the Annex), keeping within a range of - 2 per cent to + 4 per cent. In the four remaining countries, the dollar appreciated against the Turkish lira (60 per cent compared with 23 per cent in 1990), the Greek drachma (15 per cent) and the Finnish markka (6 per cent). By contrast, the Japanese yen rose by 7 per cent against the dollar.

Section B compares the data on receipts and expenditure with a number of major macroeconomic indicators -- gross domestic product, private final consumption, and exports and imports of goods and services. They cover the period 1988-1990, as comprehensive data for these indicators for 1991 are not yet available.

The comparability of the figures provided by Member countries on receipts and expenditure for international tourism is still insufficient and its improvement is a continuing priority for the Statistical Working Party of the OECD Tourism Committee.

The main source of divergence lies in the different survey methods used. Most countries use the "bank reporting method", which is based on the sales and purchases of foreign currency before or after travel abroad. The main drawback of this method is that it gives data on the currency concerned but not on the country visited. The "estimation method" is based on sample surveys carried out among residents at entry or departure points. Such surveys can provide extensive information but because of their cost are conducted by only a few countries. Lastly, some countries use a "mixed method" involving limited surveys to give adjustment factors to apply to bank-derived data. Progress towards data comparability is being made, however. (For further information, the notes in the Statistical Annex should be consulted.)

A. INTERNATIONAL TOURISM RECEIPTS AND EXPENDITURE

Various events occurred in 1991 which, while they did not directly concern the activities of those responsible for tourism policy in Member countries, nevertheless influenced international tourism growth in the OECD area. These included political and economic problems which affected certain countries and/or regions (for further details, see Chapter II) but also, in some cases, exchange rate fluctuations (see above).

Dollar receipts for the OECD area as a whole were up by 3 per cent, while dollar expenditure was down by 1 per cent (compared with growth rates of respectively 14 per cent and 8 per cent in 1990); this downturn was partly due to the slower growth in international tourism (see Chapter II), but also to the relative stability of the dollar. The decrease in expenditure affected five of the eight major OECD generating countries.

Receipts rose more than expenditure in all OECD regions, particularly in North America (by 12 per cent as against a 1 per cent rise in expenditure). In real terms, receipts in the OECD area were up by 1 per cent in 1991 as against 7 per cent in 1990.

International tourism receipts

Expressed in national currency (see Table 1), the positive and negative variations were on the whole quite moderate, with the exception of Turkey (up by 32 per cent on 1990), but this figure is not significant owing to the country's spiralling inflation (of 66 per cent in 1991). The Netherlands (up 16 per cent), Norway (up 13 per cent) and the United States (up 12 per cent) benefited from growth in international tourism. The decreases included those of Japan (down 11 per cent), the United Kingdom (down 9 per cent) and Italy (down 3 per cent).

Expressed in current dollars (see Table 2), receipts were down in 9 of the 24 OECD countries. Turkey (down 18 per cent) recorded the highest decrease for reasons that were both economic (high inflation, weakness of the currency against the dollar) and political (the Iraq conflict and the Yugoslav crisis). Sweden's and the United Kingdom's receipts were also down, by 6 and 9 per cent respectively, the main reasons being the weakness of their economies and, particularly in the case of Sweden, a decline in competitiveness. Italy recorded a 7 per cent drop in receipts and Japan one of 4 per cent. The highest gains were in the United States (up 12 per cent or $5.4 billion), the Netherlands (up 13 per cent), Norway (up 9 per cent) and Australia (up 10 per cent).

According to the preliminary estimates of the World Tourism Organisation (WTO), international tourism receipts in 1991 amounted to $259 billion, or 2 per cent more than in 1990. Receipts declined by 20 per cent in the Middle East, by 10 per cent in Africa despite a 6 per cent increased in arrivals, and by 1 per cent in Europe (as defined by the WTO). It should be noted that Europe's share in the world total declined, according to these WTO estimates, from 60 per cent in 1980 to 53 per cent in 1991. From a broader standpoint, this gave the OECD countries a 75 per cent share in the world total in 1991.

In real terms (see Table 3), i.e. after adjustment for the effects of inflation and fluctuations in exchange rates against the dollar, international tourism receipts rose by 1 per cent in the OECD area (compared with an increase of 7 per cent in each of the two previous years). Receipts rose by 7 per cent in North America but fell by 4 per cent in Australasia-Japan and by 2 per cent in Europe. The drop in Europe was partly due to a decline of 21 per cent in receipts in Turkey, 14 per cent in the

Table 1. International tourist receipts and expenditure in national currencies

In millions

	Currency	Receipts 1990	Receipts 1991	Receipts %91/90	Expenditure 1990	Expenditure 1991	Expenditure %91/90
Austria	Schilling	152 476	163 000	6.9	87 814	86 999	−0.9
Belgium-Luxembourg	Franc	123 613	124 104	0.4	181 985	190 579	4.7
Denmark	Krone	20 548	22 222	8.1	22 727	21 590	−5.0
Finland	Markka	4 470	4 821	7.9	10 538	10 672	1.3
France	Franc	109 959	120 575	9.7	67 779	69 536	2.6
Germany[2]	Deutsche Mark	17 215	17 630	2.4	47 653	51 056	7.1
Greece	Drachma	407 174	480 200	17.9	172 900	185 100	7.1
Iceland	Krona	7 121	6 944	−2.5	12 690	15 115	19.1
Ireland	Pound	875	939	7.3	701	699	−0.3
Italy[1]	Lira	23 658 000	22 853 073	−3.4	16 569 000	14 451 448	−12.8
Netherlands	Guilder	6 578	7 620	15.8	13 359	14 747	10.4
Norway	Krone	9 662	10 891	12.7	21 714	21 437	−1.3
Portugal	Escudo	502 851	539 755	7.3	122 662	148 324	20.9
Spain	Peseta	1 878 400	1 991 100	6.0	429 300	473 400	10.3
Sweden	Krona	17 196	16 523	−3.9	35 582	36 569	2.8
Switzerland	Franc	9 470	10 170	7.4	8 115	8 180	0.8
Turkey	Lira	8 405 902	11 064 289	31.6	1 355 370	2 467 995	82.1
United Kingdom	Pound	7 831	7 166	−8.5	9 916	9 834	−0.8
Canada	Dollar	6 513	6 715	3.1	12 108	13 003	7.4
United States	Dollar	43 418	48 757	12.3	37 349	36 958	−1.0
Australia	Dollar	4 691	5 153	9.8	5 333	5 032	−5.6
New Zealand	Dollar	2 551	2 615	2.5	1 672	1 720	2.9
Japan	Yen	518 756	462 188	−10.9	3 526 342	3 221 356	−8.6

Notice: for statistical coverage, see notes in table 18 in annex.
1. Break of series in 1990 due to the liberalisation of capital movements.
2. The data relate to the territory of the Federal Republic of Germany prior to 3rd October 1990.

Table 2. International tourist receipts and expenditure in current dollars

In millions

	Receipts 1990	Receipts 1991	Receipts %91/90	Expenditure 1990	Expenditure 1991	Expenditure %91/90
Austria	13 408.4	13 962.5	4.1	7 722.2	7 452.3	−3.5
Belgium-Luxembourg	3 698.5	3 632.9	−1.8	5 445.1	5 578.8	2.5
Denmark	3 321.5	3 473.5	4.6	3 673.8	3 374.8	−8.1
Finland	1 169.4	1 192.4	2.0	2 756.8	2 639.5	−4.3
France	20 191.2	21 375.5	5.9	12 445.9	12 327.3	−1.0
Germany	10 654.0	10 628.2	−0.2	29 491.4	30 779.0	4.4
Greece	2 573.4	2 637.5	2.5	1 092.7	1 016.7	−7.0
Iceland	122.0	117.5	−3.7	217.4	255.8	17.6
Ireland	1 447.2	1 510.7	4.4	1 159.4	1 124.5	−3.0
Italy	19 741.7	18 420.3	−6.7	13 826.2	11 648.3	−15.8
Netherlands	3 612.7	4 075.6	12.8	7 336.9	7 887.6	7.5
Norway	1 543.9	1 680.1	8.8	3 469.7	3 307.0	−4.7
Portugal	3 533.4	3 739.1	5.8	861.9	1 027.5	19.2
Spain	18 426.1	19 157.6	4.0	4 211.2	4 554.9	8.2
Sweden	2 905.6	2 733.1	−5.9	6 012.2	6 049.0	0.6
Switzerland	6 818.8	7 093.9	4.0	5 843.1	5 705.8	−2.3
Turkey	3 225.0	2 654.0	−17.7	520.0	592.0	13.8
United Kingdom	13 910.0	12 641.8	−9.1	17 613.6	17 348.5	−1.5
EUROPE	130 302.9	130 726.3	0.3	123 699.6	122 669.3	−0.8
Canada	5 581.2	5 858.9	5.0	10 375.4	11 345.4	9.3
United States	43 418.3	48 757.3	12.3	37 349.0	36 957.8	−1.0
NORTH AMERICA	48 999.5	54 616.2	11.5	47 724.4	48 303.2	1.2
Australia	3 659.7	4 013.3	9.7	4 160.6	3 919.0	−5.8
New Zealand	1 520.4	1 512.3	−0.5	996.5	994.7	−0.2
Japan	3 582.7	3 436.4	−4.1	24 354.0	23 951.3	−1.7
AUSTRALASIA-JAPAN	8 762.7	8 962.0	2.3	29 511.0	28 865.0	−2.2
OECD	188 065.2	194 304.5	3.3	200 935.0	199 837.6	−0.5

United Kingdom, 12 per cent in Sweden and 9 per cent in Italy and Iceland; these declines were not fully offset by the increases in receipts in the Netherlands (12 per cent), Norway (9 per cent) and France (6 per cent). Outside Europe, Japan recorded a 14 per cent fall in receipts. The marked increase in receipts in the United States (8 per cent) is to be noted.

International tourism expenditure

Expenditure in national currencies (see Table 1) was down in 9 of the 24 OECD countries. The most significant decreases concerned Italy (- 13 per cent), Japan (- 9 per cent) and Australia (- 6 per cent). The most buoyant markets in the OECD area in 1991 were Portugal (+ 21 per cent), Iceland (+ 19 per cent), Spain and the Netherlands (+ 10 per cent).

Expressed in current dollars (see Table 2), only North America recorded growth (of 1 per cent) as a result of the 9 per cent increase in spending by Canadians. Australasia-Japan was down 2 per cent and Australia alone by 6 per cent. Expenditure declined by 1 per cent in Europe where ten of the 18 Member countries noted decreases; expenditure fell markedly in countries like Italy (- 16 per cent), the United Kingdom (- 2 per cent), France (- 1 per cent) and Denmark (- 8 per cent). To be noted, however, were the increases of 19 per cent in Portugal and 18 per cent in Iceland; in addition, Germany, Europe's main generating country, was up 4 per cent.

In all, the OECD countries spent about $200 billion on international tourism, or 1 per cent less than in 1990.

The tourism balance sheet

In 1991 the OECD tourism balance was down substantially to about $6 billion. Growth in receipts exceeded growth in expenditure in all the OECD regions. Receipts in North America rose the fastest from 1981 to 1991 (by 31 per cent); as a result, this region's surplus increased eight-fold over the period to a figure of $6 billion in 1991. Over the same period, the surplus rose by only 36 per cent in Europe. By comparison, the deficit remained stable in Australasia-Japan, at around $20 billion.

B.   THE ECONOMIC IMPORTANCE OF THE "TRAVEL" ACCOUNT IN THE BALANCE OF PAYMENTS

For some years, the Tourism Committee's Statistical Working Party has been working to apply the System of National Accounts (SNA) to pinpoint the economic importance of tourism, principally in monetary terms. The SNA is the only available framework for coherent analysis of the economic contribution of tourism because it brings together commodities, supply and use, and sets them against activities and final users. It also allows links with other parts of the system, such as income and outlays.

The Manual on Tourism Economic Accounts was adopted in April 1991 by the OECD Council. It provides a basis for the compilation of data on production, consumption, value added, gross fixed capital formation and employment in the tourist industries. It will be tested over a three-year trial period which started in 1992. This system will be used as a basic tool to measure the economic importance of tourism in Member countries.

As not enough data are available at present, the Secretariat is still using other indicators which, albeit less satisfactory, are the only ones that give an idea of the macroeconomic importance of tourism.

The final section of this chapter considers the importance of tourism in individual Member countries as measured by four indicators. The tables cover the period 1988 to 1990. It should be noted that this section has not been updated from the preceding issue (except for Table 7), since the 1991 data are not yet available. Admittedly it would have been useful to include international passenger transport payments but, as only a few Member countries break down their "transport" account in this way (see Table 16 in the Statistical Annex), the data would not be comparable.

Share of "travel account" receipts in gross domestic product

"Travel account" receipts (see Table 5) amounted to 1 per cent of GDP for the entire OECD area. The increase in receipts as a proportion of GDP from 1988 to 1990 was particularly marked in Austria (from 8 to 8.5 per cent), in Iceland (from 1.8 to 2.2 per cent), and in Ireland (from 3 to 3.4 per cent). In contrast, the share of receipts in GDP fell fairly sharply in Greece (from 4.5 to 3.9 per cent) and in Spain (from 4.8 to 3.8 per cent), two countries in which tourism plays a major role in the economy.

Share of "travel account" expenditure in private final consumption

From 1988 to 1990 "travel account" expenditure as a proportion of private final consumption in the OECD area rose from 1.9 to 2.1 per cent (see Table 6). The steepest increase in this share over the last three years was in Australasia-Japan (from 1.2 to 1.6 per cent). Substantial increases also occurred in Iceland (from 6.1 to 7.2 per cent), Italy (from 1.2 to 2 per cent) and Finland (from 3.3 to 3.8 per cent). In contrast there was a marked decrease in the share for Norway (from 7.5 to 6.7 per cent) and for the Netherlands (from 5 to 4.5 per cent).

Share of "travel account" receipts in exports of goods and services

The share of international tourism receipts in exports of goods and services for the OECD area started to increase again in 1990, rising to 5 per cent. From 1988 to 1989, this share had remained steady in most countries, but 1990 saw a number of relatively sharp increases: in Greece (from 17.7 per cent to 19.4 per cent), Italy (from 6.4 to 8 per cent) and Turkey (from 13.5 to 14.7 per cent). The most notable decrease was in Spain (from 22.5 per cent to 21 per cent). At regional level, only North America was up substantially, from 5.1 per cent in 1988 to 6 per cent in 1990. The other regions remained at their 1988 level over the same period.

Share of "travel account" expenditure in imports of goods and services

In 1990 "travel account" expenditure accounted for 5.3 per cent of imports of goods and services, or slightly less than in 1988 (5.4 per cent). However, the picture varied from one region to another. In Australasia-Japan, following big increases in previous years, the share of travel account expenditure in imports was down (from 6.4 to 6.3 per cent), as it was for Europe (from 5.4 to 5.2 per cent). In contrast, the share of North America rose slightly (from 5.1 to 5.5 per cent).

Increases occurred in the case of Canada (from 5.2 to 6.3 per cent) and Australia (from 5.3 to 6.3 per cent). There were significant falls in the case of Norway (from 9.1 to 7.8 per cent), Austria (from 11.7 to 10.7 per cent) and Germany (from 7.6 to 6.6 per cent).

Table 3. Trends in international tourist receipts in real prices[1]

	1986 = 100					Relative share in percentage of total	
	1987	1988	1989	1990	1991	1990	1991
Austria	104.5	114.0	126.5	131.7	136.2	7.0	7.1
Belgium-Luxembourg	111.9	124.4	116.0	114.2	111.1	1.9	1.8
Denmark	102.5	105.1	104.1	123.1	129.6	1.6	1.7
Finland	113.5	122.1	121.2	117.1	121.3	0.5	0.6
France	102.7	115.1	140.4	144.1	153.2	10.6	11.2
Germany[5]	100.6	106.9	112.5	117.2	116.0	5.6	5.5
Greece	100.8	102.7	84.9	88.4	87.6	1.2	1.2
Iceland	114.1	131.2	142.7	143.1	130.7	0.1	0.1
Ireland	106.4	120.9	134.0	150.3	156.3	0.8	0.8
Italy[4]	102.5	99.9	95.5	129.4	117.4	9.7	8.7
Netherlands	100.7	103.7	116.9	116.0	129.3	2.0	2.2
Norway	94.1	99.9	92.2	92.8	101.2	0.7	0.8
Portugal	120.2	127.2	137.5	143.6	138.4	1.7	1.6
Spain	103.7	105.3	97.6	89.2	89.3	8.1	8.0
Sweden	110.5	116.3	124.6	118.3	103.9	1.4	1.2
Switzerland	103.6	106.3	112.3	110.3	111.9	3.5	3.6
Turkey	134.2	179.0	169.6	161.1	127.8	1.5	1.2
United Kingdom	108.6	103.5	106.8	110.0	95.1	6.8	5.8
EUROPE[1]	104.8	109.4	113.3	118.6	116.7	64.8	63.2
Canada	94.5	98.7	98.5	103.2	100.7	3.0	2.9
United States	111.0	134.4	158.1	178.1	191.9	27.4	29.3
NORTH AMERICA	108.3	128.7	148.6	166.1	177.3	30.4	32.2
Australia[3]	146.6	189.6	165.6	182.0	193.7	1.8	1.9
New Zealand[2]	101.8	166.6	158.1	168.4	168.3	0.8	0.8
Japan	124.0	152.7	175.3	202.5	174.7	2.2	1.9
AUSTRALASIA-JAPAN[1]	128.6	169.5	168.4	188.3	180.8	4.8	4.6
OECD[1]	106.5	116.1	123.7	132.5	133.6	100.0	100.0

1. After correcting for the effects of inflation in each country. For the regional and OECD totals, the receipts of the individual countries are weighted in proportion to their share in the total expressed in dollars.
2. Changes of series in 1986 and in 1987.
3. Change of statistical coverage in 1987.
4. Break of series in 1990 due to the liberalisation of capital movements.
5. The data relate to the territory of the Federal Republic of Germany prior to 3rd October 1990.

Table 4. Tourism balance sheet
In billions of current dollars

	1989	1990	1991
EUROPE			
Receipts	102.5	130.3	130.7
Expenditure	96.7	123.7	122.7
Balance[1]	*5.8*	*6.6*	*8.1*
NORTH AMERICA			
Receipts	41.6	49.0	54.6
Expenditure	40.8	47.7	48.3
Balance[1]	*0.8*	*1.3*	*6.3*
AUSTRALASIA-JAPAN			
Receipts	7.7	8.8	9.0
Expenditure	27.3	29.5	28.9
Balance[1]	*−19.7*	*−20.7*	*−19.9*
OECD			
Receipts	151.8	188.1	194.3
Expenditure	164.8	200.9	199.8
Balance[1]	*−13.0*	*−12.9*	*−5.5*

1. Minus signs indicate deficits. Due to rounding of figures, balances are not always equal to difference between receipts and expenditure.

International tourist receipts
in real terms (1)
(Shares of the various regions within the OECD)

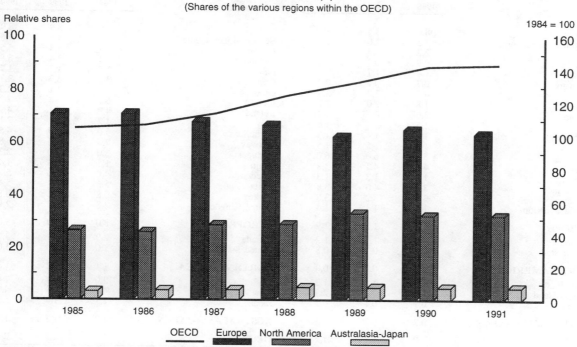

Relative shares

1984 = 100

OECD   Europe   North America   Australasia-Japan

1. New series for Italy from 1990 affecting
regional as well as overall OECD volumes.
Source: OECD

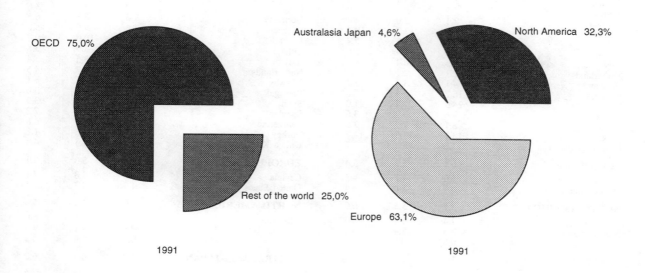

International tourist receipts
Importance of the OECD area in the world total
(in current dollars)

OECD 75,0%

Rest of the world 25,0%

1991

International tourist receipts
Share of the various regions within the OECD
(in real terms)

Australasia Japan 4,6%

North America 32,3%

Europe 63,1%

1991

Source: OECD

Source: OECD

Table 5. Ratio of the "Travel" account receipts to the gross domestic product (%)

	1988	1989	1990
Austria	8.0	8.5	8.5
Belgium-Luxembourg	2.3	2.0	1.9
Denmark	2.2	2.2	2.6
Finland	0.9	0.9	0.9
France	1.4	1.7	1.7
Germany	0.7	0.7	0.7
Greece	4.5	3.7	3.9
Iceland	1.8	2.0	2.2
Ireland	3.0	3.1	3.4
Italy	1.5	1.4	1.8
Netherlands	1.3	1.4	1.3
Norway	1.7	1.5	1.5
Portugal	5.8	6.0	6.0
Spain	4.8	4.3	3.8
Sweden	1.3	1.3	1.3
Switzerland	3.9	4.0	3.8
Turkey	3.3	3.2	3.0
United Kingdom	1.3	1.4	1.4
EUROPE	1.8	1.8	1.9
Canada	1.1	1.1	1.2
United States	0.6	0.7	0.8
NORTH AMERICA	0.7	0.8	0.8
Australia	1.3	1.1	1.2
New Zealand	2.3	2.3	2.3
Japan	0.1	0.1	0.1
AUSTRALASIA-JAPAN	0.2	0.2	0.3
OECD	1.0	1.1	1.2

Source: OECD, Balance of Payments Division and *National Accounts of OECD Member Countries.*

Table 6. Ratio of the "Travel" account expenditure to the private final consumption (%)

	1988	1989	1990
Austria	8.9	8.9	8.9
Belgium-Luxembourg	4.9	4.6	4.6
Denmark	5.4	5.3	5.5
Finland	3.3	3.4	3.8
France	1.7	1.7	1.7
Germany	3.8	3.7	3.7
Greece	2.0	2.1	2.3
Iceland	6.1	6.4	7.2
Ireland	4.9	5.1	4.9
Italy	1.2	1.3	2.1
Netherlands	5.0	4.9	4.5
Norway	7.5	6.6	6.8
Portugal	2.0	2.0	2.3
Spain	1.1	1.3	1.4
Sweden	4.8	5.0	5.2
Switzerland	5.6	5.7	5.4
Turkey	0.8	1.2	0.8
United Kingdom	2.8	2.9	2.9
EUROPE	3.0	2.9	3.0
Canada	2.9	3.1	3.7
United States	1.0	1.0	1.0
NORTH AMERICA	1.1	1.2	1.3
Australia	2.0	2.4	2.4
New Zealand	4.7	4.8	4.9
Japan	1.1	1.4	1.5
AUSTRALASIA-JAPAN	1.2	1.5	1.6
OECD	1.9	1.9	2.1

Source: OECD, Balance of Payments Division and *National Accounts of OECD Member Countries.*

Table 7. Share of "Travel" account receipts in exports of goods and services

	1988	1989	1990
Austria	18.9	18.6	18.4
Belgium-Luxembourg	2.4	1.9	1.8
Denmark	5.9	5.4	6.0
Finland	3.5	3.4	3.4
France	5.5	5.9	5.9
Germany	2.1	2.0	2.0
Greece	21.1	17.7	19.4
Iceland	5.3	5.5	5.7
Ireland	4.5	4.4	5.0
Italy	7.3	6.4	8.0
Netherlands	2.1	2.1	2.0
Norway	4.1	3.3	3.1
Portugal	16.2	15.5	15.6
Spain	24.9	22.5	21.0
Sweden	3.6	3.7	3.6
Switzerland	8.1	7.7	7.5
Turkey	13.1	13.5	14.7
United Kingdom	3.8	3.5	3.7
EUROPE	5.5	5.2	5.4
Canada	4.0	4.2	4.3
United States	5.4	5.8	6.4
NORTH AMERICA	5.1	5.5	6.0
Australia	7.4	6.4	6.9
New Zealand	8.5	8.4	8.2
Japan	0.8	0.8	0.8
AUSTRALASIA-JAPAN	1.7	1.5	1.6
OECD	4.9	4.7	5.0

Source: OECD, Balance of Payments Division.

Table 8. Share of "Travel" account expenditure in imports of goods and services

	1988	1989	1990
Austria	11.7	11.0	10.7
Belgium-Luxembourg	3.3	2.7	2.7
Denmark	7.5	6.7	6.8
Finland	6.1	5.9	6.9
France	3.9	3.7	3.6
Germany	7.6	6.8	6.5
Greece	4.6	4.6	5.0
Iceland	10.2	10.0	10.9
Ireland	4.2	3.9	3.8
Italy	3.5	3.5	5.4
Netherlands	5.2	4.7	4.5
Norway	9.1	7.5	8.1
Portugal	2.6	2.7	3.0
Spain	3.3	3.5	3.9
Sweden	7.2	7.1	7.2
Switzerland	7.7	7.0	6.8
Turkey	1.9	2.6	1.8
United Kingdom	4.6	4.4	4.4
EUROPE	5.4	5.0	5.1
Canada	5.3	5.8	7.1
United States	4.9	4.7	5.1
NORTH AMERICA	5.0	5.0	5.4
Australia	5.2	5.6	6.0
New Zealand	9.8	9.1	9.4
Japan	6.5	6.4	6.2
AUSTRALASIA-JAPAN	6.4	6.4	6.2
OECD	5.4	5.2	5.3

Source: OECD, Balance of Payments Division.

Statistical annex

NOTES AND SOURCES

TOURIST FLOWS IN THE OECD AREA

ACCOMMODATION

PAYMENTS

MOTIVES

TRANSPORT

EMPLOYMENT

PRICES

INTERNATIONAL TOURIST FLOWS FROM MAIN GENERATING COUNTRIES

INTERNATIONAL TOURIST FLOWS BY RECEIVING COUNTRY

NOTES

This Annex reproduces the main international tourism statistical series available in Member countries. For 1991, data are in certain cases provisional. It illustrates recent tourism developments in the OECD (over a two or three-year period).

Some of the data contained in the text itself may not always correspond exactly to that included in the Annex: the discrepancies can be explained by a different statistical coverage (e.g. the use of GNP instead of GDP) or by the use of material of a more analytical nature (data derived from gross figures).

Finally, certain tables are prepared from data available for other OECD work (e.g. Balance of Payments and National Accounts). In some cases, these statistics, which have been standardised to follow existing international guidelines, may differ from the ones supplied by countries in response to the annual questionnaire of the Tourism Committee.

Three tables of general interest for the use of the statistical series are presented at the beginning of the Annex:

A. Classification of travellers;
B. Series available by countries;
C. Types of establishments covered by the statistics.

Main elements of the terminology used

This section indicates the main methods used for collecting statistics and deals with international tourism.

Table A gives an overview of the international classification of travellers.

International inbound tourism (i.e. tourism performed in a given country by non-residents) is usually measured by the receiving country as monthly, quarterly or annual number of arrivals and/or nights spent, using one of three methods:

-- *Border controls*: these can provide only a limited amount of information about volumes, means of transport, etc. (as used in Japan, New Zealand and Spain);

-- *Sample surveys*: these provide a large amount of quantitative and qualitative information (as used in Canada, Portugal and the United Kingdom);

-- *Registration in means of accommodation*: this method, which is used in Finland, Italy and Switzerland among others, provides more accurate information, but with a more limited scope. However, by definition, it excludes excursionists and certain types of accommodation that are not registered for tax or other reasons, such as that provided by relatives or friends.

In estimating tourism supply, it is necessary to take account of all the goods and services required by tourism i.e. the resources, infrastructure and industries producing such goods and services, whether in the tourism field itself or indirectly related to the tourist industries.

The various means of accommodation are an essential part of this supply. They can be divided into two broad categories: hotels and similar establishments, and supplementary means of accommodation.

The first category (hotels and similar establishments) normally covers four types of establishments: hotels, motels, boarding houses and inns. However, in order to reflect the actual situation in a country more accurately, similar establishments are also often included (in which case the statistical coverage is indicated in Table C or in the methodological notes for each country).

The second category (supplementary means of accommodation) can include seven types of establishment: youth hostels, camping sites, holiday villages, mountain huts and shelters, rented rooms, houses and flats, sanatoria and health establishments and children's holiday camps. The list can also be extended in some cases.

The data on international tourism receipts and expenditure are those found under the "travel" heading in the Balance of Payments. They are available in varying degrees of disaggregation by country/region of origin or country/region of destination.

Data concerning international tourism payments follow, in practice, the recommendations of the World Tourism Organisation.

International tourism receipts: they are defined as the receipts of a country resulting from consumption expenditures, i.e., payments for goods and services, made by visitors out of foreign currency. They should, however, exclude all forms of remuneration resulting from employment, as well as international fare receipts.

International tourism expenditure: is defined as consumption expenditures, i.e., payments for goods and services, made by residents of a country visiting abroad. It should, however, exclude all forms of remuneration resulting from employment, as well as international fare payments.

Three different methods are currently used by the Member countries.

In most countries, data are collected by the central bank using a method called the *bank reporting method*. When a traveller purchases or sells currency before or after a trip abroad, the bank or authorised agency records the transaction. Under this method, data are broken down according to the currency used and not according to the traveller's country of origin or destination.

The *estimation method* is based on sample surveys that are usually carried out at the points of entry or departure for non-residents, or at the re-entry points for returning residents. Data are broken down according to tourists' country of origin or destination. These surveys provide the most reliable and most detailed statistics.

The *mixed method*, which is used by only a few countries, was developed to remedy the shortcomings of the bank reporting method. It uses parallel sources (surveys of visitors, comparison with data provided by receiving countries, etc.), allowing the statistics obtained by the bank reporting method to be adjusted.

However, these data have their limitations. First, the volumes obtained by the bank reporting method in most countries are not an accurate measure of international tourist trade, since they represent net balances and not gross volumes; tourist transactions therefore tend to be understated. Second, it was noted that items unrelated to international tourism were included under the "travel" heading. Third, large discrepancies are found when any attempt is made to compile bilateral balances by comparing a given country's receipts, broken down by country of origin, with the expenditure reported by generating countries, broken down by country of destination.

Geographic coverage

Belgium-Luxembourg: Balance-of-payments statistics refer to the Belgo-Luxembourg Economic Union.

Other OECD Europe: include OECD European countries for which no breakdown is available.

Other European countries: include non OECD European countries for which no breakdown is available.

Origin country unspecified: includes non OECD countries which cannot be broken down into any specific large geographic (other European countries, Latin America, Asia-Oceania, Africa).

Conventional signs:

/ *Break of series.*

SOURCES

The principal national bodies for each OECD Member country dealing with tourism statistics are as follows:

Australia
    Bureau of Tourism Research
    Australian Bureau of Statistics

Austria
    Osterreichisches Statistisches Zentralamt
    Osterreichische Nationalbank

Belgium
    Institut National de Statistiques
    Banque nationale de Belgique
    Institut Belgo-Luxembourgeois du Change

Canada
    Statistics Canada, International Travel Section
    Industry, Science and Technology Canada, Tourism

Denmark
    Danmarks Statistik
    Danmarks National Bank

Finland
    Central Statistical Office
    Bank of Finland

France
    Ministère du Tourisme, Direction des Industries touristiques
    Banque de France

Germany
    Statistisches Bundesamt
    Deutsche Bundesbank

Greece
    National Statistical Service of the National Tourist Organisation of Greece
    Bank of Greece

Iceland
    Icelandic Immigration Authorities
    Iceland Tourist Board
    Central Bank of Iceland

Ireland
    Central Statistics Office
    Irish Tourist Board (Bord Failte)

Italy
    Ministero del Turismo e dello Spetacolo
    Istituto Centrale di Statistica
    Banca d'Italia

Japan
    Ministry of Transport, Department of Tourism
    Japan National Tourist Organisation
    Bank of Japan

Luxembourg
    Service Central de la Statistique et des Etudes Economiques (STATEC)
    Institut Belgo-Luxembourgeois du Change

Netherlands
    Ministry of the Economy
    Central Bureau of Statistics
    Dutch Central Bank

New Zealand
    New Zealand Tourism Department

Norway
    Central Bureau of Statistics
    Bank of Norway

Portugal
    Direcçao-Geral de Turisme
    Instituto Nacional de Estatistica
    Banco de Portugal

Spain
    Instituto Nacional de Estadisticas
    Banco de Espana

Sweden
    Central Bureau of Statistics
    Central Bank of Sweden

Switzerland
   Office Fédéral de la Statistique, Section du Tourisme

Turkey
   Ministry of Tourism
   Central Bank

United Kingdom
   Department of Employment, Office of Population Censuses and Surveys
   British Tourist Authority

United States
   Department of Commerce, United States Travel and Tourism Administration (USTTA)
   Department of Commerce, Bureau of Economic Analysis

Graph A. Classification of international visitors

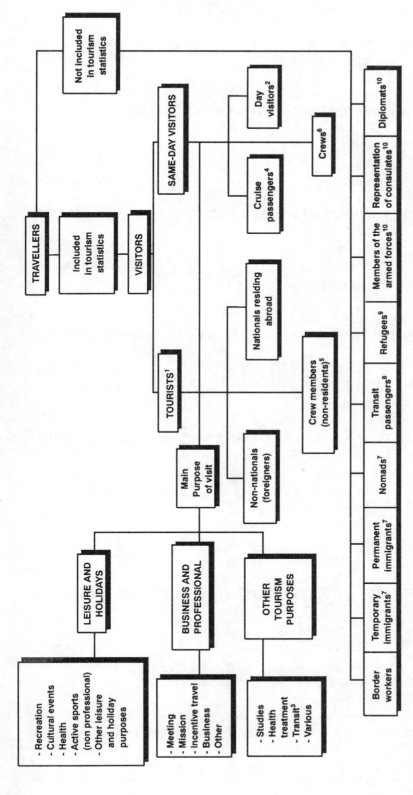

1. Visitors who spend at least one night in the country visited, but less than one year.
2. Visitors who arrive and leave the same day for pleasure, professional or other tourism purposes including transit day visitors en route to or from their destination countries.
3. Overnight visitors en route to or from their destination countries.
4. Persons who arrive in a country aboard cruise ships (as defined by the International Maritime Organization (IMO), 1965) and who spend the night aboard ship even when disembarking for one or more day visits.
5. Foreign air or ship crews docked or in lay over and who use the accommodation establishments of the country visited.
6. Crews who are not residents of the country visited and who stay in the country for the day.
7. As defined by the United Nations in the Recommendations on Statistics of International.
8. Who do not leave the transit area of the airport or the port, including transfer between airports or ports.
9. As defined by the United Nations High Commissioner for Refugees, 1967.
10. When they travel from their country of origin to the duty station and vice-versa (including household servants and dependants accompanying or joining them).

Source: World Tourism Organisation.

B. Series available by country

ARRIVALS OF FOREIGN TOURISTS AT FRONTIERS

Canada	Iceland	Portugal
France	New Zealand	United States
Greece		

ARRIVALS OF FOREIGN VISITORS AT FRONTIERS

Australia	Italy	Spain
Canada	Japan	Turkey (travellers)
Ireland	Portugal	United Kingdom

ARRIVALS OF FOREIGN TOURISTS AT HOTELS AND SIMILAR ESTABLISHMENTS

Austria	Italy*	Spain
France	Netherlands	Switzerland
Germany	Portugal	Turkey
Ireland		

ARRIVALS OF FOREIGN TOURISTS AT ALL MEANS OF ACCOMMODATION

Austria	Italy*	Switzerland
Germany	Netherlands	Turkey
Ireland	Portugal	

NIGHTS SPENT BY FOREIGN TOURISTS IN HOTELS AND SIMILAR ESTABLISHMENTS

Australia	Germany	Portugal
Austria	Ireland	Spain
Belgium*	Italy*	Sweden
Denmark	Netherlands	Switzerland
Finland	Norway	Turkey
France		

NIGHTS SPENT BY FOREIGN TOURISTS IN ALL MEANS OF ACCOMMODATION

Australia	Germany	Sweden
Austria	Ireland	Switzerland
Belgium*	Italy*	Turkey
Denmark	Netherlands	United Kingdom
France	Portugal	

*   As 1991 statistical series are not available, these tables show 1989 and 1990 data.

C. Types of accommodation covered by the statistics

Countries	Hotels and similar establishments[11]					Supplementary means of accommodation[12]							
	Hotels[1]	Motels[2]	Boarding houses[3]	Inns[4]	Others[5]	Youth hostels[6]	Camping and caravan[4] sites	Holiday villages	Mountain huts and shelters	Rented rooms, flats and houses	Sanatoria, health establishments	Recreation homes for children[8]	Others[9]
Australia	X	X	X		X	X	X	X		X			X
Austria[10]	X	X				X	X		X	X			X
Belgium	X				X		X			X	X	X	X
Canada	X	X					X				X	X	X
Denmark[10]	X				X	X	X						X
Finland	X		X		X		X	X					
France	X						X						
Germany	X	X	X	X	X	X	X	X		X	X		X
Greece	X	X	X	X	X		X						X
Ireland	X		X										
Italy	X				X	X	X			X			X
Netherlands	X	X	X		X	X	X						
Norway[10]	X				X	X	X						
Portugal	X	X	X	X	X		X					X	
Spain	X	X			X		X	X					X
Sweden	X	X	X		X	X	X	X					
Switzerland	X	X	X	X		X	X			X	X		X
Turkey	X	X	X	X	X		X	X					X

Countries not listed in this table do not dispose of data by type of accommodation.

1. Includes: Germany: hotels serving breakfast only; Belgium: motels, boarding houses and inns; Finland: motels; France: motels; Ireland: motels; Portugal: studio-hotels; Spain: "Paradores" and Casas de Huespedes"); Sweden: motels; Switzerland: boarding houses; Turkey: thermal hotels.
2. Includes: Greece: bungalows.
3. Includes: Finland: inns; Ireland: inns; Sweden: resort hotels.
4. Includes: Portugal: private and state-owned inns.
5. Includes: Australia: hotels and motels without facilities in most rooms and not necessarily providing meals and alcoholic drinks; Belgium: non-licensed establishments; Finland: lodging houses and part of youth hostels; Greece: bungalow-hotels, studio-hotels and recreation homes for children; Turkey: special licensed hotels and studio-hotels; Netherlands: youth hostels in Amsterdam; Portugal: holiday flats and villages; Spain: fondas; Sweden: boarding houses, inns, and resort hotels.
6. Includes: Germany: mountain huts and shelters.
7. Includes: Australia: cabins and flats; Finland: holiday village cottages.
8. Includes: Portugal: youth hostels.
9. Includes: Australia: rented farms, house-boats, rented camper-vans, boats, cabin cruisers, camping outside commercial grounds; Austria: mountain huts and shelters; Belgium: youth hostels, holiday villages and social tourism establishments; Canada: homes of friends or relatives, private cottages, commercial cottages and others (universities, hostels); Germany: recreation and holiday homes, institutions providing educational services; Greece: holiday centres; Italy: recreation homes for children, mountain huts and shelters, holiday homes and religious establishments; Spain: secondary residences, private apartments, chalets and bungalows; Switzerland: dormitories in recreation homes for children, tourist camps, mountain huts and shelters, holiday villages.
10. Total available without breakdown for "hotels and similar establishments".
11. Includes: Denmark: hotels with more than 40 beds.
12. Includes: Denmark: January and February (hotels only), March (hotels and campings January to march), October (hotels and campings October to December), November and December (hotels only).

1. Tourism from European Member countries [1]

	Arrivals at frontiers [2]			Arrivals at all means of accommodation [3]			Nights spent in all means of accommodation [4]		
	Volume 1991 (thousands)	% 91/90	% 90/89	Volume 1991 (thousands)	% 91/90	% 90/89	Volume 1991 (thousands)	% 91/90	% 90/89
Austria				16 989.1	6.0	0.0	94 022.1	8.4	− 2.8
Belgium									5.8
Denmark							9 588.9	14.6	10.1
Finland							1 518.2	− 1.6	− 6.0
France	49 413.0	6.5	55.1	19 483.5	3.6	4.9	313 571.0	4.3	5.7
Germany [5]				9 660.8	− 3.1	4.6	22 265.0	− 0.2	3.5
Greece	6 245.7	− 11.1	8.5						
Iceland	114.3	1.7	10.8						
Ireland	2 553.0	1.5	14.1	2 499.0	0.8	11.3	27 136.0	0.5	11.1
Italy	41 359.2	− 8.5	1.9			− 2.1			− 5.1
Luxembourg									
Netherlands				4 922.0	13.6	5.0	15 229.6	7.5	17.1
Norway							3 318.9	17.1	4.7
Portugal	8 079.9	9.6	13.4	4 248.1	12.1	7.1	20 351.0	16.4	6.3
Spain	49 319.5	4.4	− 2.8	9 874.1	4.8	− 10.4	67 241.2	17.2	− 19.0
Sweden							4 507.9	− 13.9	− 16.0
Switzerland				7 706.6	3.3	2.0	31 262.3	4.6	1.3
Turkey	1 836.9	− 36.4	7.3	1 519.1	− 50.0	2.8	7 692.6	− 33.0	14.1
United Kingdom	10 715.0	2.6	− 1.0				89 865.0	0.0	1.4
Canada	1 576.8	2.0	1.0						
United States	7 147.0	10.7	6.1						
Australia	515.2	− 2.8	3.7				18 179.0	− 3.5	24.7
New Zealand	172.2	4.8	15.6				4 721.8	15.8	13.3
Japan	482.9	− 0.3	13.1						

1. Derived from tables by receiving country (see corresponding notes).
2. *Tourist* or *visitor arrivals.* When both available: *tourist arrivals.*
3. Arrivals *in all means of accommodation* or *in hotels and similar establishments.* When both available: arrivals *in all means of accommodation.*
4. Nights spent *in all means of accommodation* or *in hotels and similar establishments.* When both available: nights spent *in all means of accommodation.*
5. The data relate to the territory of the Federal Republic of Germany prior to 3rd October 1990.

2. Tourism from Canada and the United States [1]

	Arrivals at frontiers [2]			Arrivals at all means of accommodation [3]			Nights spent in all means of accommodation [4]		
	Volume 1991 (thousands)	% 91/90	% 90/89	Volume 1991 (thousands)	% 91/90	% 90/89	Volume 1991 (thousands)	% 91/90	% 90/89
Austria				546.4	− 44.8	29.1	1 387.8	− 41.9	24.5
Belgium									7.5
Denmark							311.0	− 26.2	− 3.4
Finland							169.0	− 26.3	− 2.7
France	2 261.0	− 15.6	23.7	2 114.5	− 28.1	7.3	19 688.0	− 15.6	1.4
Germany [5]				1 777.8	− 32.7	16.8	3 715.8	− 27.8	11.0
Greece	227.5	− 34.6	− 2.8						
Iceland	23.4	− 1.3	− 2.0						
Ireland	343.0	− 21.0	4.1	356.0	− 19.6	3.7	4 310.5	− 10.7	− 4.6
Italy	1 487.5	− 21.5	6.5			5.3			3.1
Luxembourg									
Netherlands				489.1	− 20.6	9.4	1 009.6	− 18.9	11.1
Norway							280.2	− 23.1	5.0
Portugal	206.3	− 22.8	− 1.0	258.1	− 29.3	0.2	787.8	− 26.7	3.0
Spain	790.3	− 20.5	− 11.7	630.4	− 26.4	− 5.0	1 447.4	− 24.0	− 5.4
Sweden							270.8	− 27.1	− 1.2
Switzerland				876.9	− 38.3	15.0	1 998.3	− 35.1	12.1
Turkey	96.9	− 59.7	1.8	100.8	− 42.2	− 6.2	307.7	− 20.4	− 8.1
United Kingdom	2 771.0	− 26.1	7.8				31 501.0	− 17.0	4.9
Canada	12 049.6	− 1.8	0.7						
United States	18 926.6	9.6	12.4						
Australia	325.2	6.8	− 3.3				8 927.1	5.6	19.7
New Zealand	163.0	− 6.2	3.1				2 623.0	23.3	5.3
Japan	605.3	− 2.1	4.6						

1. Derived from tables by receiving country (see corresponding notes).
2. *Tourist* or *visitor arrivals.* When both available: *tourist arrivals.*
3. Arrivals *in all means of accommodation* or *in hotels and similar establishments.* When both available: arrivals *in all means of accommodation.*
4. Nights spent *in all means of accommodation* or *in hotels and similar establishments.* When both available: nights spent *in all means of accommodation.*
5. The data relate to the territory of the Federal Republic of Germany prior to 3rd October 1990.

3. Tourism from Australia, New Zealand and Japan[1]

	Arrivals at frontiers[2]			Arrivals at all means of accommodation[3]			Nights spent in all means of accommodation[4]		
	Volume 1991 (thousands)	% 91/90	% 90/89	Volume 1991 (thousands)	% 91/90	% 90/89	Volume 1991 (thousands)	% 91/90	% 90/89
Austria				276.9	− 21.0	19.2	616.4	− 15.7	20.2
Belgium									− 6.3
Denmark							93.4	− 13.5	− 8.0
Finland							57.3	− 10.1	4.6
France	458.0	− 25.9	− 19.8	1 179.1	− 18.4	1.1	3 554.0	− 24.7	5.0
Germany[5]				791.0	− 21.4	9.8	1 404.3	− 17.1	8.9
Greece	133.0	− 40.1	− 4.4						
Iceland	1.9	0.8	− 1.3						
Ireland	50.0	− 24.2	11.9	54.0	− 21.7	11.3	872.6	33.6	− 9.7
Italy	759.5	− 17.2	25.4			6.8			7.7
Luxembourg									
Netherlands				161.5	− 14.8	15.6	334.0	− 11.0	14.2
Norway							85.0	0.6	5.5
Portugal	45.9	− 15.2	8.0	54.0	− 10.3	5.6	130.1	− 4.1	3.9
Spain	253.7	− 19.4	9.5	341.7	− 31.4	5.6	629.6	− 28.1	2.1
Sweden							89.8	− 7.5	15.9
Switzerland				532.9	− 20.6	5.3	980.5	− 17.0	5.2
Turkey	46.1	− 45.9	13.0	60.2	− 37.6	7.3	112.1	− 34.5	3.1
United Kingdom	996.0	− 24.9	14.1				19 119.0	− 10.8	17.7
Canada	526.6	− 6.3	4.9						
United States	3 935.8	1.7	6.0						
Australia	1 009.1	12.3	12.5				13 228.3	− 8.2	8.7
New Zealand	460.3	− 0.8	8.1				1 311.2		
Japan	72.6	0.3	1.8						

1. Derived from tables by receiving country (see corresponding notes).
2. *Tourist* or *visitor arrivals*. When both available: *tourist arrivals*.
3. Arrivals *in all means of accommodation* or *in hotels and similar establishments*. When both available: arrivals *in all means of accommodation*.
4. Nights spent *in all means of accommodation* or *in hotels and similar establishments*. When both available: nights spent *in all means of accommodation*.
5. The data relate to the territory of the Federal Republic of Germany prior to 3rd October 1990.

4. Tourism from all OECD countries[1]

	Arrivals at frontiers[2]			Arrivals at all means of accommodation[3]			Nights spent in all means of accommodation[4]		
	Volume 1991 (thousands)	% 91/90	% 90/89	Volume 1991 (thousands)	% 91/90	% 90/89	Volume 1991 (thousands)	% 91/90	% 90/89
Austria				17 812.3	2.6	1.6	96 026.3	6.9	− 2.1
Belgium									5.7
Denmark							9 993.3	12.4	9.1
Finland							1 744.5	− 5.0	− 5.2
France	52 132.0	4.9	51.2	22 777.1	− 1.8	4.9	336 813.0	2.5	5.3
Germany[5]				12 229.5	− 10.2	7.2	27 385.1	− 6.0	5.0
Greece	6 606.2	− 13.1	7.5						
Iceland	139.6	1.1	8.2						
Ireland	2 946.0	− 2.3	12.5	2 909.0	− 2.8	10.1	32 319.1	− 0.5	8.0
Italy	43 606.3	− 9.2	2.4			− 0.7			− 4.2
Luxembourg									
Netherlands				5 572.6	8.5	5.9	16 573.2	4.9	16.5
Norway							3 684.1	12.2	4.7
Portugal	8 332.1	8.3	12.8	4 560.2	8.2	6.4	21 268.9	13.8	6.1
Spain	50 363.5	3.7	− 2.9	10 846.3	0.7	− 9.4	69 318.3	15.2	− 18.4
Sweden							4 868.6	− 14.6	− 14.8
Switzerland				9 116.4	− 4.5	4.0	34 241.1	0.3	2.3
Turkey	1 980.0	− 38.4	7.0	1 680.0	− 49.2	2.4	8 112.4	− 32.6	13.0
United Kingdom	14 482.0	− 6.7	2.2				140 485.0	− 5.9	4.3
Canada	14 153.0	− 1.5	0.9						
United States	30 009.4	8.8	9.9						
Australia	1 849.5	6.8	6.6				40 334.4	− 3.3	17.7
New Zealand	795.5	− 0.8	8.4				8 656.0	39.5	10.4
Japan	1 160.8	− 1.2	7.7						

1. Derived from tables by receiving country (see corresponding notes).
2. *Tourist* or *visitor arrivals*. When both available: *tourist arrivals*.
3. Arrivals *in all means of accommodation* or *in hotels and similar establishments*. When both available: arrivals *in all means of accommodation*.
4. Nights spent *in all means of accommodation* or *in hotels and similar establishments*. When both available: nights spent *in all means of accommodation*.
5. The data relate to the territory of the Federal Republic of Germany prior to 3rd October 1990.

5. Tourism from non-Member countries [1]

	Arrivals at frontiers [2]			Arrivals at all means of accommodation [3]			Nights spent in all means of accommodation [4]		
	Volume 1991 (thousands)	% 91/90	% 90/89	Volume 1991 (thousands)	% 91/90	% 90/89	Volume 1991 (thousands)	% 91/90	% 90/89
Austria				1 279.5	− 22.5	48.3	3 615.4	− 26.7	55.5
Belgium									8.2
Denmark							438.1	− 1.4	5.2
Finland							456.4	− 27.8	9.0
France	2 803.0	0.3	− 83.2	2 461.0	− 4.9	17.3	35 362.0	0.5	− 8.7
Germany [5]				2 065.1	2.6	3.3	5 861.0	2.7	− 2.3
Greece	1 412.7	10.8	25.8				29 873.0	− 14.7	6.3
Iceland	.8	− 7.2	7.6						
Ireland	52.0	0.0	4.0	106.0	1.9	19.5	966.9	− 20.1	− 4.9
Italy	7 710.9	− 37.1	49.2			16.6			13.6
Luxembourg									
Netherlands				269.3	− 9.8	0.4	632.7	− 5.0	8.1
Norway							232.7	− 8.4	− 14.5
Portugal	324.8	− 0.9	10.4	208.8	− 4.8	8.2	688.4	4.1	7.0
Spain	3 131.5	− 10.3	− 13.7	1 202.6	− 2.8	− 4.6	4 660.1	4.1	− 2.6
Sweden							791.8	− 9.4	− 2.0
Switzerland				968.1	− 0.2	7.1	2 742.7	0.1	6.7
Turkey	3 537.9	62.5	49.4	718.7	28.0	1.5	1 586.7	29.3	1.6
United Kingdom	2 179.7	− 12.5	16.0				40 343.0	− 14.3	6.4
Canada	797.4	− 12.6	0.5						
United States	12 740.1	6.3	4.0						
Australia	520.8	8.0	5.9				24 310.4	2.8	15.5
New Zealand	168.0	− 3.5	7.9				10 996.6	− 23.9	9.1
Japan	2 373.5	15.1	18.2	2 423.5					

1. Derived from tables by receiving country (see corresponding notes).
2. *Tourist* or *visitor arrivals.* When both available: *tourist arrivals.*
3. Arrivals *in all means of accommodation* or *in hotels and similar establishments.* When both available: arrivals *in all means of accommodation.*
4. Nights spent *in all means of accommodation* or *in hotels and similar establishments.* When both available: nights *in all means of accommodation.*
5. The data relate to the territory of the Federal Republic of Germany prior to 3rd October 1990.

6. Tourism from all countries [1]

	Arrivals at frontiers [2]			Arrivals at all means of accommodation [3]			Nights spent in all means of accommodation [4]		
	Volume 1991 (thousands)	% 91/90	% 90/89	Volume 1991 (thousands)	% 91/90	% 90/89	Volume 1991 (thousands)	% 91/90	% 90/89
Austria [5]				19 091.8	0.4	4.4	99 641.7	5.1	− 0.2
Belgium									5.9
Denmark							10 431.4	11.7	8.9
Finland							2 200.9	−10.8	− 2.0
France	54 935.0	4.6	6.0	25 238.1	− 2.1	6.0	372 175.0	2.3	3.8
Germany [7]				14 294.6	− 8.5	6.6	33 246.1	− 4.6	3.8
Greece	8 018.9	− 9.6	9.8				29 873.0	−14.7	6.3
Iceland	140.4	1.1	8.2						
Ireland	2 998.0	− 2.3	12.3	3 015.0	− 2.6	10.4	33 286.0	− 1.2	7.4
Italy	51 317.2	−14.9	9.4			1.3			− 2.5
Luxembourg									
Netherlands				5 841.9	7.5	5.5	17 205.9	4.5	16.1
Norway							3 916.8	10.7	3.1
Portugal	8 656.9	7.9	12.7	4 769.1	7.5	6.5	21 957.3	13.5	6.1
Spain	53 495.0	2.8	− 3.7	12 048.9	0.3	− 8.9	73 978.4	14.5	−17.5
Sweden							5 660.4	−13.9	−13.3
Switzerland [6]				10 084.5	− 4.1	4.2	36 983.8	0.3	2.6
Turkey [5]	5 517.9	2.4	20.9	2 398.7	−38.0	2.3	9 699.1	−26.9	11.8
United Kingdom	16 661.7	− 7.5	3.9				180 828.0	− 7.9	4.8
Canada	14 950.4	− 2.2	0.9						
United States	42 749.5	8.0	8.1						
Australia	2 370.3	7.0	6.5				64 644.8	− 1.1	16.9
New Zealand	963.5	− 1.3	8.3				19 652.6	− 4.8	9.5
Japan	3 534.4	9.2	14.2	2 423.5					

1. Derived from tables by receiving country. See corresponding notes, except for the countries mentioned in notes 5 and 6 below.
2. *Tourist* or *visitor arrivals.* When both available: *tourist arrivals.*
3. Arrivals *in all means of accommodation* or *in hotels and similar establishments.* When both available: arrivals *in all means of accommodation.*
4. Nights spent *in all means of accommodation* or *in hotels and similar establishments.* When both available: nights *in all means of accommodation.*
5. *Traveller* arrivals at frontiers.
6. *Tourist* arrivals at frontiers: estimates.
7. The data relate to the territory of the Federal Republic of Germany prior to 3rd October 1990.

7. TOURISM FROM THE UNITED STATES
EXPENDITURE OF US RESIDENTS TRAVELLING ABROAD

In millions of dollars

	1987	1988	1989	1990	1991
Expenditure abroad[1]	29 310	32 114	33 418	37 349	36 958
Canada[2]	2 939	3 232	3 396	3 541	3 704
Mexico	3 058	3 622	4 276	4 879	5 149
Total overseas	23 313	25 260	25 746	28 929	28 104
Western Europe	10 021	11 086	11 668	13 615	12 835
United Kingdom	2 974	3 325	3 319	3 657	3 599
Germany	2 203	2 423	2 664	2 671	2 520
France	1 139	1 233	1 553	1 788	1 651
Italy	1 460	1 682	1 425	1 631	1 653
Eastern Europe	230	261	299	381	341
Carribean, South and Central America	4 822	5 172	5 123	5 395	5 806
Japan	1 572	1 803	1 872	2 210	2 304
Australia, New Zealand and South Africa	894	1 019	1 049	1 249	1 262
Australia	622	694	726	867	873
Other	5 774	5 919	6 735	6 079	5 556
Fare payments					
Foreign-flag carriers	7 318	7 768	8 258	10 608	10 536

1. Exclude travel by military personnel and other Government employees stationed abroad, their dependents and United States citizens residing abroad; includes shore expenditure of United States cruise travellers.

2. Excluding fare payments and crew spending.

Source : US Department of Commerce, Bureau of Economic Analysis.

8. TOURISM FROM THE UNITED STATES
NUMBER AND EXPENDITURE OF US RESIDENTS TRAVELLING OVERSEAS

	Number of travellers In thousands			Total expenditure Millions of dollars[1]			Average expenditure per traveller		
	1989	1990[2]	1991[e]	1989	1990[2]	1991	1989	1990[2]	1991
Total overseas	14 791	15 990	14 415	25 746	28 929	28 104	1 741	1 809	1 950
Europe	6 912	7 529	n.d	11 967	13 996	13 176	1 731	1 859	n.d
Carribean, South and Central America	5 160	5 570	n.d	5 123	5 395	5 806	992	969	n.d
Other overseas countries	2 714	2 891	n.d	8 656	9 538	9 122	3 189	3 299	n.d

n.d Non available.

e. Estimate.

1. Excludes travel by military personnel and other Government employees stationed abroad, their dependents and United States citizens residing abroad and cruise travellers.

2. Includes shore expenditure of cruise travellers; excludes fares.

Source : US Department of Commerce, Bureau of Economic Analysis, based on data of the *US Department of Justice, Immigration and Naturalization Service.*

9. Average length of stay of foreign tourists

	Tourists from all foreign countries			Tourists from Europe (OECD)			Tourists from North America (OECD)			Tourists from Pacific (OECD)		
	1989	1990	1991	1989	1990	1991	1989	1990	1991	1989	1990	1991
	Average length of stay in tourist accommodation [1]											
Austria	5.2	5.0	5.2	5.6	5.4	5.5	2.5	2.4	2.5	2.1	2.1	2.2
Germany [3]	2.3	2.2	2.3	2.3	2.2	2.3	2.0	1.9	2.1	1.7	1.7	1.8
Italy	4.2	4.1		4.7	4.6		2.6	2.5		2.1	2.1	
Netherlands	2.8	3.0	2.9	2.9	3.3	3.1	2.0	2.0	2.1	2.0	2.0	2.1
Portugal [2]	4.4	4.4	4.6	4.6	4.6	4.8	2.9	2.9	3.1	2.3	2.3	2.4
Spain [2]	5.9	5.4	6.1	6.7	6.1	6.8	2.2	2.2	2.3	1.8	1.8	1.8
Switzerland	3.6	3.5	3.7	4.0	4.0	4.1	2.2	2.2	2.3	1.8	1.8	1.8
Turkey	3.1	3.4	4.0	3.4	3.8	5.1	2.3	2.2	3.1	1.9	1.8	1.9
Canada												

1. Unless otherwise stated below, the average length of stay in all means of accommodation is obtained by dividing the number of nights recorded in particular means of accommodation by the number of arrivals of tourists at the same means of accommodation (see country tables).
2. Hôtellerie.
3. The data relate to the territory of the Federal Republic of Germany prior to 3rd October 1990.

	Tourists from all foreign countries			Tourists from Europe (OECD)			Tourists from North America (OECD)			Tourists from Pacific (OECD)		
	1989	1990	1991	1989	1990	1991	1989	1990	1991	1989	1990	1991
	Average length of stay in the country visited [1]											
France	7.4			6.9			8.7			7.1		
Greece [2]												
Ireland [3]	9.2	9.2	9.9	9.1	9.3	9.9	11.1	10.5	11.4	15.2	14.4	16.3
Portugal [2]	7.7	7.4		7.7	7.4		10.3	11.3		7.5	8.0	
Turkey	9.7	8.3	6.9	11.5	10.7	11.8	9.4	8.0	12.9	12.0	9.8	12.3
United Kingdom	11.0	11.0	11.0	8.0	9.0	8.0	10.0	10.0	11.0	16.0	16.0	19.0
Canada	6.0			12.2			4.4			7.9		
Australia	30.0	32.0	29.0	43.0	50.0	55.0	25.0	29.0	29.0	17.0	18.0	14.0
Japan	13.8	13.2	12.3									
New Zealand [2]	21.0	21.0	20.0				16.0	17.0	16.0	15.0	15.0	14.0

1. Unless otherwise stated below, the average length of stay in the country visited is expressed in number of nights spent.
2. Greece, New Zealand and Portugal: number of days.
3. Ireland: visitors on overseas routes.

10. Nights spent by foreign and domestic tourists in all means of accommodation [1]

In thousands

	Nights spent by foreign tourists			Nights spent by domestic tourists			Total nights			Proportion spent by foreign tourists (%)	
	1990	1991	% 91/90	1990	1991	% 91/90	1990	1991	% 91/90	1990	1991
Austria	94 788.3	99 641.5	5.1	28 841.2	30 431.3	5.5	123 629.5	130 072.8	5.2	76.7	76.6
Belgium	12 886.2			23 953.1			36 839.3			35.0	
Denmark	9 338.0	10 430.3	11.7	13 333.6	13 436.5	0.8	22 671.7	23 866.8	5.3	41.2	43.7
Finland	2 829.8	2 549.3	−9.9	10 261.1	9 767.2	−4.8	13 090.9	12 316.5	−5.9	21.6	20.7
France	85 537.2	83 602.6	−2.3	154 794.5	150 037.3	−3.1	240 331.7	233 639.9	−2.8	35.6	35.8
Germany [3]	39 146.5	37 426.4	−4.4	234 579.0	248 014.5	5.7	273 725.5	285 440.9	4.3	14.3	13.1
Greece	36 298.6	30 521.2	−15.9	11 831.9	12 064.5	2.0	48 130.5	42 585.7	−11.5	75.4	71.7
Italy	84 719.9	86 734.9	2.4	167 496.1	173 188.9	3.4	252 216.0	259 923.8	3.1	33.6	33.4
Netherlands	16 465.1	17 205.9	4.5	39 285.7	39 140.4	−0.4	55 750.8	56 346.3	1.1	29.5	30.5
Norway	5 840.4	6 304.8	8.0	11 578.7	11 921.8	3.0	17 419.1	18 226.7	4.6	33.5	34.6
Portugal	19 349.4	21 957.3	13.5	13 206.5	13 404.1	1.5	32 555.9	35 361.4	8.6	59.4	62.1
Sweden	6 574.7	5 600.4	−14.8	27 111.9	23 237.3	−14.3	33 686.6	28 837.7	−14.4	19.5	19.4
Switzerland	36 888.8	36 983.8	0.3	38 986.0	39 817.6	2.1	75 874.8	76 801.3	1.2	48.6	48.2
Turkey [2]	13 270.6	9 699.1	−26.9	6 878.4	8 011.4	16.5	20 149.0	17 710.4	−12.1	65.9	54.8
Canada				253 673.0							
Australia	65 341.0	64 644.8	−1.1	120 867.0	117 572.0	−2.7	186 208.0	182 216.8	−2.1	35.1	35.5

1. For the "Types of accommodation covered by the statistics" see Table C.
2. Turkey: figures based on a monthly sample survey carried out amoung establishments licenced by the Ministry of Tourism.
3. The data relate to the territory of the Federal Republic of Germany prior to 3rd October 1990; from the unification, tourists from the former German Democratic Republic are regarded as domestic tourists.

11. Nights spent by foreign and domestic tourists in hotels and similar establishments [1]

In thousands

	Nights spent by foreign tourists			Nights spent by domestic tourists			Total nights			Proportion spent by foreign tourists (%)	
	1990	1991	% 91/90	1990	1991	% 91/90	1990	1991	% 91/90	1990	1991
Austria	61 893.6	64 062.1	3.5	15 152.1	16 194.6	6.9	77 045.7	80 256.7	4.2	80.3	79.8
Belgium	6 873.5			2 706.9			9 580.4			71.7	
Denmark	5 429.4	5 962.9	9.8	5 205.2	5 267.9	1.2	10 634.6	11 230.8	5.6	51.1	53.1
Finland	2 468.1	2 200.9	−10.8	8 208.9	7 798.8	−5.0	10 677.0	9 999.7	−6.3	23.1	22.0
France [2]	55 934.2	53 044.9	−5.2	90 385.9	88 012.7	−2.6	146 320.1	141 057.6	−3.6	38.2	37.6
Germany [5]	29 766.2	27 768.2	−6.7	125 620.7	132 688.9	5.6	155 387.0	160 457.1	3.3	19.2	17.3
Greece	35 012.1	29 873.0	−14.7	11 346.4	11 594.5	2.2	46 358.5	41 467.5	−10.6	75.5	72.0
Italy	66 012.1	65 842.8	−0.3	125 052.7	129 864.1	3.8	191 064.8	195 706.9	2.4	34.5	33.6
Netherlands	8 101.8	7 993.4	−1.3	6 396.1	6 758.7	5.7	14 497.9	14 752.1	1.8	55.9	54.2
Norway	3 536.6	3 916.8	10.7	8 484.9	8 908.3	5.0	12 021.5	12 825.0	6.7	29.4	30.5
Portugal	16 710.3	19 088.9	14.2	7 103.2	7 172.1	1.0	23 813.5	26 261.0	10.3	70.2	72.7
Spain	64 626.5	73 978.4	14.5	55 254.3	59 628.7	7.9	119 880.8	133 607.1	11.4	53.9	55.4
Sweden	3 193.0	2 826.2	−11.5	13 033.0	11 668.1	−10.5	16 226.0	14 494.2	−10.7	19.7	19.5
Switzerland	21 040.7	20 365.5	−3.2	13 586.9	13 871.6	2.1	34 627.7	34 237.1	−1.1	60.8	59.5
Turkey [4]	10 255.1	8 109.5	−20.9	6 091.0	7 046.6	15.7	16 346.2	15 156.1	−7.3	62.7	53.5
Canada [3]				51 514.0							
Australia	14 017.0	12 209.1	−12.9	43 370.0	43 127.0	−0.6	57 387.0	55 336.1	−3.6	24.4	22.1

1. For the "Types of accommodation covered by the statistics" see Table C.
2. France: data covering all France except 3 regions (Pays de la Loire, Champagne-Ardennes and Corse).
3. Canada: includes nights spent by canadians in the United States with final destination in Canada.
4. Turkey: does not include thermal hotels.
5. The data relate to the territory of the Federal Republic of Germany prior to 3rd October 1990; from the unification, tourists from the former German Democratic Republic are regarded as domestic tourists.

12. Nights spent by foreign and domestic tourists in supplementary means of accommodation[1]

In thousands

	Nights spent by foreign tourists			Nights spent by domestic tourists			Total nights			Proportion spent by foreign tourists (%)	
	1990	1991	% 91/90	1990	1991	% 91/90	1990	1991	% 91/90	1990	1991
Austria	32 894.7	35 579.4	8.2	13 689.1	14 236.7	4.0	46 583.8	49 816.1	6.9	70.6	71.4
Belgium	6 012.7			21 246.2			27 258.9			22.1	
Denmark	3 908.6	4 467.4	14.3	8 128.4	8 168.6	0.5	12 037.1	12 636.0	5.0	32.5	35.4
Finland	361.6	348.4	–3.7	2 052.2	1 968.3	–4.1	2 413.8	2 316.8	–4.0	15.0	15.0
France[4]	29 603.0	30 557.7	3.2	64 408.6	62 024.6	–3.7	94 011.7	92 582.4	–1.5	31.5	33.0
Germany[3]	9 380.2	9 658.2	3.0	108 958.3	115 325.6	5.8	118 338.5	124 983.8	5.6	7.9	7.7
Greece	1 286.5	648.2	–49.6	485.5	470.1	–3.2	1 772.0	1 118.2	–36.9	72.6	58.0
Italy	18 707.8	20 892.1	11.7	42 443.5	43 324.8	2.1	61 151.2	64 216.9	5.0	30.6	32.5
Netherlands	8 357.1	9 212.5	10.2	32 889.6	32 381.7	–1.5	41 246.7	41 594.2	0.8	20.3	22.1
Norway	2 303.8	2 388.1	3.7	3 093.7	3 013.6	–2.6	5 397.5	5 401.6	0.1	42.7	44.2
Portugal	2 639.1	2 868.4	8.7	6 103.3	6 232.0	2.1	8 742.3	9 100.4	4.1	30.2	31.5
Sweden	3 381.7	2 774.2	–18.0	14 079.0	11 569.3	–17.8	17 460.6	14 343.5	–17.9	19.4	19.3
Switzerland	15 848.0	16 618.3	4.9	25 399.1	25 945.9	2.2	41 247.1	42 564.2	3.2	38.4	39.0
Turkey	3 015.5	1 589.6	–47.3	787.3	964.8	22.5	3 802.8	2 554.4	–32.8	79.3	62.2
Canada[2]				202 159.0							
Australia	51 324.0	52 435.7	2.2	77 497.0	74 445.0	–3.9	128 821.0	126 880.7	–1.5	39.8	41.3
Of which: **on camping sites**											
Austria	5 377.6	5 478.8	1.9	1 240.9	1 385.1	11.6	6 618.5	6 863.9	3.7	81.3	79.8
Belgium	2 766.6			9 313.4			12 080.0			22.9	
Denmark	3 438.7	3 945.3	14.7	7 610.5	7 650.4	0.5	11 049.2	11 595.7	4.9	31.1	34.0
Finland	361.6	348.4	–3.7	2 052.2	1 968.3	–4.1	2 413.8	2 316.8	–4.0	15.0	15.0
France[4]	29 603.0	30 557.7	3.2	64 408.6	62 024.6	–3.7	94 011.7	92 582.4	–1.5	31.5	33.0
Germany[3]	4 304.9	4 180.3	–2.9	13 695.7	15 051.8	9.9	18 000.6	19 232.1	6.8	23.9	21.7
Greece	1 286.5	648.2	–49.6	485.5	470.1	–3.2	1 772.0	1 118.2	–36.9	72.6	58.0
Italy	13 753.7	15 552.9	13.1	28 218.6	29 254.9	3.7	41 972.3	44 807.8	6.8	32.8	34.7
Netherlands	3 542.4	3 819.6	7.8	14 216.8	14 256.1	0.3	17 759.2	18 075.7	1.8	19.9	21.1
Norway	2 110.7	2 189.3	3.7	2 961.1	2 880.4	–2.7	5 071.8	5 069.7	0.0	41.6	43.2
Portugal	2 548.9	2 784.2	9.2	5 021.9	5 207.4	3.7	7 570.9	7 991.7	5.6	33.7	34.8
Sweden	2 535.9	2 066.2	–18.5	10 449.0	8 332.3	–20.3	12 984.9	10 398.6	–19.9	19.5	19.9
Switzerland	2 579.1	2 697.2	4.6	5 412.1	5 544.2	2.4	7 991.2	8 241.4	3.1	32.3	32.7
Turkey	241.8	57.0	–76.4	50.9	25.4	–50.2	292.8	82.3	–71.9	82.6	69.2
Canada[2]				26 908.0							
Australia	2 432.7	2 440.6	0.3	23 398.0	22 252.0	–4.9	25 830.7	24 692.6	–4.4	9.4	9.9
Of which: **in youth hostels**											
Austria	797.2	817.6	2.6	543.1	575.7	6.0	1 340.3	1 393.2	4.0	59.5	58.7
Denmark	469.9	522.1	11.1	517.9	518.2	0.0	987.9	1 040.3	5.3	47.6	50.2
Germany[3]	1 216.4	1 139.8	–6.3	9 581.9	10 039.1	4.8	10 798.3	11 178.9	3.5	11.3	10.2
Italy	583.8	593.7	1.7	157.7	228.1	44.6	741.5	821.8	10.8	78.7	72.2
Netherlands	783.6	761.7	–2.8	336.8	321.8	–4.5	1 120.4	1 083.5	–3.3	69.9	70.3
Norway	193.1	198.8	2.9	132.7	133.2	0.4	325.8	331.9	1.9	59.3	59.9
Sweden	253.2	217.4	–14.2	831.7	790.4	–5.0	1 084.9	1 007.7	–7.1	23.3	21.6
Switzerland	558.9	553.6	–0.9	358.5	379.0	5.7	917.4	932.6	1.7	60.9	59.4
Australia	5 785.6	5 440.4	–6.0	2 268.0	2 530.0	11.6	8 053.6	7 970.4	–1.0	71.8	68.3
Of which: **in private rooms, rented apartments and houses**											
Austria	15 129.5	16 237.7	7.3	4 049.8	4 244.3	4.8	19 179.3	20 482.0	6.8	78.9	79.3
Belgium	621.2			6 235.4			6 856.6			9.1	
Germany[3]	1 737.8	1 777.2	2.3	21 899.7	23 684.5	8.1	23 637.5	25 461.7	7.7	7.4	7.0
Italy	3 274.1	3 405.5	4.0	6 754.0	6 383.2	–5.5	10 028.2	9 788.7	–2.4	32.6	34.8
Switzerland	10 400.0	11 000.0	5.8	13 400.0	13 500.0	0.7	23 800.0	24 500.0	2.9	43.7	44.9
Australia	10 205.9	9 009.9	–11.7	13 928.0	14 671.0	5.3	24 133.9	23 680.9	–1.9	42.3	38.0

1. For the "Types of accommodatiom covered by the statistics" see Table C.
2. Canada: person-nights: includes nights spent by Canadians in the United States with final destination in Canada.
3. The data relate to the territory of the Federal Republic of Germany prior to 3rd October 1990; from the unification, tourists from the former German Democratic Republic are regarded as domestic tourists.
4. France: data covering all France except 3 regions (Basse Normandie, Corse and Ile de France).

13. Capacity in hotels and similar establishments [1]

In thousands

	Hotels			Motels			Boarding houses			Inns			Others			Total		
	1990	1991	% 91/90	1990	1991	% 91/90	1990	1991	% 91/90	1990	1991	% 91/90	1990	1991	% 91/90	1990	1991	% 91/90
Austria[2]	93.7															650.6	654.1	0.5
Belgium																99.1	92.5	-6.6
Denmark[3]	82.0	85.5	4.2				15.4	15.4	0.1							99.1	100.9	3.5
Finland[4]	1 121.5	1 136.4	1.3											71.9			1 173.6	
France[5]	575.3	587.9	2.2				135.8	132.9	-2.1	240.8	239.5	-0.6	249.3	239.4	-4.0	1 201.2	1 199.7	-0.1
Germany[6]	366.4	379.7	3.6	3.5	3.2	-9.5	20.7	22.7	9.7	13.1	14.9	13.7	34.6	38.8	12.0	438.4	459.3	4.8
Greece																111.3	112.6	1.1
Netherlands													112.7	116.9	3.8	112.6	116.9	3.8
Norway[7]	88.3	94.3	6.7	1.4	1.5	6.1	45.9	46.3	1.0	4.1	3.9	-4.1	39.6	42.5	7.2	179.3	188.5	5.1
Portugal[8]																		
Spain[9]	735.7	781.6	6.2	193.8	191.2	-1.3	78.5	75.8	-3.4				94.2	97.9	3.9	1 102.2	1 146.5	4.0
Sweden[13]	113.6	116.4	2.5				46.9	49.7	6.0							160.4	166.1	3.5
Switzerland[10]	236.0	234.6	-0.6	5.5	5.3	-4.3				28.3	27.2	-3.7				269.8	267.1	-1.0
Turkey[11]	125.8	147.6	17.3	3.2	3.6	13.0	5.1	5.9	15.6	2.4	1.7	-29.9	3.7	4.9	33.6	140.2	163.7	16.8
Australia[12]	153.8	163.8	6.5	297.6	300.8	1.1										451.4	464.6	2.9
Japan	116.6	119.9	2.8							95.6	97.1	1.6						
New Zealand																		

Notice : this table contains data on available bed capacity unless otherwise stated in the following notes by country.
1. For the "Types of accommodation covered by the statistics" see Table C.
2. Austria : position at 31st August.
3. Denmark : position at 31st July.
4. Finland : position at 31st December.
5. France : position at 31st December.
6. Germany : position at April; the data relate to the territory of the Federal Republic of Germany prior to 3rd October 1990.
7. Norway : position at 31st December.
8. Portugal : position at 31st July.
9. Spain : position at 31st December.
10. Switzerland : position at 31st December.
11. Turkey : position at 31st December of accommodation establishments approved by Ministry of Culture and Tourism.
12. Australia : position at 31st December.
13. Sweden : position at December.

14. Capacity in supplementary means of accommodation[1]

In thousands

	Youth hostels			Camping sites — Places			Holiday villages			Rented rooms, houses and flats			Sanatoria and health establishments			Recreational camps			Others			Total		
	1990	1991	% 91/90	1990	1991	% 91/90	1990	1991	% 91/90	1990	1991	% 91/90	1990	1991	% 91/90	1990	1991	% 91/90	1990	1991	% 91/90	1990	1991	% 91/90
Austria	13.0	12.5	-3.5				122.9	128.7	4.7	296.4	281.9	-4.9	17.1	15.6	-8.5	28.7	28.4	-0.9	31.3	33.7	7.6	509.3	500.9	-1.7
Belgium				373.2									4.8			22.7			69.2			469.9		
Denmark	10.6	10.4	-1.9																					
France	21.0	17.6	-16.4	2 587.0	2 669.7	3.2	255.9	286.6	12.0	211.7	217.7	2.8												
Germany[4]	92.8	92.0	-0.8				23.1	25.3	9.6				128.6	132.0	2.6				159.8	160.4	0.4		3 179.9	
Greece																				206.0		615.9	627.2	1.8
Italy	8.1	6.8	-16.0	1 180.6	1 228.1	4.0				139.0	163.1	17.4							171.5	159.3	-7.1	1 499.1	1 557.4	3.9
Norway	6.1	6.5	7.7																			6.1	6.5	7.7
Portugal				261.1	265.6	1.7										10.6	10.8	1.9				271.7	276.4	1.7
Spain				571.3	575.3	0.7	45.1	45.2	0.2	384.9	402.7	4.6							7 171.0	6 629.9	-7.5	8 127.2	7 607.9	-6.4
Sweden	15.0	14.8	-1.1	395.0	395.0	0.0																455.1	455.0	0.0
Switzerland	8.1	7.9	-2.2	266.5	264.9	-0.6				360.0	360.0	0.0	6.8	6.5	-3.4							870.3	865.9	-0.5
Turkey[2]				8.2	8.3	0.5	24.8	28.7	15.6				0.0	0.0	0.0				229.0	226.6	-1.0			
Australia[3]				189.1	190.6	0.8																33.1	37.0	11.8
Japan	28.6	27.9	-2.6																					

Notice: this table contains data on available bed capacity, unless otherwise stated in the following notes by country.

1. For the "Types of accommodation covered by the statistics", see Table C.
2. Turkey: the total doesn't include licenced yacht bed capacity (9 358) and beds registered by local municipalities in social tourism establishments (223 576).
3. Australia: assuming 3 beds per place.
4. The data relate to the territory of the Federal Republic of Germany prior to 3rd October 1990.

15. Monthly hotel occupancy rates

		Austria (B)	Belgium (B)	Finland[1] (R)	Germany[10] (B)	Italy (B)	Netherlands[11] (B)	Norway[2] (B)	Portugal[8] (B)	Spain (B)	Sweden[3] (B)	Switzerland[9] (B)	Turkey[4] (B)	United Kingdom[5] (B)	Australia[6] (B)	Japan[7] (R)
1989	January		18.5	43.2	27.0	25.8	14.8	30.6	33.1	43.0	23.7	30.0	23.7	26.0	39.3	60.6
	February		22.8	52.8	33.0	28.1	18.1	39.7	41.1	48.5	32.8	40.0	27.9	33.0	30.8	73.4
	March		25.9	52.4	34.9	37.2	17.9	39.7	50.9	53.5	33.0	43.2	34.0	40.0	35.8	77.2
	April		28.3	54.1	34.5	34.1	13.1	33.6	51.0	48.2	33.7	27.5	39.2	40.0	31.7	74.4
	May		33.2	52.6	43.4	33.5	23.9	27.0	55.4	52.7	29.7	28.8	56.0	45.0	27.9	75.5
	June		30.9	54.8	46.0	42.3	21.0	43.2	55.0	53.6	35.9	37.3	54.0	53.0	30.1	73.0
	July		39.6	58.5	53.5	57.3	42.4	53.2	60.5	62.8	49.0	49.5	58.7	56.0	32.7	74.4
	August		41.4	56.5	54.0	66.2	41.2	44.9	73.7	74.8	39.0	53.0	66.4	60.0	30.9	82.9
	September		34.8	56.9	51.8	48.4	19.1	34.7	67.4	60.7	32.7	46.7	61.7	59.0	35.5	77.5
	October		32.3	52.9	44.2	37.1	20.8	29.7	53.0	51.8	28.8	32.6	51.3	51.0	34.4	82.9
	November		27.9	52.5	30.3	26.1	17.1	29.0	37.8	44.1	29.0	18.1	32.5	40.0	31.4	81.0
	December		23.7	37.4	27.2	22.1	18.4	25.2	31.0	38.4	22.5	22.2	28.5	36.0	30.2	63.9
1990	January	27.2	19.1	42.0	27.4	26.3	15.6	28.8	31.9		24.5	28.7	25.3	29.0	38.6	65.0
	February	27.2	23.0	48.6	33.0	31.2	18.6	38.9	36.5		32.2	38.7	29.6	36.0	30.1	78.0
	March	27.2	25.4	52.5	33.6	33.8	16.9	39.7	46.6		33.5	40.0	32.7	38.0	31.3	79.1
	April	27.2	32.7	47.6	38.9	37.8	17.6	30.5	57.5		29.5	32.7	46.4	47.0	33.8	77.7
	May	31.8	33.3	48.6	45.9	34.3	22.5	27.8	52.8		31.3	29.5	52.8	48.0	28.1	79.6
	June	31.8	33.9	52.0	50.6	43.4	37.4	43.4	55.2		34.8	39.8	57.2	53.0	28.8	78.5
	July	31.8	41.2	53.0	55.7	55.7	43.9	51.1	60.4		45.4	50.9	69.0	58.0	32.1	78.5
	August	31.8	42.1	52.7	56.1	70.5	46.7	43.6	76.3		36.4	54.5	67.8	61.0	30.4	84.7
	September	31.8	35.1	51.9	54.4	48.4	19.9	33.0	69.4		30.6	47.6	56.0	57.0	35.5	80.5
	October	31.8	32.1	49.6	47.0	37.5	21.3	28.7	57.8		27.2	33.0	44.2	49.0	33.1	83.3
	November	29.0	27.2	48.5	33.2	25.5	20.8	27.6	40.1		25.6	18.0	31.7	40.0	30.2	82.0
	December	29.0	23.1	33.5	30.0	26.1	20.5	23.9	31.9		17.5	23.4	28.3	34.0	28.8	64.6
1991	January	29.0		38.1	28.9	26.0	15.3	26.5		38.3	20.5	29.4	21.5		35.4	62.7
	February	29.0		45.2	34.3	30.3	17.6	39.3		41.9	28.0	41.2	22.6		27.6	78.0
	March	29.0		45.9	37.3	35.7	17.8	40.1		45.9	29.0	42.4	25.8		31.0	79.9
	April	29.0		44.6	39.0	33.1	16.2	31.3		46.8	27.2	29.2	29.3		30.4	76.6
	May	33.9		43.0	47.1	35.3	24.8	27.8		49.1	25.1	28.7	31.1		26.4	77.2
	June	33.9		48.0	50.4	44.5	22.4	44.6		53.2	30.6	37.3	36.2		28.2	75.9
	July	33.9		48.8	56.7	58.5	43.3	54.8		62.4	39.9	49.4	46.3		31.6	75.8
	August	33.9		46.3	59.4	70.5	47.8	44.9		77.6	32.2	55.3	59.0		30.3	81.1
	September	33.9		44.4	55.7	48.1	20.1	32.5		64.1	25.3	46.8	54.2		34.7	76.2
	October	33.9		41.1	48.7	37.1	21.2	29.1		52.0	23.6	33.2	41.5		34.6	82.7
	November			41.1	33.5	25.0	19.3	28.6		44.8	22.7	17.6	30.5		31.2	82.6
	December			27.8	30.4	25.4	18.2	24.0		39.2	12.8	23.8	27.3		28.8	62.4

B = Beds.
R = Rooms.
Occupancy rates registered in hotels only, unless otherwise stated.
1. Finland: room occupancy rates in hotels and similar establishments.
2. Norway: Bed occupancy rates covers registered accommodation with 20 beds or more.
3. Sweden: occupancy rates in hotels, motels, resort hotels, holiday villages and youth hostels.
4. Turkey: bed occupancy rates in hotels, motels, boarding houses, inns, holiday villages, thermal resorts and campings.
5. United Kingdom: figures apply to England only.
6. Australia: quarterly figures in bed-places in hotels and motels with facilities in most rooms.
7. Japan: rates concerning hotels which are members of the "Japan Hotel Association".
8. Portugal: bed occupancy rates in hotels, studio-hotels, motels and state-owned inns.
9. Switzerland: bed occupancy rates in hotels, motels and inns.
10. Germany: bed occupancy rates cover registered accommodation with 9 beds or more; the data relate to the territory of the Federal Republic of Germany prior to 3rd October 1990.
11. Netherlands: bed occupancy rates in all means of accommodation.

16. International fare payments

Rail, air, sea and road transport

In million dollars

	Receipts			Expenditure		
	1989	1990	1991	1989	1990	1991
Germany [1]	3 929.9	5 117.5	5 117.0	4 023.0	5 282.8	5 566.1
Greece	15.8			113.9		
Finland [2]	482.7	562.5	532.8	520.3	631.3	587.7
Ireland [2]	335.9	435.0	442.4			
Italy [2]	1.4	1.8	1.8	1.2	1.4	1.2
Spain	792.2	878.9		287.2	378.6	
Sweden [3]	874.0	976.3	816.3	773.5	963.3	832.0
Switzwerland	1 436.9	1 677.7	1 750.8	883.5	1 134.1	1 140.5
Turkey [4]	264.5	326.4	288.2	1.4	1.7	1.0
Canada	1 047.3	1 030.7	925.1	1 635.1	2 037.2	2 048.9
Australia	1 128.2	1 323.9	1 552.2	1 658.8	1 799.0	1 768.7

1. Germany: air, sea and rail transport. The data relate to the territory of the Federal Republic of Germany prior to 3rd October 1990.
2. Finland, Ireland and Italy: air and sea transport.
3. Sweden: sea and rail transport.
4. Turkey: air, sea and rail transport for receipts; rail transport only for expenditure.

17. Nominal exchange rates of national currencies against the dollar

	Exchange rates (units per dollar)			Per cent changes [1]	
	1989	1990	1991	90/89	91/90
Austria	13.23	11.37	11.67	−14.0	2.7
Belgium-Luxembourg	39.40	33.42	34.16	−15.2	2.2
Denmark	7.31	6.19	6.40	−15.4	3.4
Finland	4.29	3.82	4.04	−10.9	5.8
France	6.38	5.45	5.64	−14.6	3.6
Germany	1.88	1.62	1.66	−14.0	2.7
Greece	162.08	158.23	182.06	−2.4	15.1
Iceland	57.11	58.36	59.10	2.2	1.3
Ireland	0.71	0.60	0.62	−14.3	2.8
Italy	1 371.69	1 198.37	1 240.65	−12.6	3.5
Netherlands	2.12	1.82	1.87	−14.2	2.7
Norway	6.90	6.26	6.48	−9.3	3.6
Portugal	157.10	142.31	144.35	−9.4	1.4
Spain	118.40	101.94	103.93	−13.9	2.0
Sweden	6.45	5.92	6.05	−8.2	2.1
Switzwerland	1.64	1.39	1.43	−15.1	3.2
Turkey	2 119.96	2 606.48	4 168.91	22.9	59.9
United Kingdom	0.61	0.56	0.57	−7.9	0.7
Canada	1.18	1.17	1.15	−1.4	−1.8
United States	1.00	1.00	1.00	0.0	0.0
Australia	1.26	1.28	1.28	1.3	0.2
New Zealand	1.67	1.68	1.73	0.2	3.1
Japan	137.97	144.80	134.50	4.9	−7.1

Source: OECD Balance of Payments Division.
1. Minus signs indicate an appreciation of national currencies against the dollar.

18. International tourist receipts (R) and expenditure (E) in dollars

Regional breakdown

In million

	R/E	Europe 1990	Europe 1991	Europe % 91/90	North America 1990	North America 1991	North America % 91/90	Australasia-Japan 1990	Australasia-Japan 1991	Australasia-Japan % 91/90
Austria[1]	R	11 742.8	12 510.6	6.5	851.0	920.9	8.2	110.4	96.1	−12.9
	E	4 591.2	5 098.4	11.0	855.6	860.6	0.6	36.6	32.3	−11.7
Belgium-Luxembourg	R									
	E									
Denmark	R	2 657.3	2 817.7	6.0	410.9	443.8	8.0	13.6	17.5	28.9
	E	2 846.3	2 594.4	−8.8	525.8	563.5	7.2	6.5	4.7	−27.5
Finland	R	803.7	887.7	10.5	89.7	175.4	95.4	6.8	7.7	12.7
	E	2 029.0	2 005.6	−1.2	365.5	423.9	16.0	13.1	13.9	5.9
France	R	14 377.4	16 123.9	12.1	3 256.8	2 769.6	−15.0	742.6	651.9	−12.2
	E	7 074.9	6 939.8	−1.9	2 625.1	2 625.7	0.0	174.3	211.1	21.2
Germany[6]	R	8 119.7	8 282.5	2.0	1 006.3	936.2	−7.0	530.4	505.2	−4.7
	E	22 966.6	24 599.8	7.1	1 818.9	2 012.9	10.7	334.2	371.4	11.1
Greece	R									
	E									
Iceland	R	91.4			29.9			0.6		
	E	98.7			118.0			0.4		
Ireland[2]	R	1 099.9	1 192.1	8.4	271.2	241.3	−11.0			
	E	1 012.2	971.7	−4.0	130.7	135.1	3.4			
Italy[7]	R									
	E									
Netherlands	R	2 972.9	3 280.8	10.4	533.8	691.6	29.5	67.0	40.1	−40.1
	E	5 836.5	6 386.3	9.4	986.4	1 054.7	6.9	23.6	22.5	−4.9
Norway	R	1 308.4			184.4			8.0		
	E	2 940.6			415.0			9.4		
Portugal	R	2 678.0	2 770.4	3.5	802.5	914.3	13.9	11.5	10.3	−10.7
	E	593.2	700.4	18.1	245.2	302.1	23.2	4.0	3.2	−19.2
Spain	R									
	E									
Sweden	R	2 133.7	1 974.6	−7.5	304.1	308.8	1.5	16.6	17.9	7.9
	E	4 496.6	4 650.0	3.4	1 133.6	1 012.8	−10.7	38.4	35.6	−7.3
Switzerland	R									
	E									
Turkey	R									
	E									
United Kingdom[3]	R	5 739.2	5 994.5	4.4	3 456.6	2 639.1	−23.6	1 431.7	1 113.2	−22.2
	E	10 941.9	12 253.7	12.0	2 612.9	2 662.1	1.9	698.1	656.3	−6.0
Canada[4]	R									
	E									
United States	R									
	E									
Australia	R									
	E									
New Zealand[5]	R									
	E									
Japan	R									
	E									

Important notice: the amounts, excluding those concerning Canada, United States, Ireland, Italy, United Kingdom and Switzerland, refer to receipts and expenditure registered in foreign currency grouped regionally according to the denomination of the currency.

1. Austria: including international fare payments.

18. International tourist receipts (R) and expenditure (E) in dollars (Continued)

Regional breakdown

In million

Total OECD countries			Non-Member countries			All countries			
1990	1991	% 91/90	1990	1991	% 91/90	1990	1991	% 91/90	
12 704.1	13 527.7	6.5	704.3	434.8	−38.3	13 408.4	13 962.5	4.1	Austria [1]
5 483.5	5 991.3	9.3	2 238.7	1 461.0	−34.7	7 722.2	7 452.3	−3.5	
						3 698.5	3 632.9	−1.8	Belgium-Luxembourg
						5 445.1	5 578.8	2.5	
3 081.8	3 278.9	6.4	239.7	194.6	−18.8	3 321.5	3 473.5	4.6	Denmark
3 378.6	3 162.6	−6.4	295.2	212.1	−28.1	3 673.8	3 374.8	−8.1	
900.7	1 071.4	19.0	268.7	120.9	−55.0	1 169.4	1 192.4	2.0	Finland
2 409.9	2 446.6	1.5	346.9	192.9	−44.4	2 756.8	2 639.5	−4.3	
18 376.8	19 545.4	6.4	1 814.4	1 830.1	0.9	20 191.2	21 375.5	5.9	France
9 874.2	9 776.6	−1.0	2 571.7	2 550.7	−0.8	12 445.9	12 327.3	−1.0	
9 656.4	9 723.9	0.7	997.6	904.3	−9.4	10 654.0	10 628.2	−0.2	Germany [6]
25 119.7	26 984.1	7.4	4 371.8	3 794.9	−13.2	29 491.4	30 779.0	4.4	
						2 573.4	2 205.7	−14.3	Greece
						1 090.0	901.1	−17.3	
122.0			0.0			122.0	117.5	−3.7	Iceland
217.1			0.3			217.4	255.8	17.6	
1 371.1	1 433.4	4.5	76.1	77.2	1.5	1 447.2	1 510.7	4.4	Ireland [2]
1 142.9	1 106.9	−3.2	16.5	17.7	7.0	1 159.4	1 124.5	−3.0	
						19 741.7	18 420.3	−6.7	Italy [7]
						13 826.2	11 648.3	−15.8	
3 580.3	4 025.4	12.4	32.4	50.3	55.2	3 612.7	4 075.6	12.8	Netherlands
6 949.2	7 605.2	9.4	387.7	282.4	−27.2	7 336.9	7 887.6	7.5	
1 500.7			16.0			1 543.9	1 680.1	8.8	Norway
3 365.0			49.2			3 469.7	3 307.0	−4.7	
3 494.9	3 701.7	5.9	38.6	37.4	−3.1	3 533.4	3 739.1	5.8	Portugal
843.1	1 006.0	19.3	18.9	21.5	13.9	861.9	1 027.5	19.2	
						18 426.1	19 157.6	4.0	Spain
						4 211.2	4 554.9	8.2	
2 455.1	2 302.1	−6.2	450.5	431.1	−4.3	2 905.6	2 733.1	−5.9	Sweden
5 682.0	5 706.6	0.4	330.2	342.4	3.7	6 012.2	6 049.0	0.6	
						6 818.8	7 093.9	4.0	Switzerland
						5 843.1	5 705.8	−2.3	
						3 348.8	2 781.1	−17.0	Turkey
						522.2	601.9	15.3	
10 638.1	9 755.7	−8.3	3 271.9	2 859.7	−12.6	13 910.0	12 615.3	−9.3	United Kingdom [3]
14 261.7	15 595.0	9.3	3 351.8	3 309.5	−1.3	17 613.6	18 904.5	7.3	
						5 581.2	5 858.9	5.0	Canada [4]
						10 375.4	11 345.4	9.3	
						43 418.3	48 757.3	12.3	United States
						37 349.0	36 957.8	−1.0	
						3 659.7	3 953.3	8.0	Australia
						4 160.6	3 919.0	−5.8	
						1 520.4	1 512.3	−0.5	New Zealand [5]
						996.5	994.7	−0.2	
						3 582.7	3 436.4	−4.1	Japan
						24 354.0	23 951.3	−1.7	

2. Ireland: expenditure include international fare payments.

3. United Kingdom: including estimates for the Channel Islands receipts and expenditure, and cruise expenditure.

4. Canada: excluding crew spending.

5. New Zealand: includes international airfares payments.

6. Germany: the data relate to the territory of the Federal Republic of Germany prior to 3rd October 1990. From July 1990, data include all transactions of the former German Democratic Republic with foreign countries.

7. Italy : change of methodology in 1990.

19. Foreign tourism by purpose of visit

| | 1990 | | | | | | 1991 | | | | | |
| | Business journeys (%)[1] | Private journeys (%) | | | | Total volume in thousands | Business journeys (%)[1] | Private journeys (%) | | | | Total volume in thousands |
		Holidays	VFR[2]	Others	Total			Holidays	VFR[2]	Others	Total	
Greece[3]	9.1	82.8	3.9	4.1	90.9	8 873.3	9.4	81.0	4.0	5.6	90.6	8 036.1
Ireland[4]	16.5	43.3	34.5	5.7	83.5	3 068.0	14.8	48.9	30.3	5.9	85.2	2 997.0
Portugal[5]	2.4	92.0	0.9	4.7	97.6	8 019.9						
Spain[6]	7.9	83.2	4.0	4.9	92.1	34 666.0	13.0	56.0	12.0	19.0	87.0	35 306.7
Turkey[12]	8.0	79.4	3.2	9.4	92.0	5 389.3		76.6		23.4	100.0	5.5
United Kingdom[7]		56.9	26.7	16.3	100.0	13 527.0		55.4	27.9	16.7	100.0	12 532.0
Canada[8]												2 370.5
Australia[9]	11.9	55.7	20.6	11.8	88.1	2 214.8	11.2	59.7	20.0	9.2	88.8	2 370.5
New zealand[10]	11.3	50.2	24.1	14.5	88.7	976.0	1.1	57.0	27.1	14.8	98.9	873.8
Japan[11]	27.7	58.1		14.2	72.3	3 235.9	26.7	59.6		13.7	73.3	3 532.5

1. Includes : business, congresses, seminars, on missions, etc.
2. VFR : visits to friends and relatives.
3. Greece : number of tourists. "Others" includes journeys combining visiting relatives and holiday or business and holiday.
4. Ireland : number of visits on overseas routes.
5. Portugal : number of tourists. "Others" includes visits for cultural purposes and journeys for educational reasons.
6. Spain : number of tourists. "Others" includes journeys for educational reasons.
7. United Kingdom : number of visits. "Others" includes visits for religion, sports, health and visits of more than one purpose where none predominates.
8. Canada : number of tourists.
9. Australia : short-term visitors (less than one year). "Others" includes accompanying business traveller.
10. New Zealand : number of tourists. "Others" includes journeys for educational reasons.
11. Japan : number of visitors. "Others" includes journeys for educational reasons.
12. Turkey : "Others" includes journeys combining shopping and transit and journeys for study, health, religious and sports purposes.

20. Foreign tourism by mode of transport

| | 1990 | | | | | 1991 | | | | |
| | Breakdown of arrivals (%) | | | | Total volume in thousands | Breakdown of arrivals (%) | | | | Total volume in thousands |
	Air	Sea	Rail	Road		Air	Sea	Rail	Road	
Belgium[1]										
Iceland	96.2	3.8			141.7	94.5	5.5			143.5
Ireland[8]	62.8	37.2			3 069.0	60.0	40.0			2 997.0
Italy[2]	11.4	2.4	8.6	77.7	60 295.9	12.1	2.3	8.9	76.8	51 317.2
Portugal[2]	16.8	1.4	0.8	81.0	18 422.1					
Spain[3]	32.2	3.4	4.9	59.5	52 044.1	31.2	3.3	4.5	61.1	53 495.0
Turkey[4]	47.5	14.1	2.7	35.8	5 389.3	30.8	9.0	2.1	58.1	5 517.9
United Kingdom[2]	71.1	28.9			18 021.0	67.6	32.4			16 664.0
Canada[5]										
Australia[6]	99.6	0.4			2 214.9	99.6	0.4			2 370.4
New Zealand[5]	98.8	1.2			976.0	99.0	1.0			963.5
Japan[7]	97.0	3.0			3 504.5	97.3	2.7			3 856.0

1. Belgium: air and sea include both arrivals and departures of foreign and domestic visitors. Rail refers to international traffic only.
2. Italy, Portugal and United Kingdom : visitor arrivals.
3. Spain: visitor arrivals, including Spaniards living abroad.
4. Turkey: traveller arrivals.
5. Canada and New Zealand: tourist arrivals.
6. Australia: arrivals of short-term visitors (less than one year).
7. Japan: visitor arrivals, including those of returning residents and excluding crew members.
8. Ireland: visitors on overseas routes (average of arrivals and departure).

21. Staff employed in tourism

		1989			1990			1991		
		Total	Men %	Women %	Total	Men %	Women %	Total	Men %	Women %
Austria[1]	HR	123 047	38.0	62.0	126 034	38.7	61.3	131 240	39.4	60.6
Belgium[2]	H	13 032	47.7	52.3						
	R	59 891	47.9	52.1						
	HR	93 376	46.7	53.3						
	V	4 099	34.8	65.2						
	A	10 607	49.7	50.3						
	O	5 747	35.2	64.8						
Finland[3]	HR	73 000	20.5	78.1	75 000	24.0	76.0	69 000	23.2	76.8
Germany[4]	HR	692 700	43.2	56.8	774 400	41.5	58.5			
Norway[5]	HR	58 000			57 000					
Sweden	HR	94 500	37.6	62.4	98 000	37.8	62.2	98 000	36.7	63.3
Turkey[6]	HR	134 034			140 363			145 530		
	V	9 910	63.6	36.4	3 249			11 000		
	A	1 635	66.2	33.8	2 368	70.7	29.3	1 985	65.4	34.6
	O	1 868			1 455			2 420		
United Kingdom[7]	H	288 200	37.5	62.5	309 000	38.7	61.3	307 600	38.4	61.6
	R	287 500	38.7	61.3	303 600	40.0	60.0	286 700	38.1	61.9
	HR	575 700	38.1	61.9	612 600	39.3	60.7	594 300	38.2	61.8
	O	828 400	39.4	60.6	851 400	39.1	60.9	846 700	39.2	60.8
Canada	H	168 000	39.3	60.1						
	R	573 000	43.1	56.9						
	HR	768 000	41.7	58.2						
	V	27 000	25.9	74.1						

H: staff employed in hotels.
R: staff employed in restaurants.
HR: staff employed in hotels and restaurants.
V: staff employed in travel agencies.
A: staff employed in national tourism administrations.
O: staff employed in other sectors of tourist industry.
1. Austria: weighted average of peak season (August) and low season (November).
2. Belgium: A = tourist offices, libraries, public archives, museums, botanical gardens and zoos. O = sleeper trains and restaurant cars, youth hostels, camping sites, holiday centers and holiday homes, recreation homes for children and furnished appartments.
3. Finland: weighted average of peak season (July) and low season (January).
4. The data relate to the territory of the Federal Republic of Germany prior to 3rd October 1990.
5. Norway: average of 1st and 4th quarters.
6. Turkey: data registered at 31 December of each year, except for O registered at 31 March and V registered at 31 October. V = total number of persons (new series from 1991) which travel agencies (central and local offices) have to employ. A includes regional tourism administrations and staff working at the Ministry of Tourism. O = tourist guides whose licences have been renewed.
7. United Kingdom: data registered at September. O = "pubs", bars, night clubs, clubs, librairies, museums, art galleries, sports and other recreational services.

22. Trends in tourism prices

		%86/85	%87/86	%88/87	%89/88	%90/89	%91/90
Austria	H	3.9	3.0	3.8	2.2	3.3	
	R	4.3	4.0	2.8	2.2	3.3	
	T	1.9	0.9	2.1	2.8	3.3	3.4
	C	1.7	1.4	1.9	2.6	3.3	3.3
Belgium [1]	H	6.0	9.3	6.3	3.8	5.4	
	R	6.0	3.7	2.4	3.4	4.6	
	T	6.1	4.0	2.6	3.4	3.6	
	C	1.3	1.6	1.2	3.1	3.4	3.2
Finland [2]	H	7.0	5.0	6.0	6.0	7.0	1.0
	R	5.0	7.0	7.0	8.0	8.0	6.0
	T						
	C	2.9	4.1	5.1	6.6	6.1	4.1
France	H	5.4	9.2	7.8	6.3	6.6	
	R	5.1	7.1	5.4	5.0	6.1	
	T			5.1	5.7	5.7	
	C	2.5	3.3	2.7	3.5	3.4	3.1
Germany	H	3.2	3.4	4.3	4.4	4.8	5.3
	R	1.8	1.7	1.5	1.9	2.8	3.8
	T	4.4	1.3	1.0	1.8	0.5	1.6
	C	−0.1	0.2	1.3	2.8	2.7	3.5
Greece	H	18.0	40.0	10.0			
	R						
	T						
	C	23.0	16.4	13.5	13.7	20.4	18.9
Italy [3]	H	8.8	9.0	7.3	8.3	7.8	8.8
	R	9.7	5.8	7.2	7.9	7.8	7.9
	T	9.6	6.4	7.1	7.9	7.8	6.1
	C	6.2	4.6	5.0	6.6	6.1	6.5
Netherlands [4]	H	1.0	2.0	2.0	2.0	3.0	3.0
	R	2.0	2.0	1.0	2.0	3.0	3.0
	T						
	C	0.1	−0.7	0.7	1.1	2.5	3.9
Norway [5]	H	10.8	12.0	11.5	9.0	6.0	5.0
	R	8.2	8.6	5.7	3.9	3.0	4.7
	T						
	C	7.2	8.7	6.7	4.6	4.1	3.4
Portugal [6]	H	30.0	23.0	12.0	14.0	17.0	
	R	13.0	14.0	17.0	17.0	11.0	
	T						
	C	11.8	9.4	9.7	12.6	13.4	11.4
Spain [7]	H	11.6	13.1	10.9	10.6	13.6	7.5
	R	10.2	5.1	8.7	10.9	10.5	4.9
	T	9.6	4.8	6.9	8.6	9.7	6.9
	C	8.8	5.2	4.8	6.8	6.7	5.9
Sweden [8]	H	11.0	−1.4	5.8	6.0	14.4	9.2
	R	10.4	6.6	9.5	9.3	18.8	6.6
	T						
	C	4.2	4.2	5.8	6.4	10.5	9.3
Switzerland [9]	H	6.3	5.6	5.5	6.6	92.0	8.8
	R	3.4	2.2	3.0	4.3	51.0	5.8
	T						
	C	0.8	1.4	1.9	3.2	5.4	5.8
Turkey [10]	H						
	R						
	T	50.0					
	C	34.6	38.9	75.4	69.6	60.3	66.0
United Kingdom [11]	H	12.5	9.9	10.9	8.7	11.8	8.6
	R	7.0	7.0	6.8	6.8	8.0	10.4
	T	7.0	6.3	8.1	7.5	8.7	8.6
	C	3.4	4.1	4.9	7.8	9.5	5.9
Canada [12]	H	13.5	3.0	7.2	5.3	2.9	2.4
	R	4.7	4.0	4.6	5.3	4.9	10.9
	T	5.6	4.2	1.4	5.7	7.2	7.6
	C	4.2	4.4	4.0	5.0	4.8	5.6
Australia [13]	H	27.2	16.2	16.6			
	R	8.7	6.7	7.3			
	T	6.3	6.6	13.5	7.6	6.5	10.0
	C	8.9	8.6	7.2	7.6	7.3	3.2

NOTE TO TABLE 22

H: average increase in hotel prices.
R: average increase in restaurant prices.
T: average increase in travel prices.
C: average increase in consumer prices (CPI). Source: OECD Balance of Payments Division.

1. Belgium : H = hotels and campings, R = cafés, restaurants and bars, T = hotels, campings, cafés, restaurants, bars and package tours.
2. Finland: H = hotels, R = food and alcoholic beverages, T = transports and communications.
3. Italy: T = hotels, restaurants and public establishments (bars, night club, sea-side resorts....).
4. Netherlands: H = price of a night spent in an hotel, R = price of a certain number of typical expenses made in bars and restaurants (cup of coffee, fruit drinks, beer, jenever, croquette, fried potatoes, several hot meals, ham roll, ice cream).
5. Norway: H = approved hotels and boarding houses, R = restaurants and cafés.
6. Portugal: H = hotels of from 1 to 5 stars, R concerns Lisbon only.
7. Spain H takes into account the types of accommodation presented in the official guide R = hotels restaurants cafeteriaand bars.
8. Sweden: position at December of each year H = hotel room, R = meals not taken at home (lunch, dinner, coffee with bread, hot sausage with bread).
9. Switzerland: H = hotels and similar establishments. R is estimated.
10. Turkey: H = hotels, motels, inns, boarding houses, holiday villages, health resorts. R = 1st and 2nd class restaurants. In 1985 H and R = freely determined prices approved by the Ministry of Culture and Tourism. C concerns the city of Ankara only.
11. United Kingdom: H = all holiday accommodation. R = meals and snacks including take-away. T = accommodation, meals, food, alcohol, tobacco, durable household goods, clothes, footwear, motoring and cycling fares, entertainment and other services.
12. Canada: H = hotels and motels. R = food purchases for restaurants, T is calculated from domestic tourist spending patterns only.
13. Australia: position every fourth quarter of each year. H = change in the price of a room in hotels, motels, and similar establishments. R = change in the price of meals taken outside home and take-away food (one component of the CPI). C = weighted average of eight State capital cities. T = air, bus and rail fares, hotel, motel and caravan park charges, package tours.

INTERNATIONAL TOURIST FLOWS FROM MAIN GENERATING COUNTRIES

Tables 23 to 49 gather data available for the period 1980 to 1991 concerning physical flows to OECD Member countries and Yugoslavia.

These tables contain data on arrivals at frontiers and arrivals and nights spent at/in accommodation:

-- from all the foreign countries;
-- from the eight main generators of tourism to the OECD area (Canada, France, Germany, Italy, Japan, the Netherlands, the United Kingdom and the United States).

Data used in the synthesis tables are derived from data broken down by country of origin; when these data are not available, the tables are derived from monthly or quarterly statistics.

Methodological notes

These notes present on a country-by-country basis, and where appropriate, the main methodological and statistical changes affecting the series available between 1980 and 1991. For more detailed information, refer to the book "National and International Tourism Statistics 1974-1985", published in 1989.

Canada. Arrivals of foreign visitors at frontiers: change of series in 1980.

Finland. Arrivals of foreign visitors at frontiers: series discontinued from 1979.

France.Arrivals and nights spent at/in hotels and similar establishments: change of series in 1986.

Germany. Arrivals and nights spent at/in hotels and similar establishments and in all means of accommodation: changes of series in 1981 and in 1984.

Ireland. Arrivals and nights spent at/in hotels and similar establishments: series available from 1985.

Japan. Arrivals and nights spent at/in hotels and similar establishments: series discontinued from 1986.

Netherlands. Arrivals and nights spent at/in hotels and similar establishments: change of series in 1986. Arrivals and nights spent at/in all means of accommodations: new series from 1988.

Norway. Arrivals of foreign visitors at frontiers: series discontinued from 1984.

Portugal. Arrivals and nights spent at/in hotels and similar establishments and in all means of accommodation: change of series in 1979.

Sweden. Nights spent in all means of accommodation: change of series in 1985.

Switzerland. Arrivals of foreign tourists/visitors at frontiers: annual estimates.

Turkey. Arrivals and nights spent at/in all means of accommodation: change of series in 1980.

United States. Arrivals of foreign tourists at frontiers: estimates in 1979 and in 1980. Change of series in 1984.

Conventional signs

/ Break of series

Table/Tableau 23

ARRIVALS OF FOREIGN TOURISTS/VISITORS AT FRONTIERS
ARRIVÉES DE TOURISTES/VISITEURS ÉTRANGERS AUX FRONTIÈRES

1986=100

	T/V	Volume 1980	1981	1982	1983	1984	1985	Volume 1986	1987	1988	1989	1990	1991	Volume 1991	T/V	
France (R)	T	30 100 000	84.5	92.8	94.3	98.1	101.9	36 080 000	102.5	106.1	137.3	145.5	151.9	54 822 000	T	France (R)
Greece (N)	T	4 795 900	71.9	71.0	67.4	77.9	92.7	7 089 679	106.7	109.7	114.0	125.2	113.1	8 018 870	T	Grèce (N)
	V	5 271 115	76.0	74.4	71.6	82.1	95.9	7 339 015	109.1	112.2	110.1	120.9	109.5	8 036 127	V	
Iceland (N)	T	65 921	63.3	63.9	68.3	75.2	85.8	113 529	114.1	113.5	113.0	122.3	123.7	140 379	T	Islande (N)
Ireland (R)	V	1 679 000	92.0	96.9	97.8	103.3	105.4	1 813 000	112.5	129.4	150.7	169.2	165.4	2 998 000	V	Irlande (R)
Italy (N)	T	21 647 114												26 412 000	T	Italie (N)
	V	47 756 465	81.6	90.6	87.4	92.2	100.6	53 314 906	98.9	104.5	103.4	113.1	96.3	51 317 191	V	
Norway (N)	T	521 098													T	Norvège (N)
	V	2 708 030	55.9	58.5	68.7	76.1	92.2	5 409 201	112.8	122.5	131.6	148.3	160.0	8 656 946	V	
Portugal (N)	V	6 977 045	55.7	55.9	68.0	75.1	89.5	13 056 871	123.9	123.1	126.2	141.1	150.4	19 641 329	V	Portugal (N)
Spain (N)	V	38 026 816	84.7	88.7	87.1	90.1	90.7	47 388 793	106.7	114.3	114.1	109.8	112.9	53 494 964	V	Espagne (N)
Switzerland (R)[1]	T	10 650 000	97.8	100.0	100.0	103.0	103.5	11 500 000	101.7	101.7	109.6	114.8	109.6	12 600 000	T	Suisse (R)[1]
	V	87 250 000	80.5	80.0	84.6	91.9	91.0	111 500 000	10.6	100.6	110.2	115.9	12.3	13 700 000	V	
Turkey (N)	V	1 288 060	58.8	58.2	68.0	88.5	109.4	2 391 085	119.4	174.5	186.5	225.4	230.8	5 517 897	V	Turquie (N)
United Kingdom (R)	V	12 421 200	82.4	83.7	89.7	98.2	104.0	13 897 300	112.0	113.7	124.8	129.6	119.9	16 661 700	V	Royaume-Uni (R)
Canada (R)	T	12 785 300	82.0	78.0	80.0	83.1	84.3	15 621 300	96.1	99.1	97.0	97.7	95.9	14 988 600	T	Canada (R)
	V	40 664 000	103.7	85.0	84.7	86.2	88.8	40 459 300	97.9	97.0	93.9	93.9	91.0	36 817 700	V	
United States (R)	T	22 325 538	95.9	88.1	88.1	109.5	103.4	24 584 337	117.0	111.6	149.0	161.0	173.9	42 749 522	T	États-Unis (R)
Australia (R)	V	904 557	65.5	66.8	66.0	71.1	79.9	1 429 400	124.9	157.4	145.5	155.0	165.8	2 370 260	V	Australie (R)
Japan (N)	V	1 316 632	76.8	87.0	95.5	102.4	112.9	2 061 526	104.5	114.3	137.5	157.0	171.4	3 534 357	V	Japon (N)
New Zealand (R)	T	465 163	65.2	65.7	69.3	77.4	91.3	733 424	115.1	117.9	122.9	133.1	131.4	963 470	T	Nouvelle-Zélande (R)

V   Visitors (travellers in Austria, Germany and Turkey) / Visiteurs (voyageurs en Allemagne, en Autriche et en Turquie)
T   Tourists / Touristes
(R) Tourist count by country of residence / Recensement des touristes par pays de résidence
(N) Tourist count by country of nationality / Recensement des touristes par pays de nationalité
1.   Estimates / Estimations

Table/Tableau 24

ARRIVALS AND NIGHTS OF FOREIGN TOURISTS AT/IN HOTELS
ARRIVÉES ET NUITÉES DE TOURISTES ÉTRANGERS DANS L'HÔTELLERIE

1986=100

Country	AH/NH	Volume 1980	1981	1982	1983	1984	1985	Volume 1986	1987	1988	1989	1990	1991	Volume 1991	AH/NH	
Austria (R)	NH	55 578 296	104.2	102.6	100.8	101.8	100.1	54 532 361	101.6	103.3	112.6	113.5	117.8	64 212 549	NH	Autriche (R)
	AH	9 684 581	91.7	92.6	95.1	100.9	101.7	10 765 521	105.7	110.7	122.2	128.4	127.1	13 687 365	AH	
Belgium (R)	NH	4 378 680	82.2	89.0	92.7	98.8	104.1	5 319 029	99.9	102.0	123.6	129.2			NH	Belgique (R)
Denmark (N)	NH	4 349 100	103.2	102.5	103.8	106.2	105.8	4 338 300	103.3	100.9	112.7	125.2	137.5	5 963 100	NH	Danemark (N)
Finland (R)	NH	1 843 393	101.6	100.1	101.9	104.5	103.7	2 021 663	109.2	113.7	124.5	122.1	108.9	2 200 870	NH	Finlande (R)
France (R)[1]	NH	16 664 778	45.6	43.9	45.7	49.3	49.9	36 420 387	100.0	114.1	142.0	153.6	145.6	53 044 853	NH	France (R)[1]
	AH	5 848 181	35.6	35.7	35.9	38.2	40.6	17 069 882	100.6	114.3	142.4	151.0	147.9	25 238 061	AH	
Germany (R)	NH	19 003 302	82.8	80.7	81.6	94.8	101.8	23 472 533	103.9	107.5	120.9	126.8	118.3	27 768 232	NH	Allemagne (R)
	AH	9 110 634	81.5	81.6	84.2	98.2	104.6	11 289 691	104.3	106.8	119.3	127.7	115.5	13 044 621	AH	
Greece (N)	NH	27 608 678	80.4	78.4	74.8	86.1	101.0	33 708 170	100.1	98.9	97.7	103.9	88.6	29 873 046	NH	Grèce (N)
	AH	5 167 181	90.9	89.5	85.1	103.5	111.2	5 888 311	104.7	102.0		157.0			AH	
Iceland (N)	NH						100.1	5 273 000	104.8	117.3	144.7	161.4	174.9	9 223 000	NH	Islande (N)
Ireland (R)	NH						103.3	1 056 000	106.0	117.0	146.4	118.2	156.4	1 652 000	NH	Irlande (R)
Italy (N)	NH	66 188 494	90.5	99.2	97.3	96.8	98.2	65 150 329	108.5	108.1	104.6	118.7	100.8	65 702 498	NH	Italie (N)
	AH	14 581 731	87.5	97.7	98.6	104.1	106.1	15 165 029	112.3	115.0	116.6	117.1	112.2	17 018 456	AH	
Luxembourg (R)	NH			100.7	100.5	97.7	102.8	906 820	103.8	106.8	112.2	114.0	118.2	1 072 090	NH	Luxembourg (R)
	AH			99.8	90.1	91.1	99.4	450 457	103.0	107.7		116.3	115.5	520 179	AH	
Netherlands (R)	NH	6 065 445	85.8	88.4	84.6	92.0	94.9	7 106 500	99.1	95.1	101.0	107.2	112.5	7 993 500	NH	Pays-Bas (R)
	AH	2 757 785	83.8	88.3	86.3	95.9	99.2	3 356 800	99.9	99.0	103.9	119.4	109.8	3 686 700	AH	
Norway (N)	NH	2 430 167	75.5	69.5	71.0	104.9	112.6	3 297 715	117.2	101.8	104.1	117.0	118.8	3 916 773	NH	Norvège (N)
	AH	1 252 031	78.2	74.0	77.7	106.5	118.1	1 637 465	108.8	104.0	114.0	108.3	129.1	2 113 951	AH	
Portugal (N)	NH	9 579 589	65.5	66.9	69.2	77.2	90.6	14 286 278	101.7	105.0	108.3	118.4	133.6	19 088 928	NH	Portugal (N)
	AH	1 909 144	65.2	66.8	73.1	83.9	96.4	2 834 158	108.4	112.7	118.4	128.2	138.1	3 913 066	AH	
Spain (N)	NH	58 654 442	80.7	87.4	90.9	101.6	90.0	87 697 727	105.4	100.7	89.3	70.4	84.9	74 439 431	NH	Espagne (N)
	AH	9 228 072	77.9	82.4	84.9	95.8	91.5	13 587 330	103.9	100.4	97.0	88.4	88.7	12 048 903	AH	
Sweden (N)	NH	2 659 236	82.6	82.9	91.4	99.0	107.2	3 309 044	98.0	96.5	101.7	96.5	85.4	2 826 160	NH	Suède (N)
Switzerland (R)	NH	19 979 907	108.3	102.2	101.5	103.2	103.9	19 561 505	99.9	97.6	104.7	107.6	104.1	20 365 484	NH	Suisse (R)
	AH	6 661 098	100.7	98.9	100.1	105.8	106.5	6 881 332	102.6	101.8	115.5	115.7	107.5	7 400 292	AH	
Turkey (N)	NH	988 565	29.7	35.7	51.8	69.1	88.3	5 036 375	129.4	187.2	193.4	204.5	161.4	8 131 098	NH	Turquie (N)
	AH	393 019	32.3	38.5	55.6	69.9	87.8	1 913 738	125.4	162.0	181.2	182.6	115.8	2 216 578	AH	
Australia (R)	NH	4 190 319	70.6		66.7	69.4	79.7	8 868 000	124.6	159.6	118.9	141.5	129.7	11 503 000	NH	Australie (R)
Japan (N)	NH	1 890 625													NH	Japon (N)
	AH														AH	

AH   Arrivals at hotels and similar establishments · Arrivées dans les hôtels et les établissements assimilés
NH   Nights in hotels and similar establishments · Nuitées dans les hôtels et établissements assimilés
(R) Tourist count by country of residence · Recensement des touristes par pays de résidence
(N) Tourist count by country of nationality · Recensement des touristes par pays de nationalité
1.   Ile de France only · Ile de France seulement

Table/Tableau 25

ARRIVALS AND NIGHTS OF FOREIGN TOURISTS AT/IN ALL MEANS OF ACCOMMODATION
ARRIVÉES ET NUITÉES DE TOURISTES ÉTRANGERS DANS L'ENSEMBLE DES MOYENS D'HÉBERGEMENT

1986=100

Country	AAA/NAA	Volume 1980	1981	1982	1983	1984	1985	Volume 1986	1987	1988	1989	1990	1991	Volume 1991	AEH/NEH	
Austria (R)	NAA	90 202 611	108.3	105.3	102.4	101.5	99.6	85 403 353	100.3	102.5	111.2	111.0	116.7	99 641 723	NEH	Autriche (R)
	AAA	13 879 024	94.4	94.4	96.0	100.1	101.0	15 092 283	104.4	109.8	120.6	126.0	126.5	19 091 828	AEH	
Belgium (R)	NAA	7 171 544	73.1	86.8	90.7	94.8	99.8	9 854 546	102.1	107.3	123.5	130.8	122.6		NEH	Belgique (R)
Denmark (N)	NAA	8 226 275	104.8	108.4	112.0	107.1	105.4	8 511 241	96.3	95.4	100.7	109.7	122.6	10 431 400	NEH	Danemark (N)
France (R)	NAA	254 700 000	76.7	90.0	92.7	96.3	99.2	332 208 000	102.3	91.9	105.5	109.5	112.0	372 175 000	NEH	France (R)
	AAA	30 100 000	84.5	92.8	94.3	98.1	101.9	36 079 000	102.5						AEH	
Germany (R)	NAA	22 723 736	76.7	75.0	77.5	94.0	101.0	27 812 113	104.6	108.3	120.7	125.3	119.5	33 246 110	NEH	Allemagne (R)
	AAA	9 709 504	77.3	77.4	80.5	97.7	103.8	12 217 196	100.9	107.3	119.9	127.9	117.0	14 294 604	AEH	
Greece (N)	NAA	31 349 883	86.4	84.5	77.1	93.6	100.7	35 450 627	104.3	98.1	96.4	102.4	86.1	30 521 208	NEH	Grèce (N)
	AAA	6 316 128	95.8	94.7	89.3	107.0	109.9	6 415 487							AEH	
Ireland (R)	NAA	20 740 000	91.2	90.8	98.6	101.5	99.2	18 971 900	119.2	138.1	165.2	177.5	175.4	33 286 000	NEH	Irlande (R)
	AAA	1 731 000	89.5	91.5	91.3	97.9	103.5	1 878 000		129.1	149.3	164.9	159.1	2 987 000	AEH	
Italy (N)	NAA	103 282 488	93.0	101.5	97.9	95.8	97.2	99 286 309	93.6	93.0	87.5	85.3	88.0	87 364 180	NEH	Italie (N)
	AAA	18 121 622	86.8	96.7	96.8	101.0	103.6	19 092 676	105.7	108.0	107.8	109.3	106.2	20 283 838	AEH	
Luxembourg (R)	NAA			86.3	87.5	104.0	93.1	2 356 326	92.1	90.8					NEH	Luxembourg (R)
	AAA				82.4	96.7	96.8	711 026	100.0	102.5	106.6	114.8	116.3	826 877	AEH	
Netherlands (R)	NAA	11 327 150	84.4	91.5	88.6	99.7	99.7	13 953 086		90.6	101.6	114.8	123.3	17 205 900	NEH	Pays-Bas (R)
	AAA	4 170 745	89.3	93.8	92.3	102.2	103.4	4 828 994	101.0	101.0	106.6	118.0	121.0	5 841 900	AEH	
Norway (N)	NAA	4 374 000												6 304 825	NEH	Norvège (N)
Portugal (N)	NAA	11 488 039	70.6	71.1	71.5	76.5	89.6	16 679 986	102.6	106.6	109.3	116.0	131.6	21 957 339	NEH	Portugal (N)
	AAA	2 389 565	66.1	67.4	72.0	80.8	93.1	3 552 335	107.8	112.3	117.2	124.8	134.3	4 769 090	AEH	
Spain (N)	NAA	60 975 191													NEH	Espagne (N)
	AAA	9 390 609													AEH	
Sweden (N)	NAA	5 637 414	84.4	85.7	101.3	102.5	104.4	7 171 867	98.8	99.2	105.7	91.7	78.9	5 660 373	NEH	Suède (N)
Switzerland (R)	NAA	36 025 800	112.2	105.2	103.0	100.1	100.7	34 928 600	99.0	98.6	102.9	105.6	105.9	36 983 759	NEH	Suisse (R)
	AAA	8 872 500	102.5	100.3	100.5	103.5	104.1	9 157 500	101.8	102.1	110.2	114.9	110.1	10 084 496	AEH	
Turkey (N)	NAA	1 114 862	26.6	31.8	47.8	62.8	82.2	5 931 976	140.3	196.5	200.0	223.7	163.5	9 699 097	NEH	Turquie (N)
	AAA	412 930	31.2	37.3	54.4	68.0	86.2	2 010 529	132.4	169.7	188.2	192.4	119.3	2 398 666	AEH	
United Kingdom (R)	NAA	136 136 400	85.6	86.2	91.7	97.7	105.6	158 169 000	112.7	109.3	118.4	124.2	114.3	180 828 000	NEH	Royaume-Uni (R)
	AAA														AEH	
Canada (R)	NAA	74 494 100	83.9	79.3	76.9	84.1	84.3	91 470 500	92.8	100.5	98.4				NEH	Canada (R)
	AAA	12 785 300	82.0	78.0	80.0	83.1	84.3	15 621 300	95.9	99.1	96.7				AEH	
Australia (R)	NAA		70.6		78.1	83.7	80.5	18 075 600	124.9	114.8	309.3	361.5	357.6	64 644 800	NEH	Australie (R)
New Zealand (R)	NAA		70.6			78.2	91.3	16 138 892	112.5		116.9	128.0	119.5	19 288 595	NEH	Nouvelle-Zélande (R)

AAA Arrivals in all means of accommodation
NAA Nights in all means of accommodation
(R) Tourist count by country of residence
(N) Tourist count by country of nationality

AEH Arrivées dans l'ensemble des moyens d'hébergement
NEH Nuitées dans l'ensemble des moyens d'hébergement
(R) Recensement des touristes par pays de résidence
(N) Recensement des touristes par pays de nationalité

Table/Tableau 26

ARRIVALS OF FOREIGN TOURISTS/VISITORS AT FRONTIERS
ARRIVÉES DE TOURISTES/VISITEURS ÉTRANGERS AUX FRONTIÈRES

From Germany — *En provenance de l'Allemagne*

1986=100

Country	T/V	Volume 1980	1981	1982	1983	1984	1985	Volume 1986	1987	1988	1989	1990	1991	Volume 1991
France (R)	T	7 530 000	91.8	99.8	95.7	98.5	103.6	8 417 000	105.9	108.3	125.9	144.0	162.6	13 683 000
Greece (N)	V	692 961	54.6	52.9	63.6	75.5	91.7	1 145 000	105.2	120.7	144.5	167.9	136.3	1 561 113
Iceland (N)	T	9 046	66.8	62.6	64.4	70.7	69.3	13 601	103.0	116.9	136.0	151.7	165.3	22 477
Ireland (R)	T	109 497	86.1	84.2	95.9	93.8	99.0	97 000	104.1	115.5	155.7	177.3	200.0	194 000
Italy (N)	V	10 531 047	97.7	108.7	108.5	113.2	122.6	9 555 440	100.7	109.7	106.1	111.7	96.3	9 205 658
Norway (N)	V	90 608 / 257 639	70.0	63.6	81.5	77.0	96.5	382 562	126.1	138.4	147.6	162.4	205.6	786 496
Portugal (N)	T	300 116	71.3	67.3	82.6	80.0	96.0	430 282	122.3	132.2	142.1	158.3	198.0	851 858
Spain (N)	V	4 691 539	76.8	80.5	83.7	88.5	95.1	5 935 429	111.1	116.3	114.3	115.9	129.1	7 663 223
Turkey (N)	V	155 440	39.9	43.6	45.1	62.3	77.2	388 192	134.9	197.8	231.1	250.9	200.9	779 882
United Kingdom (R)	V	1 518 600	91.8	90.1	85.9	92.8	92.8	1 599 200	102.8	114.4	126.7	117.5	130.1	2 080 000
Canada (R)	T	189 100	100.9	92.6	82.2	85.7	78.9	198 300	120.8	132.6	132.5	129.6	139.4	276 500
Canada (R)	V	237 500	102.2	93.1	81.0	84.9	77.2	235 900	126.6	136.4	130.8	123.1	132.4	312 300
United States (R)	T	628 428	104.5	99.4	84.0	81.4	76.0	669 845	142.1	172.2	160.7	179.6	213.5	1 430 193
Australia (R)	V	35 378	93.2	92.8	82.6	81.6	89.0	41 900	127.2	157.3	162.5	177.1	185.4	77 700
Japan (N)	V	39 661	83.2	84.1	88.4	99.7	98.9	49 139	109.0	115.9	125.3	132.7	124.6	61 227
New Zealand (R)	T	7 804	72.5	74.5	79.1	79.0	88.5	12 040	136.5	167.0	197.4	249.1	284.9	34 298

V   Visitors (travellers in Turkey) — Visiteurs (voyageurs en Turquie)
T   Tourists — Touristes
(R) Tourist count by country of residence — Recensement des touristes par pays de résidence
(N) Tourist count by country of nationality — Recensement des touristes par pays de nationalité

Table/Tableau 27

ARRIVALS AND NIGHTS OF FOREIGN TOURISTS AT/IN HOTELS
ARRIVÉES ET NUITÉES DE TOURISTES ÉTRANGERS DANS L'HÔTELLERIE

From Germany
En provenance de l'Allemagne

1986=100

Country	AH/NH	Volume 1980	1981	1982	1983	1984	1985	Volume 1986	1987	1988	1989	1990	1991	Volume 1991	AH/NH	
Austria (R)	NH	38 143 140	115.1	109.8	106.5	102.2	98.9	33 177 098	99.2	100.7	107.4	102.5	115.1	38 172 969	NH	Autriche (R)
	AH	5 472 309	100.6	98.5	99.7	98.0	96.8	5 479 332	103.6	108.6	116.1	114.0	126.6	6 935 141	AH	
Belgium (R)	NH	669 701	85.3	92.8	94.7	97.8	98.1	761 452	102.3	105.3	122.5	118.0			NH	Belgique (R)
Denmark (N)	NH	1 435 600	159.1	132.7	124.2	115.0	103.9	930 700	101.4	99.8	115.3	138.4	170.5	1 587 200	NH	Danemark (N)
Finland (R)	NH	311 653	132.9	107.9	102.0	111.1	109.3	250 083	112.3	128.6	141.4	135.3	140.4	351 017	NH	Finlande (R)
France (R)[1]	NH	2 421 857	39.5	33.6	35.9	33.5	33.8	5 822 756	106.0	115.2	130.4	136.6	146.0	8 502 236	NH	France (R)[1]
	AH	877 005	30.1	26.7	28.4	25.9	27.9	2 858 917	106.6	117.3	133.0	138.0	143.6	4 104 567	AH	
Greece (N)	NH	5 605 497	74.7	67.8	64.2	76.7	96.6	7 129 880	101.0	110.4					NH	Grèce (N)
	AH	934 197	85.6	82.2	76.8	87.4	100.8	1 015 517	101.7	104.5					AH	
Iceland (N)	NH						93.3	343 000	102.6	149.9	164.4	231.8	238.2	817 000	NH	Islande (N)
Ireland (R)	NH						92.6	54 000	107.4	124.1	161.1	177.8	203.7	110 000	NH	Irlande (R)
Italy (N)	NH	27 261 922	88.2	96.8	88.4	91.7	92.8	26 850 975	105.4	105.8	96.8	89.1			NH	Italie (N)
	AH	3 996 683	78.6	89.0	88.0	90.4	92.6	4 497 592	109.7	112.2	108.5	104.8			AH	
Luxembourg (R)	NH			88.7	88.0	93.2	97.6	111 641	107.0	111.0	108.5	107.0	119.1	132 958	NH	Luxembourg (R)
	AH			95.9	85.0	92.0	97.8	63 308	110.8	111.8		109.1	116.4	73 676	AH	
Netherlands (R)	NH	1 485 218	88.3	86.3	85.0	86.9	84.5	1 629 200	96.6	90.5	93.5	101.7	114.0	1 857 900	NH	Pays-Bas (R)
	AH	608 572	86.8	84.8	70.8	88.9	88.1	690 700	96.4	96.3	97.7	105.9	115.6	798 600	AH	
Norway (N)	NH	451 489	93.9	74.6	60.5	100.1	102.9	495 983	101.9	108.7	117.1	116.9	143.8	713 212	NH	Norvège (N)
Portugal (N)	NH	1 556 951	69.1	61.8	65.9	65.4	89.9	1 890 917	108.5	108.8	110.1	124.8	171.0	3 233 873	NH	Portugal (N)
	AH	221 551	62.6	61.2	65.9	69.8	94.1	306 591	120.7	122.5	122.8	136.7	174.3	534 237	AH	
Spain (N)	NH	18 131 594	88.9	91.9	94.9	98.2	100.1	23 591 705	110.5	104.4	92.4	96.3	110.1	25 975 175	NH	Espagne (N)
	AH	1 906 378	81.5	84.9	89.9	93.2	96.1	2 600 208	109.1	103.6	95.5	90.8	112.2	2 916 982	AH	
Sweden (N)	NH	442 387	94.2	84.8	84.2	91.3	92.8	453 036	93.6	105.0	112.7	102.5	99.5	450 697	NH	Suède (N)
Switzerland (R)	NH	7 540 673	123.4	107.1	104.2	97.5	96.8	6 196 055	99.8	100.4	104.8	103.5	112.3	6 961 061	NH	Suisse (R)
	AH	2 097 576	110.3	101.7	101.2	96.9	95.5	1 919 208	102.6	105.0	111.0	109.5	116.9	2 244 199	AH	
Turkey (N)	NH			20.6	30.3	42.6	65.8	1 609 044	141.6	218.8	229.3	242.3	215.0	3 458 776	NH	Turquie (N)
	AH			23.6	36.7	46.7	68.1	519 590	136.4	172.6	182.8	184.9	108.5	563 870	AH	
Australia (R)	NH		93.0		78.0	71.9	90.6	334 000	127.2	157.2	153.1	155.7	174.2	581 800	NH	Australie (R)
Japan (N)	NH	168 008													NH	Japon (N)
	AH	62 658													AH	

AH Arrivals at hotels and similar establishments — Arrivées dans les hôtels et les établissements assimilés
NH Nights in hotels and similar establishments — Nuitées dans les hôtels et établissements assimilés
(R) Tourist count by country of residence — Recensement des touristes par pays de résidence
(N) Tourist count by country of nationality — Recensement des touristes par pays de nationalité
1. Ile de France only — Ile de France seulement

ARRIVALS AND NIGHTS OF FOREIGN TOURISTS AT/IN ALL MEANS OF ACCOMMODATION
ARRIVÉES ET NUITÉES DE TOURISTES ÉTRANGERS DANS L'ENSEMBLE DES MOYENS D'HÉBERGEMENT

From Germany
En provenance de l'Allemagne

1986=100

Country	AAA/NAA	Volume 1980	1981	1982	1983	1984	1985	Volume 1986	AEH/NEH	1987	1988	1989	1990	1991	Volume 1991	
Austria (R)	NAA	65 578 646	117.7	111.9	107.9	102.4	98.9	56 055 408	NEH	98.0	100.0	106.9	101.4	114.7	64 285 539	Autriche (R)
	AAA	8 517 509	102.8	100.5	101.0	98.6	97.0	8 393 619	AEH	102.3	107.2	115.2	112.2	126.4	10 613 343	
Belgium (R)	NAA	1 186 326	77.0	87.6	87.7	93.0	100.3	1 512 155	NEH	103.2	111.8	129.6	128.4			Belgique (R)
Denmark (N)	NAA	3 685 901	125.2	122.4	125.6	112.3	106.2	3 275 704	NEH	89.2	86.0	91.8	102.4	119.9	3 928 400	Danemark (N)
France (R)	NAA	60 240 000	81.0	98.3	95.0	96.6	100.0	76 388 000	NEH	103.3	86.0	91.8	102.4	111.2	84 956 000	France (R)
	AAA	7 530 000	91.8	99.8	95.7	96.5	103.6	8 417 000	AEH	105.9	76.5	90.0	100.7			
Greece (N)	NAA	6 419 843	80.6	73.7	69.4	82.1	96.9	7 592 937	NEH	101.6	109.5					Grèce (N)
	AAA	1 163 917	92.3	89.5	81.8	92.0	99.9	1 164 884	AEH	102.5						
Ireland (R)	NAA	1 525 080	78.0	88.4	99.0	91.9	94.9	1 331 300	NEH	114.5	132.7	167.6	208.6	241.7	3 218 000	Irlande (R)
	AAA	95 000	90.0	86.0	92.0	89.0	97.9	100 000	AEH		113.0	154.0	178.0	203.0	203 000	
Italy (N)	NAA	45 377 447	88.7	87.7	95.3	92.3	93.2	44 812 753	NEH	87.6	88.1	71.6	73.1			Italie (N)
	AAA	5 606 290	78.3	89.4	90.0	90.0	92.6	6 422 540	AEH	99.1	111.7	95.3	92.3			
Luxembourg (R)	NAA			83.4	81.5	103.9	104.7	157 452	NEH	111.7	110.5	106.3	106.3	131.1	206 440	Luxembourg (R)
	AAA					98.0	100.7	80 314	AEH					121.2	97 370	
Netherlands (R)	NAA	5 059 232	78.6	88.7	87.9	97.0	94.6	6 932 162	NEH		81.3	92.0	107.4	120.7	8 364 100	Pays-Bas (R)
	AAA	1 362 571	86.4	89.0	91.6	96.2	95.4	1 688 137	AEH		90.7	97.8	108.1	122.5	2 068 700	
Portugal (N)	NAA	2 086 049	78.5	70.5	65.7	65.8	88.6	2 532 319	NEH	110.2	109.8	108.7	117.0	156.6	3 966 162	Portugal (N)
	AAA	337 634	66.8	63.6	65.8	68.6	88.8	483 369	AEH	117.5	118.6	116.3	124.4	155.2	750 039	
Spain (N)	NAA	19 114 738							NEH							Espagne (N)
	AAA	2 043 123							AEH							
Sweden (N)	NAA	1 394 600	112.7	101.1	113.6	104.2	104.0	1 285 971	NEH	92.9	107.1	117.7	109.0	102.6	1 319 398	Suède (N)
Switzerland (R)	NAA	16 361 200	118.8	108.3	106.5	97.6	98.1	14 763 900	NEH	97.8	100.1	101.2	99.8	109.2	16 128 432	Suisse (R)
	AAA	3 100 600	108.4	102.1	102.3	96.6	96.3	2 993 500	AEH	100.9	104.5	108.6	108.2	117.5	3 517 353	
Turkey (N)	NAA	162 339	14.1	16.7	27.1	35.9	57.7	2 048 794	NEH	158.3	224.2	229.8	264.9	217.1	4 448 640	Turquie (N)
	AAA	56 917	17.9	22.2	35.3	44.3	65.5	560 044	AEH	148.7	183.7	193.2	198.9	118.1	661 497	
United Kingdom (R)	NAA	16 081 000	93.2	94.7	85.8	87.3	89.0	16 391 000	NEH	95.5	105.1	108.1	106.1	115.7	18 958 000	Royaume-Uni (R)
Canada (R)	NAA	2 693 400	106.7	103.5	89.2	92.5	82.9	2 727 200	NEH	111.4	131.3	119.1				Canada (R)
	AAA	189 100	100.9	92.6	82.2	85.7	78.9	198 300	AEH	118.1	132.6	132.5				
Australia (R)	NAA		93.8		98.2	68.8	87.7	785 400	NEH	140.0	152.3	296.8	411.0	394.3	3 096 900	Australie (R)
New Zealand (R)	NAA					70.6	77.9	410 665	NEH		152.3	180.3	215.4	276.0	1 133 327	Nouvelle-Zélande (R)

AAA Arrivals in all means of accommodation
NAA Nights in all means of accommodation
(R) Tourist count by country of residence
(N) Tourist count by country of nationality

AEH Arrivées dans l'ensemble des moyens d'hébergement
NEH Nuitées dans l'ensemble des moyens d'hébergement
(R) Recensement des touristes par pays de résidence
(N) Recensement des touristes par pays de nationalité

Table/Tableau 29

ARRIVALS OF FOREIGN TOURISTS/VISITORS AT FRONTIERS
ARRIVÉES DE TOURISTES/VISITEURS ÉTRANGERS AUX FRONTIÈRES

From Canada
1986=100

En provenance du Canada
1986=100

	T/V	Volume 1980	1981	1982	1983	1984	1985	Volume 1986	1987	1988	1989	1990	1991	Volume 1991	T/V	
France (R)	T / V	320 000	92.5	64.8	73.3	97.7	123.6	386 000	90.4	89.1		158.0	143.0	552 000	T / V	France (R)
Greece (N)	T	72 441	88.1	87.0	97.2	110.2	137.4	74 612	122.0	143.4	105.9	99.5	63.1	47 101	T	Grèce (N)
Iceland (N)	T	806	74.6	83.9	86.9	83.8	107.6	1 195	107.6	106.9	108.1	95.4	78.9	943	T	Islande (N)
Ireland (R)	V	9 598	91.3	58.0	75.0	75.0	89.3	28 000	89.3	100.0	132.1	135.7	107.1	30 000	V	Irlande (R)
Italy (N)	V	352 256	91.4	91.2	98.1	99.5	103.1	337 939	113.8	104.8	125.2	140.6	103.6	350 056	V	Italie (N)
Norway (N)	V	37 764	57.5	52.5	57.4	72.5	95.4	72 183	100.6	105.3	115.1	115.3	87.1	62 872	V	Norvège (N)
Portugal (N)	T	40 317	59.0	56.9	63.4	76.0	95.2	73 825	105.0	107.1	123.4	123.0	93.9	69 299	T	Portugal (N)
Spain (N)	V	115 019	76.8	75.4	78.3	88.0	108.0	176 880	101.0	95.0	97.4	89.2	78.0	137 950	V	Espagne (N)
Turkey (N)	V	11 561	88.0	65.3	110.0	137.8	164.3	13 101	159.0	223.0	241.1	263.9	135.0	17 680	V	Turquie (N)
United Kingdom (R)	V	387 100	70.1	73.6	93.5	102.1	113.7	555 100	107.0	117.3	115.0	126.5	93.9	521 000	V	Royaume-Uni (R)
United States (R)	T	11 384 538	99.9	95.3	109.3	100.4	99.4	10 942 753	113.5	126.5	140.4	157.8	173.0	18 926 613	T	États-Unis (R)
Australia (R)	V	28 485	65.8	69.0	70.2	73.4	87.0	47 000	112.1	141.9	115.3	114.3	113.6	53 400	V	Australie (R)
Japan (N)	V	41 045	81.3	87.4	97.1	96.0	110.6	55 222	105.5	105.3	108.2	115.6	112.8	62 306	V	Japon (N)
New Zealand (R)	T	18 556	53.4	52.5	59.6	67.1	86.9	34 326	103.6	108.2	90.1	99.0	88.2	30 276	T	Nouvelle-Zélande (R)

V   Visitors (travellers in Turkey)
T   Tourists
(R) Tourist count by country of residence
(N) Tourist count by country of nationality

V   Visiteurs (voyageurs en Turquie)
T   Touristes
(R) Recensement des touristes par pays de résidence
(N) Recensement des touristes par pays de nationalité

Table/Tableau 30

ARRIVALS AND NIGHTS OF FOREIGN TOURISTS AT/IN HOTELS
ARRIVÉES ET NUITÉES DE TOURISTES ÉTRANGERS DANS L'HÔTELLERIE

From Canada / En provenance du Canada
1986=100

From Canada	AH/NH	Volume 1980	1981	1982	1983	1984	1985	Volume 1986	1987	1988	1989	1990	1991	Volume 1991	AH/NH	En provenance du Canada
Austria (R)	NH	101 421	71.3	77.6	82.1	99.2	121.2	165 178	110.0	101.9	105.2	117.6	93.9	155 101	NH	Autriche (R)
	AH	39 835	67.2	73.9	86.9	107.9	128.8	61 537	112.1	109.4	117.5	136.1	101.8	62 626	AH	
Belgium (R)	NH	51 136	66.2	67.9	78.3	103.0	127.6	72 702	104.7	109.2	128.6	135.9			NH	Belgique (R)
Finland (R)	NH	14 433	73.2	84.0	104.4	108.3	117.6	25 439	114.2	119.6	130.6	126.0	97.9	24 895	NH	Finlande (R)
France (R)[1]	NH	271 287	37.3	40.8	49.1	57.5	69.5	808 155	92.3	93.2	118.2	127.8	93.6	756 579	NH	France (R)[1]
	AH	98 098	28.5	31.0	34.8	42.9	55.0	381 416	86.5	87.4	113.0	123.9	94.6	360 630	AH	
Germany (R)	NH	205 396	68.7	72.2	80.4	104.6	113.7	299 218	96.8	103.2	119.0	126.6	99.6	297 992	NH	Allemagne (R)
	AH	109 429	68.8	73.9	83.6	112.5	120.2	153 530	96.5	97.0	111.4	121.8	92.0	141 292	AH	
Greece (N)	NH	210 342	106.7	96.4	106.8	131.6	185.5	196 353	117.1	120.5					NH	Grèce (N)
	AH	80 102	98.1	93.0	102.1	133.6	182.2	75 635	117.2	120.7					AH	
Ireland (R)	NH							156 000	68.6	73.7	162.8	69.2	105.1	164 000	NH	Irlande (R)
	AH							28 000	82.1	85.7	132.1	75.0	103.6	29 000	AH	
Italy (N)	NH	390 855	71.2	85.3	100.8	112.4	128.2	522 814	116.1	109.7	120.3	121.2			NH	Italie (N)
	AH	148 121	66.9	81.6	100.7	118.1	130.5	204 842	115.7	113.2	118.8	123.5			AH	
Luxembourg (R)	NH														NH	Luxembourg (R)
	AH														AH	
Netherlands (R)	NH	125 411	69.3	72.6	91.9	104.9	118.3	164 300	106.1	106.8	109.7	113.0	81.7	134 200	NH	Pays-Bas (R)
	AH	67 918	64.8	66.9	92.2	105.2	121.2	93 900	105.2	109.6	100.0	97.8	67.2	63 100	AH	
Portugal (N)	NH	186 487	55.5	47.8	59.2	71.2	106.7	363 680	95.3	85.8	93.6	103.4	76.6	278 760	NH	Portugal (N)
	AH	49 322	58.4	55.8	66.5	81.5	106.5	92 409	109.2	99.3	107.8	109.1	68.5	63 328	AH	
Spain (N)	NH	242 199	81.5	85.2	104.1	120.6	141.6	341 574	66.4	53.5	52.1	48.5	35.9	122 489	NH	Espagne (N)
	AH	97 211												51 014	AH	
Sweden (N)	NH	25 316	125.0	97.4	105.2	131.0	127.7	21 985	127.7	103.9	114.1	118.1	72.6	15 959	NH	Suède (N)
Switzerland (R)	NH	170 978	70.8	75.7	88.7	100.6	121.5	261 542	91.8	80.1	83.3	89.9	67.8	177 402	NH	Suisse (R)
	AH	75 715	67.5	73.6	91.5	100.7	125.2	113 725	92.2	82.1	88.0	95.4	67.7	77 036	AH	
Turkey (N)	NH			58.9	64.0	83.9	85.2	16 401	115.9	180.5	187.8	171.0	119.0	19 522	NH	Turquie (N)
	AH			40.2	63.0	71.9	79.3	7 001	109.9	150.6	225.7	186.4	113.6	7 950	AH	
Australia (R)	NH	90 496	61.3		90.0	62.7	84.7	419 500	112.1	141.9	92.4	115.6	87.2	365 700	NH	Australie (R)
Japan (N)	NH	90 496													NH	Japon (N)
	AH	38 131													AH	

AH Arrivals at hotels and similar establishments — Arrivées dans les hôtels et les établissements assimilés
NH Nights in hotels and similar establishments — Nuitées dans les hôtels et établissements assimilés
(R) Tourist count by country of residence — Recensement des touristes par pays de résidence
(N) Tourist count by country of nationality — Recensement des touristes par pays de nationalié
1. Ile de France only — Ile de France seulement

117

Table/Tableau 31

ARRIVALS AND NIGHTS OF FOREIGN TOURISTS AT/IN ALL MEANS OF ACCOMMODATION
ARRIVÉES ET NUITÉES DE TOURISTES ÉTRANGERS DANS L'ENSEMBLE DES MOYENS D'HÉBERGEMENT

From Canada
1986=100

En provenance du Canada
1986=100

Country	AAA/NAA	Volume 1980	1981	1982	1983	1984	1985	Volume 1986	1987	1988	1989	1990	1991	Volume 1991	AEH/NEH	Pays
Austria (R)	NAA	141 581	71.8	80.7	84.3	100.1	117.3	209 691	108.5	106.6	105.2	118.6	93.6	196 294	NEH	Autriche (R)
	AAA	50 315	66.2	73.7	84.1	105.4	123.8	76 545	110.4	110.5	117.5	135.7	101.6	77 774	AEH	
Belgium (R)	NAA	60 672	63.3	67.2	75.4	98.1	120.8	87 716	98.0	103.4	120.0	129.5			NEH	Belgique (R)
	AAA														AEH	
France (R)	NAA	3 200 000	60.7	60.4	72.5	91.3	113.0	5 884 000	96.6	106.4	88.7	107.3	95.4	5 614 000	NEH	France (R)
	AAA														AEH	
Germany (R)	NAA	320 000	92.5	64.8	73.3	97.7	123.6	386 000	90.4	89.1	119.2	126.2	98.8	335 562	NEH	Allemagne (R)
	AAA	222 000	61.9	65.1	72.6	103.1	112.0	339 652	96.4	103.2	111.1	121.8	91.3	160 568	AEH	
Greece (N)	NAA	115 702	60.5	64.9	73.5	110.0	116.6	175 802	95.5	96.7					NEH	Grèce (N)
	AAA														AEH	
Ireland (R)	NAA	238 894	113.3	112.2	112.2	190.3	184.0	202 484	116.2	119.0				436 450	NEH	Irlande (R)
	AAA	90 365	104.9	100.0	108.5	142.6	180.3	78 091	116.6	119.3				35 000	AEH	
Italy (N)	NAA	574 194	80.9	93.8	102.5	111.5	123.1	657 843	107.0	102.6	111.8	113.0			NEH	Italie (N)
	AAA	171 601	68.5	81.6	99.3	115.7	126.4	230 982	113.1	112.2	116.8	121.5			AEH	
Luxembourg (R)	NAA														NEH	Luxembourg (R)
	AAA														AEH	
Netherlands (R)	NAA	163 520	79.0	82.0	98.6	111.8	123.4	180 471		113.3	116.9	122.7	91.7	165 500	NEH	Pays-Bas (R)
	AAA	86 417	74.5	76.4	99.0	112.5	126.4	103 712		118.4	104.8	104.8	76.7	79 500	AEH	
Portugal (N)	NAA	202 793	57.3	49.3	60.6	72.5	107.2	374 163	95.7	86.5	94.0	103.7	76.9	287 805	NEH	Portugal (N)
	AAA	54 640	60.2	57.1	67.8	82.5	106.9	96 124	109.3	99.8	108.4	110.5	69.7	67 003	AEH	
Sweden (N)	NAA	28 674	119.6	95.8	104.7	126.9	124.0	25 168	122.3	102.5	111.7	115.9	73.0	18 376	NEH	Suède (N)
	AAA														AEH	
Switzerland (R)	NAA	211 600	72.9	77.8	88.9	100.3	119.6	314 500	92.7	81.3	85.4	90.7	70.6	221 938	NEH	Suisse (R)
	AAA	95 500	70.6	76.2	91.9	108.7	123.5	137 200	91.5	83.2	89.2	95.6	70.3	96 413	AEH	
Turkey (N)	NAA	5 450	33.9	57.8	63.4	83.7	85.2	16 802	118.8	184.9	188.3	174.2	120.1	20 181	NEH	Turquie (N)
	AAA	2 067	35.6	39.9	62.8	71.8	80.3	7 085	113.2	157.5	227.7	189.9	117.0	8 286	AEH	
United Kingdom (R)	NAA	5 870 000	76.9	83.2	94.2	98.6	106.5	8 557 000	96.2	103.5	100.3	109.3	86.0	7 355 000	NEH	Royaume-Uni (R)
	AAA														AEH	
Australia (R)	NAA		79.8	153.7		92.3	89.5	862 400	112.1	141.9	208.3	309.9	265.4	2 288 900	NEH	Australie (R)
New Zealand (R)	NAA													666 285	NEH	Nouvelle-Zélande (R)

AAA Arrivals in all means of accommodation
NAA Nights in all means of accommodation
(R) Tourist count by country of residence
(N) Tourist count by country of nationality

AEH Arrivées dans l'ensemble des moyens d'hébergement
NEH Nuitées dans l'ensemble des moyens d'hébergement
(R) Recensement des touristes par pays de résidence
(N) Recensement des touristes par pays de nationalité

Table/Tableau 32

ARRIVALS OF FOREIGN TOURISTS/VISITORS AT FRONTIERS
ARRIVÉES DE TOURISTES/VISITEURS ÉTRANGERS AUX FRONTIÈRES

From the United States / En provenance des États-Unis

1986=100

Country	T/V	Volume 1980	1981	1982	1983	1984	1985	Volume 1986	1987	1988	1989	1990	1991	Volume 1991	T/V	
France (R)	T / V	1 190 000	82.1	81.2	122.9	152.2	166.5	1 668 000	108.0	116.9	129.9	124.1	102.4	1 708 000	T / V	France (R)
Greece (N)	T	288 647	156.9	162.7	198.8	232.0	227.8	204 667	127.0	144.1	136.3	133.8	88.2	180 429	T	Grèce (N)
Iceland (N)	T	15 260	54.8	63.7	76.2	83.5	96.7	32 700	109.1	87.8	70.2	69.2	68.8	22 506	T	Islande (N)
Ireland (R)	V	241 142	81.6	101.3	89.9	101.7	126.8	298 000	120.1	125.2	127.5	132.9	105.0	313 000	V	Irlande (R)
Italy (N)	V	1 724 167	90.7	100.7	107.9	111.5	115.3	1 591 542	93.2	84.9	85.2	89.3	71.5	1 137 441	V	Italie (N)
Norway (N)	V	81 079	95.3	111.4	100.5	144.6	144.1	114 419	132.5	169.7	163.2	160.7	125.4	143 459	V	Norvège (N)
Portugal (N)	T	115 431	94.6	102.9	124.7	139.8	153.2	149 808	130.2	149.0	157.2	168.3	118.9	178 133	T	Portugal (N)
Spain (N)	V	817 376	100.3	98.5	105.4	121.6	129.6	769 785	112.4	111.6	123.9	108.6	84.7	652 338	V	Espagne (N)
Turkey (N)	V	118 669	130.2	131.5	237.3	268.0	246.5	79 614	164.0	207.8	256.9	258.5	99.6	79 256	V	Turquie (N)
United Kingdom (R)	V	1 694 600	75.0	75.4	101.3	120.8	138.4	2 288 300	122.4	114.5	124.2	133.2	98.3	2 250 000	V	Royaume-Uni (R)
Canada (R)	T	10 963 300	80.6	76.9	80.2	83.0	84.9	13 608 400	93.5	93.8	89.5	90.1	88.5	12 049 600	T	Canada (R)
Canada (R)	V	38 501 000	104.2	84.9	85.0	86.3	89.3	38 199 500	96.7	94.6	90.9	90.9	87.9	33 577 200	V	
Australia (R)	V	110 815	46.4	51.1	56.9	65.4	80.1	245 400	125.9	131.3	106.2	102.2	110.8	271 800	V	Australie (R)
Japan (N)	V	319 017	64.0	74.4	83.5	92.6	101.1	552 182	99.7	93.5	96.3	100.5	98.3	543 025	V	Japon (N)
New Zealand (R)	T	77 796	49.9	49.6	56.3	65.6	79.9	153 974	117.1	108.8	89.3	90.7	86.2	132 690	T	Nouvelle-Zélande (R)

V   Visitors (travellers in Turkey)
T   Tourists
(R)   Tourist count by country of residence
(N)   Tourist count by country of nationality

V   Visiteurs (voyageurs en Turquie)
T   Touristes
(R)   Recensement des touristes par pays de résidence
(N)   Recensement des touristes par pays de nationalité

Table/Tableau 33

ARRIVALS AND NIGHTS OF FOREIGN TOURISTS AT/IN HOTELS
ARRIVÉES ET NUITÉES DE TOURISTES ÉTRANGERS DANS L'HÔTELLERIE

From the United States — *En provenance des États-Unis*

1986=100

Country	AH/NH	Volume 1980	1981	1982	1983	1984	1985	Volume 1986	1987	1988	1989	1990	1991	Volume 1991
Austria (R)	NH	1 187 466	81.8	103.4	126.4	161.4	174.0	1 254 379	123.7	113.8	122.1	156.2	84.8	1 063 374
Austria (R)	AH	512 520	87.6	107.7	139.7	191.4	202.0	458 116	133.6	122.8	133.9	178.0	91.4	418 515
Belgium (R)	NH	464 660	77.4	90.6	96.9	114.7	128.6	600 249	89.8	77.3	92.3	97.6		
Denmark (N)	NH	362 200	81.5	99.8	121.2	128.1	138.3	414 200	107.2	91.3	100.1	96.5	70.4	291 500
Finland (R)	NH	84 927	61.3	72.0	94.1	98.8	115.9	159 467	125.2	127.4	127.0	123.7	90.4	144 098
Finland (R)	AH													
France (R) [1]	NH	1 858 505	61.5	63.7	79.3	104.1	117.9	3 267 007	110.0	121.1	160.3	173.6	119.9	3 917 294
France (R) [1]	AH	672 159	51.2	57.4	67.5	91.0	101.0	1 410 281	108.4	124.9	163.8	175.1	124.4	1 753 891
Germany (R)	NH	2 697 126	67.9	77.9	96.3	124.8	135.2	3 585 433	112.6	101.9	111.1	124.0	88.7	3 179 799
Germany (R)	AH	1 446 086	70.9	81.6	102.6	135.7	143.4	1 769 815	111.7	100.9	110.9	130.4	86.9	1 538 400
Greece (N)	NH	1 286 314	244.7	254.5	321.0	384.1	328.4	508 795	155.5	162.8				
Greece (N)	AH	497 639	261.6	272.4	352.4	442.3	387.7	185 863	174.3	192.2				
Iceland (N)	NH							1 614 000	124.7	132.2	120.7	126.4	111.1	1 793 000
Ireland (R)	NH							312 000	122.1	121.8	121.2	119.9	91.3	285 000
Ireland (R)	AH													
Italy (N)	NH	3 650 976	101.6	122.8	154.1	181.5	194.0	3 389 713	140.4	135.4	143.0	147.2		
Italy (N)	AH	1 481 541	106.8	131.4	170.1	207.3	220.1	1 281 687	147.1	145.4	151.5	159.5		
Luxembourg (R)	NH							74 557	103.5	85.0	80.0	80.0	59.5	44 371
Luxembourg (R)	AH							42 909	104.2	77.5	77.1	77.1	54.5	23 402
Netherlands (R)	NH	654 167	80.1	68.6	94.6	128.6	129.2	832 900	100.4	90.8	98.4	109.7	91.8	764 600
Netherlands (R)	AH	324 157	75.3	70.0	93.0	113.0	134.2	420 700	101.5	90.6	98.0	108.3	87.0	366 200
Norway (N)	NH	329 603	81.5	91.2	109.0	136.4	156.4	411 183	111.2	84.6	84.5	88.7	68.2	280 250
Norway (N)	AH	458 402	92.8	94.0	131.8	143.2	159.0	495 972	126.5	131.1	136.6	135.5	97.9	485 490
Portugal (N)	NH	159 923	97.3	98.4	140.1	156.6	169.5	172 178	134.5	139.2	147.5	146.5	108.0	186 020
Portugal (N)	AH													
Spain (N)	NH	1 372 458	106.2	111.0	136.5	166.3	171.0	1 485 026	128.4	118.3	116.4	118.0	87.1	1 293 788
Spain (N)	AH	550 860	88.2	91.8	121.4	127.6	174.7	710 486	113.4	109.1	101.8	111.4	81.6	579 414
Sweden (N)	NH	249 332	83.8	90.3	114.7	121.4	148.2	325 670	107.0	100.0	101.8	100.4	73.2	238 495
Switzerland (R)	NH	1 728 423	84.7	99.7	124.1	147.3	156.9	2 078 955	112.2	98.1	107.0	120.8	75.8	1 576 724
Switzerland (R)	AH	809 947	87.0	104.6		162.8	170.0	893 656	116.1	103.8	115.5	134.7	80.1	715 637
Turkey (N)	NH		68.3	65.6	87.5	116.3	122.4	218 786	122.3	143.9	174.0	159.4	129.1	282 437
Turkey (N)	AH				93.8	104.0	116.0	76 163	121.9	155.0	220.0	208.0	119.9	91 288
Australia (R)	NH	1 116 656	42.7		57.6	50.2	77.0	2 157 400	125.9	131.3	94.9	97.2	97.8	2 110 400
Japan (N)	NH	493 592												
Japan (N)	AH													

AH Arrivals at hotels and similar establishments — Arrivées dans les hôtels et les établissements assimilés
NH Nights in hotels and similar establishments — Nuitées dans les hôtels et établissements assimilés
(R) Tourist count by country of residence — Recensement des touristes par pays de résidence
(N) Tourist count by country of nationality — Recensement des touristes par pays de nationalité
1. Ile de France only — Ile de France seulement

Table/Tableau 34

ARRIVALS AND NIGHTS OF FOREIGN TOURISTS AT/IN ALL MEANS OF ACCOMMODATION
ARRIVÉES ET NUITÉES DE TOURISTES ÉTRANGERS DANS L'ENSEMBLE DES MOYENS D'HÉBERGEMENT

From the United States

En provenance des États-Unis

1986=100

Country	AAA/NAA	Volume 1980	1981	1982	1983	1984	1985	Volume 1986	1987	1988	1989	1990	1991	AEH/NEH	Volume 1991	
Austria (R)	NAA	1 332 572	83.1	102.1	123.6	156.4	168.7	1 408 803	122.1	113.0	120.5	151.8	84.6	NEH	1 191 496	Autriche
	AAA	553 705	86.6	105.1	134.9	182.8	193.9	509 472	131.8	121.7	132.7	173.8	92.0	AEH	468 646	
Belgium (R)	NAA	487 640	61.3	70.7	75.6	92.5	111.5	800 408	91.5	71.6	73.8	79.3		NEH		Belgique (R)
Denmark (N)	NAA	390 482	83.2	100.9	120.2	126.8	136.5	436 384	107.1	91.4	100.0	96.5	71.3	NEH	311 000	Danemark (N)
France (R)	NAA	9 520 000	47.2	64.9	98.1	117.7	133.3	23 202 000	109.8	63.6	76.7	73.4	60.7	NEH	14 074 000	France (R)
	AAA	1 190 000	82.1	81.2	122.9	152.2	166.5	1 668 000	108.0					AEH		
Germany (R)	NAA	2 857 558	65.1	74.5	92.9	123.9	134.1	3 795 838	112.5	102.1	111.5	124.2	89.1	NEH	3 380 246	Allemagne (R)
	AAA	1 503 072	68.1	78.3	98.6	134.9	142.0	1 852 229	111.8	101.4	111.6	131.1	87.3	AEH	1 617 196	
Greece (N)	NAA	1 413 846	256.0	263.6	329.9	398.5	322.6	521 723	153.3	160.3				NEH		Grèce (N)
	AAA	524 512	268.0	278.9	358.6	453.3	382.3	189 790	172.7					AEH		
Ireland (R)	NAA	2 980 000	79.2	93.6	108.6	102.0	124.4	3 291 100	121.6	124.9	138.1	134.7	117.7	NEH	3 874 000	Irlande (R)
	AAA	234 000	72.6	84.5	83.4	92.7	114.3	343 000		112.2	112.2	117.2	93.6	AEH	321 000	
Italy (N)	NAA	4 417 108	103.7	122.8	149.7	171.8	182.3	4 031 381	126.6	122.1	128.3	132.6		NEH		Italie (N)
	AAA	1 561 205	106.5	129.9	167.0	202.1	214.7	1 354 268	144.4	147.1	148.7	156.9		AEH		
Luxembourg (R)	NAA			65.8	89.4	115.4	131.7	80 502	105.5	87.2	107.3	82.7	65.1	NEH	52 401	Luxembourg (R)
	AAA				85.9	112.6	131.9	47 251	105.9	81.3	105.7	78.8	58.3	AEH	27 545	
Netherlands (R)	NAA	749 832	89.1	107.7	113.2	145.9	137.6	847 822		98.0		120.7	99.6	NEH	844 100	Pays-Bas (R)
	AAA	377 303	85.1	107.7	117.5	142.0	146.2	429 913	100.7	100.7	105.7	105.7	95.3	AEH	409 600	
Portugal (N)	NAA	479 437	93.9	95.1	120.8	154.6	158.0	510 556	127.6	130.6	135.7	135.7	97.9	NEH	500 018	Portugal (N)
	AAA	167 328	97.7	98.5	130.8		167.7	177 479	134.1	138.6	146.6	146.6	107.7	AEH	191 100	
Spain (N)	NAA	1 646 158												NEH		Espagne (N)
	AAA	656 062												AEH		
Sweden (N)	NAA	262 361	83.8	90.1	119.8	126.7	146.6	340 841	106.9	99.7	102.0	100.4	74.1	NEH	252 448	Suède (N)
Switzerland (R)	NAA	1 922 400	85.0	99.2	112.4	142.6	152.6	2 327 700	110.5	98.0	106.5	120.0	76.3	NEH	1 776 377	Suisse (R)
	AAA	885 200	88.5	105.3	123.3	158.9	166.6	967 200	115.5	103.9	115.1	133.5	80.7	AEH	780 515	
Turkey (N)	NAA	65 382	46.5	67.7	86.7	115.9	121.7	222 872	122.9	144.4	174.5	160.3	129.0	NEH	287 511	Turquie (N)
	AAA	23 616	47.0	65.4	93.4	104.2	116.2	77 112	123.3	156.7	220.4	208.9	120.0	AEH	92 496	
United Kingdom (R)	NAA	18 401 000	73.4	78.0	94.0	108.4	126.8	24 613 000	117.6	103.7	112.2	116.3	98.1	NEH	24 146 000	Royaume-Uni (R)
Canada (R)	NAA	50 423 000	81.3	74.7	76.4	83.7	85.0	63 320 800	87.4	88.8	84.6			NEH		Canada (R)
	AAA	10 963 300	80.6	76.9	80.2	83.0	84.9	13 608 400	93.5	93.8	89.5			AEH		
Australia (R)	NAA	3 347 800				63.4	87.9		107.2	98.8	157.4	172.8	198.3	NEH	6 638 200	Australie (R)
New Zealand (R)	NAA	2 285 043	50.7		66.5	68.3	86.2		98.8		88.4	93.1	83.3	NEH	1 903 738	Nouvelle-Zélande (R)

AAA Arrivals in all means of accommodation
NAA Nights in all means of accommodation
(R) Tourist count by country of residence
(N) Tourist count by country of nationality

AEH Arrivées dans l'ensemble des moyens d'hébergement
NEH Nuitées dans l'ensemble des moyens d'hébergement
(R) Recensement des touristes par pays de résidence
(N) Recensement des touristes par pays de nationalité

Table/Tableau 35

ARRIVALS OF FOREIGN TOURISTS/VISITORS AT FRONTIERS
ARRIVÉES DE TOURISTES/VISITEURS ÉTRANGERS AUX FRONTIÈRES

From France
1986=100

En provenance de la France
1986=100

Country	T/V	Volume 1980	1981	1982	1983	1984	1985	Volume 1986	1987	1988	1989	1990	1991	Volume 1991	T/V	
Greece (N)	T	299 791	63.3	71.6	63.9	86.6	94.2	468 499	108.9	100.1	102.0	120.7	100.5	470 945	T	Grèce (N)
Iceland (N)	T	3 581	75.7	78.8	69.8	86.3	79.8	5 617	94.6	109.3	145.8	178.4	179.3	10 071	T	Islande (N)
Ireland (R)	V	72 748	100.5	109.1	94.2	94.2	108.1	86 000	129.1	124.4	158.1	227.9	254.7	219 000	V	Irlande (R)
Italy (N)	V	7 402 441	87.1	98.9	92.1	98.7	101.6	8 570 229	105.5	104.7	109.6	107.6	106.4	9 114 554	V	Italie (N)
Norway (N)	V	25 224	67.1	82.0	92.7	91.8	94.0	340 608	121.5	166.0	179.4	181.4	195.9	667 122	V	Norvège (N)
Portugal (N)	T	223 205	68.2	82.4	93.6	93.3	99.2	350 134	124.2	169.5	184.7	188.0	203.2	711 493	T	Portugal (N)
Spain (N)	V	10 062 052	94.5	96.4	91.6	88.5	97.5	11 279 741	103.5	107.1	106.3	103.0	106.9	12 052 767	V	Espagne (N)
Turkey (N)	V	87 342	67.2	69.0	61.3	71.8	104.2	143 971	117.1	171.4	196.9	215.9	81.3	117 070	V	Turquie (N)
United Kingdom (R)	V	1 603 100	80.5	86.5	86.3	92.9	92.3	1 756 100	114.4	112.2	128.7	131.5	130.5	2 292 000	V	Royaume-Uni (R)
Canada (R)	T	114 000	84.7	84.2	64.6	79.0	76.5	140 300	135.3	163.7	173.1	185.0	218.9	307 100	T	Canada (R)
United States (R)	V	134 600	87.9	85.0	64.1	78.2	75.2	155 900	135.2	160.6	167.9	176.8	207.8	323 900	V	États-Unis (R)
United States (R)	T	360 670	93.5	96.3	69.3	75.2	76.3	439 611	123.8	140.7	148.7	162.9	175.2	770 230	T	États-Unis (R)
Australia (R)	V	8 118	60.3	73.7	71.9	80.6	86.3	13 900	123.0	151.1	144.6	151.8	163.3	22 700	V	Australie (R)
Japan (N)	V	25 860	78.2	83.8	81.6	96.6	112.3	35 322	105.3	114.5	133.8	144.4	141.9	50 119	V	Japon (N)
New Zealand (R)	T	2 000	70.6	69.0	72.7	83.6	91.6	2 651	143.8	129.6	153.7	129.3	175.1	4 643	T	Nouvelle-Zélande (R)

V   Visitors (travellers in Turkey)
T   Tourists
(R)   Tourist count by country of residence
(N)   Tourist count by country of nationality

V   Visiteurs (voyageurs en Turquie)
T   Touristes
(R)   Recensement des touristes par pays de résidence
(N)   Recensement des touristes par pays de nationalité

Table/Tableau 36

ARRIVALS AND NIGHTS OF FOREIGN TOURISTS AT/IN HOTELS
ARRIVÉES ET NUITÉES DE TOURISTES ÉTRANGERS DANS L'HÔTELLERIE

From France / En provenance de la France
1986=100

Country	AH/NH	Volume 1980	1981	1982	1983	1984	1985	Volume 1986	1987	1988	1989	1990	1991	Volume 1991
Austria (R)	NH	1 160 109	66.1	74.3	65.5	84.4	90.1	2 121 711	98.3	97.8	106.9	111.8	116.7	2 475 837
Belgium (R)	AH	366 517	75.2	79.2	68.4	86.8	91.5	574 618	96.5	97.5	107.9	114.1	116.0	666 335
Belgium (R)	NH	545 782	89.0	96.0	81.6	89.4	97.4	592 496	102.3	110.9	132.4	139.1		
Denmark (N)	NH	85 500	112.1	117.4	94.3	105.6	109.9	76 600	100.1	99.0	103.1	107.7	111.2	85 200
Finland (R)	NH	46 866	86.3	93.3	85.5	108.2	106.4	54 377	113.8	122.2	131.1	153.9	148.7	80 840
Germany (R)	NH	1 111 229	98.6	92.1	80.1	90.4	95.9	1 162 686	102.1	105.1	119.8	126.2	120.7	1 403 608
Germany (R)	AH	592 989	98.8	93.8	81.7	92.0	97.0	613 039	101.5	104.4	118.4	124.1	119.0	729 664
Greece (N)	NH	1 937 418	77.7	84.1	70.4	96.0	109.2	2 415 036	105.6	101.2				
Greece (N)	AH	640 504	81.9	89.5	72.7	99.5	105.5	763 052	102.0	94.6				
Iceland (N)	NH													892 000
Ireland (R)	NH													137 000
Italy (N)	NH	5 547 970	92.3	105.3	85.3	90.4	94.1	5 591 791	102.7	98.9	91.8	89.8		
Italy (N)	AH	1 728 968	89.9	103.4	84.6	93.8	95.3	1 732 782	104.0	103.6	101.6	99.7		
Luxembourg (R)	NH			99.5	79.8	86.5	96.6	68 693	110.5	123.8		157.3	144.6	99 333
Luxembourg (R)	AH			112.0	79.0	84.7	92.9	38 812	108.8	123.8		141.3	131.9	51 188
Netherlands (R)	NH	435 488	94.4	99.5	77.4	88.8	90.2	445 500	103.0	99.8	104.3	122.5	111.2	495 500
Netherlands (R)	AH	235 855	89.7	97.6	78.0	90.9	91.3	256 000	103.2	100.7	101.2	118.9	101.5	259 800
Norway (N)	NH	82 544	79.9	81.6	67.1	93.2	92.9	109 718	108.9	109.3	127.6	155.6	190.0	208 419
Portugal (N)	NH	521 317	71.7	78.0	68.9	87.1	89.9	748 879	90.6		110.2	110.2	130.9	980 151
Portugal (N)	AH	165 792	66.9	75.0	67.5	84.8	87.9	250 548	101.2		106.8	123.7	139.9	350 410
Spain (N)	NH	5 520 890	98.2	100.2	97.1	102.6	96.6	6 202 529	109.8	111.8	118.6	105.6	108.5	6 727 747
Spain (N)	AH	1 248 763	88.6	88.9	89.1	88.4	86.5	1 558 503	107.5	114.7	113.7	97.2	101.6	1 582 876
Sweden (N)	NH	88 423	95.8	95.5	82.8	94.4	95.7	88 221	95.5	110.9	112.0	111.4	104.9	92 503
Switzerland (R)	NH	1 783 260	113.5	102.5	88.9	95.1	95.1	1 695 151	96.6	91.9	109.0	90.6	91.2	1 545 634
Switzerland (R)	AH	584 011	112.2	103.4	86.0	94.3	94.1	563 879		95.7	93.0	99.7	99.1	558 860
Turkey (N)	NH			40.3	48.2	55.7	86.1	630 525	134.4	177.8	179.8	191.0	74.2	467 794
Turkey (N)	AH			37.6	47.1	55.6	86.1	345 697	131.6	156.9	189.7	182.8	53.2	183 950
Australia (R)	NH		81.2	84.0	84.0	106.5	98.4	85 000		151.1				
Japan (N)	NH	130 354												
Japan (N)	AH	49 536												

AH Arrivals at hotels and similar establishments — Arrivées dans les hôtels et les établissements assimilés
NH Nights in hotels and similar establishments — Nuitées dans les hôtels et établissements assimilés
(R) Tourist count by country of residence — Recensement des touristes par pays de résidence
(N) Tourist count by country of nationality — Recensement des touristes par pays de nationalité

Table/Tableau 37

ARRIVALS AND NIGHTS OF FOREIGN TOURISTS AT/IN ALL MEANS OF ACCOMMODATION
ARRIVÉES ET NUITÉES DE TOURISTES ÉTRANGERS DANS L'ENSEMBLE DES MOYENS D'HÉBERGEMENT

From France
En provenance de la France
1986=100

Country	AAA/NAA	Volume 1980	1981	1982	1983	1984	1985	Volume 1986	1987	1988	1989	1990	1991	Volume 1991	AEH/NEH	
Austria (R)	NAA	1 609 695	71.0	79.6	67.9	87.4	91.7	2 702 647	98.7	98.1	107.2	113.8	117.3	3 169 839	NEH	Autriche (R)
	AAA	474 202	76.5	81.6	68.0	88.4	92.0	722 937	95.9	97.0	107.7	115.8	117.0	845 483	AEH	
Belgium (R)	NAA	873 649	90.9	103.4	92.1	98.4	97.2	972 144	100.0	104.0	124.5	129.9			NEH	Belgique (R)
Denmark (N)	NAA	143 380	112.0	117.2	86.5	113.6	109.4	131 504	104.2	105.6	108.9	112.8	115.8	152 300	NEH	Danemark (N)
Germany (R)	NAA	1 257 870	89.1	83.7	72.9	90.0	96.2	1 345 326	103.8	109.0	123.2	130.3	124.3	1 671 571	NEH	Allemagne (R)
	AAA	615 113	91.5	86.7	75.6	91.8	96.9	672 897	102.2	106.2	120.1	126.2	120.9	813 348	AEH	
Greece (N)	NAA	2 396 801	91.1	98.3	81.9	107.7	108.4	2 580 603	105.8	100.5					NEH	Grèce (N)
	AAA	770 091	88.4	96.9	79.1	105.5	104.3	840 921	101.2						AEH	
Ireland (R)	NAA	1 298 000	97.5	104.7	103.0	82.9	104.3	1 047 300	138.6	149.6	206.1	297.9	289.2	3 029 000	NEH	Irlande (R)
	AAA	83 300	102.2	103.3	90.0	96.7	105.6	90 000		123.3	153.3	220.0	244.4	220 000	AEH	
Italy (N)	NAA	8 047 324	98.4	110.8	88.7	92.4	95.3	7 591 419	94.4	90.1	83.1	81.1			NEH	Italie (N)
	AAA	2 073 441	91.0	104.4	85.4	94.4	96.2	2 061 736	102.1	101.2	98.6	96.5			AEH	
Luxembourg (R)	NAA			98.3	75.9	89.9	98.5	88 273	108.5	122.9		151.2	148.4	131 028	NEH	Luxembourg (R)
	AAA				74.9		94.5	44 947	107.1	123.4		142.5	135.0	60 668	AEH	
Netherlands (R)	NAA	618 280	103.6	105.8	84.1	99.9	97.1	583 536		106.0	115.3	136.3	130.8	763 500	NEH	Pays-Bas (R)
	AAA	333 398	98.3	103.6	83.3	98.6	96.3	331 493		109.7	105.4	123.2	111.8	370 600	AEH	
Portugal (N)	NAA	918 708	87.0	91.3	78.9	84.0	86.2	1 188 571	95.5	105.5	111.9	110.8	124.9	1 484 551	NEH	Portugal (N)
	AAA	273 484	69.0	77.3	68.4	79.8	81.7	412 885	102.0	110.8	116.9	119.2	129.7	535 406	AEH	
Spain (N)	NAA	6 273 239													NEH	Espagne (N)
	AAA	1 371 364													AEH	
Sweden (N)	NAA	142 012	91.8	92.7	75.8	96.1	91.0	156 808	93.6	96.5	106.3	116.3	105.0	164 724	NEH	Suède (N)
Switzerland (R)	NAA	2 774 800	114.1	108.9	91.5	93.7	94.1	2 664 300	97.9	93.5	92.8	91.6	94.2	2 508 996	NEH	Suisse (R)
	AAA	748 000	109.7	104.0	86.0	93.7	93.4	746 900	97.1	96.3	99.0	100.5	101.1	755 029	AEH	
Turkey (N)	NAA	166 177	27.1	34.9	45.2	51.8	79.1	826 635	132.0	185.0	178.7	191.9	76.4	631 272	NEH	Turquie (N)
	AAA	65 646	29.3	36.0	46.1	54.1	84.9	372 800	131.9	159.5	190.4	186.3	55.3	206 269	AEH	
United Kingdom (R)	NAA	11 975 000	85.5	91.5	92.3	106.8	104.8	12 212 000	136.8	115.0	132.8	139.2	121.8	14 872 000	NEH	Royaume-Uni (R)
Canada (R)	NAA	1 358 600	88.6	83.5	66.9	78.4	75.9	1 807 900	128.5	157.2	161.6				NEH	Canada (R)
	AAA	114 000	84.7	84.2	64.6	79.0	76.5	140 300	133.7	163.7	173.1				AEH	
Australia (R)	NAA		86.3		76.8	117.0	91.0	192 700						92 267	NEH	Australie (R)
New Zealand (R)	NAA														NEH	Nouvelle-Zélande (R)

AAA   Arrivals in all means of accommodation
NAA   Nights in all means of accommodation
(R)   Tourist count by country of residence
(N)   Tourist count by country of nationality

AEH   Arrivées dans l'ensemble des moyens d'hébergement
NEH   Nuitées dans l'ensemble des moyens d'hébergement
(R)   Recensement des touristes par pays de résidence
(N)   Recensement des touristes par pays de nationalité

Table/Tableau 38

ARRIVALS OF FOREIGN TOURISTS/VISITORS AT FRONTIERS
ARRIVÉES DE TOURISTES/VISITEURS ÉTRANGERS AUX FRONTIÈRES

From Italy
1986=100

En provenance de l'Italie
1986=100

	T/V	Volume 1980	1981	1982	1983	1984	1985	Volume 1986	1987	1988	1989	1990	1991	Volume 1991	T/V	
France (R)	T	1 560 000	49.7	71.5	78.4	90.9	94.6	2 798 000	112.8	123.0	187.3	201.8	243.8	6 821 000	T	France (R)
	V														V	
Greece (N)	T	197 006	51.2	50.9	74.5	74.7	82.8	440 000	105.7	123.6	129.3	141.1	117.5	517 145	T	Grèce (N)
Iceland (N)	T	935	38.7	42.6	49.7	48.9	55.2	2 119	127.4	133.2	140.7	170.6	226.9	4 808	T	Islande (N)
Norway (N)	V	7 266													V	Norvège (N)
Portugal (N)	T	45 212	51.8	60.2	59.5	65.6	91.3	90 635	132.7	153.1	184.5	209.0	276.4	250 478	T	Portugal (N)
	V	72 681	62.9	66.8	60.9	66.1	86.1	108 545	123.8	142.5	170.6	203.7	268.1	290 971	V	
Spain (N)	V	482 674	51.3	60.3	61.4	74.7	93.8	1 089 996	109.4	122.3	138.7	152.0	162.2	1 767 599	V	Espagne (N)
Turkey (N)	V	63 215	77.3	50.9	65.7	75.2	85.4	87 622	116.8	164.7	175.8	178.4	73.2	64 134	V	Turquie (N)
United Kingdom (R)	V	408 400	82.9	80.5	92.8	96.2	100.1	493 800	138.3	133.8	143.4	144.6	144.6	714 000	V	Royaume-Uni (R)
Canada (R)	T	49 600	78.2	72.2	70.1	81.6	84.7	65 200	118.3	132.4	142.3	139.4	136.7	89 100	T	Canada (R)
United States (R)	V	65 800	81.7	77.3	71.6	81.5	81.0	80 500	128.6	133.7	133.4	125.6	124.1	99 900	V	États-Unis (R)
	T	203 834	85.5	86.6	74.0	81.4	82.1	268 270	118.8	132.9	132.3	147.6	178.5	478 853	T	
Australia (R)	V	12 291	70.3	69.9	69.4	77.5	83.8	17 300	111.6	145.7	118.5	141.0	140.5	24 300	V	Australie (R)
Japan (N)	V	12 439	77.9	72.7	75.6	83.5	114.7	18 820	110.9	124.7	147.0	158.3	160.5	30 199	V	Japon (N)
New Zealand (R)	T	1 120	58.6	53.5	50.5	55.8	73.6	1 712	152.5	164.4	153.5	184.1	209.1	3 580	T	Nouvelle-Zélande (R)

V Visitors (travellers in Turkey)
T Tourists
(R) Tourist count by country of residence
(N) Tourist count by country of nationality

V Visiteurs (voyageurs en Turquie)
T Touristes
(R) Recensement des touristes par pays de résidence
(N) Recensement des touristes par pays de nationalité

Table/Tableau 39

ARRIVALS AND NIGHTS OF FOREIGN TOURISTS AT/IN HOTELS
ARRIVÉES ET NUITÉES DE TOURISTES ÉTRANGERS DANS L'HÔTELLERIE

From Italy — En provenance de l'Italie
1986=100

From Italy	AH/NH	Volume 1980	1981	1982	1983	1984	1985	Volume 1986	1987	1988	1989	1990	1991	Volume 1991	AH/NH	En provenance de l'Italie
Austria (R)	NH	588 588	52.8	59.5	64.3	77.2	82.2	1 319 797	110.8	139.7	184.9	203.8	212.7	2 806 764	NH	Autriche (R)
	AH	280 859	56.0	61.1	65.5	78.7	82.4	573 659	110.5	136.7	173.3	185.8	182.0	1 044 017	AH	
Belgium (R)	NH	186 173	84.8	84.9	91.5	95.8	100.9	217 880	110.0	122.2	147.8	158.2			NH	Belgique (R)
Denmark (N)	NH	77 100	111.1	107.4	104.7	103.6	100.3	78 400	113.0	132.5	138.8	162.1	181.5	142 300	NH	Danemark (N)
Finland (R)	NH	30 306	61.0	74.7	78.5	88.9	93.0	50 577	133.0	161.8	171.8	156.7	161.8	81 830	NH	Finlande (R)
France (R)¹	NH	1 220 509	36.1	34.5	35.5	37.7	36.9	3 619 883	109.3	145.3	188.2	193.6	193.4	7 000 617	NH	France (R)¹
	AH	417 341	29.5	27.8	27.5	29.5	30.2	1 614 344	109.3	136.4	183.2	192.8	194.4	3 137 722	AH	
Germany (R)	NH	757 132	72.1	75.8	79.4	86.9	91.4	1 100 322	106.9	120.9	143.2	153.5	157.8	1 735 885	NH	Allemagne (R)
	AH	391 788	71.8	76.5	79.8	87.9	92.6	566 637	107.8	122.8	144.4	154.9	158.6	898 795	AH	
Greece (N)	NH	849 357	63.9	67.4	73.4	83.6	102.7	1 345 869	103.0	122.6					NH	Grèce (N)
	AH	275 570	65.0	70.1	80.2	89.4	101.7	434 679	114.9	114.5					AH	
Ireland (R)	NH													571 000	NH	Irlande (R)
	AH													79 000	AH	
Luxembourg (R)	NH													157 003	NH	Luxembourg (R)
Netherlands (R)	NH	196 969	76.7	78.5	71.4	78.9	82.8	268 900	115.7	134.5	152.9	226.8	200.3	538 600	NH	Pays-Bas (R)
	AH	83 554	72.6	75.4	71.4	80.3	86.8	125 500	113.7	131.4	166.5	238.4	196.7	246 800	AH	
Norway (N)	NH	143 034	52.4	60.1	61.4	68.6	86.2	246 329	123.3	142.4	153.9	186.6	243.1	598 905	NH	Norvège (N)
Portugal (N)	NH	47 599	47.6	55.4	60.6	67.9	85.5	94 730	125.2	142.3	155.5	185.1	245.4	232 422	NH	Portugal (N)
Spain (N)	NH	1 089 161	36.9	46.8	60.9	92.1	105.1	3 894 029	110.7	119.4	117.8	109.9	118.9	4 631 878	NH	Espagne (N)
	AH	359 636	41.3	51.2	61.8	86.1	96.4	1 105 393	98.3	101.8	108.4	95.6	101.2	1 118 199	AH	
Sweden (N)	NH	58 198	76.7	83.2	79.4	88.8	96.4	78 925	121.4	121.5	149.3	156.4	149.9	118 347	NH	Suède (N)
Switzerland (R)	NH	786 094	89.8	88.6	86.1	91.3	93.4	977 582	106.1	112.2	129.7	139.6	144.0	1 407 635	NH	Suisse (R)
	AH	386 811	87.5	86.1	85.7	90.9	93.2	486 635	105.0	110.0	126.2	131.0	135.5	659 526	AH	
Turkey (N)	NH			44.2	74.4	79.4	90.6	239 656	131.2	163.2	158.0	167.3	122.3	293 218	NH	Turquie (N)
	AH			43.7	71.5	78.2	92.8	114 377	133.4	163.7	172.6	181.3	100.6	115 068	AH	
Australia (R)	NH		57.1		36.5	55.1	71.6	130 400	111.6	145.6					NH	Australie (R)
Japan (N)	NH	59 027													NH	Japon (N)
	AH	20 765													AH	

AH Arrivals at hotels and similar establishments
NH Nights in hotels and similar establishments
(R) Tourist count by country of residence
(N) Tourist count by country of nationality

AH Arrivées dans les hôtels et les établissements assimilés
NH Nuitées dans les hôtels et établissements assimilés
(R) Recensement des touristes par pays de résidence
(N) Recensement des touristes par pays de nationalité

Table/Tableau 40

ARRIVALS AND NIGHTS OF FOREIGN TOURISTS AT/IN ALL MEANS OF ACCOMMODATION
ARRIVÉES ET NUITÉES DE TOURISTES ÉTRANGERS DANS L'ENSEMBLE DES MOYENS D'HÉBERGEMENT

From Italy
En provenance de l'Italie

1986=100

	AAA/NAA	Volume 1980	1981	1982	1983	1984	1985	Volume 1986	1987	1988	1989	1990	1991	Volume 1991	AEH/NEH	
Austria (R)	NAA	702 625	54.7	61.2	69.2	82.0	83.3	1 518 736	111.3	137.7	183.5	203.5	217.8	3 307 567	NEH	Autriche (R)
Belgium (R)	AAA	316 938	56.3	62.1	67.7	84.3	83.4	641 313	110.3	135.1	171.7	184.8	185.0	1 186 432	AEH	Belgique (R)
Denmark (N)	NAA	210 833	86.5	85.9	92.0	96.7	100.9	247 856	108.8	122.8	145.8	156.3			NEH	Danemark (N)
France (R)	NAA	104 088	100.1	100.8	102.8	102.0	102.7	117 668	117.0	130.4	141.6	159.5	186.1	218 937	NEH	France (R)
France (R)	AAA	9 360 000	36.0	73.0	78.1	87.5	89.5	23 146 000	115.2	108.6	143.3	152.9	183.0	42 350 000	AEH	
Germany (R)	NAA	1 560 000	49.7	71.5	76.3	85.7	90.8	2 798 000	112.8	123.0	142.9	153.0			NEH	Allemagne (R)
Germany (R)	AAA	793 919	69.4	73.1	77.2	87.1	90.8	1 165 248	107.0	121.3	144.4	154.9	157.4	1 833 624	AEH	
Greece (N)	NAA	398 210	69.5	74.0	77.2	96.9	92.1	588 691	108.0	123.1	153.0	154.9	158.5	933 023	NEH	Grèce (N)
Greece (N)	AAA	1 104 707	72.7	76.2	80.3	96.6	103.6	1 517 462	115.8	118.1	144.4				AEH	
Ireland (R)	NAA	357 197	71.3	77.4	87.4	96.6	102.6	495 437	72.3	110.6				1 309 440	NEH	Irlande (R)
Luxembourg (R)	AAA													96 000	AEH	Luxembourg (R)
Netherlands (R)	NAA	255 303	79.1	82.7	80.1	89.1	89.0	334 521		138.2	159.6	229.5	206.8	691 900	NEH	Pays-Bas (R)
Netherlands (R)	AAA	109 888	75.4	79.8	78.4	89.3	92.7	157 113		136.1	165.0	231.4	196.9	309 300	AEH	
Portugal (N)	NAA	195 140	60.5	66.9	61.5	62.8	83.6	321 724	115.7	132.6	144.1	166.5	220.5	709 291	NEH	Portugal (N)
Spain (N)	AAA	60 923	46.8	53.8	58.3	62.5	83.3	122 159	117.6	132.3	145.7	166.4	221.4	270 509	AEH	Espagne (N)
Spain (N)	NAA	1 089 161													NEH	
Spain (N)	AAA	359 636													AEH	
Sweden (N)	NAA	62 260	75.2	81.4	78.9	89.4	94.6	87 685	123.4	125.7	154.9	160.7	153.0	134 119	NEH	Suède (N)
Switzerland (R)	NAA	996 400	85.5	86.0	86.3	91.2	92.9	1 321 500	106.6	114.7	130.8	143.9	151.0	1 995 680	NEH	Suisse (R)
Switzerland (R)	AAA	436 000	84.8	84.6	85.2	90.7	93.1								AEH	
Turkey (N)	NAA	72 962	41.3	41.2	72.2	78.1	89.4	569 600	104.5	110.0	124.9	131.2	136.5	777 516	NEH	Turquie (N)
Turkey (N)	AAA	30 180	38.8	43.1	71.1	78.6	92.8	264 298	143.4	186.2	185.3	201.9	138.8	366 916	AEH	
United Kingdom (R)	NAA	6 499 000	92.3	85.3	103.9	101.4	113.6	6 128 000	150.7	138.8	135.1	136.6	146.9	9 001 000	NEH	Royaume-Uni (R)
United Kingdom (R)	AAA							117 039	147.2	182.4	192.5	200.9	106.8	124 941	AEH	
Canada (R)	NAA	590 600	80.6	87.8	64.9	87.4	90.3	836 400	119.5	128.0	120.4				NEH	Canada (R)
Australia (R)	NAA	302 000	47.7		43.9	43.8	47.5	302 000	111.6	145.7					NEH	Australie (R)

AAA   Arrivals in all means of accommodation
NAA   Nights in all means of accommodation
(R)   Tourist count by country of residence
(N)   Tourist count by country of nationality

AEH   Arrivées dans l'ensemble des moyens d'hébergement
NEH   Nuitées dans l'ensemble des moyens d'hébergement
(R)   Recensement des touristes par pays de résidence
(N)   Recensement des touristes par pays de nationalité

Table/Tableau 41

ARRIVALS OF FOREIGN TOURISTS/VISITORS AT FRONTIERS
ARRIVÉES DE TOURISTES/VISITEURS ÉTRANGERS AUX FRONTIÈRES

From Japan
1986=100

En provenance du Japon
1986=100

	T/V	Volume 1980	1981	1982	1983	1984	1985	Volume 1986	1987	1988	1989	1990	1991	Volume 1991		T/V
France (R)	T	400 000	87.6			100.4	103.9	508 000	112.5	130.3	151.8	121.7	90.2	458 000	France (R)	T
Greece (N)	T	75 666	88.3	87.9	96.4	101.6	109.1	85 075	108.1	123.4	122.2	126.6	68.1	57 902	Grèce (N)	T
Iceland (N)	T	366	39.6	45.0	52.9	62.9	83.5	857	116.7	115.9	146.3	135.8	146.3	1 254	Islande (N)	T
Italy (N)	V	348 560	65.6	75.6	81.5	84.8	83.5	401 278	95.9	95.9	113.8	158.7	139.5	559 665	Italie (N)	V
Norway (N)	V	8 463	59.0	53.5	59.6	73.1	83.6	22 014	125.3	128.1	136.7	148.4	120.8	26 587	Norvège (N)	V
Portugal (N)	T	10 186	63.6	59.5	61.7	83.9	86.0	23 246	123.0	127.6	138.2	152.4	122.3	28 422	Portugal (N)	T
Spain (N)	V	88 035	71.6	66.3	78.4	89.7	104.6	121 072	107.8	140.6	178.8	201.3	154.0	186 485	Espagne (N)	V
Turkey (N)	V	6 865	41.5	37.5	46.5	78.0	100.4	16 740	125.8	167.3	192.9	211.2	110.4	18 479	Turquie (N)	V
United Kingdom (R)	V	162 400	79.7	77.7	82.9	97.7	102.6	205 400	144.7	189.0	245.8	278.5	214.2	440 000	Royaume-Uni (R)	V
Canada (R)	T	122 700	57.6	58.3	59.2	68.6	74.0	197 100	126.4	164.4	197.7	209.3	201.7	397 500	Canada (R)	T
United States (R)	V	162 300	62.3	59.3	59.0	69.0	74.2	235 200	132.5	172.0	196.7	201.6	204.2	480 300	États-Unis (R)	V
United States (R)	T	1 198 016	80.5	85.4	76.3	84.2	89.0	1 681 071	126.6	150.7	183.2	192.2	197.5	3 319 934	États-Unis (R)	T
Australia (R)	V	48 813	36.9	41.5	49.3	60.4	73.9	145 600	148.1	242.0	240.0	329.6	363.0	528 500	Australie (R)	V
New Zealand (R)	T	19 196	41.1	43.6	51.8	66.9	80.2	62 656	121.5	149.7	155.3	172.1	183.1	114 718	Nouvelle-Zélande (R)	T

V Visitors (travellers in Austria, Germany and Turkey)
T Tourists
(R) Tourist count by country of residence
(N) Tourist count by country of nationality
1. Estimates

V Visiteurs (voyageurs en Allemagne, en Autriche et en Turquie)
T Touristes
(R) Recensement des touristes par pays de résidence
(N) Recensement des touristes par pays de nationalité
1. Estimations

128

Table/Tableau 42

ARRIVALS AND NIGHTS OF FOREIGN TOURISTS AT/IN HOTELS
ARRIVÉES ET NUITÉES DE TOURISTES ÉTRANGERS DANS L'HÔTELLERIE

From Japan / En provenance du Japon
1986=100

Country / Pays	AH/NH	Volume 1980	1981	1982	1983	1984	1985	Volume 1986	1987	1988	1989	1990	1991	Volume 1991	AH/NH
Austria (R) / Autriche (R)	NH	127 367	67.7	72.1	78.9	85.8	101.7	230 233	133.9	139.2	160.9	203.6	179.5	413 186	NH
	AH	61 393	61.7	70.9	76.5	89.7	105.9	118 585	137.4	140.2	161.9	198.8	160.3	190 073	AH
Belgium (R) / Belgique (R)	NH	67 824	85.5	83.0	75.9	89.3	98.8	95 327	111.6	126.4	175.7	162.8			NH
Denmark (N) / Danemark (N)	NH	82 000	113.7	106.0	117.1	113.4	111.3	70 100	118.3	153.6	167.5	154.1	133.2	93 400	NH
Finland (R) / Finlande (R)	NH	22 602	59.1	62.4	95.5	108.6	114.6	38 550	133.1	144.7	157.9	165.2	148.5	57 258	NH
France (R)1 / France (R)1	AH	1 209 784	96.8	94.0	95.9	89.8	86.2	1 195 101	114.6	142.8	240.5	223.8	183.3	2 190 904	AH
Germany (R) / Allemagne (R)	AH	432 840	81.8	86.4	84.1	82.4	86.5	543 696	112.6	142.4	231.1	232.6	187.0	1 016 778	AH
	NH	528 653	71.6	75.1	76.1	83.0	98.4	839 238	112.1	120.3	144.9	157.5	132.5	1 111 909	NH
Greece (N) / Grèce (N)	NH	287 391	68.2	72.6	73.9	83.1	99.1	478 810	118.9	125.1	153.6	168.2	133.5	639 365	NH
	AH	207 731	98.1	103.8	105.8	114.4	124.0	207 356	115.0	126.0					AH
Italy (N) / Italie (N)		86 331	94.0	96.1	100.2	107.4	121.0	91 861	114.9	130.4					
	NH	446 732	72.5	82.5	88.2	90.3	89.0	655 336	143.7	175.4	219.7	239.8			NH
	AH	222 541	68.5	77.2	81.3	87.4	86.0	322 926	146.6	177.2	219.1	235.0			AH
Luxembourg (R) / Luxembourg (R)															
Netherlands (R) / Pays-Bas (R)	NH	126 670	83.0	95.8	85.5	81.2	98.3	155 800	95.5	102.8	104.4	119.3	111.9	174 300	NH
	AH	60 954	88.8	104.8	89.8	96.1	104.5	73 700	107.5	113.8	114.5	130.0	118.5	87 300	AH
Norway (N) / Norvège (N)	NH	40 835	85.7	90.4	115.1	136.7	139.8	46 046	163.2	144.9	173.9	183.5	184.6	85 001	NH
Portugal (N) / Portugal (N)	NH	31 096	64.0	62.2	67.9	94.0	93.3	53 176	121.6	135.8	137.9	144.4	136.7	72 679	NH
Spain (N) / Espagne (N)	AH	11 637	54.3	55.9	64.7	93.6	94.1	24 563	123.8	131.5	135.0	139.2	129.9	31 904	AH
	NH	255 738	73.7	73.1	74.3	80.4	92.6	421 857	139.9	151.5	203.2	208.0	146.2	616 909	NH
Sweden (N) / Suède (N)	NH	117 167	59.9	58.2	61.5	73.5	88.4	232 371	141.0	153.4	152.7	176.6	147.1	341 745	NH
	AH	55 638	94.7	104.2	97.6	109.5	108.2	53 421	116.4	139.1	145.7	152.4	157.4	84 110	AH
Switzerland (R) / Suisse (R)	NH	402 832	78.5	83.8	90.6	92.5	96.1	536 992	116.3	121.6	150.7	158.8	135.0	724 962	NH
	AH	216 197	72.4	78.0	85.4	89.7	94.1	313 295	117.8	127.0	151.1	150.6	132.5	414 987	AH
Turkey (N) / Turquie (N)	NH			36.6	52.7	50.2	80.4	89 156	110.3	131.3	172.2	178.9	101.9	90 890	NH
	AH			32.3	53.0	51.2	76.5	43 074	121.0	146.4			115.2	49 623	AH
Australia (R) / Australie (R)	NH		27.6	51.9	51.9	75.2	87.7	725 100	148.1	242.0	260.6	350.6	368.9	2 674 800	NH

AH   Arrivals at hotels and similar establishments — Arrivées dans les hôtels et les établissements assimilés
NH   Nights in hotels and similar establishments — Nuitées dans les hôtels et établissements assimilés
(R) Tourist count by country of residence — Recensement des touristes par pays de résidence
(N) Tourist count by country of nationality — Recensement des touristes par pays de nationalité
1.   Ile de France only — Ile de France seulement

129

Table/Tableau 43

ARRIVALS AND NIGHTS OF FOREIGN TOURISTS AT/IN ALL MEANS OF ACCOMMODATION
ARRIVÉES ET NUITÉES DE TOURISTES ÉTRANGERS DANS L'ENSEMBLE DES MOYENS D'HÉBERGEMENT

From Japan / En provenance du Japon
1986=100

	AAA/NAA	AEH/NEH	Volume 1980	1981	1982	1983	1984	1985	Volume 1986	1987	1988	1989	1990	1991	Volume 1991	
Austria (R)	NAA	NEH	127 367	67.7	72.1	78.9	85.8	101.7	230 233	133.9	139.2	160.9	203.6	179.5	413 186	Autriche (R)
	AAA	AEH	61 393	61.7	70.9	76.5	89.7	105.9	118 585	137.4	140.2	161.9	198.8	160.3	190 073	
Belgium (R)	NAA	NEH	71 851	85.0	81.9	75.7	89.6	99.3	98 906	111.4	126.8	175.1	164.0			Belgique (R)
Denmark (N)	NAA	NEH								115.0	85.8	121.7	127.7		93 400	Danemark (N)
France (R)	NAA	NEH	1 600 000	84.7	73.0	74.2	97.6	100.5	3 694 000	112.6	130.3	145.7	159.0	96.2	3 554 000	France (R)
	AAA	AEH	400 000	87.6	70.5	71.8	100.4	103.9	508 000	112.5	121.5	154.3	170.2			
Germany (R)	NAA	NEH	544 057	69.6		71.8	83.2	98.2	868 420	119.1	126.0			133.3	1 157 976	Allemagne (R)
	AAA	AEH	289 189	66.2			83.0	98.8	494 333	114.9	125.9			134.7	665 625	
Greece (N)	NAA	NEH	211 690	99.6	107.0	107.4	115.9	124.0	207 683	114.8	130.3					Grèce (N)
	AAA	AEH	87 786	95.5	98.3	101.3	108.8	121.0	92 030							
Italy (N)	NAA	NEH	493 441	73.2	82.6	87.0	89.4	88.4	710 862	137.5	167.3	208.0	227.6			Italie (N)
	AAA	AEH	228 229	68.2	76.7	80.8	87.0	85.9	332 085	145.3	175.6	216.5	232.7			
Luxembourg (R)	NAA	NEH														Luxembourg (R)
	AAA	AEH														
Netherlands (R)	NAA	NEH	132 292	90.6	103.2	93.8	89.0	106.1	148 942		110.8	112.5	130.0	120.8	179 900	Pays-Bas (R)
	AAA	AEH	64 658	96.7	112.6	97.1	104.4	112.6	71 383		122.7	122.0	139.8	126.9	90 600	
Portugal (N)	NAA	NEH	32 177	65.0	63.9	68.6	94.2	93.7	54 012	121.7	136.6	138.4	146.9	137.3	74 152	Portugal (N)
	AAA	AEH	12 115	55.3	56.9	65.3	93.8	94.2	24 939	123.8	133.1	135.6	142.1	130.5	32 550	
Spain (N)	NAA	NEH	255 738													Espagne (N)
	AAA	AEH	117 167													
Sweden (N)	NAA	NEH	56 821	95.0	104.2	99.3	110.0	109.6	54 689	117.5	140.0	153.3	177.6	164.3	89 841	Suède (N)
Switzerland (R)	NAA	NEH	424 700	78.7	83.3	89.7	92.0	95.8	561 800	116.0	121.0	144.7	151.3	134.4	755 297	Suisse (R)
	AAA	AEH	226 800	72.7	77.6	85.0	89.3	94.1	326 300	117.3	126.5	150.0	157.9	131.5	429 152	
Turkey (N)	NAA	NEH	17 715	23.6	36.6	52.7	50.3	80.4	89 494	112.1	131.3	151.2	151.0	101.8	91 097	Turquie (N)
	AAA	AEH	7 779	20.0	32.3	52.9	51.2	76.5	43 244	122.6	146.2	172.1	179.1	114.9	49 707	
United Kingdom (R)	NAA	NEH	1 129 000	69.5	62.7	56.2	87.4	136.7	1 754 000	132.9	167.8	187.6	225.4	230.4	4 041 000	Royaume-Uni (R)
Canada (R)	NAA	NEH	883 900	59.2	56.1	48.5	66.4	60.8	1 527 500	115.3	145.9	166.2				Canada (R)
Australia (R)	NAA	NEH		34.3		51.9	67.7	95.8	956 600	148.1	242.0	449.0	610.0	445.5	4 262 000	Australie (R)
New Zealand (R)	NAA	NEH													1 298 393	Nouvelle-Zélande (R)

AAA Arrivals in all means of accommodation
NAA Nights in all means of accommodation
(R) Tourist count by country of residence
(N) Tourist count by country of nationality

AEH Arrivées dans l'ensemble des moyens d'hébergement
NEH Nuitées dans l'ensemble des moyens d'hébergement
(R) Recensement des touristes par pays de résidence
(N) Recensement des touristes par pays de nationalité

130

Table/Tableau 44

ARRIVALS OF FOREIGN TOURISTS/VISITORS AT FRONTIERS
ARRIVÉES DE TOURISTES/VISITEURS ÉTRANGERS AUX FRONTIÈRES

From the Netherlands

1986=100

En provenance des Pays-Bas

1986=100

	T/V	Volume 1980	1981	1982	1983	1984	1985	Volume 1986	1987	1988	1989	1990	1991	Volume 1991	T/V	
France (R)	T	3 420 000	73.0	96.9	94.9	93.9	91.1	4 012 000	98.1	100.9	99.4	99.0	88.4	3 546 000	T	France (R)
	V														V	
Greece (N)	T	179 842	51.5	42.2	46.6	58.4	84.9	330 000	104.5	117.9	129.7	150.2	136.4	450 065	T	Grèce (N)
Iceland (N)	T	1 850	68.0	73.9	65.2	69.7	71.6	2 309	104.8	122.7	109.0	129.7	127.8	2 952	T	Islande (N)
Ireland (R)	V	119 013													V	Irlande (R)
Italy (N)	V	1 836 370	88.5	101.8	97.8	101.1	95.2	1 743 102	79.7	103.4	105.6	121.7	88.0	1 533 360	V	Italie (N)
Norway (N)	V	37 026													V	Norvège (N)
Portugal (N)	T	114 056	72.2	69.9	89.5	87.3	92.7	163 346	125.6	168.6	193.9	183.0	199.3	325 586	T	Portugal (N)
	V	127 713	75.0	72.6	91.0	88.4	95.4	171 724	124.7	166.1	193.8	191.9	209.9	360 452	V	
Spain (N)	V	1 368 435	88.7	87.1	84.5	89.0	91.0	1 556 851	108.2	128.8	130.7	125.5	138.6	2 157 079	V	Espagne (N)
Turkey (N)	V	19 051	58.4	56.5	66.6	68.7	79.1	39 450	126.5	205.4	270.5	381.1	271.3	107 018	V	Turquie (N)
United Kingdom (R)	V	910 400	96.9	91.2	95.5	96.4	99.1	768 900	111.2	114.6	122.3	128.9	139.2	1 070 000	V	Royaume-Uni (R)
Canada (R)	T	87 000	115.3	104.4	92.3	88.6	85.1	68 600	113.6	128.3	130.8	126.8	129.9	89 100	T	Canada (R)
	V	98 000	116.1	104.6	91.1	88.2	84.4	75 700	116.9	130.6	127.9	123.2	125.9	95 300	V	
United States (R)	T	178 631	121.3	116.7	89.2	82.5	80.7	162 740	123.9	152.3	160.3	174.5	194.5	316 609	T	États-Unis (R)
Australia (R)	V	18 262	113.3	105.4	93.7	88.7	96.9	15 900	108.8	140.9	126.4	132.7	134.6	21 400	V	Australie (R)
Japan (N)	V	10 902	83.7	79.1	88.5	97.8	106.4	14 484	109.8	109.4	113.4	121.3	124.6	18 044	V	Japon (N)
New Zealand (R)	T	4 972	89.5	88.9	83.3	89.2	93.5	5 788	109.2	122.0	123.1	134.4	131.0	7 584	T	Nouvelle-Zélande (R)

V   Visitors (travellers in Turkey)
T   Tourists
(R)   Tourist count by country of residence
(N)   Tourist count by country of nationality

V   Visiteurs (voyageurs en Turquie)
T   Touristes
(R)   Recensement des touristes par pays de résidence
(N)   Recensement des touristes par pays de nationalité

131

Table/Tableau 45

ARRIVALS AND NIGHTS OF FOREIGN TOURISTS AT/IN HOTELS
ARRIVÉES ET NUITÉES DE TOURISTES ÉTRANGERS DANS L'HÔTELLERIE

From the Netherlands
1986=100

En provenance des Pays-Bas
1986=100

	AH/NH	Volume 1980	1981	1982	1983	1984	1985	Volume 1986	1987	1988	1989	1990	1991	Volume 1991	AH/NH	
Austria (R)	NH	5 766 463	117.5	110.3	102.6	105.4	100.9	5 036 307	101.4	99.3	104.3	99.1	102.3	5 153 046	NH	Autriche (R)
	AH	784 665	111.1	105.0	100.1	102.9	100.8	732 879	104.2	105.9	111.7	108.6	108.6	795 892	AH	
Belgium (R)	NH	487 263	67.4	77.0	90.2	97.8	97.3	676 711	105.4	109.5	136.4	139.8			NH	Belgique (R)
Denmark (N)	NH	121 100	127.4	122.5	128.5	115.5	104.5	93 800	107.1	108.8	115.0	121.3	167.1	156 700	NH	Danemark (N)
Finland (R)	NH	48 355	114.4	97.5	99.4	119.3	109.2	36 985	112.9	125.1	141.1	149.0	142.8	52 823	NH	Finlande (R)
France (R)¹	NH	1 064 891	47.6	41.9	41.3	43.6	39.1	1 933 971	105.9	117.8	125.3	120.7	125.2	2 421 424	NH	France (R)¹
	AH	423 490	35.0	31.3	30.6	30.3	28.7	1 034 898	106.9	122.4	122.4	121.2	129.2	1 337 046	AH	
Germany (R)	NH	3 265 485	102.5	97.4	90.2	94.2	95.1	3 316 589	103.8	103.6	103.6	106.5	105.4	3 494 580	NH	Allemagne (R)
	AH	1 456 473	103.6	98.3	93.8	98.2	98.7	1 461 823	105.2	106.6	106.6	109.4	106.2	1 551 966	AH	
Greece (N)	NH	1 059 240	54.5	50.4	46.6	65.4	96.7	1 950 202	84.5	85.0	109.2				NH	Grèce (N)
	AH	185 611	67.4	63.2	59.6	78.0	102.7	274 513	94.4	93.9	109.9				AH	
Ireland (R)	NH							131 000	82.4	95.4	152.7	166.4	230.5	302 000	NH	Irlande (R)
	AH							22 000	90.9	113.6	150.0	181.8	227.3	50 000	AH	
Italy (N)	NH	1 899 173	106.6	109.5	99.9	81.0	87.9	1 283 125	143.5	117.4	107.5	106.0			NH	Italie (N)
	AH	340 362	94.5	103.2	97.5	86.8	94.5	277 610	110.8	122.7	120.4	124.2			AH	
Luxembourg (R)	NH														NH	Luxembourg (R)
	AH														AH	
Norway (N)	NH	184 572	151.0	106.0	98.4	124.3	119.9	110 812	108.9	97.3	106.7	113.7	135.7	150 398	NH	Norvège (N)
Portugal (N)	NH	984 829	99.9	94.1	79.0	89.0	91.4	815 526	107.5	146.6	158.1	175.2	207.6	1 693 066	NH	Portugal (N)
	AH	104 512	85.7	86.2	86.2	93.3	96.8	110 053	117.7	154.1	166.9	188.4	207.2	228 008	AH	
Spain (N)	NH	2 901 509	92.5	92.9	87.6	100.6	88.0	3 895 455	87.1	85.3	72.1	53.6	62.5	2 434 054	NH	Espagne (N)
	AH	408 568												357 129	AH	
Sweden (N)	NH	126 720	172.9	141.0	164.3	114.4	105.1	73 314	95.5	94.5	103.8	106.3	93.8	68 784	NH	Suède (N)
Switzerland (R)	NH	1 257 487	148.7	122.7	111.4	97.2	94.6	846 833	97.5	94.6	101.5	101.8	105.4	892 630	NH	Suisse (R)
	AH	348 703	132.3	117.0	109.1	98.2	94.2	253 410	98.0	97.6	105.2	104.3	107.8	273 230	AH	
Australia (R)	NH		118.3		90.4	88.3	119.9	60 700	108.9	140.9					NH	Australie (R)
Japan (N)	NH	46 854													NH	Japon (N)
	AH	17 198													AH	

AH Arrivals at hotels and similar establishments
NH Nights in hotels and similar establishments
(R) Tourist count by country of residence
(N) Tourist count by country of nationality
1. Ile de France only

AH Arrivées dans les hôtels et les établissements assimilés
NH Nuitées dans les hôtels et établissements assimilés
(R) Recensement des touristes par pays de résidence
(N) Recensement des touristes par pays de nationalité
1. Ile de France seulement

Table/Tableau 46

ARRIVALS AND NIGHTS OF FOREIGN TOURISTS AT/IN ALL MEANS OF ACCOMMODATION
ARRIVÉES ET NUITÉES DE TOURISTES ÉTRANGERS DANS L'ENSEMBLE DES MOYENS D'HÉBERGEMENT

From the Netherlands — *En provenance des Pays-Bas*
1986=100

	AAA/NAA	Volume 1980	1981	1982	1983	1984	1985	Volume 1986	1987	1988	1989	1990	1991	Volume 1991	AEH/NEH	
Austria (R)	NAA	9 767 692	112.7	106.0	98.6	101.9	100.0	9 175 793	101.6	101.0	105.3	99.3	100.7	9 242 866	NEH	Autriche (R)
	AAA	1 254 707	108.1	101.9	96.8	100.7	100.3	1 243 350	104.5	107.1	112.9	108.2	106.4	1 322 987	AEH	
Belgium (R)	NAA	1 913 379	57.6	83.8	92.6	92.6	95.3	3 323 080	108.1	122.5	134.9	144.6			NEH	Belgique (R)
Denmark (N)	NAA	583 926	114.7	129.1	148.5	121.2	112.1	598 256	90.3	85.1	88.0	85.3	105.4	630 364	NEH	Danemark (N)
France (R)	NAA	23 940 000	59.3	96.9	95.1	97.0	90.5	34 580 000	95.2	79.3	88.0	98.3	88.4	30 567 000	NEH	France (R)
	AAA	3 420 000	73.0	96.9	94.9	93.9	91.1	4 012 000	98.1	100.9					AEH	
Germany (R)	NAA	5 398 430	86.6	82.9	83.8	93.4	94.7	5 336 089	105.7	106.6	111.8	108.0	112.9	6 025 416	NEH	Allemagne (R)
	AAA	1 727 507	94.6	90.0	89.1	97.2	97.6	1 749 511	106.1	107.4	111.7	109.5	110.2	1 927 880	AEH	
Greece (N)	NAA	1 231 764	61.2	57.1	52.1	74.9	97.2	2 061 030	85.2	85.0					NEH	Grèce (N)
	AAA	233 937	74.2	71.2	65.1	86.1	102.4	312 017	93.7	92.6					AEH	
Ireland (R)	NAA													984 380	NEH	Irlande (R)
	AAA													83 000	AEH	
Italy (N)	NAA	5 401 870	116.5	118.6	97.3	84.2	90.7	3 660 822	93.0	97.2	88.2	83.6			NEH	Italie (N)
	AAA	634 574	98.3	104.8	93.5	85.0	92.2	524 741	105.6	111.9	106.8	105.3			AEH	
Luxembourg (R)	NAA														NEH	Luxembourg (R)
	AAA														AEH	
Portugal (N)	NAA	1 222 858	98.0	93.0	77.7	84.0	89.4	1 131 892	107.9	145.8	154.1	163.4	190.2	2 152 918	NEH	Portugal (N)
	AAA	155 339	75.6	77.2	73.9	78.6	90.1	195 873	111.4	142.8	150.7	158.1	174.7	342 131	AEH	
Sweden (N)	NAA	421 915	146.7	125.2	189.6	137.7	124.6	378 104	99.2	91.0	105.7	100.6	84.9	321 133	NEH	Suède (N)
Switzerland (R)	NAA	4 007 900	142.5	120.5	109.6	96.8	90.8	3 057 800	97.4	97.5	103.3	109.3	110.6	3 380 760	NEH	Suisse (R)
	AAA	675 100	133.6	118.8	110.7	99.9	91.5	519 800	98.5	99.8	106.9	110.9	113.7	590 913	AEH	
United Kingdom (R)	NAA	6 351 000	122.1	101.0	108.4	104.3	122.9	4 373 000	118.0	127.3	118.7	126.2	139.1	6 083 000	NEH	Royaume-Uni (R)
Canada (R)	NAA	1 269 600	127.0	119.5	103.8	99.1	94.5	969 500	113.2	124.5	118.5				NEH	Canada (R)
Australia (R)	NAA		118.1		157.8	109.0	99.0	148 500	108.8	140.9					NEH	Australie (R)
New Zealand (R)	NAA													320 272	NEH	Nouvelle-Zélande (R)

AAA   Arrivals in all means of accommodation
NAA   Nights in all means of accommodation
(R)   Tourist count by country of residence
(N)   Tourist count by country of nationality

AEH   Arrivées dans l'ensemble des moyens d'hébergement
NEH   Nuitées dans l'ensemble des moyens d'hébergement
(R)   Recensement des touristes par pays de résidence
(N)   Recensement des touristes par pays de nationalité

ARRIVALS OF FOREIGN TOURISTS/VISITORS AT FRONTIERS
ARRIVÉES DE TOURISTES/VISITEURS ÉTRANGERS AUX FRONTIÈRES

From the United Kingdom
1986=100

En provenance du Royaume-Uni
1986=100

	T/V	Volume 1980	1981	1982	1983	1984	1985	Volume 1986	1987	1988	1989	1990	1991	Volume 1991	T/V	
France (R)	T / V	3 460 000	57.5	95.5	94.2	87.0	93.1	6 299 000	101.1	105.5	112.6	110.8	108.6	6 840 000	T / V	France (R)
Greece (N)	T	768 215	56.4	59.8	52.0	61.0	77.7	1 710 000	115.8	104.7	95.4	96.3	97.9	1 674 875	T	Grèce (N)
Iceland (N)	T	6 876	76.8	70.9	86.4	91.6	94.7	10 264	103.1	102.5	116.8	133.9	142.8	14 662	T	Islande (N)
Ireland (R)	V	1 057 643	94.7	99.3	104.2	109.6	101.8	1 084 000	111.5	135.1	153.9	164.8	159.5	1 729 000	V	Irlande (R)
Italy (N)	V	2 045 068	88.2	90.1	92.3	87.3	86.5	2 047 774	97.6	88.8	93.1	100.0	83.6	1 711 634	V	Italie (N)
Norway (N)	V	132 895													V	Norvège (N)
Portugal (N)	T	370 146	44.8	51.3	55.8	64.3	76.1	992 697	114.6	107.2	103.5	106.9	117.0	1 161 863	T	Portugal (N)
	V	483 944	51.3	53.4	58.9	66.4	82.3	1 069 087	112.6	106.6	106.4	112.5	122.3	1 307 312	V	
Spain (N)	V	3 590 094	63.2	75.4	80.7	93.7	78.3	6 429 099	117.4	118.9	114.3	97.8	95.6	6 145 003	V	Espagne (N)
Turkey (N)	V	62 192	39.1	38.6	54.7	58.2	80.8	154 231	173.1	301.6	263.2	227.9	130.2	200 813	V	Turquie (N)
Canada (R)	T	489 400	121.4	106.6	91.0	87.6	78.6	399 500	111.7	132.0	140.5	140.0	134.4	537 000	T	Canada (R)
	V	553 200	123.1	107.9	91.3	87.7	78.6	439 300	115.3	133.3	139.9	137.1	132.2	580 700	V	
United States (R)	T	1 302 207	138.9	114.1	89.7	81.8	75.9	1 133 683	120.2	160.4	196.0	197.9	220.1	2 495 354	T	États-Unis (R)
Australia (R)	V	127 468	80.8	98.4	83.9	82.7	87.2	176 000	113.0	147.9	155.1	157.9	149.9	263 800	V	Australie (R)
Japan (N)	V	90 867	85.5	107.5	122.8	117.6	128.6	142 106	104.4	108.8	124.7	150.9	154.4	219 425	V	Japon (N)
New Zealand (R)	T	34 101	76.6	76.4	78.7	80.9	87.8	49 675	122.9	146.4	149.6	175.7	177.0	87 944	T	Nouvelle-Zélande (R)

V   Visitors (travellers in Turkey)
T   Tourists
(R) Tourist count by country of residence
(N) Tourist count by country of nationality

V   Visiteurs (voyageurs en Turquie)
T   Touristes
(R) Recensement des touristes par pays de résidence
(N) Recensement des touristes par pays de nationalité

Table/Tableau 48

ARRIVALS AND NIGHTS OF FOREIGN TOURISTS AT/IN HOTELS
ARRIVÉES ET NUITÉES DE TOURISTES ÉTRANGERS DANS L'HÔTELLERIE

From the United Kingdom — En provenance du Royaume-Uni

1986=100

Country / Pays	AH/NH	Volume 1980	1981	1982	1983	1984	1985	Volume 1986	1987	1988	1989	1990	1991	Volume 1991
Austria (R) / Autriche (R)	NH	1 981 157	61.6	82.9	94.4	102.2	97.9	3 825 162	98.7	97.3	109.2	114.7	95.8	3 664 186
	AH	447 657	70.8	88.8	98.3	108.7	103.5	673 727	99.1	97.3	111.6	121.9	100.2	675 168
Belgium (R) / Belgique (R)	NH	860 034	91.9	98.7	108.7	107.6	107.6	976 216	92.8	87.7	108.1	122.9		
Denmark (N) / Danemark (N)	NH	315 700	108.0	116.6	109.3	96.4	106.9	311 700	97.7	93.0	98.0	107.0	101.5	316 500
Finland (R) / Finlande (R)	NH	82 539	90.6	93.0	100.7	104.6	104.8	103 347	112.8	127.4	136.7	137.5	127.4	131 699
France (R)¹ / France (R)¹	NH	1 746 656	31.3	31.8	32.9	35.6	36.8	5 899 361	97.0	114.5	150.9	185.8	172.4	10 170 853
	AH	706 706	25.1	25.2	25.5	26.2	28.4	3 101 760	99.2	112.9	148.9	157.1	165.6	5 137 632
Germany (R) / Allemagne (R)	NH	2 036 697	80.2	79.3	80.3	91.8	95.8	2 378 761	96.3	97.5	113.5	126.8	114.0	2 712 231
	AH	933 934	81.1	84.7	85.6	96.1	98.9	1 122 306	97.9	99.5	113.7	128.7	108.8	1 221 558
Greece (N) / Grèce (N)	NH	5 619 627	79.5	72.5	60.1	72.4	87.7	8 603 214	97.9	83.9	113.5			
	AH	786 062	90.3	81.5	68.2	79.0	93.5	984 162	100.2	89.1	113.7			
Iceland (N) / Islande (N)	NH													
Ireland (R) / Irlande (R)	NH		91.0	100.3	101.5	88.4	86.5	1 895 000	97.4	110.7	153.1	139.4	188.0	3 562 000
	AH		91.2	98.9	100.6	92.6	92.1	444 000	96.4	119.1	152.7	160.6	172.5	766 000
Italy (N) / Italie (N)	NH	6 264 472	91.0	100.3	101.5	88.4	84.6	5 803 582	95.4	89.3	96.1	88.4		
	AH	1 209 040	91.2	98.9	100.6	92.6	90.3	1 169 164	101.0	99.4	107.3	105.0		
Luxembourg (R)	NH		85.1	92.3	82.4	90.9	84.8	53 946	95.4	103.2		119.0	116.7	62 975
	AH		83.9	91.4	90.7	90.4	97.8	26 889	95.3	104.8			118.9	31 964
Netherlands (R) / Pays-Bas (R)	NH	1 055 845	85.1	92.3	83.6	90.9	96.8	1 335 400	93.7	92.1	101.7	113.8	113.7	1 519 000
	AH	461 361	83.9	91.4	84.3	90.4	95.8	619 200	97.0	97.5	104.8	115.7	113.6	703 400
Norway (N) / Norvège (N)	NH	310 311	92.6	88.2	81.9	117.1	123.2	365 138	95.0	92.4	92.4	92.4	95.1	347 278
Portugal (N)	NH	2 681 063	51.4	56.4	61.4	67.2	84.9	5 831 208	95.5	90.4	87.4	90.2	96.3	5 618 270
	AH	325 605	51.2	55.3	63.4	72.2	91.0	706 871	97.8	92.5	91.6	98.4	101.6	718 435
Spain (N) / Espagne (N)	NH	18 110 142	70.4	82.8	88.7	103.9	74.0	33 824 655	99.8	92.5	74.7	57.8	56.3	19 045 083
	AH	2 187 894	71.5	83.5	86.5	98.8	74.0	3 754 685	99.6	92.1	79.5	59.0	62.3	2 339 168
Sweden (N) / Suède (N)	NH	236 571	100.0	99.6	103.3	103.7	105.1	246 460	91.6	97.1	107.9	109.9	92.6	228 135
Switzerland (R) / Suisse (R)	NH	1 351 959	87.1	87.6	100.1	96.9	95.9	2 016 612	90.3	88.0	95.4	100.3	91.6	1 847 021
	AH	426 647	95.6	100.9	101.8	101.8	98.5	539 592	96.4	97.2	104.8	112.0	99.4	536 230
Turkey (N) / Turquie (N)	NH		26.3	26.3	45.9	50.4	77.3	328 187	155.0	271.5	235.9	193.5	115.4	378 702
	AH		33.3	33.3	50.3	61.8	82.0	103 239	137.9	213.6	197.4	169.1	91.2	94 170
Australia (R) / Australie (R)	NH	205 802	30.5	52.8	52.8	52.8	67.0	1 117 100	113.0	147.9	128.4	196.7	120.8	1 349 700
Japan (N) / Japon (N)	NH	75 255												
	AH													

AH Arrivals at hotels and similar establishments — Arrivées dans les hôtels et les établissements assimilés
NH Nights in hotels and similar establishments — Nuitées dans les hôtels et établissements assimilés
(R) Tourist count by country of residence — Recensement des touristes par pays de résidence
(N) Tourist count by country of nationality — Recensement des touristes par pays de nationalité
1. Ile de France only — Ile de France seulement

Table/Tableau 49

ARRIVALS AND NIGHTS OF FOREIGN TOURISTS AT/IN ALL MEANS OF ACCOMMODATION
ARRIVÉES ET NUITÉES DE TOURISTES ÉTRANGERS DANS L'ENSEMBLE DES MOYENS D'HÉBERGEMENT

From the United Kingdom   *En provenance du Royaume-Uni*

1986=100   1986=100

	AAA/NAA	Volume 1980	1981	1982	1983	1984	1985	Volume 1986	1987	1988	1989	1990	1991	Volume 1991	AEH/NEH	
Austria (R)	NAA	2 207 847	62.4	82.8	94.5	100.9	98.5	4 297 861	98.9	98.0	109.8	114.7	97.8	4 204 954	NEH	Autriche (R)
	AAA	507 107	71.5	88.0	97.8	106.4	103.0	772 650	99.0	97.5	111.8	121.1	101.8	786 300	AEH	
Belgium (R)	NAA	1 111 849	96.9	101.1	109.5	109.3	107.3	1 150 214	93.9	84.7	102.9	117.4			NEH	Belgique (R)
Denmark (N)	NAA	391 898	113.4	120.8	114.5	101.5	108.6	375 085	95.6	92.8	96.1	105.5	97.8	366 900	NEH	Danemark (N)
France (R)	NAA	31 140 000	55.6	88.0	88.8	85.3	90.5	58 598 000	103.3	73.1	86.5	88.2	85.7	50 223 000	NEH	France (R)
	AAA	3 460 000	57.5	95.5	94.2	87.0	93.1	6 299 000	101.1						AEH	
Germany (R)	NAA	2 209 717	75.8	75.3	76.5	91.5	96.2	2 577 554	98.8	99.3	115.0	126.6	115.7	2 982 207	NEH	Allemagne (R)
	AAA	985 890	77.5	80.9	81.9	96.4	99.5	1 184 524	99.2	100.1	114.4	128.8	110.0	1 303 110	AEH	
Greece (N)	NAA	5 957 748	83.7	75.8	63.3	78.3	87.8	8 692 375	97.9	83.8					NEH	Grèce (N)
	AAA	855 596	95.1	85.7	72.2	85.9	93.5	1 006 513	100.0						AEH	
Ireland (R)	NAA	11 162 006	96.9	96.7	103.1	111.1	98.2	9 747 800	123.6	141.6	165.5	159.9	151.0	14 723 000	NEH	Irlande (R)
	AAA	1 068 000	89.4	91.5	93.1	99.4	99.3	1 127 000	133.8	133.8	152.3	158.4	151.7	1 710 000	AEH	
Italy (N)	NAA	7 482 898	93.6	100.8	101.4	87.3	84.1	7 121 770	124.3	86.1	89.8	84.4			NEH	Italie (N)
	AAA	1 365 127	92.5	98.5	99.9	91.7	89.0	1 340 632	100.0	98.6	106.5	103.1			AEH	
Luxembourg (R)	NAA				89.7	97.8	93.5	72 411	100.7	107.0		124.0	120.1	86 961	NEH	Luxembourg (R)
	AAA				95.2	99.3	98.7	35 066	99.0	106.2		125.1	123.3	43 222	AEH	
Netherlands (R)	NAA	1 308 174	90.8	99.1	89.9	99.3	103.0	1 535 574	98.4	98.4	110.1	125.5	126.4	1 940 900	NEH	Pays-Bas (R)
	AAA	569 905	93.0	100.7	92.6	100.2	104.0	681 971	104.3	104.3	110.1	121.4	122.0	831 800	AEH	
Portugal (N)	NAA	2 784 776	52.7	57.6	62.2	67.5	84.9	5 992 652	95.8	90.4	87.4	90.5	96.5	5 782 887	NEH	Portugal (N)
	AAA	350 495	53.1	57.0	64.3	72.5	90.9	739 656	98.0	92.4	91.6	98.3	101.4	750 236	AEH	
Spain (N)	NAA	18 415 844	124.4	106.7	106.0	104.5	103.9								NEH	Espagne (N)
	AAA	2 238 371	85.0	92.0	96.8	94.3	94.2								AEH	
Sweden (N)	NAA	341 249	98.2	100.9	102.0	100.7	97.4	333 103	90.5	93.6	102.4	100.9	82.6	275 157	NEH	Suède (N)
Switzerland (R)	NAA	1 871 700						2 901 600	91.9	89.2	93.9	96.6	87.7	2 543 400	NEH	Suisse (R)
	AAA	559 200						693 800	96.3	95.5	103.1	108.1	96.6	669 897	AEH	
Turkey (N)	NAA	60 997	24.0	25.0	44.8	48.1	75.3	353 020	168.4	277.7	238.4	191.2	118.8	419 471	NEH	Turquie (N)
	AAA	20 416	30.9	32.5	49.5	60.5	80.6	106 892	142.2	216.9	200.3	170.2	95.8	102 374	AEH	
Canada (R)	NAA	6 732 000	117.4	107.8	93.6	90.4	80.3	5 737 000	99.3	118.8	119.1				NEH	Canada (R)
	AAA	489 400	121.4	106.6	91.0	87.6	78.6	399 500	110.0	132.0	140.3				AEH	
Australia (R)	NAA		33.8		89.6	55.9	51.1	2 674 800	120.1	136.0	477.4	583.5	563.9	15 082 100	NEH	Australie (R)
New Zealand (R)	NAA					81.4	88.4	2 138 679			133.7	149.3	146.7	3 137 433	NEH	Nouvelle-Zélande (R)

AAA   Arrivals in all means of accommodation
NAA   Nights in all means of accommodation
(R)   Tourist count by country of residence
(N)   Tourist count by country of nationality

AEH   Arrivées dans l'ensemble des moyens d'hébergement
NEH   Nuitées dans l'ensemble des moyens d'hébergement
(R)   Recensement des touristes par pays de résidence
(N)   Recensement des touristes par pays de nationalité

AUSTRALIA

ARRIVALS OF FOREIGN VISITORS AT FRONTIERS[1]

(by country of residence)

	1990	Relative share	1991	Relative share	% Variation over 1990
Austria	9 600	0.4	10 300	0.4	7.3
Belgium	4 200	0.2	4 100	0.2	−2.4
Denmark	9 900	0.4	9 900	0.4	0.0
Finland	5 800	0.3	5 700	0.2	−1.7
France	21 100	1.0	22 700	1.0	7.6
Germany [2]	74 200	3.4	77 700	3.3	4.7
Greece	7 500	0.3	5 800	0.2	−22.7
Iceland	200	0.0	100	0.0	−50.0
Ireland	10 600	0.5	9 600	0.4	−9.4
Italy	24 400	1.1	24 300	1.0	−0.4
Luxembourg	200	0.0	300	0.0	50.0
Netherlands	21 100	1.0	21 400	0.9	1.4
Norway	4 400	0.2	4 100	0.2	−6.8
Portugal	1 400	0.1	1 200	0.1	−14.3
Spain	4 300	0.2	4 000	0.2	−7.0
Sweden	22 000	1.0	19 100	0.8	−13.2
Switzerland	29 500	1.3	29 600	1.2	0.3
Turkey	1 500	0.1	1 500	0.1	0.0
United Kingdom	277 900	12.5	263 800	11.1	−5.1
Other OECD-Europe	..	..	..	..	
Total Europe	529 800	23.9	515 200	21.7	−2.8
Canada	53 700	2.4	53 400	2.3	−0.6
United States	250 700	11.3	271 800	11.5	8.4
Total North America	304 400	13.7	325 200	13.7	6.8
Australia	..	..	..	..	
New Zealand	418 400	18.9	480 600	20.3	14.9
Japan	479 900	21.7	528 500	22.3	10.1
Total Australasia and Japan	898 300	40.6	1 009 100	42.6	12.3
Total OECD Countries	**1 732 500**	**78.2**	**1 849 500**	**78.0**	**6.8**
Yugoslavia	5 800	0.3	4 900	0.2	−15.5
Other European countries	14 200	0.6	10 700	0.5	−24.6
Bulgaria	400	0.0	300	0.0	−25.0
Czechoslovakia	1 100	0.0	1 300	0.1	18.2
Germany (D. R.)	100	0.0	..	..	
Hungary	1 900	0.1	1 400	0.1	−26.3
Poland	3 700	0.2	2 200	0.1	−40.5
Rumania	600	0.0	500	0.0	−16.7
USSR	5 300	0.2	4 300	0.2	−18.9
Latin America	12 600	0.6	10 800	0.5	−14.3
Argentina	2 400	0.1	2 600	0.1	8.3
Brazil	2 900	0.1	2 500	0.1	−13.8
Chile	1 600	0.1	1 300	0.1	−18.8
Colombia	400	0.0	500	0.0	25.0
Mexico	1 700	0.1	1 600	0.1	−5.9
Venezuela	200	0.0	300	0.0	50.0
Asia-Oceania	428 900	19.4	472 560	19.9	10.2
China	23 700	1.1	16 400	0.7	−30.8
Hong Kong	54 500	2.5	62 800	2.6	15.2
India	11 000	0.5	9 800	0.4	−10.9
Iran	1 500	0.1	1 300	0.1	−13.3
Israel	5 300	0.2	4 900	0.2	−7.5
Republic of Korea	14 100	0.6	23 600	1.0	67.4
Lebanon	1 700	0.1	1 300	0.1	−23.5
Malaysia	46 600	2.1	48 000	2.0	3.0
Pakistan	1 900	0.1	1 300	0.1	−31.6
Philippines	13 600	0.6	15 700	0.7	15.4
Saudi Arabia	2 200	0.1	2 000	0.1	−9.1
Singapore	75 900	3.4	87 500	3.7	15.3
Taiwan	25 300	1.1	34 700	1.5	37.2
Thailand	19 600	0.9	24 700	1.0	26.0
Africa	18 400	0.8	18 300	0.8	−0.5
Algeria	100	0.0	0	0.0	−100.0
Egypt	1 100	0.0	900	0.0	−18.2
Morocco	100	0.0	0	0.0	−100.0
South Africa	9 100	0.4	9 200	0.4	1.1
Origin country undetermined	2 500	0.1	3 500	0.1	40.0
Total non-OECD Countries	**482 400**	**21.8**	**520 760**	**22.0**	**8.0**
TOTAL	**2 214 900**	**100.0**	**2 370 260**	**100.0**	**7.0**

1. Includes a small number of "in transit" passengers who leave the port or airport, but do not necessarily stay overnight in Australia.
2. Germany includes Federal and Democratic Republics.

AUSTRALIA

NIGHTS SPENT BY FOREIGN TOURISTS IN HOTELS[1]

(by country of residence)

	1990	Relative share	1991	Relative share	% Variation over 1990
Austria	..	..	..	..	..
Belgium	..	..	..	..	..
Denmark	..	..	..	..	..
Finland	..	..	..	..	..
France	..	..	..	..	..
Germany	520 000	4.1	581 800	5.1	11.9
Greece	..	..	..	..	..
Iceland	..	..	..	..	..
Ireland	..	..	..	..	..
Italy	..	..	..	..	..
Luxembourg	..	..	..	..	..
Netherlands	..	..	..	..	..
Norway	..	..	..	..	..
Portugal	..	..	..	..	..
Spain	..	..	..	..	..
Sweden	..	..	..	..	..
Switzerland	..	..	..	..	..
Turkey	..	..	..	..	..
United Kingdom[2]	2 196 800	17.5	1 349 700	11.7	−38.6
Other OECD-Europe	..	..	..	..	..
Total Europe	2 716 800	21.7	1 931 500	16.8	−28.9
Canada	485 000	3.9	365 700	3.2	−24.6
United States	2 096 000	16.7	2 110 400	18.3	0.7
Total North America	2 581 000	20.6	2 476 100	21.5	−4.1
Australia	..	..	..	..	..
New Zealand	1 744 300	13.9	1 568 700	13.6	−10.1
Japan	2 542 000	20.3	2 674 800	23.3	5.2
Total Australasia and Japan	4 286 300	34.2	4 243 500	36.9	−1.0
Total OECD Countries	**9 584 100**	**76.4**	**8 651 100**	**75.2**	**−9.7**
Yugoslavia	..	..	..	..	..
Origin country undetermined	2 964 400	23.6	2 851 900	24.8	−3.8
Total non-OECD Countries	**2 964 400**	**23.6**	**2 851 900**	**24.8**	**−3.8**
TOTAL	**12 548 500**	**100.0**	**11 503 000**	**100.0**	**−8.3**

1. Includes nights spent by tourists aged 15 years and above.
2. United Kingdom includes Ireland.

AUSTRALIA

NIGHTS SPENT BY FOREIGN TOURISTS IN REGISTERED TOURIST ACCOMMODATION[1]

(by country of residence)

	1990	Relative share	1991	Relative share	% Variation over 1990
Austria	..	..	..	..	..
Belgium	..	..	..	..	..
Denmark	..	..	..	..	..
Finland	..	..	..	..	..
France	..	..	..	..	..
Germany	3 227 900	4.9	3 096 900	4.8	−4.1
Greece	..	..	..	..	..
Iceland	..	..	..	..	..
Ireland	..	..	..	..	..
Italy	..	..	..	..	..
Luxembourg	..	..	..	..	..
Netherlands	..	..	..	..	..
Norway	..	..	..	..	..
Portugal	..	..	..	..	..
Spain	..	..	..	..	..
Sweden	..	..	..	..	..
Switzerland	..	..	..	..	..
Turkey	..	..	..	..	..
United Kingdom[2]	15 608 200	23.9	15 082 100	23.3	−3.4
Other OECD-Europe	..	..	..	..	..
Total Europe	18 836 100	28.8	18 179 000	28.1	−3.5
Canada	2 672 600	4.1	2 288 900	3.5	−14.4
United States	5 783 600	8.9	6 638 200	10.3	14.8
Total North America	8 456 200	12.9	8 927 100	13.8	5.6
Australia	..	..	..	..	
New Zealand	8 572 100	13.1	8 966 300	13.9	4.6
Japan	5 835 000	8.9	4 262 000	6.6	−27.0
Total Australasia and Japan	14 407 100	22.0	13 228 300	20.5	−8.2
Total OECD Countries	**41 699 400**	**63.8**	**40 334 400**	**62.4**	**−3.3**
Yugoslavia	..	..	..	..	..
Origin country undetermined	23 641 600	36.2	24 310 400	37.6	2.8
Total non-OECD Countries	**23 641 600**	**36.2**	**24 310 400**	**37.6**	**2.8**
TOTAL	**65 341 000**	**100.0**	**64 644 800**	**100.0**	**−1.1**

1. Covers only commercial accommodation (ie excluding stays with friends/relatives).
2. United Kingdom includes Ireland.

AUSTRIA

ARRIVALS OF FOREIGN TOURISTS AT HOTELS

(by country of residence)

	1990	Relative share	1991	Relative share	% Variation over 1990
Austria	..	..	..	..	..
Belgium[1]	320 314	2.3	329 237	2.4	2.8
Denmark	131 655	1.0	128 751	0.9	−2.2
Finland	66 128	0.5	55 818	0.4	−15.6
France	655 594	4.7	666 335	4.9	1.6
Germany	6 244 499	45.2	6 935 141	50.7	11.1
Greece	67 674	0.5	46 220	0.3	−31.7
Iceland[2]					
Ireland	11 243	0.1	10 608	0.1	−5.6
Italy	1 066 073	7.7	1 044 017	7.6	−2.1
Luxembourg[1]					
Netherlands	795 641	5.8	795 892	5.8	0.0
Norway	65 502	0.5	46 384	0.3	−29.2
Portugal	23 306	0.2	17 040	0.1	−26.9
Spain	262 856	1.9	270 059	2.0	2.7
Sweden	263 681	1.9	249 932	1.8	−5.2
Switzerland	673 853	4.9	673 355	4.9	−0.1
Turkey	27 960	0.2	25 739	0.2	−7.9
United Kingdom	821 061	5.9	675 168	4.9	−17.8
Other OECD-Europe	..	..	..	..	..
Total Europe	11 497 040	83.1	11 969 696	87.5	4.1
Canada	83 732	0.6	62 626	0.5	−25.2
United States	815 640	5.9	418 515	3.1	−48.7
Total North America	899 372	6.5	481 141	3.5	−46.5
Australia[3]	114 728	0.8	86 799	0.6	−24.3
New Zealand[3]	..	..	..	..	..
Japan	235 705	1.7	190 073	1.4	−19.4
Total Australasia and Japan	350 433	2.5	276 872	2.0	−21.0
Total OECD Countries	**12 746 845**	**92.2**	**12 727 709**	**93.0**	**−0.2**
Yugoslavia	184 394	1.3	179 083	1.3	−2.9
Other European countries[2]	328 679	2.4	435 133	3.2	32.4
Bulgaria	10 359	0.1	12 576	0.1	21.4
Czechoslovakia	83 702	0.6	88 984	0.7	6.3
Hungary	145 899	1.1	152 582	1.1	4.6
Poland	43 596	0.3	60 788	0.4	39.4
Rumania	16 675	0.1	15 990	0.1	−4.1
USSR	28 448	0.2	32 838	0.2	15.4
Latin America	78 236	0.6	71 375	0.5	−8.8
Asia-Oceania	167 038	1.2	155 095	1.1	−7.1
Africa	24 955	0.2	22 609	0.2	−9.4
Origin country undetermined	297 200	2.1	96 361	0.7	−67.6
Total non-OECD Countries	**1 080 502**	**7.8**	**959 656**	**7.0**	**−11.2**
TOTAL	**13 827 347**	**100.0**	**13 687 365**	**100.0**	**−1.0**

1. Belgium includes Luxembourg.
2. "Other European countries" includes Iceland.
3. Australia includes New Zealand.

AUSTRIA

ARRIVALS OF FOREIGN TOURISTS AT REGISTERED TOURIST ACCOMMODATION

(by country of residence)

	1990	Relative share	1991	Relative share	% Variation over 1990
Austria					
Belgium[1]	445 673	2.3	450 111	2.4	1.0
Denmark	201 144	1.1	198 706	1.0	−1.2
Finland	66 128	0.3	55 818	0.3	−15.6
France	837 297	4.4	845 483	4.4	1.0
Germany	9 418 695	49.5	10 613 343	55.6	12.7
Greece	72 194	0.4	49 995	0.3	−30.7
Iceland[2]					
Ireland	11 243	0.1	10 608	0.1	−5.6
Italy	1 184 841	6.2	1 186 432	6.2	0.1
Luxembourg[1]					
Netherlands	1 345 130	7.1	1 322 987	6.9	−1.6
Norway	65 502	0.3	46 384	0.2	−29.2
Portugal	23 306	0.1	17 040	0.1	−26.9
Spain	262 856	1.4	270 059	1.4	2.7
Sweden	340 459	1.8	327 683	1.7	−3.8
Switzerland	782 779	4.1	782 365	4.1	−0.1
Turkey	27 960	0.1	25 739	0.1	−7.9
United Kingdom	935 476	4.9	786 300	4.1	−15.9
Other OECD-Europe					
Total Europe	16 020 683	84.3	16 989 053	89.0	6.0
Canada	103 847	0.5	77 774	0.4	−25.1
United States	885 337	4.7	468 646	2.5	−47.1
Total North America	989 184	5.2	546 420	2.9	−44.8
Australia[3]	114 728	0.6	86 799	0.5	−24.3
New Zealand[3]					
Japan	235 705	1.2	190 073	1.0	−19.4
Total Australasia and Japan	350 433	1.8	276 872	1.5	−21.0
Total OECD Countries	**17 360 300**	**91.3**	**17 812 345**	**93.3**	**2.6**
Yugoslavia	217 487	1.1	212 205	1.1	−2.4
Other European countries[2]	475 021	2.5	538 838	2.8	13.4
Bulgaria	11 757	0.1	14 018	0.1	19.2
Czechoslovakia	136 488	0.7	147 884	0.8	8.3
Hungary	199 109	1.0	215 081	1.1	8.0
Poland	77 882	0.4	105 738	0.6	35.8
Rumania	21 337	0.1	19 159	0.1	−10.2
USSR	28 448	0.1	36 958	0.2	29.9
Latin America	78 236	0.4	71 376	0.4	−8.8
Asia-Oceania	174 774	0.9	163 355	0.9	−6.5
Africa	24 955	0.1	22 609	0.1	−9.4
Origin country undetermined	680 625	3.6	271 100	1.4	−60.2
Total non-OECD Countries	**1 651 098**	**8.7**	**1 279 483**	**6.7**	**−22.5**
TOTAL	**19 011 398**	**100.0**	**19 091 828**	**100.0**	**0.4**

1. Belgium includes Luxembourg.
2. "Other European countries" includes Iceland.
3. Australia includes New Zealand.

AUSTRIA

NIGHTS SPENT BY FOREIGN TOURISTS IN HOTELS

(by country of residence)

	1990	Relative share	1991	Relative share	% Variation over 1990
Austria	..	..	..	..	..
Belgium[1]	1 868 555	3.0	1 983 728	3.1	6.2
Denmark	663 815	1.1	651 684	1.0	−1.8
Finland	253 043	0.4	235 233	0.4	−7.0
France	2 372 949	3.8	2 475 837	3.9	4.3
Germany	34 019 547	55.0	38 172 969	59.4	12.2
Greece[2]	167 710	0.3	128 042	0.2	−23.7
Iceland[2]	..	..	..	..	..
Ireland	61 078	0.1	55 764	0.1	−8.7
Italy	2 689 615	4.3	2 806 764	4.4	4.4
Luxembourg[1]					
Netherlands	4 992 080	8.1	5 153 046	8.0	3.2
Norway	228 795	0.4	157 324	0.2	−31.2
Portugal	44 440	0.1	34 108	0.1	−23.2
Spain	534 001	0.9	563 629	0.9	5.5
Sweden	1 045 470	1.7	1 050 578	1.6	0.5
Switzerland	2 580 244	4.2	2 645 338	4.1	2.5
Turkey	85 293	0.1	71 156	0.1	−16.6
United Kingdom	4 388 522	7.1	3 664 186	5.7	−16.5
Other OECD-Europe	..	..	..	..	..
Total Europe	55 995 157	90.5	59 849 386	93.2	6.9
Canada	194 198	0.3	155 101	0.2	−20.1
United States	1 959 781	3.2	1 063 374	1.7	−45.7
Total North America	2 153 979	3.5	1 218 475	1.9	−43.4
Australia[3]	262 280	0.4	203 224	0.3	−22.5
New Zealand[3]	..	..	..	..	..
Japan	468 795	0.8	413 186	0.6	−11.9
Total Australasia and Japan	731 075	1.2	616 410	1.0	−15.7
Total OECD Countries	**58 880 211**	**95.1**	**61 684 271**	**96.1**	**4.8**
Yugoslavia	449 691	0.7	500 254	0.8	11.2
Other European countries[2]	932 892	1.5	1 107 134	1.7	18.7
Bulgaria	33 212	0.1	33 357	0.1	0.4
Czechoslovakia	192 210	0.3	209 727	0.3	9.1
Hungary	331 550	0.5	359 468	0.6	8.4
Poland	152 322	0.2	159 941	0.2	5.0
Rumania	66 461	0.1	61 378	0.1	−7.6
USSR	157 137	0.3	132 833	0.2	−15.5
Latin America	158 433	0.3	150 430	0.2	−5.1
Asia-Oceania	424 800	0.7	410 712	0.6	−3.3
Africa	99 424	0.2	87 097	0.1	−12.4
Origin country undetermined	948 161	1.5	272 651	0.4	−71.2
Total non-OECD Countries	**3 013 401**	**4.9**	**2 528 278**	**3.9**	**−16.1**
TOTAL	**61 893 612**	**100.0**	**64 212 549**	**100.0**	**3.7**

1. Belgium includes Luxembourg.
2. "Other European countries" includes Iceland.
3. Australia includes New Zealand.

AUSTRIA

NIGHTS SPENT BY FOREIGN TOURISTS IN REGISTERED TOURIST ACCOMMODATION

(by country of residence)

	1990	Relative share	1991	Relative share	% Variation over 1990
Austria	..	..	..	..	..
Belgium [1]	2 762 052	2.9	2 889 874	2.9	4.6
Denmark	1 000 770	1.1	1 006 058	1.0	0.5
Finland	253 043	0.3	235 233	0.2	−7.0
France	3 076 393	3.2	3 169 839	3.2	3.0
Germany	56 819 027	59.9	64 285 539	64.5	13.1
Greece	183 728	0.2	144 773	0.1	−21.2
Iceland [2]	..	..	..	..	..
Ireland	61 078	0.1	55 764	0.1	−8.7
Italy	3 090 858	3.3	3 307 567	3.3	7.0
Luxembourg [1]	..	..	..	..	..
Netherlands	9 112 348	9.6	9 242 866	9.3	1.4
Norway	228 795	0.2	157 324	0.2	−31.2
Portugal	44 440	0.0	34 108	0.0	−23.2
Spain	534 001	0.6	563 629	0.6	5.5
Sweden	1 382 316	1.5	1 414 429	1.4	2.3
Switzerland	3 172 139	3.3	3 239 015	3.3	2.1
Turkey	85 293	0.1	71 156	0.1	−16.6
United Kingdom	4 931 102	5.2	4 204 954	4.2	−14.7
Other OECD-Europe	..	..	..	..	..
Total Europe	86 737 383	91.5	94 022 128	94.4	8.4
Canada	248 783	0.3	196 294	0.2	−21.1
United States	2 139 202	2.3	1 191 496	1.2	−44.3
Total North America	2 387 985	2.5	1 387 790	1.4	−41.9
Australia [3]	262 280	0.3	203 224	0.2	−22.5
New Zealand [3]					
Japan	468 795	0.5	413 186	0.4	−11.9
Total Australasia and Japan	731 075	0.8	616 410	0.6	−15.7
Total OECD Countries	**89 856 443**	**94.8**	**96 026 328**	**96.4**	**6.9**
Yugoslavia	620 565	0.7	708 816	0.7	14.2
Other European countries [2]	1 366 722	1.4	1 444 333	1.4	5.7
Bulgaria	42 289	0.0	44 518	0.0	5.3
Czechoslovakia	307 862	0.3	344 798	0.3	12.0
Hungary	512 596	0.5	568 833	0.6	11.0
Poland	241 482	0.3	260 790	0.3	8.0
Rumania	105 356	0.1	75 926	0.1	−27.9
USSR	157 137	0.2	149 468	0.2	−4.9
Latin America	158 433	0.2	150 430	0.2	−5.1
Asia-Oceania	453 839	0.5	442 348	0.4	−2.5
Africa	99 424	0.1	87 097	0.1	−12.4
Origin country undetermined	2 232 864	2.4	782 371	0.8	−65.0
Total non-OECD Countries	**4 931 847**	**5.2**	**3 615 395**	**3.6**	**−26.7**
TOTAL	**94 788 290**	**100.0**	**99 641 723**	**100.0**	**5.1**

1. Belgium includes Luxembourg.
2. "Other European countries" includes Iceland.
3. Australia includes New Zealand.

BELGIUM

NIGHTS SPENT BY FOREIGN TOURISTS IN HOTELS

(by country of residence)

	1989	Relative share	1990	Relative share	% Variation over 1989
Austria	54 406	0.8	52 739	0.8	−3.1
Belgium	..	..	..	..	..
Denmark	79 270	1.2	85 638	1.2	8.0
Finland [1]	..	..	..	..	..
France	784 345	11.9	824 150	12.0	5.1
Germany	932 731	14.2	898 645	13.1	−3.7
Greece	79 823	1.2	77 631	1.1	−2.7
Iceland [1]	..	..	..	..	..
Ireland	41 576	0.6	48 324	0.7	16.2
Italy	321 965	4.9	344 602	5.0	7.0
Luxembourg	87 955	1.3	91 219	1.3	3.7
Netherlands	922 728	14.0	945 765	13.8	2.5
Norway	50 725	0.8	59 811	0.9	17.9
Portugal	72 881	1.1	80 494	1.2	10.4
Spain	238 159	3.6	251 056	3.7	5.4
Sweden	128 775	2.0	137 442	2.0	6.7
Switzerland	100 969	1.5	98 415	1.4	−2.5
Turkey	19 717	0.3	25 268	0.4	28.2
United Kingdom	1 055 331	16.1	1 199 470	17.5	13.7
Other OECD-Europe	..	..	..	..	..
Total Europe	4 971 356	75.6	5 220 669	76.0	5.0
Canada	93 477	1.4	98 828	1.4	5.7
United States	554 027	8.4	586 137	8.5	5.8
Total North America	647 504	9.8	684 965	10.0	5.8
Australia [2]	..	..	..	..	..
New Zealand [2]	..	..	..	..	..
Japan	167 454	2.5	155 174	2.3	−7.3
Total Australasia and Japan	167 454	2.5	155 174	2.3	−7.3
Total OECD Countries	**5 786 314**	**88.0**	**6 060 808**	**88.2**	**4.7**
Yugoslavia	..	..	..	..	..
Other European countries [1]	200 565	3.1	243 822	3.5	21.6
USSR	22 997	0.3	32 227	0.5	40.1
Latin America	57 145	0.9	54 294	0.8	−5.0
Mexico [3]	34 499	0.5	31 323	0.5	−9.2
Asia-Oceania [2]	226 107	3.4	217 906	3.2	−3.6
Africa	247 144	3.8	233 148	3.4	−5.7
Origin country undetermined	57 496	0.9	63 550	0.9	10.5
Total non-OECD Countries	**788 457**	**12.0**	**812 720**	**11.8**	**3.1**
TOTAL	**6 574 771**	**100.0**	**6 873 528**	**100.0**	**4.5**

1. "Other European countries" includes Finland and Iceland.
2. "Asia-Oceania" includes Australia and New Zealand.
3. Mexico includes Central America.

BELGIUM

NIGHTS SPENT BY FOREIGN TOURISTS IN REGISTERED TOURIST ACCOMMODATION

(by country of residence)

	1989	Relative share	1990	Relative share	% Variation over 1989
Austria	64 674	0.5	65 325	0.5	1.0
Belgium	..		..		
Denmark	104 872	0.9	115 240	0.9	9.9
Finland [1]	..		..		
France	1 210 213	9.9	1 262 842	9.8	4.3
Germany	1 959 329	16.1	1 940 991	15.1	−0.9
Greece	82 445	0.7	82 628	0.6	0.2
Iceland [1]	..		..		
Ireland	49 913	0.4	55 914	0.4	12.0
Italy	361 299	3.0	387 409	3.0	7.2
Luxembourg	191 093	1.6	183 047	1.4	−4.2
Netherlands	4 484 153	36.9	4 805 065	37.3	7.2
Norway	60 789	0.5	67 765	0.5	11.5
Portugal	83 242	0.7	92 908	0.7	11.6
Spain	272 359	2.2	289 430	2.2	6.3
Sweden	143 998	1.2	149 758	1.2	4.0
Switzerland	108 888	0.9	107 516	0.8	−1.3
Turkey	22 115	0.2	28 068	0.2	26.9
United Kingdom	1 183 534	9.7	1 350 314	10.5	14.1
Other OECD-Europe	..		..		
Total Europe	10 382 916	85.3	10 984 220	85.2	5.8
Canada	105 273	0.9	113 574	0.9	7.9
United States	590 724	4.9	634 543	4.9	7.4
Total North America	695 997	5.7	748 117	5.8	7.5
Australia [2]	..	..	..	..	..
New Zealand [2]	..	..	..	..	..
Japan	173 172	1.4	162 249	1.3	−6.3
Total Australasia and Japan	173 172	1.4	162 249	1.3	−6.3
Total OECD Countries	**11 252 085**	**92.5**	**11 894 586**	**92.3**	**5.7**
Yugoslavia	..		..		
Other European countries [1]	244 104	2.0	306 563	2.4	25.6
USSR	25 346	0.2	38 311	0.3	51.2
Latin America	63 625	0.5	60 759	0.5	−4.5
Mexico [3]	38 615	0.3	44 293	0.3	14.7
Asia-Oceania [2]	252 385	2.1	251 164	1.9	−0.5
Africa	282 681	2.3	287 442	2.2	1.7
Origin country undetermined	73 423	0.6	85 735	0.7	16.8
Total non-OECD Countries	**916 218**	**7.5**	**991 663**	**7.7**	**8.2**
TOTAL	**12 168 303**	**100.0**	**12 886 249**	**100.0**	**5.9**

1. "Other European countries" includes Finland and Iceland.
2. "Asia-Oceania" includes Australia and New Zealand.
3. Mexico includes Central America.

CANADA

ARRIVALS OF FOREIGN TOURISTS AT FRONTIERS

(by country of residence)

	1990	Relative share	1991	Relative share	% Variation over 1990
Austria	22 000	0.1	22 300	0.1	1.4
Belgium [1]	28 400	0.2	31 000	0.2	9.2
Denmark	20 300	0.1	18 700	0.1	−7.9
Finland	17 800	0.1	15 600	0.1	−12.4
France [2]	259 600	1.7	307 100	2.0	18.3
Germany	257 000	1.7	276 500	1.8	7.6
Greece	18 200	0.1	14 800	0.1	−18.7
Iceland	1 100	0.0	1 200	0.0	9.1
Ireland	19 700	0.1	14 000	0.1	−28.9
Italy	90 900	0.6	89 100	0.6	−2.0
Luxembourg [1]	1 500	0.0	2 000	0.0	33.3
Netherlands	87 000	0.6	89 100	0.6	2.4
Norway	13 600	0.1	12 600	0.1	−7.4
Portugal	15 500	0.1	13 000	0.1	−16.1
Spain	24 500	0.2	24 600	0.2	0.4
Sweden	29 600	0.2	26 500	0.2	−10.5
Switzerland	75 100	0.5	77 700	0.5	3.5
Turkey	3 600	0.0	3 600	0.0	0.0
United Kingdom	559 400	3.7	537 000	3.6	−4.0
Other OECD-Europe	..	..	..	..	..
Total Europe	1 544 800	10.1	1 576 400	10.5	2.0
Canada	..	..	..	..	..
United States	12 267 000	80.4	12 049 600	80.4	−1.8
Total North America	12 267 000	80.4	12 049 600	80.4	−1.8
Australia [4]	112 300	0.7	100 000	0.7	−11.0
New Zealand	37 300	0.2	29 100	0.2	−22.0
Japan	412 500	2.7	397 500	2.7	−3.6
Total Australasia and Japan	562 100	3.7	526 600	3.5	−6.3
Total OECD Countries	**14 373 900**	**94.2**	**14 152 600**	**94.4**	**−1.5**
Yugoslavia	13 000	0.1	12 100	0.1	−6.9
Other European countries	88 500	0.6	67 700	0.5	−23.5
Bulgaria [1]	2 100	0.0	900	0.0	−57.1
Czechoslovakia	10 500	0.1	9 500	0.1	−9.5
Hungary	8 900	0.1	7 800	0.1	−12.4
Poland	31 400	0.2	21 400	0.1	−31.8
Rumania [1]	2 800	0.0	2 600	0.0	−7.1
USSR	24 900	0.2	21 200	0.1	−14.9
Latin America [3]	166 600	1.1	162 900	1.1	−2.2
Argentina	30 100	0.2	24 100	0.2	−19.9
Brazil	33 600	0.2	34 100	0.2	1.5
Chile	6 400	0.0	5 900	0.0	−7.8
Colombia	5 500	0.0	5 000	0.0	−9.1
Mexico	63 900	0.4	65 500	0.4	2.5
Venezuela	10 500	0.1	11 100	0.1	5.7
Asia-Oceania	450 700	3.0	439 800	2.9	−2.4
China [6]	25 600	0.2	26 600	0.2	3.9
Hong Kong	125 100	0.8	121 900	0.8	−2.6
India [1]	46 300	0.3	39 400	0.3	−14.9
Iran [1]	4 100	0.0	4 600	0.0	12.2
Israel	56 900	0.4	56 600	0.4	−0.5
Republic of Korea [1]	35 500	0.2	39 800	0.3	12.1
Lebanon	3 800	0.0	3 300	0.0	−13.2
Malaysia [1]	17 300	0.1	15 800	0.1	−8.7
Pakistan [1]	8 800	0.1	7 700	0.1	−12.5
Philippines [1]	20 800	0.1	19 800	0.1	−4.8
Saudi Arabia [1]	7 800	0.1	7 100	0.0	−9.0
Singapore [1]	18 600	0.1	20 200	0.1	8.6
Taiwan	39 300	0.3	41 200	0.3	4.8
Thailand [1]	9 800	0.1	9 400	0.1	−4.1
Africa	49 700	0.3	46 300	0.3	−6.8
Algeria [1]	1 400	0.0	1 300	0.0	−7.1
Egypt [1]	5 400	0.0	4 900	0.0	−9.3
Morocco [1]	5 200	0.0	4 500	0.0	−13.5
South Africa	11 300	0.1	11 000	0.1	−2.7
Origin country undetermined [5]	115 400	0.8	107 200	0.7	−7.1
Total non-OECD Countries	**883 900**	**5.8**	**836 000**	**5.6**	**−5.4**
TOTAL [1]	**15 257 800**	**100.0**	**14 988 600**	**100.0**	**−1.8**

1. Estimate.
2. France includes Andorra and Monaco.
3. Latin America includes South America and Mexico.
4. Australia includes Papua New Guinea, Solomon, Caroline and Christmas islands.
5. Origin country undetermined includes Bermuda, Caribbean, Central America, Greenland and St. Pierre and Miquelon.
6. China includes Mongolia and Tibet.

CANADA

ARRIVALS OF FOREIGN VISITORS AT FRONTIERS
(by country of residence)

	1990	Relative share	1991	Relative share	% Variation over 1990
Austria	23 600	0.1	23 600	0.1	0.0
Belgium[1]	32 500	0.1	32 800	0.1	0.9
Denmark	21 900	0.1	20 200	0.1	-7.8
Finland	19 000	0.1	16 700	0.0	-12.1
France[2]	275 700	0.7	323 900	0.9	17.5
Germany	290 500	0.8	312 300	0.8	7.5
Greece	19 500	0.1	16 400	0.0	-15.9
Iceland	1 200	0.0	1 300	0.0	8.3
Ireland	20 900	0.1	15 200	0.0	-27.3
Italy	101 100	0.3	99 900	0.3	-1.2
Luxembourg[1]	1 500	0.0	2 000	0.0	33.3
Netherlands	93 300	0.2	95 300	0.3	2.1
Norway	14 500	0.0	13 600	0.0	-6.2
Portugal	16 000	0.0	13 500	0.0	-15.6
Spain	27 000	0.1	27 000	0.1	0.0
Sweden	31 900	0.1	28 600	0.1	-10.3
Switzerland	79 700	0.2	82 200	0.2	3.1
Turkey	3 900	0.0	3 900	0.0	0.0
United Kingdom	602 400	1.6	580 700	1.6	-3.6
Other OECD-Europe	..	..	..	..	..
Total Europe	1 676 100	4.4	1 709 100	4.6	2.0
Canada	..	..	..	..	..
United States	34 734 100	91.4	33 577 200	91.2	-3.3
Total North America	34 734 100	91.4	33 577 200	91.2	-3.3
Australia[4]	122 300	0.3	109 400	0.3	-10.5
New Zealand	39 500	0.1	31 300	0.1	-20.8
Japan	474 100	1.2	480 300	1.3	1.3
Total Australasia and Japan	635 900	1.7	621 000	1.7	-2.3
Total OECD Countries	**37 046 100**	**97.5**	**35 907 300**	**97.5**	**-3.1**
Yugoslavia	13 500	0.0	13 100	0.0	-3.0
Other European countries	89 800	0.2	70 600	0.2	-21.4
Bulgaria[1]	2 100	0.0	900	0.0	-57.1
Czechoslovakia	11 100	0.0	10 100	0.0	-9.0
Hungary	9 100	0.0	8 100	0.0	-11.0
Poland	32 200	0.1	22 500	0.1	-30.1
Rumania[1]	3 000	0.0	2 800	0.0	-6.7
USSR	25 100	0.1	21 600	0.1	-13.9
Latin America[3]	179 700	0.5	178 400	0.5	-0.7
Argentina	30 900	0.1	25 600	0.1	-17.2
Brazil	35 500	0.1	36 400	0.1	2.5
Chile	6 800	0.0	6 400	0.0	-5.9
Colombia	6 300	0.0	5 700	0.0	-9.5
Mexico	71 000	0.2	74 000	0.2	4.2
Venezuela	11 400	0.0	12 400	0.0	8.8
Asia-Oceania	491 300	1.3	488 900	1.3	-0.5
China[6]	28 200	0.1	30 300	0.1	7.4
Hong Kong	129 600	0.3	127 100	0.3	-1.9
India[1]	54 600	0.1	49 100	0.1	-10.1
Iran[1]	4 200	0.0	4 800	0.0	14.3
Israel	63 700	0.2	65 900	0.2	3.5
Republic of Korea[1]	41 700	0.1	46 400	0.1	11.3
Lebanon	4 400	0.0	3 800	0.0	-13.6
Malaysia[1]	19 600	0.1	18 400	0.0	-6.1
Pakistan[1]	10 000	0.0	9 400	0.0	-6.0
Philippines[1]	23 000	0.1	22 100	0.1	-3.9
Saudi Arabia[1]	8 100	0.0	7 800	0.0	-3.7
Singapore[1]	19 800	0.1	21 700	0.1	9.6
Taiwan	41 000	0.1	43 100	0.1	5.1
Thailand[1]	10 700	0.0	10 500	0.0	-1.9
Africa	51 000	0.1	48 000	0.1	-5.9
Algeria[1]	1 400	0.0	1 300	0.0	-7.1
Egypt[1]	5 600	0.0	5 200	0.0	-7.1
Morocco[1]	5 200	0.0	4 600	0.0	-11.5
South Africa	11 300	0.0	11 600	0.0	2.7
Origin country undetermined[5]	119 100	0.3	111 400	0.3	-6.5
Total non-OECD Countries	**944 400**	**2.5**	**910 400**	**2.5**	**-3.6**
TOTAL[1]	**37 990 500**	**100.0**	**36 817 700**	**100.0**	**-3.1**

1. Estimate.
2. France includes Andorra and Monaco.
3. Latin America includes South America and Mexico.
4. Australia includes Papua New Guinea, Solomon, Caroline and Christmas islands.
5. Origin country undetermined includes Bermuda, Caribbean, Central America, Greenland and St. Pierre and Miquelon.
6. China includes Mongolia and Tibet.

DENMARK

NIGHTS SPENT BY FOREIGN TOURISTS IN HOTELS

(by country of nationality)

	1990	Relative share	1991	Relative share	% Variation over 1990
Austria [1]	..	..	..	..	..
Belgium [1]	..	..	..	..	..
Denmark	..	..	..	..	..
Finland	128 600	2.4	136 700	2.3	6.3
France	82 500	1.5	85 200	1.4	3.3
Germany	1 288 200	23.7	1 587 200	26.6	23.2
Greece [1]	..	..	..	..	..
Iceland [1]	..	..	..	..	..
Ireland [1]	..	..	..	..	..
Italy	127 100	2.3	142 300	2.4	12.0
Luxembourg [1]	..	..	..	..	..
Netherlands	113 800	2.1	156 700	2.6	37.7
Norway	709 800	13.1	746 800	12.5	5.2
Portugal [1]	..	..	..	..	..
Spain [1]	..	..	..	..	..
Sweden	1 477 500	27.2	1 746 200	29.3	18.2
Switzerland [1]	..	..	..	..	..
Turkey [1]	..	..	..	..	..
United Kingdom	333 500	6.1	316 500	5.3	–5.1
Other OECD-Europe [1]	277 900	5.1	308 200	5.2	10.9
Total Europe	4 538 900	83.6	5 225 800	87.6	15.1
Canada [2]	..	..	..	..	..
United States	399 500	7.4	291 500	4.9	–27.0
Total North America	399 500	7.4	291 500	4.9	–27.0
Australia [2]	..	..	..	..	..
New Zealand [2]	..	..	..	..	..
Japan	108 000	2.0	93 400	1.6	–13.5
Total Australasia and Japan	108 000	2.0	93 400	1.6	–13.5
Total OECD Countries	**5 046 400**	**92.9**	**5 610 700**	**94.1**	**11.2**
Yugoslavia	..	..	..	..	..
Origin country undetermined [2]	383 000	7.1	352 400	5.9	–8.0
Total non-OECD Countries	**383 000**	**7.1**	**352 400**	**5.9**	**–8.0**
TOTAL	**5 429 400**	**100.0**	**5 963 100**	**100.0**	**9.8**

1. Other OECD-Europe includes Austria, Belgium, Greece, Iceland, Ireland, Luxembourg, Portugal, Spain, Switzerland, Turkey as well as European non-member countries.
2. Origin country undetermined includes Australia, Canada and New Zealand.

DENMARK

NIGHTS SPENT BY FOREIGN TOURISTS IN REGISTERED TOURIST ACCOMMODATION

(by country of nationality)

	1990	Relative share	1991	Relative share	% Variation over 1990
Austria [1]	..	..	..	..	..
Belgium [1]	..	..	..	..	..
Denmark					
Finland	225 555	2.4	232 634	2.2	3.1
France	148 374	1.6	152 300	1.5	2.6
Germany	3 353 577	35.9	3 928 400	37.7	17.1
Greece [1]	..	..	..	..	..
Iceland [1]	..	..	..	..	..
Ireland [1]	..	..	..	..	..
Italy	187 630	2.0	218 937	2.1	16.7
Luxembourg [1]					
Netherlands	510 547	5.5	630 364	6.0	23.5
Norway	1 023 492	11.0	1 062 800	10.2	3.8
Portugal [1]	..	..	..	..	..
Spain [1]					
Sweden	2 128 500	22.8	2 567 700	24.6	20.6
Switzerland [1]	..	..	..	..	..
Turkey [1]					
United Kingdom	395 567	4.2	366 900	3.5	–7.2
Other OECD-Europe [1]	391 508	4.2	428 888	4.1	9.5
Total Europe	8 364 750	89.6	9 588 923	91.9	14.6
Canada [2]					
United States	421 281	4.5	311 000	3.0	–26.2
Total North America	421 281	4.5	311 000	3.0	–26.2
Australia [2]	..	..	..	..	..
New Zealand [2]					
Japan [3]	108 000	1.2	93 400	0.9	–13.5
Total Australasia and Japan	108 000	1.2	93 400	0.9	–13.5
Total OECD Countries	**8 894 031**	**95.2**	**9 993 323**	**95.8**	**12.4**
Yugoslavia					
Origin country undetermined [2]	444 169	4.8	438 077	4.2	–1.4
Total non-OECD Countries	**444 169**	**4.8**	**438 077**	**4.2**	**–1.4**
TOTAL	**9 338 200**	**100.0**	**10 431 400**	**100.0**	**11.7**

1. Other OECD-Europe includes Austria, Belgium, Greece, Iceland, Ireland, Luxembourg, Portugal, Spain, Switzerland, Turkey as well as European non-member countries.
2. Origin country undetermined includes Australia, Canada and New Zealand.
3. Japan includes only nights spent in hotels.

FINLAND

NIGHTS SPENT BY FOREIGN TOURISTS IN HOTELS
(by country of residence)

	1990	Relative share	1991	Relative share	% Variation over 1990
Austria	24 272	1.0	22 123	1.0	−8.9
Belgium	15 168	0.6	16 994	0.8	12.0
Denmark	75 211	3.0	65 565	3.0	−12.8
Finland	..	..	..	..	..
France	83 691	3.4	80 840	3.7	−3.4
Germany	338 261	13.7	351 017	15.9	3.8
Greece [1]	..	..	..	..	..
Iceland	7 036	0.3	5 434	0.2	−22.8
Ireland [2]	..	..	..	..	..
Italy	79 275	3.2	81 830	3.7	3.2
Luxembourg [1]	..	..	..	..	..
Netherlands	55 126	2.2	52 823	2.4	−4.2
Norway	99 228	4.0	91 700	4.2	−7.6
Portugal [3]	..	..	..	..	..
Spain [3]	32 962	1.3	31 607	1.4	−4.1
Sweden	518 101	21.0	524 299	23.8	1.2
Switzerland	72 498	2.9	62 271	2.8	−14.1
Turkey [1]	..	..	..	..	..
United Kingdom [2]	142 102	5.8	131 699	6.0	−7.3
Other OECD-Europe	..	..	..	..	..
Total Europe	1 542 931	62.5	1 518 202	69.0	−1.6
Canada	32 056	1.3	24 895	1.1	−22.3
United States	197 318	8.0	144 098	6.5	−27.0
Total North America	229 374	9.3	168 993	7.7	−26.3
Australia	..	..	..	..	..
New Zealand	..	..	..	..	..
Japan	63 669	2.6	57 258	2.6	−10.1
Total Australasia and Japan	63 669	2.6	57 258	2.6	−10.1
Total OECD Countries	**1 835 974**	**74.4**	**1 744 453**	**79.3**	**−5.0**
Yugoslavia	..	..	..	..	..
Other European countries [1]	425 246	17.2	279 412	12.7	−34.3
Bulgaria [4]	17 117	0.7	11 178	0.5	−34.7
Czechoslovakia	13 893	0.6	14 448	0.7	4.0
Hungary	16 816	0.7	12 313	0.6	−26.8
Poland	21 602	0.9	19 624	0.9	−9.2
USSR	355 818	14.4	221 849	10.1	−37.7
Origin country undetermined [5]	206 912	8.4	177 005	8.0	−14.5
Total non-OECD Countries	**632 158**	**25.6**	**456 417**	**20.7**	**−27.8**
TOTAL	**2 468 132**	**100.0**	**2 200 870**	**100.0**	**−10.8**

1. "Other European countries" includes Greece, Luxembourg and Turkey.
2. United Kingdom includes Ireland.
3. Spain includes Portugal.
4. Bulgaria includes Rumania.
5. "Origin country undetermined" includes Latin America, Asia-Oceania and Africa.

FRANCE

ARRIVALS OF FOREIGN TOURISTS AT FRONTIERS [1]

(by country of residence)

	1990	Relative share	1991	Relative share	% Variation over 1990
Austria	422 000	0.8	410 000	0.7	−2.8
Belgium	6 883 000	13.1	7 657 000	13.9	11.2
Denmark	474 000	0.9	549 000	1.0	15.8
Finland	186 000	0.4	194 000	0.4	4.3
France	..	..	..	..	
Germany	12 117 000	23.1	13 683 000	24.9	12.9
Greece	197 000	0.4	122 000	0.2	−38.1
Iceland	16 000	0.0	13 000	0.0	−18.8
Ireland	307 000	0.6	258 000	0.5	−16.0
Italy	5 645 000	10.8	6 821 000	12.4	20.8
Luxembourg	303 000	0.6	339 000	0.6	11.9
Netherlands	3 972 000	7.6	3 546 000	6.5	−10.7
Norway	215 000	0.4	239 000	0.4	11.2
Portugal	522 000	1.0	527 000	1.0	1.0
Spain	2 637 000	5.0	2 458 000	4.5	−6.8
Sweden	719 000	1.4	803 000	1.5	11.7
Switzerland	4 810 000	9.2	4 954 000	9.0	3.0
Turkey	..	..	..	..	
United Kingdom	6 978 000	13.3	6 840 000	12.5	−2.0
Other OECD-Europe	..	..	..	..	
Total Europe	46 403 000	88.4	49 413 000	89.9	6.5
Canada	610 000	1.2	552 000	1.0	−9.5
United States	2 070 000	3.9	1 709 000	3.1	−17.4
Total North America	2 680 000	5.1	2 261 000	4.1	−15.6
Australia	..	..	..	..	..
New Zealand	..	..	..	..	..
Japan	618 000	1.2	458 000	0.8	−25.9
Total Australasia and Japan	618 000	1.2	458 000	0.8	−25.9
Total OECD Countries	**49 701 000**	**94.7**	**52 132 000**	**94.9**	**4.9**
Yugoslavia	..		..		..
Origin country undetermined	2 794 000	5.3	2 803 000	5.1	0.3
Total non-OECD Countries	**2 794 000**	**5.3**	**2 803 000**	**5.1**	**0.3**
TOTAL	**52 495 000**	**100.0**	**54 935 000**	**100.0**	**4.6**

1. Estimates of number of "trips", the same person coming perhaps several times in one year.

FRANCE[1]

ARRIVALS OF FOREIGN TOURISTS AT HOTELS

(by country of residence)

	1990	Relative share	1991	Relative share	% Variation over 1990
Austria[4]	..	..	..	..	..
Belgium[2]	1 655 391	6.4	1 719 837	6.8	3.9
Denmark[4]	..	..	..	..	..
Finland[4]	..	..	..	..	..
France	..	..	..	..	..
Germany	3 944 278	15.3	4 104 567	16.3	4.1
Greece[4]	..	..	..	..	..
Iceland[4]	..	..	..	..	..
Ireland[3]	..	..	..	..	..
Italy	3 112 773	12.1	3 137 722	12.4	0.8
Luxembourg[2]	..	..	..	..	..
Netherlands	1 254 164	4.9	1 337 046	5.3	6.6
Norway[4]	..	..	..	..	..
Portugal[4]	..	..	..	..	..
Spain	1 391 514	5.4	1 413 675	5.6	1.6
Sweden[4]	..	..	..	..	..
Switzerland	1 107 120	4.3	1 128 411	4.5	1.9
Turkey[4]	..	..	..	..	..
United Kingdom[3]	4 872 717	18.9	5 137 632	20.4	5.4
Other OECD-Europe[4]	1 461 552	5.7	1 504 589	6.0	2.9
Total Europe	18 799 509	72.9	19 483 479	77.2	3.6
Canada	472 754	1.8	360 630	1.4	−23.7
United States	2 468 889	9.6	1 753 891	6.9	−29.0
Total North America	2 941 643	11.4	2 114 521	8.4	−28.1
Australia[5]	180 759	0.7	162 282	0.6	−10.2
New Zealand[5]	..	..	..	..	..
Japan	1 264 895	4.9	1 016 778	4.0	−19.6
Total Australasia and Japan	1 445 654	5.6	1 179 060	4.7	−18.4
Total OECD Countries	**23 186 806**	**90.0**	**22 777 060**	**90.2**	**−1.8**
Yugoslavia	..	..	..	..	..
Latin America[6]	343 099	1.3	313 934	1.2	−8.5
Asia-Oceania[7]	593 968	2.3	589 015	2.3	−0.8
Africa	519 123	2.0	479 083	1.9	−7.7
Origin country undetermined	1 131 212	4.4	1 078 969	4.3	−4.6
Total non-OECD Countries	**2 587 402**	**10.0**	**2 461 001**	**9.8**	**−4.9**
TOTAL	**25 774 208**	**100.0**	**25 238 061**	**100.0**	**−2.1**

1. Data covering all France except 3 regions (Pays de la Loire and Champagne-Ardenne).
2. Belgium includes Luxembourg.
3. United Kingdom includes Ireland.
4. "Other OECD-Europe" includes Austria, Denmark, Greece, Iceland, Finland, Norway, Portugal, Sweden, Turkey and countries of Central and Eastern Europe.
5. Australia includes New Zealand and Oceania.
6. Latin America includes Central America.
7. Asia only.

FRANCE[1]

NIGHTS SPENT BY FOREIGN TOURISTS IN HOTELS
(by country of residence)

	1990	Relative share	1991	Relative share	% Variation over 1990
Austria[4]					
Belgium[2]	3 498 661	6.3	3 609 053	6.8	3.2
Denmark[4]	..	..	..	..	..
Finland[4]	..	..	..	..	..
France	..	..	..	..	..
Germany	7 953 923	14.2	8 502 236	16.0	6.9
Greece[4]	..	..	..	..	..
Iceland[4]	..	..	..	..	..
Ireland[3]	..	..	..	..	..
Italy	7 007 067	12.5	7 000 617	13.2	−0.1
Luxembourg[2]					
Netherlands	2 334 752	4.2	2 421 424	4.6	3.7
Norway[4]	..	..	..	..	..
Portugal[4]					
Spain	2 764 800	4.9	2 755 953	5.2	−0.3
Sweden[4]					
Switzerland	2 346 506	4.2	2 319 286	4.4	−1.2
Turkey[4]					
United Kingdom[3]	10 961 596	19.6	10 170 853	19.2	−7.2
Other OECD-Europe[4]	3 682 712	6.6	3 699 926	7.0	0.5
Total Europe	40 550 017	72.5	40 479 348	76.3	−0.2
Canada	1 032 776	1.8	756 579	1.4	−26.7
United States	5 672 261	10.1	3 917 294	7.4	−30.9
Total North America	6 705 037	12.0	4 673 873	8.8	−30.3
Australia[5]	408 044	0.7	341 490	0.6	−16.3
New Zealand[5]					
Japan	2 675 010	4.8	2 190 904	4.1	−18.1
Total Australasia and Japan	3 083 054	5.5	2 532 394	4.8	−17.9
Total OECD Countries	**50 338 108**	**90.0**	**47 685 615**	**89.9**	**−5.3**
Yugoslavia					
Latin America[6]	902 754	1.6	773 213	1.5	−14.3
Asia-Oceania[7]	1 444 525	2.6	1 343 449	2.5	−7.0
Africa	1 357 807	2.4	1 239 616	2.3	−8.7
Origin country undetermined	1 890 959	3.4	2 002 960	3.8	5.9
Total non-OECD Countries	**5 596 045**	**10.0**	**5 359 238**	**10.1**	**−4.2**
TOTAL	**55 934 153**	**100.0**	**53 044 853**	**100.0**	**−5.2**

1. Data covering all France except 3 regions (Pays de la Loire and Champagne-Ardenne).
2. Belgium includes Luxembourg.
3. United Kingdom includes Ireland.
4. "Other OECD-Europe" includes Austria, Denmark, Finland, Greece, Iceland, Norway, Portugal, Sweden, Turkey and countries of Central and Eastern Europe.
5. Australia includes New Zealand and Oceania.
6. Latin America includes Central America.
7. Asia only.

FRANCE

NIGHTS SPENT BY FOREIGN TOURISTS IN TOURIST ACCOMMODATION[1]

(by country of residence)

	1990	Relative share	1991	Relative share	% Variation over 1990
Austria	2 946 000	0.8	2 825 000	0.8	−4.1
Belgium	39 213 000	10.8	41 893 000	11.3	6.8
Denmark	3 395 000	0.9	3 886 000	1.0	14.5
Finland	1 089 000	0.3	1 109 000	0.3	1.8
France	..	..	..	..	..
Germany	76 936 000	21.1	84 956 000	22.8	10.4
Greece	2 028 000	0.6	1 242 000	0.3	−38.8
Iceland	100 000	0.0	81 000	0.0	−19.0
Ireland	2 271 000	0.6	1 890 000	0.5	−16.8
Italy	35 380 000	9.7	42 350 000	11.4	19.7
Luxembourg	1 727 000	0.5	1 855 000	0.5	7.4
Netherlands	34 007 000	9.3	30 567 000	8.2	−10.1
Norway	1 390 000	0.4	1 498 000	0.4	7.8
Portugal	4 440 000	1.2	4 695 000	1.3	5.7
Spain	13 335 000	3.7	12 419 000	3.3	−6.9
Sweden	4 720 000	1.3	5 055 000	1.4	7.1
Switzerland	25 894 000	7.1	27 027 000	7.3	4.4
Turkey	..	..	..	..	..
United Kingdom	51 689 000	14.2	50 223 000	13.5	−2.8
Other OECD-Europe	..	..	..	..	..
Total Europe	300 560 000	82.6	313 571 000	84.3	4.3
Canada	6 314 000	1.7	5 614 000	1.5	−11.1
United States	17 021 000	4.7	14 074 000	3.8	−17.3
Total North America	23 335 000	6.4	19 688 000	5.3	−15.6
Australia	..	..	..	..	..
New Zealand	..	..	..	..	..
Japan	4 718 000	1.3	3 554 000	1.0	−24.7
Total Australasia and Japan	4 718 000	1.3	3 554 000	1.0	−24.7
Total OECD Countries	**328 613 000**	**90.3**	**336 813 000**	**90.5**	**2.5**
Yugoslavia	..	..	..	..	..
Origin country undetermined	35 196 000	9.7	35 362 000	9.5	0.5
Total non-OECD Countries	**35 196 000**	**9.7**	**35 362 000**	**9.5**	**0.5**
TOTAL	**363 809 000**	**100.0**	**372 175 000**	**100.0**	**2.3**

1. The figures are based on an update of the findings of the 1989 frontier survey.

GERMANY [1]

ARRIVALS OF FOREIGN TOURISTS AT HOTELS [2]

(by country of residence)

	1990	Relative share	1991	Relative share	% Variation over 1990
Austria	534 216	3.7	549 730	4.2	2.9
Belgium	461 318	3.2	483 699	3.7	4.9
Denmark	619 911	4.3	573 979	4.4	−7.4
Finland	196 786	1.4	164 201	1.3	−16.6
France	760 774	5.3	729 664	5.6	−4.1
Germany	..	..	..	..	..
Greece	123 462	0.9	104 304	0.8	−15.5
Iceland	22 002	0.2	18 765	0.1	−14.7
Ireland	34 748	0.2	33 961	0.3	−2.3
Italy	877 688	6.1	898 795	6.9	2.4
Luxembourg	66 983	0.5	67 002	0.5	0.0
Netherlands	1 598 614	11.1	1 551 966	11.9	−2.9
Norway	296 761	2.1	256 382	2.0	−13.6
Portugal	45 869	0.3	49 971	0.4	8.9
Spain	301 900	2.1	302 256	2.3	0.1
Sweden	968 834	6.7	962 108	7.4	−0.7
Switzerland	710 690	4.9	709 493	5.4	−0.2
Turkey	91 779	0.6	93 685	0.7	2.1
United Kingdom	1 444 579	10.0	1 221 558	9.4	−15.4
Other OECD-Europe	..	..	..	..	..
Total Europe	9 156 914	63.5	8 771 519	67.2	−4.2
Canada	187 001	1.3	141 292	1.1	−24.4
United States	2 308 179	16.0	1 538 400	11.8	−33.4
Total North America	2 495 180	17.3	1 679 692	12.9	−32.7
Australia	105 369	0.7	80 413	0.6	−23.7
New Zealand	15 257	0.1	10 734	0.1	−29.6
Japan	805 462	5.6	639 365	4.9	−20.6
Total Australasia and Japan	926 088	6.4	730 512	5.6	−21.1
Total OECD Countries	**12 578 182**	**87.2**	**11 181 723**	**85.7**	**−11.1**
Yugoslavia	226 048	1.6	192 530	1.5	−14.8
Other European countries	465 670	3.2	555 838	4.3	19.4
Bulgaria	20 283	0.1	20 543	0.2	1.3
Czechoslovakia	93 007	0.6	117 387	0.9	26.2
Hungary	98 902	0.7	109 471	0.8	10.7
Poland	127 345	0.9	169 281	1.3	32.9
Rumania	25 934	0.2	27 201	0.2	4.9
USSR	100 199	0.7	111 955	0.9	11.7
Latin America	140 850	1.0	130 692	1.0	−7.2
Argentina	26 301	0.2	26 591	0.2	1.1
Brazil	69 053	0.5	65 732	0.5	−4.8
Chile	8 655	0.1	8 368	0.1	−3.3
Mexico	36 841	0.3	30 001	0.2	−18.6
Asia-Oceania	117 635	0.8	107 018	0.8	−9.0
Israel	117 635	0.8	107 018	0.8	−9.0
Africa	43 080	0.3	38 737	0.3	−10.1
South Africa	43 080	0.3	38 737	0.3	−10.1
Origin country undetermined	849 569	5.9	838 083	6.4	−1.4
Total non-OECD Countries	**1 842 852**	**12.8**	**1 862 898**	**14.3**	**1.1**
TOTAL	**14 421 034**	**100.0**	**13 044 621**	**100.0**	**−9.5**

1. The data relate to the territory of the Federal Republic of Germany prior to 3rd October 1990; as of 1990, tourists from the former German Democratic Republic will be regarded as domestic tourists.
2. Arrivals at hotels (including "bed and breakfast"), boarding houses and inns.

GERMANY[1]

ARRIVALS OF FOREIGN TOURISTS AT REGISTERED TOURIST ACCOMMODATION[2]

(by country of residence)

	1990	Relative share	1991	Relative share	% Variation over 1990
Austria	555 146	3.6	570 437	4.0	2.8
Belgium	505 724	3.2	527 539	3.7	4.3
Denmark	690 983	4.4	656 480	4.6	−5.0
Finland	211 811	1.4	176 800	1.2	−16.5
France	849 395	5.4	813 348	5.7	−4.2
Germany	..	..	..	..	..
Greece	127 189	0.8	107 412	0.8	−15.5
Iceland	24 507	0.2	20 743	0.1	−15.4
Ireland	40 992	0.3	41 532	0.3	1.3
Italy	911 931	5.8	933 023	6.5	2.3
Luxembourg	73 483	0.5	73 428	0.5	−0.1
Netherlands	1 915 925	12.3	1 927 880	13.5	0.6
Norway	314 131	2.0	270 365	1.9	−13.9
Portugal	49 436	0.3	53 670	0.4	8.6
Spain	320 687	2.1	323 010	2.3	0.7
Sweden	1 007 987	6.5	1 018 859	7.1	1.1
Switzerland	743 299	4.8	742 967	5.2	−0.0
Turkey	97 086	0.6	100 158	0.7	3.2
United Kingdom	1 526 140	9.8	1 303 110	9.1	−14.6
Other OECD-Europe	..	..	..	..	..
Total Europe	9 965 852	63.8	9 660 761	67.6	−3.1
Canada	214 145	1.4	160 568	1.1	−25.0
United States	2 428 067	15.5	1 617 196	11.3	−33.4
Total North America	2 642 212	16.9	1 777 764	12.4	−32.7
Australia	143 503	0.9	110 263	0.8	−23.2
New Zealand	21 436	0.1	15 116	0.1	−29.5
Japan	841 462	5.4	665 625	4.7	−20.9
Total Australasia and Japan	1 006 401	6.4	791 004	5.5	−21.4
Total OECD Countries	**13 614 465**	**87.1**	**12 229 529**	**85.6**	**−10.2**
Yugoslavia	234 417	1.5	202 558	1.4	−13.6
Other European countries	537 648	3.4	660 100	4.6	22.8
Bulgaria	21 991	0.1	22 211	0.2	1.0
Czechoslovakia	107 751	0.7	141 086	1.0	30.9
Hungary	111 617	0.7	122 686	0.9	9.9
Poland	154 415	1.0	216 884	1.5	40.5
Rumania	28 261	0.2	29 623	0.2	4.8
USSR	113 613	0.7	127 610	0.9	12.3
Latin America	158 032	1.0	148 568	1.0	−6.0
Argentina	29 543	0.2	30 854	0.2	4.4
Brazil	78 239	0.5	74 908	0.5	−4.3
Chile	10 196	0.1	10 107	0.1	−0.9
Mexico	40 054	0.3	32 699	0.2	−18.4
Asia-Oceania	124 760	0.8	112 957	0.8	−9.5
Israel	124 760	0.8	112 957	0.8	−9.5
Africa	49 258	0.3	43 082	0.3	−12.5
South Africa	49 258	0.3	43 082	0.3	−12.5
Origin country undetermined	908 278	5.8	897 810	6.3	−1.2
Total non-OECD Countries	**2 012 393**	**12.9**	**2 065 075**	**14.4**	**2.6**
TOTAL	**15 626 858**	**100.0**	**14 294 604**	**100.0**	**−8.5**

1. The data relate to the territory of the Federal Republic of Germany prior to 3rd October 1990; as of 1990, tourists from the former German Democratic Republic will be regarded as domestic tourists.
2. Arrivals at hotels and similar establishments, holiday villages, sanatoria and recreation and holiday homes.

GERMANY [1]

NIGHTS SPENT BY FOREIGN TOURISTS IN HOTELS [2]

(by country of residence)

	1990	Relative share	1991	Relative share	% Variation over 1990
Austria	1 099 101	3.7	1 113 448	4.0	1.3
Belgium	1 049 860	3.5	1 154 343	4.2	10.0
Denmark	1 136 133	3.8	1 084 394	3.9	−4.6
Finland	353 954	1.2	295 353	1.1	−16.6
France	1 467 218	4.9	1 403 608	5.1	−4.3
Germany	..	..	..	..	..
Greece	301 582	1.0	267 403	1.0	−11.3
Iceland	49 133	0.2	41 895	0.2	−14.7
Ireland	84 489	0.3	89 891	0.3	6.4
Italy	1 689 032	5.7	1 735 885	6.3	2.8
Luxembourg	181 833	0.6	190 830	0.7	4.9
Netherlands	3 531 524	11.9	3 494 580	12.6	−1.0
Norway	488 571	1.6	413 516	1.5	−15.4
Portugal	114 959	0.4	129 679	0.5	12.8
Spain	612 458	2.1	603 097	2.2	−1.5
Sweden	1 532 032	5.1	1 515 960	5.5	−1.0
Switzerland	1 441 737	4.8	1 458 229	5.3	1.1
Turkey	242 253	0.8	239 400	0.9	−1.2
United Kingdom	3 015 443	10.1	2 712 231	9.8	−10.1
Other OECD-Europe	..	..	..	..	..
Total Europe	18 391 312	61.8	17 943 742	64.6	−2.4
Canada	378 723	1.3	297 992	1.1	−21.3
United States	4 444 619	14.9	3 179 799	11.5	−28.5
Total North America	4 823 342	16.2	3 477 791	12.5	−27.9
Australia	209 208	0.7	164 855	0.6	−21.2
New Zealand	32 331	0.1	26 218	0.1	−18.9
Japan	1 321 676	4.4	1 111 909	4.0	−15.9
Total Australasia and Japan	1 563 215	5.3	1 302 982	4.7	−16.6
Total OECD Countries	**24 777 869**	**83.2**	**22 724 515**	**81.8**	**−8.3**
Yugoslavia	525 638	1.8	504 533	1.8	−4.0
Other European countries	1 485 272	5.0	1 724 788	6.2	16.1
Bulgaria	58 330	0.2	63 357	0.2	8.6
Czechoslovakia	236 193	0.8	309 456	1.1	31.0
Hungary	257 990	0.9	301 623	1.1	16.9
Poland	495 669	1.7	558 425	2.0	12.7
Rumania	88 794	0.3	94 009	0.3	5.9
USSR	348 296	1.2	397 918	1.4	14.2
Latin America	336 544	1.1	311 408	1.1	−7.5
Argentina	67 214	0.2	65 703	0.2	−2.2
Brazil	165 972	0.6	154 819	0.6	−6.7
Chile	21 999	0.1	22 275	0.1	1.3
Mexico	81 359	0.3	68 611	0.2	−15.7
Asia-Oceania	323 528	1.1	306 968	1.1	−5.1
Israel	323 528	1.1	306 968	1.1	−5.1
Africa	109 385	0.4	103 223	0.4	−5.6
South Africa	109 385	0.4	103 223	0.4	−5.6
Origin country undetermined	2 207 995	7.4	2 092 797	7.5	−5.2
Total non-OECD Countries	**4 988 362**	**16.8**	**5 043 717**	**18.2**	**1.1**
TOTAL	**29 766 231**	**100.0**	**27 768 232**	**100.0**	**−6.7**

1. The data relate to the territory of the Federal Republic of Germany prior to 3rd October 1990; as of 1990, tourists from the former German Democratic Republic will be regarded as domestic tourists.
2. Nights spent in hotels (including "bed and breakfast"), boarding houses and inns.

GERMANY[1]

NIGHTS SPENT BY FOREIGN TOURISTS IN REGISTERED TOURIST ACCOMMODATION[2]

(by country of residence)

	1990	Relative share	1991	Relative share	% Variation over 1990
Austria	1 174 296	3.4	1 187 296	3.6	1.1
Belgium	1 257 479	3.6	1 373 545	4.1	9.2
Denmark	1 433 058	4.1	1 410 580	4.2	−1.6
Finland	382 995	1.1	320 091	1.0	−16.4
France	1 752 874	5.0	1 671 571	5.0	−4.6
Germany	..	..	..	..	..
Greece	316 083	0.9	280 807	0.8	−11.2
Iceland	63 323	0.2	51 488	0.2	−18.7
Ireland	97 366	0.3	104 535	0.3	7.4
Italy	1 782 457	5.1	1 833 624	5.5	2.9
Luxembourg	223 486	0.6	229 273	0.7	2.6
Netherlands	5 760 363	16.5	6 025 416	18.1	4.6
Norway	526 147	1.5	447 926	1.3	−14.9
Portugal	132 796	0.4	148 747	0.4	12.0
Spain	665 608	1.9	664 389	2.0	−0.2
Sweden	1 626 785	4.7	1 674 275	5.0	2.9
Switzerland	1 575 520	4.5	1 595 294	4.8	1.3
Turkey	265 330	0.8	263 941	0.8	−0.5
United Kingdom	3 263 549	9.4	2 982 207	9.0	−8.6
Other OECD-Europe	..	..	..	..	..
Total Europe	22 299 515	64.0	22 265 005	67.0	−0.2
Canada	428 709	1.2	335 562	1.0	−21.7
United States	4 714 849	13.5	3 380 246	10.2	−28.3
Total North America	5 143 558	14.8	3 715 808	11.2	−27.8
Australia	271 047	0.8	213 422	0.6	−21.3
New Zealand	41 748	0.1	32 914	0.1	−21.2
Japan	1 381 195	4.0	1 157 976	3.5	−16.2
Total Australasia and Japan	1 693 990	4.9	1 404 312	4.2	−17.1
Total OECD Countries	**29 137 063**	**83.6**	**27 385 125**	**82.4**	**−6.0**
Yugoslavia	562 697	1.6	541 136	1.6	−3.8
Other European countries	1 892 265	5.4	2 225 500	6.7	17.6
Bulgaria	63 835	0.2	69 189	0.2	8.4
Czechoslovakia	271 044	0.8	359 079	1.1	32.5
Hungary	295 330	0.8	340 927	1.0	15.4
Poland	755 832	2.2	851 536	2.6	12.7
Rumania	96 911	0.3	104 993	0.3	8.3
USSR	409 313	1.2	499 776	1.5	22.1
Latin America	374 108	1.1	350 386	1.1	−6.3
Argentina	73 928	0.2	74 826	0.2	1.2
Brazil	186 654	0.5	174 028	0.5	−6.8
Chile	25 450	0.1	26 872	0.1	5.6
Mexico	88 076	0.3	74 660	0.2	−15.2
Asia-Oceania	355 016	1.0	334 273	1.0	−5.8
Israel	355 016	1.0	334 273	1.0	−5.8
Africa	123 631	0.4	114 587	0.3	−7.3
South Africa	123 631	0.4	114 587	0.3	−7.3
Origin country undetermined	2 396 759	6.9	2 295 103	6.9	−4.2
Total non-OECD Countries	**5 704 476**	**16.4**	**5 860 985**	**17.6**	**2.7**
TOTAL	**34 841 539**	**100.0**	**33 246 110**	**100.0**	**−4.6**

1. The data relate to the territory of the Federal Republic of Germany prior to 3rd October 1990; as of 1990, tourists from the former German Democratic Republic will be regarded as domestic tourists.
2. Nights spent in hotels and similar establishments, holiday villages, sanatoria, and recreation and holiday homes.

GREECE

ARRIVALS OF FOREIGN TOURISTS AT FRONTIERS[1]
(by country of nationality)

	1990	Relative share	1991	Relative share	% Variation over 1990
Austria	286 525	3.2	288 317	3.6	0.6
Belgium[2]	201 807	2.3	179 754	2.2	–10.9
Denmark	281 598	3.2	211 883	2.6	–24.8
Finland	238 020	2.7	216 131	2.7	–9.2
France	565 407	6.4	470 945	5.9	–16.7
Germany	1 922 029	21.7	1 561 113	19.5	–18.8
Greece	..	..	..	..	..
Iceland[3]	..	..	..	..	..
Ireland	67 835	0.8	44 085	0.5	–35.0
Italy	620 766	7.0	517 145	6.4	–16.7
Luxembourg[2]	..	..	..	..	..
Netherlands	495 699	5.6	450 065	5.6	–9.2
Norway	91 755	1.0	68 396	0.9	–25.5
Portugal	27 408	0.3	16 586	0.2	–39.5
Spain	127 516	1.4	104 655	1.3	–17.9
Sweden	259 669	2.9	261 946	3.3	0.9
Switzerland	151 695	1.7	126 241	1.6	–16.8
Turkey	43 406	0.5	53 531	0.7	23.3
United Kingdom	1 647 361	18.6	1 674 875	20.9	1.7
Other OECD-Europe	..	..	..	..	..
Total Europe	7 028 496	79.2	6 245 668	77.9	–11.1
Canada	74 218	0.8	47 101	0.6	–36.5
United States	273 849	3.1	180 429	2.3	–34.1
Total North America	348 067	3.9	227 530	2.8	–34.6
Australia	101 142	1.1	66 566	0.8	–34.2
New Zealand[4]	12 948	0.1	8 489	0.1	–34.4
Japan	107 694	1.2	57 902	0.7	–46.2
Total Australasia and Japan	221 784	2.5	132 957	1.7	–40.1
Total OECD Countries	**7 598 347**	**85.6**	**6 606 155**	**82.4**	**–13.1**
Yugoslavia	580 733	6.5	518 644	6.5	–10.7
Other European countries[3]	445 164	5.0	703 672	8.8	58.1
Bulgaria	133 767	1.5	157 910	2.0	18.0
Czechoslovakia	28 766	0.3	130 129	1.6	352.4
Hungary	60 692	0.7	107 685	1.3	77.4
Poland	61 073	0.7	47 535	0.6	–22.2
Rumania	11 258	0.1	17 919	0.2	59.2
USSR	40 956	0.5	78 194	1.0	90.9
Argentina	4 506	0.1	5 092	0.1	13.0
Brazil	11 313	0.1	8 523	0.1	–24.7
Mexico	6 264	0.1	3 642	0.0	–41.9
Asia-Oceania[4]	165 321	1.9	106 852	1.3	–35.4
Iran	4 451	0.1	4 226	0.1	–5.1
Israel	32 772	0.4	36 989	0.5	12.9
Lebanon	23 836	0.3	15 637	0.2	–34.4
Africa	83 745	0.9	83 547	1.0	–0.2
Egypt	23 056	0.3	20 020	0.2	–13.2
South Africa	19 982	0.2	13 527	0.2	–32.3
Total non-OECD Countries	**1 274 963**	**14.4**	**1 412 715**	**17.6**	**10.8**
TOTAL	**8 873 310**	**100.0**	**8 018 870**	**100.0**	**–9.6**

1. Excluding Greek nationals residing abroad and cruise passengers.
2. Belgium includes Luxembourg.
3. ''Other European countries'' includes Iceland.
4. ''Asia-Oceania'' includes New Zealand.

ICELAND

ARRIVALS OF FOREIGN TOURISTS AT FRONTIERS [1]

(by country of nationality)

	1990	Relative share	1991	Relative share	% Variation over 1990
Austria	3 614	2.6	4 036	2.9	11.7
Belgium	941	0.7	1 060	0.8	12.6
Denmark	15 176	10.9	13 777	9.8	−9.2
Finland	4 769	3.4	4 079	2.9	−14.5
France	10 021	7.2	10 071	7.2	0.5
Germany	20 638	14.9	22 477	16.0	8.9
Greece	111	0.1	183	0.1	64.9
Iceland	..	..	..	..	
Ireland	570	0.4	491	0.3	−13.9
Italy	3 614	2.6	4 808	3.4	33.0
Luxembourg	314	0.2	508	0.4	61.8
Netherlands	2 994	2.2	2 952	2.1	−1.4
Norway	10 256	7.4	10 391	7.4	1.3
Portugal	204	0.1	248	0.2	21.6
Spain	1 103	0.8	1 173	0.8	6.3
Sweden	18 612	13.4	16 295	11.6	−12.4
Switzerland	5 651	4.1	7 003	5.0	23.9
Turkey	90	0.1	82	0.1	−8.9
United Kingdom	13 745	9.9	14 662	10.4	6.7
Other OECD-Europe	..	..	..	..	
Total Europe	112 423	81.0	114 296	81.4	1.7
Canada	1 140	0.8	943	0.7	−17.3
United States	22 616	16.3	22 506	16.0	−0.5
Total North America	23 756	17.1	23 449	16.7	−1.3
Australia	502	0.4	465	0.3	−7.4
New Zealand	183	0.1	144	0.1	−21.3
Japan	1 164	0.8	1 254	0.9	7.7
Total Australasia and Japan	1 849	1.3	1 863	1.3	0.8
Total OECD Countries	**138 028**	**99.4**	**139 608**	**99.5**	**1.1**
Yugoslavia	227	0.2	339	0.2	49.3
Other European countries	108	0.1	39	0.0	−63.9
Bulgaria	87	0.1	31	0.0	−64.4
Czechoslovakia	264	0.2	253	0.2	−4.2
Hungary	267	0.2	136	0.1	−49.1
Poland	441	0.3	645	0.5	46.3
Rumania	26	0.0	16	0.0	−38.5
USSR	452	0.3	420	0.3	−7.1
Latin America	170	0.1	131	0.1	−22.9
Argentina	30	0.0	45	0.0	50.0
Brazil	58	0.0	89	0.1	53.4
Chile	53	0.0	46	0.0	−13.2
Colombia	27	0.0	28	0.0	3.7
Mexico	28	0.0	94	0.1	235.7
Venezuela	14	0.0	17	0.0	21.4
Asia-Oceania	134	0.1	108	0.1	−19.4
China	122	0.1	127	0.1	4.1
Hong Kong	7	0.0	14	0.0	100.0
India	70	0.1	83	0.1	18.6
Iran	32	0.0	17	0.0	−46.9
Israel	177	0.1	167	0.1	−5.6
Republic of Korea	42	0.0	75	0.1	78.6
Lebanon	11	0.0	19	0.0	72.7
Malaysia	22	0.0	27	0.0	22.7
Pakistan	14	0.0	12	0.0	−14.3
Philippines	154	0.1	123	0.1	−20.1
Saudi Arabia	4	0.0	5	0.0	25.0
Singapore	23	0.0	26	0.0	13.0
Taiwan	131	0.1	184	0.1	40.5
Thailand	104	0.1	143	0.1	37.5
Africa	168	0.1	125	0.1	−25.6
Algeria	26	0.0	26	0.0	0.0
Egypt	20	0.0	25	0.0	25.0
Morocco	45	0.0	12	0.0	−73.3
South Africa	108	0.1	174	0.1	61.1
Origin country undetermined	24	0.0	29	0.0	20.8
Total non-OECD Countries	**831**	**0.6**	**771**	**0.5**	**−7.2**
TOTAL	**138 859**	**100.0**	**140 379**	**100.0**	**1.1**

1. Excluding shore excursionists.

IRELAND

ARRIVALS OF FOREIGN VISITORS AT FRONTIERS[1]

(by country of residence)

	1990	Relative share	1991	Relative share	% Variation over 1990
Austria[4]	..	..	..	..	..
Belgium[4]	..	..	..	..	..
Denmark[4]	..	..	..	..	..
Finland[4]	..	..	..	..	..
France	196 000	6.4	219 000	7.3	11.7
Germany	172 000	5.6	194 000	6.5	12.8
Greece[4]	..	..	..	..	..
Iceland[4]	..	..	..	..	..
Ireland	..	..	..	..	..
Italy[4]	..	..	..	..	..
Luxembourg[4]	..	..	..	..	..
Netherlands[4]	..	..	..	..	..
Norway[4]	..	..	..	..	..
Portugal[4]	..	..	..	..	..
Spain[4]	..	..	..	..	..
Sweden[4]	..	..	..	..	..
Switzerland[4]	..	..	..	..	..
Turkey[4]	..	..	..	..	..
United Kingdom	1 786 000	58.2	1 729 000	57.7	-3.2
Other OECD-Europe[4]	362 000	11.8	411 000	13.7	13.5
Total Europe	2 516 000	82.0	2 553 000	85.2	1.5
Canada	38 000	1.2	30 000	1.0	-21.1
United States	396 000	12.9	313 000	10.4	-21.0
Total North America	434 000	14.1	343 000	11.4	-21.0
Australia[2]	66 000	2.2	50 000	1.7	-24.2
New Zealand[2]	..	..	..	..	..
Japan[3]	..	..	..	..	..
Total Australasia and Japan	66 000	2.2	50 000	1.7	-24.2
Total OECD Countries	**3 016 000**	**98.3**	**2 946 000**	**98.3**	**-2.3**
Yugoslavia	..		..		..
Origin country unspecified[3]	52 000	1.7	52 000	1.7	0.0
Total non-OECD Countries	**52 000**	**1.7**	**52 000**	**1.7**	**0.0**
TOTAL	**3 068 000**	**100.0**	**2 998 000**	**100.0**	**-2.3**

1. Visitors arrivals on overseas routes only.
2. Australia includes New Zealand.
3. Origin country unspecified includes Japan.
4. Included in Other OECD-Europe.

IRELAND

ARRIVALS OF FOREIGN TOURISTS AT HOTELS

(by country of residence)

	1990	Relative share	1991	Relative share	% Variation over 1990
Austria	..	..	..	..	..
Belgium	20 000	1.2	17 000	1.0	−15.0
Denmark	..	..	..	..	..
Finland	..	..	..	..	..
France	130 000	7.9	137 000	8.2	5.4
Germany	96 000	5.8	110 000	6.6	14.6
Greece	..	..	..	..	..
Iceland	..	..	..	..	..
Ireland	..	..	..	..	..
Italy	49 000	3.0	79 000	4.7	61.2
Luxembourg	..	..	..	..	..
Netherlands	40 000	2.4	50 000	3.0	25.0
Norway	..	..	..	..	..
Portugal	..	..	..	..	..
Spain	..	..	..	..	..
Sweden	..	..	..	..	..
Switzerland	32 000	1.9	29 000	1.7	−9.4
Turkey	..	..	..	..	..
United Kingdom [1]	713 000	43.2	766 000	45.8	7.4
Other OECD-Europe	..	..	..	..	..
Total Europe	1 080 000	65.4	1 188 000	71.0	10.0
Canada	21 000	1.3	29 000	1.7	38.1
United States	374 000	22.6	285 000	17.0	−23.8
Total North America	395 000	23.9	314 000	18.8	−20.5
Australia	52 000	3.1	41 000	2.5	−21.2
New Zealand	..	..	..	..	..
Japan	..	..	..	..	..
Total Australasia and Japan	52 000	3.1	41 000	2.5	−21.2
Total OECD Countries	**1 527 000**	**92.4**	**1 543 000**	**92.2**	**1.0**
Yugoslavia	..	..	..	..	..
Origin country undetermined	125 000	7.6	130 000	7.8	4.0
Total non-OECD Countries	**125 000**	**7.6**	**130 000**	**7.8**	**4.0**
TOTAL	**1 652 000**	**100.0**	**1 673 000**	**100.0**	**1.3**

1. Excludes Northern Ireland.

IRELAND

ARRIVALS OF FOREIGN TOURISTS IN TOURIST ACCOMMODATION

(by country of residence)

	1990	Relative share	1991	Relative share	% Variation over 1990
Austria	..	..	..	..	..
Belgium	37 000	1.2	33 000	1.1	–10.8
Denmark	16 000	0.5	19 000	0.6	18.8
Finland	..	..	..	..	..
France	198 000	6.4	220 000	7.4	11.1
Germany	178 000	5.7	203 000	6.8	14.0
Greece	..	..	..	..	..
Iceland	..	..	..	..	..
Ireland	..	..	..	..	..
Italy	73 000	2.4	96 000	3.2	31.5
Luxembourg	..	..	..	..	..
Netherlands	72 000	2.3	83 000	2.8	15.3
Norway	26 000	0.8	27 000	0.9	3.8
Portugal	..	..	..	..	..
Spain	54 000	1.7	62 000	2.1	14.8
Sweden	..	..	..	..	..
Switzerland	41 000	1.3	46 000	1.5	12.2
Turkey	..	..	..	..	..
United Kingdom [1]	1 785 000	57.7	1 710 000	57.2	–4.2
Other OECD-Europe	..	..	..	..	..
Total Europe	2 480 000	80.1	2 499 000	83.7	0.8
Canada	41 000	1.3	35 000	1.2	–14.6
United States	402 000	13.0	321 000	10.7	–20.1
Total North America	443 000	14.3	356 000	11.9	–19.6
Australia	..	..	..	..	..
New Zealand [2]	69 000	2.2	54 000	1.8	–21.7
Japan	..	..	..	..	..
Total Australasia and Japan	69 000	2.2	54 000	1.8	–21.7
Total OECD Countries	**2 992 000**	**96.6**	**2 909 000**	**97.4**	**–2.8**
Yugoslavia	..	..	..	..	..
Origin country undetermined	104 000	3.4	78 000	2.6	–25.0
Total non-OECD Countries	**104 000**	**3.4**	**78 000**	**2.6**	**–25.0**
TOTAL	**3 096 000**	**100.0**	**2 987 000**	**100.0**	**–3.5**

1. Excludes Northern Ireland.
2. New Zealand includes all others countries not specified.

IRELAND

NIGHTS SPENT BY FOREIGN TOURISTS IN HOTELS

(by country of residence)

	1990	Part relative	1991	Part relative	Variation en % par rapport à 1990
Autriche	..	..	..	..	..
Belgique	91 000	1.1	85 000	0.9	−6.6
Danemark	..	..	..	..	..
Finlande	..	..	..	..	..
France	943 000	11.4	892 000	9.7	−5.4
Allemagne	795 000	9.6	817 000	8.9	2.8
Grèce	..	..	..	..	..
Islande	..	..	..	..	..
Irlande					
Italie	299 000	3.6	571 000	6.2	91.0
Luxembourg					
Pays-Bas	218 000	2.6	302 000	3.3	38.5
Norvège	..	..	..	..	..
Portugal	..	..	..	..	..
Espagne	..	..	..	..	..
Suède	..	..	..	..	..
Suisse	187 000	2.3	189 000	2.0	1.1
Turquie					
United Kingdom [1]	2 642 000	31.9	3 562 000	38.6	34.8
Autres OCDE-Europe	..	..	..	..	..
Total Europe	5 175 000	62.5	6 418 000	69.6	24.0
Canada	108 000	1.3	164 000	1.8	51.9
États-Unis	2 040 000	24.6	1 793 000	19.4	−12.1
Total Amérique du Nord	2 148 000	26.0	1 957 000	21.2	−8.9
Australie	302 000	3.6	253 000	2.7	−16.2
Nouvelle-Zélande	..	..	..	..	..
Japon	..	..	..	..	..
Total Australasie et Japon	302 000	3.6	253 000	2.7	−16.2
Total Pays OCDE	**7 625 000**	**92.1**	**8 628 000**	**93.5**	**13.2**
Yougoslavie	..	..	..	..	..
Pays d'origine indéterminé	652 000	7.9	595 000	6.5	−8.7
Total Pays non-OCDE	**652 000**	**7.9**	**595 000**	**6.5**	**−8.7**
TOTAL	**8 277 000**	**100.0**	**9 223 000**	**100.0**	**11.4**

1. Excludes Northern Ireland.

IRELAND

NIGHTS SPENT BY FOREIGN TOURISTS IN TOURIST ACCOMMODATION

(by country of residence)

	1990	Part relative	1991	Part relative	Variation en % par rapport à 1990
Autriche					
Belgique	696 000	2.1	335 280	1.0	−51.8
Danemark	..	..	..	..	..
Finlande	..	..	..	..	..
France	3 120 000	9.3	3 029 000	9.1	−2.9
Allemagne	2 777 000	8.2	3 218 000	9.7	15.9
Grèce	..	..	..	..	..
Islande	..	..	..	..	..
Irlande					
Italie	1 040 000	3.1	1 309 440	3.9	25.9
Luxembourg					
Pays-Bas	798 000	2.4	984 380	3.0	23.4
Norvège	..	..	..	..	..
Portugal					
Espagne	..	..	..	..	..
Suède	..	..	..	..	..
Suisse	456 000	1.4	628 820	1.9	37.9
Turquie					
United Kingdom [1]	15 583 000	46.3	14 723 000	44.2	−5.5
Autres OCDE-Europe	2 526 000	7.5	2 908 080	8.7	15.1
Total Europe	26 996 000	80.1	27 136 000	81.5	0.5
Canada	391 000	1.2	436 450	1.3	11.6
États-Unis	4 434 000	13.2	3 874 000	11.6	−12.6
Total Amérique du Nord	4 825 000	14.3	4 310 450	12.9	−10.7
Australie					
New Zealand [2]	653 000	1.9	872 640	2.6	33.6
Japon					
Total Australasie et Japon	653 000	1.9	872 640	2.6	33.6
Total Pays OCDE	**32 474 000**	**96.4**	**32 319 090**	**97.1**	**−0.5**
Yougoslavie					
Pays d'origine indéterminé	1 210 000	3.6	966 910	2.9	−20.1
Total Pays non-OCDE	**1 210 000**	**3.6**	**966 910**	**2.9**	**−20.1**
TOTAL	**33 684 000**	**100.0**	**33 286 000**	**100.0**	**−1.2**

1. Excludes Northern Ireland.
2. New Zealand includes all other countries not specified.

ITALY

ARRIVALS OF FOREIGN VISITORS AT FRONTIERS[1]
(by country of nationality)

	1990	Relative share	1991	Relative share	% Variation over 1990
Austria	6 056 982	10.0	5 540 654	10.8	−8.5
Belgium	1 173 345	1.9	953 229	1.9	−18.8
Denmark	623 414	1.0	421 444	0.8	−32.4
Finland	313 204	0.5	220 537	0.4	−29.6
France	9 219 317	15.3	9 114 554	17.8	−1.1
Germany	10 676 781	17.7	9 205 658	17.9	−13.8
Greece	519 016	0.9	521 864	1.0	0.5
Iceland[2]	..	..	..	..	..
Ireland	172 656	0.3	136 410	0.3	−21.0
Italy	..	..	..	..	..
Luxembourg	129 728	0.2	135 443	0.3	4.4
Netherlands	2 122 099	3.5	1 533 360	3.0	−27.7
Norway	242 641	0.4	215 136	0.4	−11.3
Portugal	205 152	0.3	179 060	0.3	−12.7
Spain	679 487	1.1	601 966	1.2	−11.4
Sweden	517 249	0.9	469 974	0.9	−9.1
Switzerland	10 331 451	17.1	10 228 678	19.9	−1.0
Turkey	195 146	0.3	169 639	0.3	−13.1
United Kingdom	2 047 838	3.4	1 711 634	3.3	−16.4
Other OECD-Europe	..	..	..	..	..
Total Europe	45 225 506	75.0	41 359 240	80.6	−8.5
Canada	475 191	0.8	350 056	0.7	−26.3
United States	1 420 888	2.4	1 137 441	2.2	−19.9
Total North America	1 896 079	3.1	1 487 497	2.9	−21.5
Australia	279 924	0.5	199 877	0.4	−28.6
New Zealand	..	..	..	..	..
Japan	636 961	1.1	559 665	1.1	−12.1
Total Australasia and Japan	916 885	1.5	759 542	1.5	−17.2
Total OECD Countries	**48 038 470**	**79.7**	**43 606 279**	**85.0**	**−9.2**
Yugoslavia	8 942 065	14.8	4 367 181	8.5	−51.2
Other European countries[2]	1 767 130	2.9	1 962 826	3.8	11.1
USSR	83 709	0.1	73 675	0.1	−12.0
Latin America	616 785	1.0	578 389	1.1	−6.2
Argentina	142 699	0.2	137 193	0.3	−3.9
Brazil	154 373	0.3	144 218	0.3	−6.6
Mexico	95 894	0.2	74 152	0.1	−22.7
Venezuela	80 935	0.1	79 102	0.2	−2.3
Asia-Oceania	169 644	0.3	150 558	0.3	−11.3
Israel	79 952	0.1	69 956	0.1	−12.5
Africa	93 421	0.2	90 599	0.2	−3.0
Egypt	44 967	0.1	43 333	0.1	−3.6
South Africa	48 454	0.1	47 266	0.1	−2.5
Origin country undetermined	668 408	1.1	561 359	1.1	−16.0
Total non-OECD Countries	**12 257 453**	**20.3**	**7 710 912**	**15.0**	**−37.1**
TOTAL	**60 295 923**	**100.0**	**51 317 191**	**100.0**	**−14.9**

1. Includes about 53% of excursionists.
2. "Other European countries" includes Iceland.

ITALY

ARRIVALS OF FOREIGN TOURISTS AT HOTELS
(by country of nationality)

	1989	Relative share	1990	Relative share	% Variation over 1989
Austria	832 178	4.7	850 627	4.7	2.2
Belgium	408 033	2.3	403 802	2.3	−1.0
Denmark	130 233	0.7	128 651	0.7	−1.2
Finland	116 398	0.7	107 534	0.6	−7.6
France	1 760 124	10.0	1 727 012	9.6	−1.9
Germany	4 879 953	27.6	4 714 956	26.3	−3.4
Greece	206 741	1.2	212 743	1.2	2.9
Iceland [1]	..	..	..	..	..
Ireland	52 630	0.3	64 188	0.4	22.0
Italy	..	..	..	..	..
Luxembourg	32 301	0.2	28 710	0.2	−11.1
Netherlands	334 176	1.9	344 882	1.9	3.2
Norway	68 517	0.4	74 408	0.4	8.6
Portugal	79 678	0.5	90 628	0.5	13.7
Spain	830 489	4.7	848 208	4.7	2.1
Sweden	240 141	1.4	228 805	1.3	−4.7
Switzerland	1 056 180	6.0	969 123	5.4	−8.2
Turkey	72 977	0.4	89 861	0.5	23.1
United Kingdom	1 264 964	7.2	1 227 388	6.8	−3.0
Other OECD-Europe	..	..	..	..	..
Total Europe	12 365 713	69.9	12 111 526	67.6	−2.1
Canada	243 361	1.4	252 987	1.4	4.0
United States	1 941 418	11.0	2 044 360	11.4	5.3
Total North America	2 184 779	12.4	2 297 347	12.8	5.2
Australia	248 932	1.4	260 889	1.5	4.8
New Zealand	..	..	..	..	..
Japan	707 377	4.0	758 729	4.2	7.3
Total Australasia and Japan	956 309	5.4	1 019 618	5.7	6.6
Total OECD Countries	**15 506 801**	**87.7**	**15 428 491**	**86.1**	**−0.5**
Yugoslavia	193 036	1.1	290 590	1.6	50.5
Other European countries [1]	377 072	2.1	502 999	2.8	33.4
USSR	94 908	0.5	94 731	0.5	−0.2
Latin America	526 467	3.0	583 713	3.3	10.9
Argentina	101 183	0.6	116 975	0.7	15.6
Brazil	198 185	1.1	220 140	1.2	11.1
Mexico	93 530	0.5	98 133	0.5	4.9
Venezuela	28 022	0.2	31 360	0.2	11.9
Asia-Oceania	218 355	1.2	204 195	1.1	−6.5
Israel	137 439	0.8	124 941	0.7	−9.1
Africa	61 411	0.3	67 371	0.4	9.7
Egypt	22 305	0.1	21 752	0.1	−2.5
South Africa	39 126	0.2	45 617	0.3	16.6
Origin country undetermined	799 449	4.5	847 061	4.7	6.0
Total non-OECD Countries	**2 175 790**	**12.3**	**2 495 929**	**13.9**	**14.7**
TOTAL	**17 682 591**	**100.0**	**17 924 420**	**100.0**	**1.4**

1. "Other European countries" includes Iceland.

ITALY

ARRIVALS OF FOREIGN TOURISTS AT REGISTERED TOURIST ACCOMMODATION

(by country of nationality)

	1989	Relative share	1990	Relative share	% Variation over 1989
Austria	988 551	4.8	1 038 425	5.0	5.0
Belgium	478 324	2.3	469 665	2.3	−1.8
Denmark	201 556	1.0	189 769	0.9	−5.8
Finland	132 516	0.6	120 974	0.6	−8.7
France	2 033 431	9.9	1 988 570	9.5	−2.2
Germany	6 120 000	29.7	5 926 824	28.4	−3.2
Greece	213 171	1.0	219 726	1.1	3.1
Iceland [1]	..	..	..	..	..
Ireland	60 910	0.3	74 384	0.4	22.1
Italy	..	..	..	..	..
Luxembourg	35 887	0.2	32 594	0.2	−9.2
Netherlands	560 578	2.7	552 572	2.6	−1.4
Norway	83 198	0.4	89 048	0.4	7.0
Portugal	92 546	0.4	104 402	0.5	12.8
Spain	898 275	4.4	921 142	4.4	2.5
Sweden	295 935	1.4	276 264	1.3	−6.6
Switzerland	1 198 913	5.8	1 099 527	5.3	−8.3
Turkey	79 236	0.4	97 635	0.5	23.2
United Kingdom	1 427 626	6.9	1 382 807	6.6	−3.1
Other OECD-Europe	..	..	..	..	..
Total Europe	14 900 653	72.4	14 584 328	69.9	−2.1
Canada	269 871	1.3	280 716	1.3	4.0
United States	2 015 103	9.8	2 124 345	10.2	5.4
Total North America	2 284 974	11.1	2 405 061	11.5	5.3
Australia	297 191	1.4	312 315	1.5	5.1
New Zealand	..	..	..	..	..
Japan	718 881	3.5	772 608	3.7	7.5
Total Australasia and Japan	1 016 072	4.9	1 084 923	5.2	6.8
Total OECD Countries	**18 201 699**	**88.4**	**18 074 312**	**86.7**	**−0.7**
Yugoslavia	203 492	1.0	304 948	1.5	49.9
Other European countries [1]	474 834	2.3	665 081	3.2	40.1
USSR	96 595	0.5	97 406	0.5	0.8
Latin America	561 682	2.7	616 344	3.0	9.7
Argentina	110 357	0.5	127 458	0.6	15.5
Brazil	210 868	1.0	236 693	1.1	12.2
Mexico	98 896	0.5	103 936	0.5	5.1
Venezuela	29 738	0.1	32 860	0.2	10.5
Asia-Oceania	228 982	1.1	215 170	1.0	−6.0
Israel	144 877	0.7	131 649	0.6	−9.1
Africa	68 743	0.3	75 986	0.4	10.5
Egypt	23 549	0.1	23 686	0.1	0.6
South Africa	45 194	0.2	52 300	0.3	15.7
Origin country undetermined	845 130	4.1	901 124	4.3	6.6
Total non-OECD Countries	**2 382 863**	**11.6**	**2 778 653**	**13.3**	**16.6**
TOTAL	**20 584 562**	**100.0**	**20 852 965**	**100.0**	**1.3**

1. "Other European countries" includes Iceland.

ITALY

NIGHTS SPENT BY FOREIGN TOURISTS IN HOTELS

(by country of nationality)

	1989	Relative share	1990	Relative share	% Variation over 1989
Austria	3 393 894	5.0	3 397 075	5.1	0.1
Belgium	1 919 674	2.8	1 802 579	2.7	−6.1
Denmark	588 382	0.9	557 274	0.8	−5.3
Finland	598 030	0.9	545 843	0.8	−8.7
France	5 133 599	7.5	5 021 561	7.6	−2.2
Germany	25 983 133	38.1	23 917 334	36.2	−8.0
Greece	463 657	0.7	479 734	0.7	3.5
Iceland [1]	..	..	..	..	..
Ireland	197 635	0.3	212 288	0.3	7.4
Italy	..	..	..	..	..
Luxembourg	216 456	0.3	180 353	0.3	−16.7
Netherlands	1 379 476	2.0	1 359 948	2.1	−1.4
Norway	254 640	0.4	286 121	0.4	12.4
Portugal	202 009	0.3	236 488	0.4	17.1
Spain	1 712 432	2.5	1 849 029	2.8	8.0
Sweden	965 097	1.4	888 336	1.3	−8.0
Switzerland	4 632 885	6.8	4 113 049	6.2	−11.2
Turkey	197 874	0.3	264 527	0.4	33.7
United Kingdom	5 577 226	8.2	5 128 645	7.8	−8.0
Other OECD-Europe	..	..	..	..	..
Total Europe	53 416 099	78.4	50 240 184	76.1	−5.9
Canada	629 007	0.9	633 774	1.0	0.8
United States	4 848 656	7.1	4 990 826	7.6	2.9
Total North America	5 477 663	8.0	5 624 600	8.5	2.7
Australia	563 393	0.8	592 012	0.9	5.1
New Zealand	..	..	..	..	..
Japan	1 439 456	2.1	1 571 358	2.4	9.2
Total Australasia and Japan	2 002 849	2.9	2 163 370	3.3	8.0
Total OECD Countries	**60 896 611**	**89.4**	**58 028 154**	**87.9**	**−4.7**
Yugoslavia	524 693	0.8	804 468	1.2	53.3
Other European countries [1]	1 941 772	2.8	1 973 870	3.0	1.7
USSR	771 261	1.1	498 451	0.8	−35.4
Latin America	1 471 890	2.2	1 737 936	2.6	18.1
Argentina	285 743	0.4	342 544	0.5	19.9
Brazil	561 256	0.8	666 024	1.0	18.7
Mexico	214 801	0.3	235 845	0.4	9.8
Venezuela	90 557	0.1	100 037	0.2	10.5
Asia-Oceania	580 031	0.9	561 399	0.9	−3.2
Israel	304 139	0.4	280 265	0.4	−7.8
Africa	209 706	0.3	233 782	0.4	11.5
Egypt	97 245	0.1	105 737	0.2	8.7
South Africa	112 461	0.2	128 945	0.2	14.7
Origin country undetermined	2 508 366	3.7	2 672 521	4.0	6.5
Total non-OECD Countries	**7 236 458**	**10.6**	**7 983 976**	**12.1**	**10.3**
TOTAL	**68 133 069**	**100.0**	**66 012 130**	**100.0**	**−3.1**

1. "Other European countries" includes Iceland.

ITALY

NIGHTS SPENT BY FOREIGN TOURISTS IN REGISTERED TOURIST ACCOMMODATION

(by country of nationality)

	1989	Relative share	1990	Relative share	% Variation over 1989
Austria	4 445 976	5.1	4 725 296	5.6	6.3
Belgium	2 513 411	2.9	2 358 769	2.8	−6.2
Denmark	1 108 873	1.3	1 011 955	1.2	−8.7
Finland	694 126	0.8	612 209	0.7	−11.8
France	6 307 542	7.3	6 153 510	7.3	−2.4
Germany	35 104 255	40.4	32 775 705	38.7	−6.6
Greece	492 260	0.6	510 212	0.6	3.6
Iceland [1]	..		..		..
Ireland	227 181	0.3	247 286	0.3	8.8
Italy	..		..		..
Luxembourg	246 666	0.3	210 937	0.2	−14.5
Netherlands	3 228 744	3.7	3 059 868	3.6	−5.2
Norway	348 424	0.4	375 761	0.4	7.8
Portugal	235 945	0.3	275 823	0.3	16.9
Spain	1 913 070	2.2	2 052 122	2.4	7.3
Sweden	1 345 490	1.5	1 209 377	1.4	−10.1
Switzerland	5 706 003	6.6	5 119 153	6.0	−10.3
Turkey	230 652	0.3	306 885	0.4	33.1
United Kingdom	6 497 012	7.5	6 008 759	7.1	−7.5
Other OECD-Europe	..		..		..
Total Europe	70 645 630	81.3	67 013 627	79.1	−5.1
Canada	735 273	0.8	743 264	0.9	1.1
United States	5 170 408	6.0	5 345 414	6.3	3.4
Total North America	5 905 681	6.8	6 088 678	7.2	3.1
Australia	679 640	0.8	707 351	0.8	4.1
New Zealand	..		..		..
Japan	1 478 535	1.7	1 617 994	1.9	9.4
Total Australasia and Japan	2 158 175	2.5	2 325 345	2.7	7.7
Total OECD Countries	**78 709 486**	**90.6**	**75 427 650**	**89.0**	**−4.2**
Yugoslavia	576 732	0.7	872 848	1.0	51.3
Other European countries [1]	2 382 840	2.7	2 650 119	3.1	11.2
USSR	780 728	0.9	511 662	0.6	−34.5
Latin America	1 622 125	1.9	1 916 773	2.3	18.2
Argentina	329 218	0.4	391 086	0.5	18.8
Brazil	617 128	0.7	726 211	0.9	17.7
Mexico	229 886	0.3	253 954	0.3	10.5
Venezuela	108 726	0.1	120 252	0.1	10.6
Asia-Oceania	616 711	0.7	604 039	0.7	−2.1
Israel	323 575	0.4	297 311	0.4	−8.1
Africa	255 718	0.3	272 552	0.3	6.6
Egypt	107 605	0.1	119 380	0.1	10.9
South Africa	148 113	0.2	153 172	0.2	3.4
Origin country undetermined	2 723 560	3.1	2 975 819	3.5	9.3
Total non-OECD Countries	**8 177 686**	**9.4**	**9 292 150**	**11.0**	**13.6**
TOTAL	**86 887 172**	**100.0**	**84 719 800**	**100.0**	**−2.5**

1. "Other European countries" includes Iceland.

JAPAN

ARRIVALS OF FOREIGN VISITORS AT FRONTIERS

(by country of nationality)

	1990	Relative share	1991	Relative share	% Variation over 1990
Austria	8 144	0.3	7 957	0.2	−2.3
Belgium	8 818	0.3	8 013	0.2	−9.1
Denmark	7 788	0.2	7 806	0.2	0.2
Finland	8 941	0.3	9 192	0.3	2.8
France	51 014	1.6	50 119	1.4	−1.8
Germany	65 218	2.0	61 227	1.7	−6.1
Greece	3 763	0.1	3 970	0.1	5.5
Iceland	419	0.0	554	0.0	32.2
Ireland	4 650	0.1	5 221	0.1	12.3
Italy	29 798	0.9	30 199	0.9	1.3
Luxembourg	473	0.0	442	0.0	−6.6
Netherlands	17 573	0.5	18 044	0.5	2.7
Norway	5 088	0.2	5 263	0.1	3.4
Portugal	5 787	0.2	5 539	0.2	−4.3
Spain	16 150	0.5	16 554	0.5	2.5
Sweden	15 648	0.5	14 763	0.4	−5.7
Switzerland	16 472	0.5	15 385	0.4	−6.6
Turkey	4 041	0.1	3 188	0.1	−21.1
United Kingdom	214 413	6.6	219 425	6.2	2.3
Other OECD-Europe	..	..	..	..	..
Total Europe	484 198	15.0	482 861	13.7	−0.3
Canada	63 850	2.0	62 306	1.8	−2.4
United States	554 753	17.1	543 025	15.4	−2.1
Total North America	618 603	19.1	605 331	17.1	−2.1
Australia	56 238	1.7	54 520	1.5	−3.1
New Zealand	16 197	0.5	18 120	0.5	11.9
Japan	..	..	..	..	..
Total Australasia and Japan	72 435	2.2	72 640	2.1	0.3
Total OECD Countries	**1 175 236**	**36.3**	**1 160 832**	**32.8**	**−1.2**
Yugoslavia	1 550	0.0	1 756	0.0	13.3
Other European countries	35 310	1.1	37 949	1.1	7.5
Bulgaria	1 159	0.0	623	0.0	−46.2
Hungary	2 050	0.1	2 038	0.1	−0.6
Poland	3 588	0.1	2 182	0.1	−39.2
Rumania	620	0.0	609	0.0	−1.8
USSR	24 706	0.8	31 828	0.9	28.8
Latin America	92 807	2.9	121 691	3.4	31.1
Argentina	4 963	0.2	5 025	0.1	1.2
Brazil	55 126	1.7	69 503	2.0	26.1
Chile	1 434	0.0	1 954	0.1	36.3
Colombia	2 252	0.1	2 708	0.1	20.2
Mexico	9 744	0.3	9 216	0.3	−5.4
Venezuela	1 259	0.0	1 699	0.0	34.9
Asia-Oceania	1 916 952	59.2	2 197 095	62.2	14.6
China	105 993	3.3	130 487	3.7	23.1
Hong Kong	40 077	1.2	38 526	1.1	−3.9
India	27 878	0.9	26 978	0.8	−3.2
Iran	31 832	1.0	48 901	1.4	53.6
Israel	7 644	0.2	9 010	0.3	17.9
Republic of Korea	740 441	22.9	861 820	24.4	16.4
Lebanon	435	0.0	488	0.0	12.2
Malaysia	57 752	1.8	77 423	2.2	34.1
Pakistan	6 412	0.2	6 575	0.2	2.5
Philippines	108 108	3.3	114 383	3.2	5.8
Singapore	43 015	1.3	42 882	1.2	−0.3
Taiwan	607 721	18.8	658 106	18.6	8.3
Thailand	74 678	2.3	107 770	3.0	44.3
Africa	12 135	0.4	12 915	0.4	6.4
Egypt	1 743	0.1	1 405	0.0	−19.4
South Africa	1 982	0.1	2 433	0.1	22.8
Origin country undetermined	2 762	0.1	2 119	0.1	−23.3
Total non-OECD Countries	**2 061 516**	**63.7**	**2 373 525**	**67.2**	**15.1**
TOTAL	**3 236 752**	**100.0**	**3 534 357**	**100.0**	**9.2**

NETHERLANDS

ARRIVALS OF FOREIGN TOURISTS AT HOTELS

(by country of residence)

	1990	Relative share	1991	Relative share	% Variation over 1990
Austria[3]	..	..	..	..	..
Belgium	160 400	4.1	159 800	4.3	−0.4
Denmark	69 600	1.8	60 800	1.6	−12.6
Finland	35 800	0.9	31 800	0.9	−11.2
France	304 300	7.8	259 800	7.0	−14.6
Germany	731 600	18.7	798 600	21.7	9.2
Greece[3]	..	..	..	..	..
Iceland[3]	..	..	..	..	..
Ireland	24 900	0.6	27 200	0.7	9.2
Italy	299 200	7.7	246 800	6.7	−17.5
Luxembourg	13 300	0.3	13 100	0.4	−1.5
Netherlands					
Norway	46 000	1.2	46 000	1.2	0.0
Portugal[1]	..	..	..	..	..
Spain[1]	151 900	3.9	154 200	4.2	1.5
Sweden	114 700	2.9	113 100	3.1	−1.4
Switzerland	100 300	2.6	95 000	2.6	−5.3
Turkey	..	..	..	..	..
United Kingdom	716 300	18.4	703 400	19.1	−1.8
Other OECD-Europe[3]	169 700	4.3	189 400	5.1	11.6
Total Europe	2 938 000	75.3	2 899 000	78.6	−1.3
Canada	91 800	2.4	63 100	1.7	−31.3
United States	455 600	11.7	366 200	9.9	−19.6
Total North America	547 400	14.0	429 300	11.6	−21.6
Australia[2]	59 200	1.5	39 900	1.1	−32.6
New Zealand[2]	..	..	..	..	..
Japan	95 800	2.5	87 300	2.4	−8.9
Total Australasia and Japan	155 000	4.0	127 200	3.5	−17.9
Total OECD Countries	**3 640 400**	**93.3**	**3 455 500**	**93.7**	**−5.1**
Yugoslavia					
Latin America	64 500	1.7	51 600	1.4	−20.0
Asia-Oceania	151 100	3.9	134 700	3.7	−10.9
Africa	47 100	1.2	44 900	1.2	−4.7
Total non-OECD Countries	**262 700**	**6.7**	**231 200**	**6.3**	**−12.0**
TOTAL	**3 903 100**	**100.0**	**3 686 700**	**100.0**	**−5.5**

1. Spain includes Portugal.
2. Australia includes New Zealand.
3. Other OECD-Europe includes Austria, Greece, Iceland and all non-OECD European countries.

NETHERLANDS

ARRIVALS OF FOREIGN TOURISTS AT REGISTERED TOURIST ACCOMMODATION

(by country of residence)

	1990	Relative share	1991	Relative share	% Variation over 1990
Austria [3]	..	..	..	..	..
Belgium	331 300	5.7	353 000	6.0	6.5
Denmark	109 000	1.9	95 400	1.6	−12.5
Finland	44 700	0.8	40 000	0.7	−10.5
France	408 400	7.0	370 600	6.3	−9.3
Germany	1 824 800	31.5	2 068 700	35.4	13.4
Greece [3]	..	..	..	..	..
Iceland [3]					
Ireland	30 600	0.5	34 600	0.6	13.1
Italy	363 500	6.3	309 300	5.3	−14.9
Luxembourg	14 400	0.2	14 400	0.2	0.0
Netherlands					
Norway	57 000	1.0	56 400	1.0	−1.1
Portugal [1]	..	..	..	..	..
Spain [1]	197 200	3.4	201 000	3.4	1.9
Sweden	144 300	2.5	144 500	2.5	0.1
Switzerland	126 800	2.2	131 800	2.3	3.9
Turkey	..	..	..	..	..
United Kingdom	828 200	14.3	831 800	14.2	0.4
Other OECD-Europe [3]	210 700	3.6	270 500	4.6	28.4
Total Europe	4 690 900	80.9	4 922 000	84.3	4.9
Canada	108 700	1.9	79 500	1.4	−26.9
United States	507 300	8.8	409 600	7.0	−19.3
Total North America	616 000	10.6	489 100	8.4	−20.6
Australia [2]	89 800	1.5	70 900	1.2	−21.0
New Zealand [2]	..	..	..	..	..
Japan	99 800	1.7	90 600	1.6	−9.2
Total Australasia and Japan	189 600	3.3	161 500	2.8	−14.8
Total OECD Countries	**5 496 500**	**94.8**	**5 572 600**	**95.4**	**1.4**
Yugoslavia	..	..	..	..	..
Latin America	74 400	1.3	62 900	1.1	−15.5
Asia-Oceania	166 500	2.9	150 900	2.6	−9.4
Africa	57 700	1.0	55 500	1.0	−3.8
Total non-OECD Countries	**298 600**	**5.2**	**269 300**	**4.6**	**−9.8**
TOTAL	**5 795 100**	**100.0**	**5 841 900**	**100.0**	**0.8**

1. Spain includes Portugal.
2. Australia includes New Zealand.
3. Other OECD-Europe includes Austria, Greece, Iceland and non-OECD European countries.

NETHERLANDS

NIGHTS SPENT BY FOREIGN TOURISTS IN HOTELS

(by country of residence)

	1990	Relative share	1991	Relative share	% Variation over 1990
Austria[3]	..	..	..	..	..
Belgium	293 800	3.6	305 600	3.8	4.0
Denmark	141 000	1.7	128 300	1.6	−9.0
Finland	72 600	0.9	69 000	0.9	−5.0
France	545 600	6.7	495 500	6.2	−9.2
Germany	1 657 200	20.5	1 857 900	23.2	12.1
Greece[3]	..	..	..	..	..
Iceland[3]	..	..	..	..	..
Ireland	55 500	0.7	59 800	0.7	7.7
Italy	609 800	7.5	538 600	6.7	−11.7
Luxembourg	29 800	0.4	27 400	0.3	−8.1
Netherlands	..	..	..	..	..
Norway	91 000	1.1	92 600	1.2	1.8
Portugal[1]	..	..	..	..	..
Spain[1]	319 100	3.9	331 100	4.1	3.8
Sweden	217 700	2.7	228 800	2.9	5.1
Switzerland	205 600	2.5	202 300	2.5	−1.6
Turkey	..	..	..	..	..
United Kingdom	1 519 400	18.8	1 519 000	19.0	−0.0
Other OECD-Europe[3]	368 500	4.5	425 600	5.3	15.5
Total Europe	6 126 600	75.6	6 281 500	78.6	2.5
Canada	185 600	2.3	134 200	1.7	−27.7
United States	913 800	11.3	764 600	9.6	−16.3
Total North America	1 099 400	13.6	898 800	11.2	−18.2
Australia[2]	112 300	1.4	87 000	1.1	−22.5
New Zealand[2]	..	..	..	..	..
Japan	185 900	2.3	174 300	2.2	−6.2
Total Australasia and Japan	298 200	3.7	261 300	3.3	−12.4
Total OECD Countries	**7 524 200**	**92.9**	**7 441 600**	**93.1**	**−1.1**
Yugoslavia	..	..	..	..	..
Latin America	141 400	1.7	121 300	1.5	−14.2
Asia-Oceania	330 700	4.1	324 900	4.1	−1.8
Africa	105 500	1.3	105 700	1.3	0.2
Total non-OECD Countries	**577 600**	**7.1**	**551 900**	**6.9**	**−4.4**
TOTAL	**8 101 800**	**100.0**	**7 993 500**	**100.0**	**−1.3**

1. Spain includes Portugal.
2. Australia includes New Zealand.
3. Other OECD-Europe includes Austria, Greece, Iceland and all non-OECD European countries.

NETHERLANDS

NIGHTS SPENT BY FOREIGN TOURISTS IN REGISTERED TOURIST ACCOMMODATION

(by country of residence)

	1990	Relative share	1991	Relative share	% Variation over 1990
Austria [3]	..	..	..	..	..
Belgium	1 145 100	7.0	1 219 500	7.1	6.5
Denmark	268 400	1.6	246 600	1.4	−8.1
Finland	93 900	0.6	85 900	0.5	−8.5
France	795 600	4.8	763 500	4.4	−4.0
Germany	7 443 000	45.2	8 364 100	48.6	12.4
Greece [3]	..	..	..	..	..
Iceland [3]	..	..	..	..	..
Ireland	73 800	0.4	80 500	0.5	9.1
Italy	767 800	4.7	691 900	4.0	−9.9
Luxembourg	34 900	0.2	32 600	0.2	−6.6
Netherlands					
Norway	117 500	0.7	116 200	0.7	−1.1
Portugal [1]	..	..	..	..	..
Spain [1]	434 800	2.6	452 400	2.6	4.0
Sweden	289 300	1.8	296 500	1.7	2.5
Switzerland	289 400	1.8	313 200	1.8	8.2
Turkey					
United Kingdom	1 927 300	11.7	1 940 900	11.3	0.7
Other OECD-Europe [3]	491 700	3.0	625 800	3.6	27.3
Total Europe	14 172 500	86.1	15 229 600	88.5	7.5
Canada	221 400	1.3	165 500	1.0	−25.2
United States	1 023 500	6.2	844 100	4.9	−17.5
Total North America	1 244 900	7.6	1 009 600	5.9	−18.9
Australia [2]	181 800	1.1	154 100	0.9	−15.2
New Zealand [2]	..	..	..	..	..
Japan	193 600	1.2	179 900	1.0	−7.1
Total Australasia and Japan	375 400	2.3	334 000	1.9	−11.0
Total OECD Countries	**15 792 800**	**96.0**	**16 573 200**	**96.3**	**4.9**
Yugoslavia	..	..	..	..	..
Latin America	161 600	1.0	142 900	0.8	−11.6
Asia-Oceania	368 500	2.2	362 000	2.1	−1.8
Africa	135 700	0.8	127 800	0.7	−5.8
Total non-OECD Countries	**665 800**	**4.0**	**632 700**	**3.7**	**−5.0**
TOTAL	**16 458 600**	**100.0**	**17 205 900**	**100.0**	**4.5**

1. Spain includes Portugal.
2. Australia includes New Zealand.
3. Other OECD-Europe includes Austria, Greece, Iceland and non-OECD European countries.

NEW ZEALAND

ARRIVALS OF FOREIGN TOURISTS AT FRONTIERS

(by country of residence)

	1990	Relative share	1991	Relative share	% Variation over 1990
Austria	2 565	0.3	2 839	0.3	10.7
Belgium	1 001	0.1	824	0.1	−17.7
Denmark	3 401	0.3	3 342	0.3	−1.7
Finland	1 499	0.2	2 011	0.2	34.2
France	3 429	0.4	4 643	0.5	35.4
Germany	29 992	3.1	34 298	3.6	14.4
Greece	311	0.0	295	0.0	−5.1
Iceland	66	0.0	32	0.0	−51.5
Ireland	1 578	0.2	1 632	0.2	3.4
Italy	3 152	0.3	3 580	0.4	13.6
Luxembourg	130	0.0	111	0.0	−14.6
Netherlands	7 780	0.8	7 584	0.8	−2.5
Norway	1 614	0.2	2 037	0.2	26.2
Portugal	113	0.0	203	0.0	79.6
Spain	1 155	0.1	925	0.1	−19.9
Sweden	8 476	0.9	7 992	0.8	−5.7
Switzerland	10 642	1.1	11 717	1.2	10.1
Turkey	214	0.0	192	0.0	−10.3
United Kingdom	87 255	8.9	87 944	9.1	0.8
Other OECD-Europe	..	..	..	..	..
Total Europe	164 373	16.8	172 201	17.9	4.8
Canada	33 983	3.5	30 276	3.1	−10.9
United States	139 664	14.3	132 690	13.8	−5.0
Total North America	173 647	17.8	162 966	16.9	−6.2
Australia	341 713	35.0	338 509	35.1	−0.9
New Zealand [1]	14 368	1.5	7 062	0.7	−50.8
Japan	107 840	11.0	114 718	11.9	6.4
Total Australasia and Japan	463 921	47.5	460 289	47.8	−0.8
Total OECD Countries	**801 941**	**82.2**	**795 456**	**82.6**	**−0.8**
Yugoslavia	267	0.0	231	0.0	−13.5
Bulgaria	45	0.0	32	0.0	−28.9
Czechoslovakia	70	0.0	149	0.0	112.9
Hungary	139	0.0	180	0.0	29.5
Poland	123	0.0	94	0.0	−23.6
Rumania	64	0.0	83	0.0	29.7
USSR	4 519	0.5	2 807	0.3	−37.9
Latin America	..	..	5 415	0.6	..
Argentina	1 458	0.1	1 715	0.2	17.6
Brazil	924	0.1	1 143	0.1	23.7
Chile	437	0.0	478	0.0	9.4
Colombia	172	0.0	184	0.0	7.0
Mexico	928	0.1	735	0.1	−20.8
Venezuela	152	0.0	144	0.0	−5.3
China	3 082	0.3	2 596	0.3	−15.8
Hong Kong	15 460	1.6	18 564	1.9	20.1
India	2 190	0.2	1 495	0.2	−31.7
Iran	392	0.0	191	0.0	−51.3
Israel	1 089	0.1	1 172	0.1	7.6
Republic of Korea	4 184	0.4	6 369	0.7	52.2
Lebanon	42	0.0	29	0.0	−31.0
Malaysia	10 021	1.0	8 776	0.9	−12.4
Pakistan	356	0.0	173	0.0	−51.4
Philippines	2 880	0.3	2 237	0.2	−22.3
Saudi Arabia	792	0.1	483	0.1	−39.0
Singapore	15 207	1.6	17 342	1.8	14.0
Taiwan	12 845	1.3	14 811	1.5	15.3
Thailand	5 568	0.6	6 897	0.7	23.9
Africa	..	..	3 235	0.3	..
Algeria	0	0.0	0	0.0	..
Egypt	114	0.0	84	0.0	−26.3
Morocco	22	0.0	10	0.0	−54.5
South Africa	1 921	0.2	2 045	0.2	6.5
Origin country undetermined	173 802	17.8	159 133	16.5	−8.4
Total non-OECD Countries	**174 069**	**17.8**	**168 014**	**17.4**	**−3.5**
TOTAL	**976 010**	**100.0**	**963 470**	**100.0**	**−1.3**

1. New Zealanders who have lived abroad for less than 12 months and who return for a short stay.

NORWAY

NIGHTS SPENT BY FOREIGN TOURISTS IN HOTELS

(by country of nationality)

	1990	Relative share	1991	Relative share	% Variation over 1990
Austria [1]	..	..	..	..	..
Belgium [1]	..	..	..	..	..
Denmark	623 812	17.6	701 634	17.9	12.5
Finland	105 311	3.0	118 141	3.0	12.2
France	170 685	4.8	208 419	5.3	22.1
Germany	579 869	16.4	713 212	18.2	23.0
Greece [1]	..	..	..	..	..
Iceland [1]	..	..	..	..	..
Ireland [1]	..	..	..	..	..
Italy [1]	103 215	2.9	157 003	4.0	52.1
Luxembourg [1]	..	..	..	..	..
Netherlands	126 030	3.6	150 398	3.8	19.3
Norway	..	..	..	..	..
Portugal [1]	..	..	..	..	..
Spain [1]	32 607	0.9	40 201	1.0	23.3
Sweden	566 595	16.0	680 972	17.4	20.2
Switzerland [1]	42 324	1.2	47 404	1.2	12.0
Turkey [1]	..	..	..	..	..
United Kingdom	340 890	9.6	347 278	8.9	1.9
Other OECD-Europe	142 244	4.0	154 193	3.9	8.4
Total Europe	2 833 582	80.1	3 318 855	84.7	17.1
Canada [1]	..	..	..	..	..
United States	364 544	10.3	280 250	7.2	−23.1
Total North America	364 544	10.3	280 250	7.2	−23.1
Australia [1]	..	..	..	..	..
New Zealand [1]	..	..	..	..	..
Japan	84 495	2.4	85 001	2.2	0.6
Total Australasia and Japan	84 495	2.4	85 001	2.2	0.6
Total OECD Countries	**3 282 621**	**92.8**	**3 684 106**	**94.1**	**12.2**
Yugoslavia (S.F.R.) [1]	..	..	..	..	..
Origin country undetermined [1]	254 010	7.2	232 667	5.9	−8.4
Total non-OECD Countries	**254 010**	**7.2**	**232 667**	**5.9**	**−8.4**
TOTAL	**3 536 631**	**100.0**	**3 916 773**	**100.0**	**10.7**

1. Included in "Origin country undetermined".

PORTUGAL

ARRIVALS OF FOREIGN TOURISTS AT FRONTIERS

(by country of nationality)

	1990	Relative share	1991	Relative share	% Variation over 1990
Austria	37 082	0.5	41 439	0.5	11.7
Belgium	168 273	2.1	188 296	2.2	11.9
Denmark	100 739	1.3	107 486	1.2	6.7
Finland	87 231	1.1	148 154	1.7	69.8
France	617 873	7.7	667 122	7.7	8.0
Germany	621 418	7.7	786 496	9.1	26.6
Greece [1]	..	..	..	..	..
Iceland [1]	..	..	..	..	..
Ireland	69 204	0.9	73 783	0.9	6.6
Italy	189 390	2.4	250 478	2.9	32.3
Luxembourg	10 145	0.1	16 010	0.2	57.8
Netherlands	298 941	3.7	325 586	3.8	8.9
Norway	27 746	0.3	23 509	0.3	−15.3
Portugal	..	..	..	..	..
Spain	3 924 340	48.9	4 111 089	47.5	4.8
Sweden	88 168	1.1	105 188	1.2	19.3
Switzerland	69 311	0.9	73 366	0.8	5.9
Turkey [1]	..	..	..	..	..
United Kingdom	1 061 136	13.2	1 161 863	13.4	9.5
Other OECD-Europe	..	..	..	..	..
Total Europe	7 370 997	91.9	8 079 865	93.3	9.6
Canada	83 238	1.0	62 872	0.7	−24.5
United States	183 886	2.3	143 459	1.7	−22.0
Total North America	267 124	3.3	206 331	2.4	−22.8
Australia [2]	21 481	0.3	19 322	0.2	−10.1
New-Zealand [2]	..	..	..	..	..
Japan	32 665	0.4	26 587	0.3	−18.6
Total Australasia and Japan	54 146	0.7	45 909	0.5	−15.2
Total OECD Countries	**7 692 267**	**95.9**	**8 332 105**	**96.2**	**8.3**
Yugoslavia (S.F.R.) [1]	..	..	..	..	..
Other European countries [1]	52 474	0.7	57 295	0.7	9.2
Africa	102 030	1.3	101 006	1.2	−1.0
Origin country undetermined	173 148	2.2	166 540	1.9	−3.8
Total non-OECD Countries	**327 652**	**4.1**	**324 841**	**3.8**	**−0.9**
TOTAL	**8 019 919**	**100.0**	**8 656 946**	**100.0**	**7.9**

1. "Other European countries" includes Greece, Iceland, Turkey and Yugoslavia.
2. Australia includes New Zealand.

PORTUGAL

ARRIVALS OF FOREIGN VISITORS AT FRONTIERS

(by country of nationality)

	1990	Relative share	1991	Relative share	% Variation over 1990
Austria	40 295	0.2	48 745	0.2	21.0
Belgium	173 062	0.9	198 434	1.0	14.7
Denmark	104 627	0.6	112 220	0.6	7.3
Finland	93 650	0.5	149 205	0.8	59.3
France	658 198	3.6	711 493	3.6	8.1
Germany	680 971	3.7	851 858	4.3	25.1
Greece	16 481	0.1	16 068	0.1	−2.5
Iceland	2 448	0.0	3 251	0.0	32.8
Ireland	71 784	0.4	76 182	0.4	6.1
Italy	221 113	1.2	290 971	1.5	31.6
Luxembourg	10 177	0.1	17 521	0.1	72.2
Netherlands	329 457	1.8	360 452	1.8	9.4
Norway	31 314	0.2	26 393	0.1	−15.7
Portugal	..	..	..	..	..
Spain	13 806 281	74.9	14 583 216	74.2	5.6
Sweden	97 577	0.5	114 315	0.6	17.2
Switzerland	78 029	0.4	79 890	0.4	2.4
Turkey	3 495	0.0	3 365	0.0	−3.7
United Kingdom	1 202 874	6.5	1 307 312	6.7	8.7
Other OECD-Europe	..		..		..
Total Europe	17 621 833	95.7	18 950 891	96.5	7.5
Canada	90 830	0.5	69 299	0.4	−23.7
United States	252 057	1.4	178 133	0.9	−29.3
Total North America	342 887	1.9	247 432	1.3	−27.8
Australia	17 645	0.1	16 457	0.1	−6.7
New Zealand	5 999	0.0	4 966	0.0	−17.2
Japan	35 433	0.2	28 422	0.1	−19.8
Total Australasia and Japan	59 077	0.3	49 845	0.3	−15.6
Total OECD Countries	**18 023 797**	**97.8**	**19 248 168**	**98.0**	**6.8**
Yugoslavia	8 393	0.0	6 777	0.0	−19.3
Other European countries	61 916	0.3	64 012	0.3	3.4
Bulgaria	2 173	0.0	2 509	0.0	15.5
Czechoslovakia	3 003	0.0	6 487	0.0	116.0
Germany (D. R.)	4 298	0.0	..	..	..
Hungary	2 394	0.0	3 407	0.0	42.3
Poland	6 917	0.0	12 262	0.1	77.3
Rumania	1 586	0.0	1 155	0.0	−27.2
USSR	39 076	0.2	36 435	0.2	−6.8
Latin America	169 544	0.9	161 525	0.8	−4.7
Argentina	9 731	0.1	10 694	0.1	9.9
Brazil	118 926	0.6	114 053	0.6	−4.1
Chile	3 233	0.0	3 009	0.0	−6.9
Colombia	2 424	0.0	2 319	0.0	−4.3
Mexico	7 525	0.0	4 578	0.0	−39.2
Venezuela	17 985	0.1	17 802	0.1	−1.0
Asia-Oceania	49 268	0.3	52 993	0.3	7.6
China	2 885	0.0	2 469	0.0	−14.4
Hong Kong	1 097	0.0	950	0.0	−13.4
India	7 179	0.0	9 435	0.0	31.4
Iran	837	0.0	845	0.0	1.0
Israel	6 281	0.0	7 284	0.0	16.0
Republic of Korea	6 552	0.0	5 444	0.0	−16.9
Lebanon	632	0.0	556	0.0	−12.0
Malaysia	935	0.0	1 012	0.0	8.2
Pakistan	1 410	0.0	1 627	0.0	15.4
Philippines	14 040	0.1	17 124	0.1	22.0
Saudi Arabia	405	0.0	362	0.0	−10.6
Singapore	1 155	0.0	989	0.0	−14.4
Thailand	1 182	0.0	1 143	0.0	−3.3
Africa	106 452	0.6	105 837	0.5	−0.6
Algeria	1 993	0.0	1 287	0.0	−35.4
Egypt	1 030	0.0	1 115	0.0	8.3
Morocco	6 407	0.0	4 255	0.0	−33.6
South Africa	14 018	0.1	14 503	0.1	3.5
Origin country undetermined	2 708	0.0	2 017	0.0	−25.5
Total non-OECD Countries	**398 281**	**2.2**	**393 161**	**2.0**	**−1.3**
TOTAL	**18 422 078**	**100.0**	**19 641 329**	**100.0**	**6.6**

PORTUGAL

ARRIVALS OF FOREIGN TOURISTS AT HOTELS[1]

(by country of residence)

	1990	Relative share	1991	Relative share	% Variation over 1990
Austria	34 711	1.0	45 622	1.2	31.4
Belgium	90 078	2.5	101 959	2.6	13.2
Denmark	60 180	1.7	62 208	1.6	3.4
Finland	78 333	2.2	126 322	3.2	61.3
France	309 988	8.5	350 410	9.0	13.0
Germany	419 054	11.5	534 237	13.7	27.5
Greece	9 114	0.3	9 647	0.2	5.8
Iceland	2 162	0.1	2 744	0.1	26.9
Ireland	34 664	1.0	47 337	1.2	36.6
Italy	175 326	4.8	232 422	5.9	32.6
Luxembourg	4 570	0.1	6 143	0.2	34.4
Netherlands	207 358	5.7	228 008	5.8	10.0
Norway	25 465	0.7	23 198	0.6	−8.9
Portugal	..	..	..	..	..
Spain	692 587	19.1	734 127	18.8	6.0
Sweden	92 784	2.6	104 888	2.7	13.0
Switzerland	95 336	2.6	96 881	2.5	1.6
Turkey	1 458	0.0	1 154	0.0	−20.9
United Kingdom	695 680	19.2	718 435	18.4	3.3
Other OECD-Europe	..	..	..	..	..
Total Europe	3 028 848	83.4	3 425 742	87.5	13.1
Canada	100 852	2.8	63 328	1.6	−37.2
United States	252 185	6.9	186 020	4.8	−26.2
Total North America	353 037	9.7	249 348	6.4	−29.4
Australia	10 048	0.3	9 169	0.2	−8.7
New Zealand	1 917	0.1	1 758	0.0	−8.3
Japan	34 199	0.9	31 904	0.8	−6.7
Total Australasia and Japan	46 164	1.3	42 831	1.1	−7.2
Total OECD Countries	**3 428 049**	**94.4**	**3 717 921**	**95.0**	**8.5**
Yugoslavia	2 574	0.1	2 282	0.1	−11.3
Other European countries	13 640	0.4	12 311	0.3	−9.7
Bulgaria	662	0.0	755	0.0	14.0
Czechoslovakia	1 665	0.0	2 008	0.1	20.6
Hungary	985	0.0	1 702	0.0	72.8
Poland	1 137	0.0	1 499	0.0	31.8
Rumania	505	0.0	718	0.0	42.2
USSR	7 805	0.2	4 654	0.1	−40.4
Latin America	111 793	3.1	106 745	2.7	−4.5
Argentina	5 365	0.1	6 895	0.2	28.5
Brazil	92 712	2.6	85 821	2.2	−7.4
Chile	954	0.0	1 142	0.0	19.7
Colombia	914	0.0	810	0.0	−11.4
Mexico	3 989	0.1	3 778	0.1	−5.3
Venezuela	4 643	0.1	5 350	0.1	15.2
Asia-Oceania	18 069	0.5	19 286	0.5	6.7
China	1 716	0.0	1 405	0.0	−18.1
Iran	410	0.0	129	0.0	−68.5
Israel	7 579	0.2	9 709	0.2	28.1
Lebanon	255	0.0	244	0.0	−4.3
Philippines	1 187	0.0	1 103	0.0	−7.1
Saudi Arabia	761	0.0	600	0.0	−21.2
Africa	58 117	1.6	54 521	1.4	−6.2
Egypt	650	0.0	623	0.0	−4.2
Morocco	4 130	0.1	2 458	0.1	−40.5
South Africa	17 972	0.5	18 105	0.5	0.7
Total non-OECD Countries	**204 193**	**5.6**	**195 145**	**5.0**	**−4.4**
TOTAL	**3 632 242**	**100.0**	**3 913 066**	**100.0**	**7.7**

1. Includes arrivals at hotels, studio-hotels, holiday-flats, villages, motels, inns and boarding-houses.

PORTUGAL

ARRIVALS OF FOREIGN TOURISTS AT REGISTERED TOURIST ACCOMMODATION[1]

(by country of residence)

	1990	Relative share	1991	Relative share	% Variation over 1990
Austria	45 584	1.0	58 100	1.2	27.5
Belgium	122 430	2.8	140 401	2.9	14.7
Denmark	74 560	1.7	75 732	1.6	1.6
Finland	80 601	1.8	128 641	2.7	59.6
France	492 144	11.1	535 406	11.2	8.8
Germany	601 528	13.6	750 039	15.7	24.7
Greece	9 519	0.2	10 000	0.2	5.1
Iceland	2 190	0.0	2 768	0.1	26.4
Ireland	36 437	0.8	49 491	1.0	35.8
Italy	203 320	4.6	270 509	5.7	33.0
Luxembourg	5 393	0.1	6 756	0.1	25.3
Netherlands	309 771	7.0	342 131	7.2	10.4
Norway	26 539	0.6	24 395	0.5	−8.1
Portugal	..	..	..	..	..
Spain	849 633	19.2	886 357	18.6	4.3
Sweden	96 369	2.2	108 218	2.3	12.3
Switzerland	105 600	2.4	107 663	2.3	2.0
Turkey	1 567	0.0	1 261	0.0	−19.5
United Kingdom	726 768	16.4	750 236	15.7	3.2
Other OECD-Europe	..	..	..	..	..
Total Europe	3 789 953	85.5	4 248 104	89.1	12.1
Canada	106 216	2.4	67 003	1.4	−36.9
United States	258 920	5.8	191 100	4.0	−26.2
Total North America	365 136	8.2	258 103	5.4	−29.3
Australia	18 173	0.4	15 551	0.3	−14.4
New Zealand	6 619	0.1	5 938	0.1	−10.3
Japan	35 438	0.8	32 550	0.7	−8.1
Total Australasia and Japan	60 230	1.4	54 039	1.1	−10.3
Total OECD Countries	**4 215 319**	**95.1**	**4 560 246**	**95.6**	**8.2**
Yugoslavia	3 459	0.1	2 950	0.1	−14.7
Other European countries	16 207	0.4	17 082	0.4	5.4
Bulgaria	788	0.0	842	0.0	6.9
Czechoslovakia	2 009	0.0	2 717	0.1	35.2
Hungary	1 879	0.0	2 930	0.1	55.9
Poland	1 998	0.0	3 806	0.1	90.5
Rumania	526	0.0	877	0.0	66.7
USSR	7 874	0.2	4 873	0.1	−38.1
Latin America	117 485	2.6	111 255	2.3	−5.3
Argentina	5 762	0.1	7 280	0.2	26.3
Brazil	96 919	2.2	89 244	1.9	−7.9
Chile	1 193	0.0	1 246	0.0	4.4
Colombia	968	0.0	883	0.0	−8.8
Mexico	4 223	0.1	3 916	0.1	−7.3
Venezuela	4 892	0.1	5 476	0.1	11.9
Asia-Oceania	18 968	0.4	19 951	0.4	5.2
China	1 756	0.0	1 429	0.0	−18.6
Iran	458	0.0	155	0.0	−66.2
Israel	7 737	0.2	9 906	0.2	28.0
Lebanon	267	0.0	248	0.0	−7.1
Philippines	1 192	0.0	1 106	0.0	−7.2
Saudi Arabia	769	0.0	644	0.0	−16.3
Africa	63 290	1.4	57 606	1.2	−9.0
Egypt	662	0.0	634	0.0	−4.2
Morocco	6 077	0.1	3 503	0.1	−42.4
South Africa	19 190	0.4	19 118	0.4	−0.4
Total non-OECD Countries	**219 409**	**4.9**	**208 844**	**4.4**	**−4.8**
TOTAL	**4 434 728**	**100.0**	**4 769 090**	**100.0**	**7.5**

1. Includes arrivals at hotels, studio-hotels, holiday-flats, villages, motels, inns, boarding-houses, recreation centres for children and camping-sites.

PORTUGAL

NIGHTS SPENT BY FOREIGN TOURISTS IN HOTELS[1]

(by country of residence)

	1990	Relative share	1991	Relative share	% Variation over 1990
Austria	142 782	0.9	189 455	1.0	32.7
Belgium	393 473	2.4	457 021	2.4	16.2
Denmark	404 479	2.4	384 222	2.0	−5.0
Finland	532 914	3.2	898 993	4.7	68.7
France	825 493	4.9	980 151	5.1	18.7
Germany	2 360 295	14.1	3 233 873	16.9	37.0
Greece	26 356	0.2	25 511	0.1	−3.2
Iceland	18 278	0.1	21 236	0.1	16.2
Ireland	271 603	1.6	372 567	2.0	37.2
Italy	459 771	2.8	598 905	3.1	30.3
Luxembourg	24 770	0.1	41 469	0.2	67.4
Netherlands	1 428 931	8.6	1 693 066	8.9	18.5
Norway	167 464	1.0	141 375	0.7	−15.6
Portugal	..	..	..	..	..
Spain	1 738 193	10.4	1 870 917	9.8	7.6
Sweden	549 742	3.3	698 078	3.7	27.0
Switzerland	341 358	2.0	360 374	1.9	5.6
Turkey	4 595	0.0	4 183	0.0	−9.0
United Kingdom	5 260 390	31.5	5 618 270	29.4	6.8
Other OECD-Europe	..	..	..	..	..
Total Europe	14 950 887	89.5	17 589 666	92.1	17.6
Canada	375 915	2.2	278 760	1.5	−25.8
United States	672 205	4.0	485 490	2.5	−27.8
Total North America	1 048 120	6.3	764 250	4.0	−27.1
Australia	23 030	0.1	25 427	0.1	10.4
New Zealand	4 971	0.0	4 096	0.0	−17.6
Japan	76 787	0.5	72 679	0.4	−5.3
Total Australasia and Japan	104 788	0.6	102 202	0.5	−2.5
Total OECD Countries	**16 103 795**	**96.4**	**18 456 118**	**96.7**	**14.6**
Yugoslavia	8 343	0.0	9 854	0.1	18.1
Other European countries	41 577	0.2	42 312	0.2	1.8
Bulgaria	2 423	0.0	3 422	0.0	41.2
Czechoslovakia	5 006	0.0	7 393	0.0	47.7
Hungary	3 543	0.0	5 138	0.0	45.0
Poland	5 093	0.0	6 025	0.0	18.3
Rumania	2 211	0.0	1 980	0.0	−10.4
USSR	19 546	0.1	15 419	0.1	−21.1
Latin America	288 089	1.7	287 295	1.5	−0.3
Argentina	13 593	0.1	20 250	0.1	49.0
Brazil	238 759	1.4	226 645	1.2	−5.1
Chile	2 996	0.0	3 740	0.0	24.8
Colombia	2 208	0.0	2 336	0.0	5.8
Mexico	8 740	0.1	8 953	0.0	2.4
Venezuela	13 374	0.1	16 713	0.1	25.0
Asia-Oceania	49 104	0.3	55 618	0.3	13.3
China	6 132	0.0	4 641	0.0	−24.3
Iran	1 703	0.0	426	0.0	−75.0
Israel	16 968	0.1	25 847	0.1	52.3
Lebanon	842	0.0	720	0.0	−14.5
Philippines	2 740	0.0	2 811	0.0	2.6
Saudi Arabia	3 635	0.0	2 146	0.0	−41.0
Africa	219 424	1.3	237 731	1.2	8.3
Egypt	1 988	0.0	2 589	0.0	30.2
Morocco	12 263	0.1	7 170	0.0	−41.5
South Africa	56 185	0.3	65 947	0.3	17.4
Total non-OECD Countries	**606 537**	**3.6**	**632 810**	**3.3**	**4.3**
TOTAL	**16 710 332**	**100.0**	**19 088 928**	**100.0**	**14.2**

1. Includes nights spent at hotels, studio-hotels, holiday-flats, villages, motels, inns and boarding-houses.

PORTUGAL

NIGHTS SPENT BY FOREIGN TOURISTS IN REGISTERED TOURIST ACCOMMODATION[1]

(by country of residence)

	1990	Relative share	1991	Relative share	% Variation over 1990
Austria	170 710	0.9	224 875	1.0	31.7
Belgium	505 463	2.6	584 922	2.7	15.7
Denmark	459 741	2.4	436 316	2.0	−5.1
Finland	543 694	2.8	915 288	4.2	68.3
France	1 316 761	6.8	1 484 551	6.8	12.7
Germany	2 963 668	15.3	3 966 162	18.1	33.8
Greece	27 643	0.1	27 228	0.1	−1.5
Iceland	18 359	0.1	21 299	0.1	16.0
Ireland	278 212	1.4	381 733	1.7	37.2
Italy	535 542	2.8	709 291	3.2	32.4
Luxembourg	27 039	0.1	43 664	0.2	61.5
Netherlands	1 849 867	9.6	2 152 918	9.8	16.4
Norway	171 971	0.9	147 844	0.7	−14.0
Portugal	..	..	..	..	..
Spain	2 245 750	11.6	2 365 405	10.8	5.3
Sweden	563 279	2.9	711 686	3.2	26.3
Switzerland	370 429	1.9	390 295	1.8	5.4
Turkey	4 919	0.0	4 625	0.0	−6.0
United Kingdom	5 423 920	28.0	5 782 887	26.3	6.6
Other OECD-Europe	..	..	..	..	..
Total Europe	17 476 967	90.3	20 350 989	92.7	16.4
Canada	388 130	2.0	287 805	1.3	−25.8
United States	687 311	3.6	500 018	2.3	−27.3
Total North America	1 075 441	5.6	787 823	3.6	−26.7
Australia	40 909	0.2	42 163	0.2	3.1
New Zealand	15 453	0.1	13 822	0.1	−10.6
Japan	79 364	0.4	74 152	0.3	−6.6
Total Australasia and Japan	135 726	0.7	130 137	0.6	−4.1
Total OECD Countries	**18 688 134**	**96.6**	**21 268 949**	**96.9**	**13.8**
Yugoslavia	10 611	0.1	12 244	0.1	15.4
Other European countries	49 231	0.3	55 662	0.3	13.1
Bulgaria	3 130	0.0	3 833	0.0	22.5
Czechoslovakia	5 768	0.0	9 214	0.0	59.7
Hungary	6 584	0.0	8 860	0.0	34.6
Poland	7 045	0.0	10 671	0.0	51.5
Rumania	2 785	0.0	3 001	0.0	7.8
USSR	19 640	0.1	16 943	0.1	−13.7
Latin America	301 909	1.6	303 892	1.4	0.7
Argentina	14 439	0.1	21 435	0.1	48.5
Brazil	249 299	1.3	240 140	1.1	−3.7
Chile	3 771	0.0	4 073	0.0	8.0
Colombia	2 294	0.0	2 478	0.0	8.0
Mexico	9 105	0.0	9 312	0.0	2.3
Venezuela	13 892	0.1	17 082	0.1	23.0
Asia-Oceania	50 831	0.3	58 003	0.3	14.1
China	6 208	0.0	4 774	0.0	−23.1
Iran	1 871	0.0	516	0.0	−72.4
Israel	17 214	0.1	27 173	0.1	57.9
Lebanon	927	0.0	730	0.0	−21.3
Philippines	2 766	0.0	2 817	0.0	1.8
Saudi Arabia	3 647	0.0	2 264	0.0	−37.9
Africa	248 670	1.3	258 589	1.2	4.0
Egypt	2 027	0.0	2 610	0.0	28.8
Morocco	19 729	0.1	11 890	0.1	−39.7
South Africa	59 207	0.3	68 803	0.3	16.2
Total non-OECD Countries	**661 252**	**3.4**	**688 390**	**3.1**	**4.1**
TOTAL	**19 349 386**	**100.0**	**21 957 339**	**100.0**	**13.5**

1. Includes nights spent at hotels, studio-hotels, holiday-flats, villages, motels, inns, boarding-houses, recreation centres for children and camping-sites.

SPAIN

ARRIVALS OF FOREIGN VISITORS AT FRONTIERS[1]

(by country of nationality)

	1990	Relative share	1991	Relative share	% Variation over 1990
Austria	279 034	0.5	320 040	0.6	14.7
Belgium	1 261 204	2.4	1 369 365	2.6	8.6
Denmark	482 583	0.9	412 702	0.8	−14.5
Finland	457 201	0.9	411 762	0.8	−9.9
France	11 623 555	22.3	12 052 767	22.5	3.7
Germany	6 880 240	13.2	7 663 223	14.3	11.4
Greece	106 547	0.2	94 787	0.2	−11.0
Iceland	18 700	0.0	19 854	0.0	6.2
Ireland	178 058	0.3	177 339	0.3	−0.4
Italy	1 656 906	3.2	1 767 599	3.3	6.7
Luxembourg	80 292	0.2	79 818	0.1	−0.6
Netherlands	1 953 887	3.8	2 157 079	4.0	10.4
Norway	350 690	0.7	301 541	0.6	−14.0
Portugal	10 106 114	19.4	10 535 848	19.7	4.3
Spain[2]	3 299 309	6.3	3 471 896	6.5	5.2
Sweden	782 599	1.5	781 837	1.5	−0.1
Switzerland	1 086 079	2.1	1 167 088	2.2	7.5
Turkey	19 193	0.0	17 041	0.0	−11.2
United Kingdom	6 286 433	12.1	6 145 003	11.5	−2.2
Other OECD-Europe[3]	335 315	0.6	372 904	0.7	11.2
Total Europe	47 243 939	90.8	49 319 493	92.2	4.4
Canada	157 756	0.3	137 950	0.3	−12.6
United States	836 292	1.6	652 338	1.2	−22.0
Total North America	994 048	1.9	790 288	1.5	−20.5
Australia	53 872	0.1	48 709	0.1	−9.6
New Zealand	16 985	0.0	18 539	0.0	9.1
Japan	243 775	0.5	186 485	0.3	−23.5
Total Australasia and Japan	314 632	0.6	253 733	0.5	−19.4
Total OECD Countries	**48 552 619**	**93.3**	**50 363 514**	**94.1**	**3.7**
Yugoslavia	79 456	0.2	57 287	0.1	−27.9
Other European countries	283 351	0.5	306 285	0.6	8.1
Bulgaria	7 601	0.0	12 596	0.0	65.7
Czechoslovakia	14 297	0.0	36 389	0.1	154.5
Hungary	14 031	0.0	18 215	0.0	29.8
Poland	33 002	0.1	47 167	0.1	42.9
Rumania	10 485	0.0	15 134	0.0	44.3
USSR	203 962	0.4	176 784	0.3	−13.3
Latin America	503 141	1.0	479 850	0.9	−4.6
Argentina	105 327	0.2	102 684	0.2	−2.5
Brazil	114 419	0.2	104 047	0.2	−9.1
Chile	24 685	0.0	24 111	0.0	−2.3
Colombia	27 230	0.1	31 378	0.1	15.2
Mexico	65 876	0.1	62 334	0.1	−5.4
Venezuela	53 712	0.1	51 509	0.1	−4.1
Asia-Oceania	218 701	0.4	211 944	0.4	−3.1
Africa	2 397 938	4.6	2 067 996	3.9	−13.8
Origin country undetermined	8 850	0.0	8 088	0.0	−8.6
Total non-OECD Countries	**3 491 437**	**6.7**	**3 131 450**	**5.9**	**−10.3**
TOTAL	**52 044 056**	**100.0**	**53 494 964**	**100.0**	**2.8**

1. Includes about 34% of arrivals of excursionists.
2. Spanish nationals residing abroad.
3. ''Other OECD-Europe'' includes Andorra, Cyprus, Malta, Monaco, and the Vatican States.

SPAIN

ARRIVALS OF FOREIGN TOURISTS AT HOTELS[1]

(by country of nationality)

	1990	Relative share	1991	Relative share	% Variation over 1990
Austria	411 340	3.4	..	..	..
Belgium	411 340	3.4	432 358	3.6	5.1
Denmark	133 286	1.1	130 780	1.1	−1.9
Finland	..	..	..	..	..
France	1 515 138	12.6	1 582 876	13.1	4.5
Germany	2 361 519	19.7	2 916 982	24.2	23.5
Greece	39 550	0.3	31 595	0.3	−20.1
Iceland	..	..	..	..	..
Ireland	29 532	0.2	33 610	0.3	13.8
Italy	1 056 418	8.8	1 118 199	9.3	5.8
Luxembourg	20 214	0.2	26 961	0.2	33.4
Netherlands	324 924	2.7	357 129	3.0	9.9
Norway	57 955	0.5	59 325	0.5	2.4
Portugal	323 356	2.7	325 444	2.7	0.6
Spain	..	..	..	..	..
Sweden	198 126	1.6	180 619	1.5	−8.8
Switzerland	322 702	2.7	339 093	2.8	5.1
Turkey	..	..	..	..	..
United Kingdom	2 214 403	18.4	2 339 168	19.4	5.6
Other OECD-Europe	..	..	..	..	..
Total Europe	9 419 803	78.4	9 874 139	82.0	4.8
Canada	64 991	0.5	51 014	0.4	−21.5
United States	791 753	6.6	579 414	4.8	−26.8
Total North America	856 744	7.1	630 428	5.2	−26.4
Australia	..	..	..	..	..
New Zealand	..	..	..	..	..
Japan	498 027	4.1	341 745	2.8	−31.4
Total Australasia and Japan	498 027	4.1	341 745	2.8	−31.4
Total OECD Countries	**10 774 574**	**89.7**	**10 846 312**	**90.0**	**0.7**
Yugoslavia	..	..	..	..	..
Other European countries	319 476	2.7	357 219	3.0	11.8
Latin America	442 397	3.7	406 744	3.4	−8.1
Origin country undetermined	475 538	4.0	438 628	3.6	−7.8
Total non-OECD Countries	**1 237 411**	**10.3**	**1 202 591**	**10.0**	**−2.8**
TOTAL	**12 011 985**	**100.0**	**12 048 903**	**100.0**	**0.3**

1. Arrivals recorded in hotels with "estrellas de oro" (golden stars) and "estrellas de plata" (silver stars).

SPAIN

NIGHTS SPENT BY FOREIGN TOURISTS IN HOTELS[1]

(by country of nationality)

	1990	Relative share	1991	Relative share	% Variation over 1990
Austria	..	..	..	..	..
Belgium	3 081 674	4.3	3 226 737	4.3	4.7
Denmark	973 155	1.4	816 016	1.1	−16.1
Finland	..	..	..	..	..
France	6 550 276	9.1	6 727 747	9.0	2.7
Germany	22 728 327	31.7	25 975 175	34.9	14.3
Greece	83 826	0.1	68 231	0.1	−18.6
Iceland	..	..	..	..	..
Ireland	135 417	0.2	171 090	0.2	26.3
Italy	4 280 342	6.0	4 631 878	6.2	8.2
Luxembourg	191 898	0.3	237 371	0.3	23.7
Netherlands	2 089 521	2.9	2 434 054	3.3	16.5
Norway	327 473	0.5	297 735	0.4	−9.1
Portugal	718 861	1.0	792 452	1.1	10.2
Spain	..	..	..	..	..
Sweden	1 265 228	1.8	1 072 574	1.4	−15.2
Switzerland	2 182 125	3.0	2 254 496	3.0	3.3
Turkey	..	..	..	..	..
United Kingdom	19 566 838	27.3	19 045 083	25.6	−2.7
Other OECD-Europe	..	..	..	..	..
Total Europe	64 174 961	89.5	67 750 639	91.0	5.6
Canada	165 665	0.2	122 489	0.2	−26.1
United States	1 752 844	2.4	1 293 788	1.7	−26.2
Total North America	1 918 509	2.7	1 416 277	1.9	−26.2
Australia	..	..	..	..	..
New Zealand	..	..	..	..	..
Japan	877 387	1.2	616 909	0.8	−29.7
Total Australasia and Japan	877 387	1.2	616 909	0.8	−29.7
Total OECD Countries	**66 970 857**	**93.4**	**69 783 825**	**93.7**	**4.2**
Yugoslavia					
Other European countries	2 251 486	3.1	2 355 504	3.2	4.6
Latin America	1 049 197	1.5	959 712	1.3	−8.5
Argentina	220 761	0.3	216 550	0.3	−1.9
Mexico	177 471	0.2	152 515	0.2	−14.1
Venezuela	62 389	0.1	54 877	0.1	−12.0
Origin country undetermined	1 469 928	2.0	1 340 390	1.8	−8.8
Total non-OECD Countries	**4 770 611**	**6.6**	**4 655 606**	**6.3**	**−2.4**
TOTAL	**71 741 468**	**100.0**	**74 439 431**	**100.0**	**3.8**

1. Nights recorded in hotels with "estrellas de oro" (golden stars) and "estrellas de plata" (silver stars).

SWEDEN

NIGHTS SPENT BY FOREIGN TOURISTS IN HOTELS

(by country of nationality)

	1990	Relative share	1991	Relative share	% Variation over 1990
Austria [1]	..	..	..	..	..
Belgium [1]	..	..	..	..	..
Denmark	198 396	6.2	189 246	6.7	−4.6
Finland	368 287	11.5	367 849	13.0	−0.1
France	98 268	3.1	92 503	3.3	−5.9
Germany	464 483	14.5	450 697	15.9	−3.0
Greece [1]	..	..	..	..	..
Iceland [1]	..	..	..	..	..
Ireland [1]	..	..	..	..	..
Italy	123 467	3.9	118 347	4.2	−4.1
Luxembourg [1]	..	..	..	..	..
Netherlands	77 938	2.4	68 784	2.4	−11.7
Norway	464 483	14.5	370 781	13.1	−20.2
Portugal [1]	..	..	..	..	..
Spain [1]	..	..	..	..	..
Sweden					
Switzerland	61 462	1.9	57 027	2.0	−7.2
Turkey [1]	..	..	..	..	..
United Kingdom	270 767	8.5	228 135	8.1	−15.7
Other OECD-Europe	..	..	..	..	..
Total Europe	2 127 551	66.6	1 943 369	68.8	−8.7
Canada	25 972	0.8	15 959	0.6	−38.6
United States	326 900	10.2	238 495	8.4	−27.0
Total North America	352 872	11.1	254 454	9.0	−27.9
Australia [2]	..	..	..	..	..
New Zealand [2]	..	..	..	..	..
Japan	94 350	3.0	84 110	3.0	−10.9
Total Australasia and Japan	94 350	3.0	84 110	3.0	−10.9
Total OECD Countries	**2 574 773**	**80.6**	**2 281 933**	**80.7**	**−11.4**
Yugoslavia	..	..	..	..	..
Other European countries [1]	285 941	9.0	230 840	8.2	−19.3
Origin country undetermined [2]	332 448	10.4	313 387	11.1	−5.7
Total non-OECD Countries	**618 389**	**19.4**	**544 227**	**19.3**	**−12.0**
TOTAL	**3 193 162**	**100.0**	**2 826 160**	**100.0**	**−11.5**

1. Included in "Other European countries".
2. Included in "Origin country undetermined".

SWEDEN

NIGHTS SPENT BY FOREIGN TOURISTS IN REGISTERED TOURIST ACCOMMODATION

(by country of nationality)

	1990	Relative share	1991	Relative share	% Variation over 1990
Austria [1]	..	..	..	..	..
Belgium [1]	..	..	..	..	..
Denmark	586 946	8.9	579 934	10.2	−1.2
Finland	579 758	8.8	556 958	9.8	−3.9
France	182 423	2.8	164 724	2.9	−9.7
Germany	1 402 342	21.3	1 319 398	23.3	−5.9
Greece [1]	..	..	..	..	..
Iceland [1]	..	..	..	..	..
Ireland [1]	..	..	..	..	..
Italy	140 935	2.1	134 119	2.4	−4.8
Luxembourg [1]	..	..	..	..	..
Netherlands	380 364	5.8	321 133	5.7	−15.6
Norway	1 546 139	23.5	1 083 756	19.1	−29.9
Portugal [1]	..	..	..	..	..
Spain [1]	..	..	..	..	..
Sweden	..	..	..	..	..
Switzerland	77 931	1.2	72 733	1.3	−6.7
Turkey [1]	..	..	..	..	..
United Kingdom	336 192	5.1	275 157	4.9	−18.2
Other OECD-Europe	..	..	..	..	..
Total Europe	5 233 030	79.6	4 507 912	79.6	−13.9
Canada	29 159	0.4	18 376	0.3	−37.0
United States	342 216	5.2	252 448	4.5	−26.2
Total North America	371 375	5.6	270 824	4.8	−27.1
Australia [2]	..	..	..	..	..
New Zealand [2]	..	..	..	..	..
Japan	97 126	1.5	89 841	1.6	−7.5
Total Australasia and Japan	97 126	1.5	89 841	1.6	−7.5
Total OECD Countries	**5 701 531**	**86.7**	**4 868 577**	**86.0**	**−14.6**
Yugoslavia	..	..	..	..	..
Other European countries [1]	431 156	6.6	389 292	6.9	−9.7
Origin country undetermined [2]	442 980	6.7	402 504	7.1	−9.1
Total non-OECD Countries	**874 136**	**13.3**	**791 796**	**14.0**	**−9.4**
TOTAL	**6 575 667**	**100.0**	**5 660 373**	**100.0**	**−13.9**

1. Included in "Other European countries".
2. Included in "Origin country undetermined".

SWITZERLAND

ARRIVALS OF FOREIGN TOURISTS AT HOTELS

(by country of residence)

	1990	Relative share	1991	Relative share	% Variation over 1990
Austria	168 479	2.1	175 759	2.4	4.3
Belgium	215 508	2.7	225 038	3.0	4.4
Denmark	41 627	0.5	43 764	0.6	5.1
Finland	39 239	0.5	32 836	0.4	−16.3
France	562 131	7.1	558 860	7.6	−0.6
Germany	2 102 289	26.4	2 244 199	30.3	6.8
Greece	58 435	0.7	58 566	0.8	0.2
Iceland [1]	..	..	..	..	..
Ireland	15 355	0.2	15 092	0.2	−1.7
Italy	637 318	8.0	659 526	8.9	3.5
Luxembourg	26 381	0.3	32 646	0.4	23.7
Netherlands	264 285	3.3	273 230	3.7	3.4
Norway	33 641	0.4	30 110	0.4	−10.5
Portugal	42 052	0.5	37 578	0.5	−10.6
Spain	262 749	3.3	251 835	3.4	−4.2
Sweden	111 876	1.4	109 527	1.5	−2.1
Switzerland			..	..	..
Turkey	35 420	0.4	31 750	0.4	−10.4
United Kingdom	604 448	7.6	536 230	7.2	−11.3
Other OECD-Europe	..	..	..	..	..
Total Europe	5 221 233	65.6	5 316 546	71.8	1.8
Canada	108 491	1.4	77 036	1.0	−29.0
United States	1 204 047	15.1	715 637	9.7	−40.6
Total North America	1 312 538	16.5	792 673	10.7	−39.6
Australia [2]	95 629	1.2	70 051	0.9	−26.7
New Zealand [2]	..	..	..	..	..
Japan	497 648	6.2	414 987	5.6	−16.6
Total Australasia and Japan	593 277	7.5	485 038	6.6	−18.2
Total OECD Countries	**7 127 048**	**89.5**	**6 594 257**	**89.1**	**−7.5**
Yugoslavia	52 384	0.7	55 173	0.7	5.3
Other European countries [1]	111 866	1.4	126 879	1.7	13.4
Germany (D. R.)	14 854	0.2	..	..	..
USSR	19 280	0.2	24 054	0.3	24.8
Latin America	142 508	1.8	131 865	1.8	−7.5
Argentina	19 651	0.2	20 549	0.3	4.6
Brazil	57 154	0.7	53 432	0.7	−6.5
Mexico	20 554	0.3	16 026	0.2	−22.0
Asia-Oceania	398 245	5.0	378 448	5.1	−5.0
India	35 953	0.5	29 292	0.4	−18.5
Iran	12 806	0.2	10 089	0.1	−21.2
Israel	117 728	1.5	120 149	1.6	2.1
Africa	131 108	1.6	113 670	1.5	−13.3
Egypt	19 297	0.2	17 600	0.2	−8.8
South Africa	31 449	0.4	25 403	0.3	−19.2
Total non-OECD Countries	**836 111**	**10.5**	**806 035**	**10.9**	**−3.6**
TOTAL	**7 963 159**	**100.0**	**7 400 292**	**100.0**	**−7.1**

1. "Other European countries" includes Iceland.
2. Australia includes New Zealand.

SWITZERLAND

ARRIVALS OF FOREIGN TOURISTS AT REGISTERED TOURIST ACCOMMODATION

(by country of residence)

	1990	Relative share	1991	Relative share	% Variation over 1990
Austria	209 131	2.0	222 094	2.2	6.2
Belgium	353 932	3.4	363 154	3.6	2.6
Denmark	60 883	0.6	64 240	0.6	5.5
Finland	49 529	0.5	42 360	0.4	−14.5
France	750 857	7.1	755 029	7.5	0.6
Germany	3 237 677	30.8	3 517 353	34.9	8.6
Greece	61 086	0.6	61 682	0.6	1.0
Iceland [1]	..	..	..	..	..
Ireland	20 324	0.2	19 935	0.2	−1.9
Italy	747 238	7.1	777 516	7.7	4.1
Luxembourg	35 720	0.3	42 848	0.4	20.0
Netherlands	576 476	5.5	590 913	5.9	2.5
Norway	39 753	0.4	35 607	0.4	−10.4
Portugal	49 221	0.5	44 356	0.4	−9.9
Spain	341 964	3.3	334 688	3.3	−2.1
Sweden	136 802	1.3	131 994	1.3	−3.5
Switzerland					
Turkey	36 773	0.3	32 953	0.3	−10.4
United Kingdom	750 315	7.1	669 897	6.6	−10.7
Other OECD-Europe	..	..	..	..	..
Total Europe	7 457 681	70.9	7 706 619	76.4	3.3
Canada	131 135	1.2	96 413	1.0	−26.5
United States	1 290 729	12.3	780 515	7.7	−39.5
Total North America	1 421 864	13.5	876 928	8.7	−38.3
Australia [2]	156 055	1.5	103 736	1.0	−33.5
New Zealand [2]	..	..	..	..	..
Japan	515 181	4.9	429 152	4.3	−16.7
Total Australasia and Japan	671 236	6.4	532 888	5.3	−20.6
Total OECD Countries	**9 550 781**	**90.8**	**9 116 435**	**90.4**	**−4.5**
Yugoslavia	60 024	0.6	62 359	0.6	3.9
Other European countries [1]	150 514	1.4	206 758	2.1	37.4
Latin America	160 570	1.5	148 865	1.5	−7.3
Argentina	22 186	0.2	23 681	0.2	6.7
Brazil	64 990	0.6	60 453	0.6	−7.0
Mexico	23 323	0.2	17 778	0.2	−23.8
Asia-Oceania	443 418	4.2	421 322	4.2	−5.0
India	38 326	0.4	31 185	0.3	−18.6
Iran	13 694	0.1	10 622	0.1	−22.4
Israel	131 191	1.2	131 101	1.3	−0.1
Africa	155 124	1.5	128 757	1.3	−17.0
Egypt	20 042	0.2	18 264	0.2	−8.9
South Africa	39 005	0.4	31 064	0.3	−20.4
Total non-OECD Countries	**969 650**	**9.2**	**968 061**	**9.6**	**−0.2**
TOTAL	**10 520 431**	**100.0**	**10 084 496**	**100.0**	**−4.1**

1. "Other European countries" includes Iceland.
2. Australia includes New Zealand.

SWITZERLAND

NIGHTS SPENT BY FOREIGN TOURISTS IN HOTELS

(by country of residence)

	1990	Relative share	1991	Relative share	% Variation over 1990
Austria	386 147	1.8	414 303	2.0	7.3
Belgium	863 649	4.1	924 226	4.5	7.0
Denmark	101 685	0.5	104 856	0.5	3.1
Finland	91 757	0.4	78 523	0.4	−14.4
France	1 535 088	7.3	1 545 634	7.6	0.7
Germany	6 415 768	30.5	6 961 061	34.2	8.5
Greece	139 765	0.7	138 616	0.7	−0.8
Iceland [1]	..	..	..	..	..
Ireland	37 901	0.2	38 821	0.2	2.4
Italy	1 364 828	6.5	1 407 635	6.9	3.1
Luxembourg	99 427	0.5	120 624	0.6	21.3
Netherlands	861 937	4.1	892 630	4.4	3.6
Norway	73 991	0.4	69 843	0.3	−5.6
Portugal	89 556	0.4	80 933	0.4	−9.6
Spain	470 186	2.2	460 630	2.3	−2.0
Sweden	268 942	1.3	252 161	1.2	−6.2
Switzerland	..	..	..	..	..
Turkey	141 378	0.7	104 820	0.5	−25.9
United Kingdom	2 023 310	9.6	1 847 021	9.1	−8.7
Other OECD-Europe	..	..	..	..	..
Total Europe	14 965 315	71.1	15 442 337	75.8	3.2
Canada	235 059	1.1	177 402	0.9	−24.5
United States	2 510 625	11.9	1 576 724	7.7	−37.2
Total North America	2 745 684	13.0	1 754 126	8.6	−36.1
Australia [2]	209 688	1.0	158 954	0.8	−24.2
New Zealand [2]	..	..	..	..	
Japan	818 604	3.9	724 962	3.6	−11.4
Total Australasia and Japan	1 028 292	4.9	883 916	4.3	−14.0
Total OECD Countries	**18 739 291**	**89.1**	**18 080 379**	**88.8**	**−3.5**
Yugoslavia	139 924	0.7	180 702	0.9	29.1
Other European countries [1]	352 254	1.7	373 446	1.8	6.0
Germany (D. R.)	38 221	0.2	..	..	..
USSR	79 603	0.4	95 401	0.5	19.8
Latin America	342 309	1.6	326 654	1.6	−4.6
Argentina	49 925	0.2	49 201	0.2	−1.5
Brazil	134 575	0.6	126 426	0.6	−6.1
Mexico	44 672	0.2	37 405	0.2	−16.3
Asia-Oceania	1 036 590	4.9	986 081	4.8	−4.9
India	94 192	0.4	82 244	0.4	−12.7
Iran	44 368	0.2	37 026	0.2	−16.5
Israel	303 112	1.4	296 310	1.5	−2.2
Africa	430 375	2.0	418 222	2.1	−2.8
Egypt	69 296	0.3	65 856	0.3	−5.0
South Africa	82 511	0.4	70 451	0.3	−14.6
Total non-OECD Countries	**2 301 452**	**10.9**	**2 285 105**	**11.2**	**−0.7**
TOTAL	**21 040 743**	**100.0**	**20 365 484**	**100.0**	**−3.2**

1. "Other European countries" includes Iceland.
2. Australia includes New Zealand.

SWITZERLAND

NIGHTS SPENT BY FOREIGN TOURISTS IN REGISTERED TOURIST ACCOMMODATION
(by country of residence)

	1990	Relative share	1991	Relative share	% Variation over 1990
Austria	536 668	1.5	583 509	1.6	8.7
Belgium	1 998 423	5.4	2 049 503	5.5	2.6
Denmark	191 429	0.5	200 773	0.5	4.9
Finland	117 584	0.3	104 106	0.3	−11.5
France	2 440 748	6.6	2 508 996	6.8	2.8
Germany	14 728 783	39.9	16 128 432	43.6	9.5
Greece	151 326	0.4	149 316	0.4	−1.3
Iceland [1]	..	..	..	..	..
Ireland	50 815	0.1	52 304	0.1	2.9
Italy	1 902 280	5.2	1 995 680	5.4	4.9
Luxembourg	181 201	0.5	208 790	0.6	15.2
Netherlands	3 343 426	9.1	3 380 760	9.1	1.1
Norway	91 248	0.2	88 405	0.2	−3.1
Portugal	109 335	0.3	97 288	0.3	−11.0
Spain	703 461	1.9	713 123	1.9	1.4
Sweden	388 364	1.1	345 956	0.9	−10.9
Switzerland	..	..	..	..	..
Turkey	151 189	0.4	111 947	0.3	−26.0
United Kingdom	2 802 159	7.6	2 543 400	6.9	−9.2
Other OECD-Europe	..	..	..	..	..
Total Europe	29 888 439	81.0	31 262 288	84.5	4.6
Canada	285 392	0.8	221 938	0.6	−22.2
United States	2 793 601	7.6	1 776 377	4.8	−36.4
Total North America	3 078 993	8.3	1 998 315	5.4	−35.1
Australia [2]	331 984	0.9	225 199	0.6	−32.2
New Zealand [2]	..	..	..	..	..
Japan	849 971	2.3	755 297	2.0	−11.1
Total Australasia and Japan	1 181 955	3.2	980 496	2.7	−17.0
Total OECD Countries	**34 149 387**	**92.6**	**34 241 099**	**92.6**	**0.3**
Yugoslavia	167 186	0.5	208 969	0.6	25.0
Other European countries [1]	468 640	1.3	549 525	1.5	17.3
Latin America	392 802	1.1	371 454	1.0	−5.4
Argentina	55 222	0.1	56 208	0.2	1.8
Brazil	155 791	0.4	143 469	0.4	−7.9
Mexico	49 914	0.1	41 288	0.1	−17.3
Asia-Oceania	1 202 762	3.3	1 129 674	3.1	−6.1
India	101 044	0.3	87 737	0.2	−13.2
Iran	47 796	0.1	39 961	0.1	−16.4
Israel	383 127	1.0	360 433	1.0	−5.9
Africa	507 985	1.4	483 038	1.3	−4.9
Egypt	73 818	0.2	69 188	0.2	−6.3
South Africa	108 325	0.3	91 608	0.2	−15.4
Total non-OECD Countries	**2 739 375**	**7.4**	**2 742 660**	**7.4**	**0.1**
TOTAL	**36 888 762**	**100.0**	**36 983 759**	**100.0**	**0.3**

1. "Other European countries" includes Iceland.
2. Australia includes New Zealand.

TURKEY

ARRIVALS OF FOREIGN TRAVELLERS AT FRONTIERS
(by country of nationality)

	1990	Relative share	1991	Relative share	% Variation over 1990
Austria	196 561	3.6	102 071	1.8	−48.1
Belgium	56 258	1.0	33 763	0.6	−40.0
Denmark	34 507	0.6	32 320	0.6	−6.3
Finland	104 321	1.9	80 511	1.5	−22.8
France	310 809	5.8	117 070	2.1	−62.3
Germany	973 914	18.1	779 882	14.1	−19.9
Greece	227 709	4.2	138 918	2.5	−39.0
Iceland [1]	..	..	..	..	..
Ireland [1]	..	..	..	..	..
Italy	156 342	2.9	64 134	1.2	−59.0
Luxembourg [1]	..	..	..	..	..
Netherlands	150 337	2.8	107 018	1.9	−28.8
Norway	39 889	0.7	24 590	0.4	−38.4
Portugal [1]	..	..	..	..	..
Spain	62 220	1.2	24 944	0.5	−59.9
Sweden	110 204	2.0	69 344	1.3	−37.1
Switzerland	76 368	1.4	41 606	0.8	−45.5
Turkey	..	..	..	..	..
United Kingdom	351 458	6.5	200 813	3.6	−42.9
Other OECD-Europe [1]	35 359	0.7	19 939	0.4	−43.6
Total Europe	2 886 256	53.6	1 836 923	33.3	−36.4
Canada	34 575	0.6	17 680	0.3	−48.9
United States	205 831	3.8	79 256	1.4	−61.5
Total North America	240 406	4.5	96 936	1.8	−59.7
Australia	37 045	0.7	20 707	0.4	−44.1
New Zealand	12 937	0.2	6 950	0.1	−46.3
Japan	35 358	0.7	18 479	0.3	−47.7
Total Australasia and Japan	85 340	1.6	46 136	0.8	−45.9
Total OECD Countries	**3 212 002**	**59.6**	**1 979 995**	**35.9**	**−38.4**
Yugoslavia	325 703	6.0	158 699	2.9	−51.3
Other European countries	1 134 160	21.0	2 751 666	49.9	142.6
Bulgaria	72 741	1.3	943 250	17.1	1196.7
Czechoslovakia	66 224	1.2	217 232	3.9	228.0
Germany (D. R.)	10 512	0.2	0	0.0	−100.0
Hungary	172 357	3.2	164 903	3.0	−4.3
Poland	206 682	3.8	184 008	3.3	−11.0
Rumania	377 275	7.0	503 785	9.1	33.5
USSR	223 211	4.1	731 869	13.3	227.9
Latin America	30 470	0.6	11 428	0.2	−62.5
Argentina	2 491	0.0	2 218	0.0	−11.0
Brazil	5 336	0.1	3 094	0.1	−42.0
Chile	878	0.0	523	0.0	−40.4
Mexico	6 162	0.1	2 100	0.0	−65.9
Asia-Oceania	590 822	11.0	552 913	10.0	−6.4
Iran	253 452	4.7	253 260	4.6	−0.1
Israel	40 064	0.7	46 043	0.8	14.9
Lebanon	14 655	0.3	14 140	0.3	−3.5
Pakistan	15 252	0.3	9 370	0.2	−38.6
Saudi Arabia	16 417	0.3	15 083	0.3	−8.1
Africa	89 924	1.7	59 943	1.1	−33.3
Algeria	9 737	0.2	6 286	0.1	−35.4
Egypt	11 102	0.2	8 343	0.2	−24.9
Morocco	5 695	0.1	2 621	0.0	−54.0
Origin country undetermined [2]	6 225	0.1	3 253	0.1	−47.7
Total non-OECD Countries	**2 177 304**	**40.4**	**3 537 902**	**64.1**	**62.5**
TOTAL	**5 389 306**	**100.0**	**5 517 897**	**100.0**	**2.4**

1. "Other OECD-Europe" includes Iceland, Ireland, Luxembourg and Portugal.
2. "Origin country undetermined" includes Other North America and Stateless persons.

TURKEY

ARRIVALS OF FOREIGN TOURISTS AT HOTELS

(by country of nationality)

	1990	Relative share	1991	Relative share	% Variation over 1990
Austria	114 267	3.3	56 650	2.6	−50.4
Belgium [1]	206 345	5.9	110 029	5.0	−46.7
Denmark [2]	169 596	4.9	89 246	4.0	−47.4
Finland [2]	..	..	..	..	
France	631 868	18.1	183 950	8.3	−70.9
Germany	960 575	27.5	563 870	25.4	−41.3
Greece	65 124	1.9	21 920	1.0	−66.3
Iceland	..	..	..	..	
Ireland	..	..			
Italy	207 337	5.9	115 068	5.2	−44.5
Luxembourg [1]	..	..	..	..	..
Netherlands [1]	..	..	..	..	..
Norway [2]	..	..	..	..	..
Portugal	..	..			
Spain	92 355	2.6	80 674	3.6	−12.6
Sweden [2]	..	..	..	..	
Switzerland	65 089	1.9	30 708	1.4	−52.8
Turkey	..	..			
United Kingdom	174 624	5.0	94 170	4.2	−46.1
Other OECD-Europe	..	..	..	..	
Total Europe	2 687 180	76.9	1 346 285	60.7	−49.9
Canada	13 050	0.4	7 950	0.4	−39.1
United States	158 428	4.5	91 288	4.1	−42.4
Total North America	171 478	4.9	99 238	4.5	−42.1
Australia	17 612	0.5	10 299	0.5	−41.5
New Zealand	..	..	..	..	
Japan	77 046	2.2	49 623	2.2	−35.6
Total Australasia and Japan	94 658	2.7	59 922	2.7	−36.7
Total OECD Countries	**2 953 316**	**84.5**	**1 505 445**	**67.9**	**−49.0**
Yugoslavia	48 721	1.4	39 387	1.8	−19.2
Other European countries	144 781	4.1	315 646	14.2	118.0
Bulgaria	10 825	0.3	92 607	4.2	755.5
Hungary	41 868	1.2	38 816	1.8	−7.3
Poland	37 109	1.1	75 641	3.4	103.8
Rumania	27 959	0.8	37 700	1.7	34.8
USSR	27 020	0.8	70 882	3.2	162.3
Asia-Oceania [3]	115 702	3.3	100 403	4.5	−13.2
Iran	45 111	1.3	44 098	2.0	−2.2
Lebanon	6 440	0.2	6 528	0.3	1.4
Pakistan	7 836	0.2	4 527	0.2	−42.2
Saudi Arabia	21 334	0.6	20 459	0.9	−4.1
Africa	14 190	0.4	14 721	0.7	3.7
Egypt	5 279	0.2	5 957	0.3	12.8
Origin country undetermined	218 634	6.3	240 976	10.9	10.2
Total non-OECD Countries	**542 028**	**15.5**	**711 133**	**32.1**	**31.2**
TOTAL	**3 495 344**	**100.0**	**2 216 578**	**100.0**	**−36.6**

1. Belgium includes Luxembourg and Netherlands.
2. Denmark includes Finland, Norway and Sweden.
3. Asia-Oceania includes Iraq, Kuwait, Lebanon, Syria, Saudi Arabia, Jordan, Iran and Pakistan.

TURKEY

ARRIVALS OF FOREIGN TOURISTS AT REGISTERED TOURIST ACCOMMODATION

(by country of nationality)

	1990	Relative share	1991	Relative share	% Variation over 1990
Austria	167 894	4.3	69 762	2.9	−58.4
Belgium [1]	223 308	5.8	121 197	5.1	−45.7
Denmark [2]	176 140	4.6	91 781	3.8	−47.9
Finland [2]	..	..	..	..	..
France	694 566	18.0	206 269	8.6	−70.3
Germany	1 113 735	28.8	661 497	27.6	−40.6
Greece	66 293	1.7	22 093	0.9	−66.7
Iceland	..	..	..	..	..
Ireland	..	..	..	..	..
Italy	235 140	6.1	124 941	5.2	−46.9
Luxembourg [1]	..	..	..	..	..
Netherlands [1]	..	..	..	..	..
Norway [2]	..	..	..	..	..
Portugal	..	..	..	..	..
Spain	93 659	2.4	81 349	3.4	−13.1
Sweden [2]	..	..	..	..	..
Switzerland	84 103	2.2	37 788	1.6	−55.1
Turkey					
United Kingdom	181 942	4.7	102 374	4.3	−43.7
Other OECD-Europe	..	..	..	..	..
Total Europe	3 036 780	78.5	1 519 051	63.3	−50.0
Canada	13 454	0.3	8 286	0.3	−38.4
United States	161 058	4.2	92 496	3.9	−42.6
Total North America	174 512	4.5	100 782	4.2	−42.2
Australia	18 912	0.5	10 470	0.4	−44.6
New Zealand	..	..	..	..	..
Japan	77 464	2.0	49 707	2.1	−35.8
Total Australasia and Japan	96 376	2.5	60 177	2.5	−37.6
Total OECD Countries	**3 307 668**	**85.5**	**1 680 010**	**70.0**	**−49.2**
Yugoslavia	49 286	1.3	39 588	1.7	−19.7
Other European countries	151 801	3.9	317 763	13.2	109.3
Bulgaria	11 091	0.3	92 713	3.9	735.9
Hungary	43 625	1.1	39 578	1.7	−9.3
Poland	40 468	1.0	76 530	3.2	89.1
Rumania	29 037	0.8	37 930	1.6	30.6
USSR	27 580	0.7	71 012	3.0	157.5
Asia-Oceania [3]	120 694	3.1	100 935	4.2	−16.4
Iran	46 313	1.2	44 187	1.8	−4.6
Lebanon	6 667	0.2	6 879	0.3	3.2
Pakistan	7 958	0.2	4 534	0.2	−43.0
Saudi Arabia	23 712	0.6	20 474	0.9	−13.7
Africa	14 451	0.4	14 763	0.6	2.2
Egypt	5 501	0.1	5 967	0.2	8.5
Origin country undetermined	225 266	5.8	245 607	10.2	9.0
Total non-OECD Countries	**561 498**	**14.5**	**718 656**	**30.0**	**28.0**
TOTAL	**3 869 166**	**100.0**	**2 398 666**	**100.0**	**−38.0**

1. Belgium includes Luxembourg and Netherlands.
2. Denmark includes Finland, Norway and Sweden.
3. Asia-Oceania includes Iraq, Kuwait, Lebanon, Syria, Saudi Arabia, Jordan, Iran and Pakistan.

TURKEY

NIGHTS SPENT BY FOREIGN TOURISTS IN HOTELS

(by country of nationality)

	1990	Relative share	1991	Relative share	% Variation over 1990
Austria	486 455	4.7	295 750	3.6	−39.2
Belgium [1]	640 452	6.2	435 325	5.4	−32.0
Denmark [2]	751 576	7.3	500 365	6.2	−33.4
Finland [2]	..	..	..	..	..
France	1 204 113	11.7	467 794	5.8	−61.2
Germany	3 898 518	37.8	3 458 776	42.5	−11.3
Greece	129 816	1.3	52 451	0.6	−59.6
Iceland	..	..	..	..	..
Ireland	..	..	..	..	..
Italy	400 878	3.9	293 218	3.6	−26.9
Luxembourg [1]	..	..	..	..	..
Netherlands [1]	..	..	..	..	..
Norway [2]	..	..	..	..	..
Portugal	..	..	..	..	..
Spain	185 758	1.8	146 571	1.8	−21.1
Sweden [2]	..	..	..	..	..
Switzerland	249 466	2.4	129 740	1.6	−48.0
Turkey					
United Kingdom	635 154	6.2	378 702	4.7	−40.4
Other OECD-Europe	..	..	..	..	..
Total Europe	8 582 186	83.3	6 158 692	75.7	−28.2
Canada	28 044	0.3	19 522	0.2	−30.4
United States	348 767	3.4	282 437	3.5	−19.0
Total North America	376 811	3.7	301 959	3.7	−19.9
Australia	32 576	0.3	20 418	0.3	−37.3
New Zealand	..	..	..	..	..
Japan	134 267	1.3	90 890	1.1	−32.3
Total Australasia and Japan	166 843	1.6	111 308	1.4	−33.3
Total OECD Countries	**9 125 840**	**88.6**	**6 571 959**	**80.8**	**−28.0**
Yugoslavia	81 503	0.8	64 856	0.8	−20.4
Other European countries	337 269	3.3	647 200	8.0	91.9
Bulgaria	15 422	0.1	134 755	1.7	773.8
Hungary	96 717	0.9	77 163	0.9	−20.2
Poland	98 717	1.0	190 010	2.3	92.5
Rumania	65 556	0.6	84 919	1.0	29.5
USSR	60 857	0.6	160 353	2.0	163.5
Asia-Oceania [3]	262 305	2.5	245 534	3.0	−6.4
Iran	113 151	1.1	110 289	1.4	−2.5
Lebanon	12 980	0.1	15 379	0.2	18.5
Pakistan	14 292	0.1	9 527	0.1	−33.3
Saudi Arabia	46 509	0.5	49 398	0.6	6.2
Africa	36 225	0.4	45 922	0.6	26.8
Egypt	13 967	0.1	19 287	0.2	38.1
Origin country undetermined	457 432	4.4	555 627	6.8	21.5
Total non-OECD Countries	**1 174 734**	**11.4**	**1 559 139**	**19.2**	**32.7**
TOTAL	**10 300 574**	**100.0**	**8 131 098**	**100.0**	**−21.1**

1. Belgium includes Luxembourg and Netherlands.
2. Denmark includes Finland, Norway and Sweden.
3. Asia-Oceania includes Iraq, Kuwait, Lebanon, Syria, Saudi Arabia, Jordan, Iran and Pakistan.

TURKEY

NIGHTS SPENT BY FOREIGN TOURISTS IN REGISTERED TOURIST ACCOMMODATION

(by country of nationality)

	1990	Relative share	1991	Relative share	% Variation over 1990
Austria	1 004 432	7.6	421 862	4.3	−58.0
Belgium [1]	737 729	5.6	500 657	5.2	−32.1
Denmark [2]	802 997	6.1	514 268	5.3	−36.0
Finland [2]	..	..	..	..	..
France	1 586 354	12.0	631 272	6.5	−60.2
Germany	5 426 311	40.9	4 448 640	45.9	−18.0
Greece	132 419	1.0	52 862	0.5	−60.1
Iceland	..	..	..	..	..
Ireland					
Italy	533 676	4.0	366 916	3.8	−31.2
Luxembourg [1]	..	..	..	..	..
Netherlands [1]	..	..	..	..	..
Norway [2]	..	..	..	..	..
Portugal	..	..	..	..	..
Spain	191 621	1.4	147 729	1.5	−22.9
Sweden [2]	..	..	..	..	..
Switzerland	394 564	3.0	188 880	1.9	−52.1
Turkey	..	..	..	..	..
United Kingdom	675 111	5.1	419 471	4.3	−37.9
Other OECD-Europe	..	..	..	..	..
Total Europe	11 485 214	86.5	7 692 557	79.3	−33.0
Canada	29 266	0.2	20 181	0.2	−31.0
United States	357 293	2.7	287 511	3.0	−19.5
Total North America	386 559	2.9	307 692	3.2	−20.4
Australia	36 207	0.3	21 048	0.2	−41.9
New Zealand	..	..	..	..	..
Japan	135 101	1.0	91 097	0.9	−32.6
Total Australasia and Japan	171 308	1.3	112 145	1.2	−34.5
Total OECD Countries	**12 043 081**	**90.7**	**8 112 394**	**83.6**	**−32.6**
Yugoslavia	82 633	0.6	65 323	0.7	−20.9
Other European countries	353 297	2.7	651 883	6.7	84.5
Bulgaria	15 823	0.1	134 907	1.4	752.6
Hungary	101 001	0.8	78 098	0.8	−22.7
Poland	106 780	0.8	192 765	2.0	80.5
Rumania	67 617	0.5	85 321	0.9	26.2
USSR	62 076	0.5	160 792	1.7	159.0
Asia-Oceania [3]	274 000	2.1	246 496	2.5	−10.0
Iran	115 569	0.9	110 675	1.1	−4.2
Lebanon	13 480	0.1	15 786	0.2	17.1
Pakistan	14 439	0.1	9 549	0.1	−33.9
Saudi Arabia	51 728	0.4	49 431	0.5	−4.4
Africa	36 803	0.3	46 160	0.5	25.4
Egypt	14 465	0.1	19 331	0.2	33.6
Libyan Arab Jamahiriya	22 338	0.2	..	..	..
Origin country undetermined	480 827	3.6	576 841	5.9	20.0
Total non-OECD Countries	**1 227 560**	**9.3**	**1 586 703**	**16.4**	**29.3**
TOTAL	**13 270 641**	**100.0**	**9 699 097**	**100.0**	**−26.9**

1. Belgium includes Luxembourg and Netherlands.
2. Denmark includes Finland, Norway and Sweden.
3. Asia-Oceania includes Iraq, Kuwait, Lebanon, Syria, Saudi Arabia, Jordan, Iran and Pakistan.

UNITED KINGDOM

ARRIVALS OF FOREIGN VISITORS AT FRONTIERS

(by country of residence)

	1990	Relative share	1991	Relative share	% Variation over 1990
Austria	154 000	0.9	156 000	0.9	1.3
Belgium	546 000	3.0	653 000	3.9	19.6
Denmark	228 000	1.3	236 000	1.4	3.5
Finland	134 000	0.7	109 000	0.7	−18.7
France	2 309 000	12.8	2 292 000	13.8	−0.7
Germany	1 879 000	10.4	2 080 000	12.5	10.7
Greece	134 000	0.7	116 000	0.7	−13.4
Iceland	50 000	0.3	29 000	0.2	−42.0
Ireland	1 317 000	7.3	1 314 000	7.9	−0.2
Italy	714 000	4.0	714 000	4.3	0.0
Luxembourg	26 000	0.1	27 000	0.2	3.8
Netherlands	991 000	5.5	1 070 000	6.4	8.0
Norway	272 000	1.5	267 000	1.6	−1.8
Portugal	105 000	0.6	100 000	0.6	−4.8
Spain	605 000	3.4	619 000	3.7	2.3
Sweden	470 000	2.6	444 000	2.7	−5.5
Switzerland	446 000	2.5	428 000	2.6	−4.0
Turkey	65 000	0.4	61 000	0.4	−6.2
United Kingdom	..	..	..	..	..
Other OECD-Europe	..	..	..	..	..
Total Europe	10 445 000	58.0	10 715 000	64.3	2.6
Canada	702 000	3.9	521 000	3.1	−25.8
United States	3 049 000	16.9	2 250 000	13.5	−26.2
Total North America	3 751 000	20.8	2 771 000	16.6	−26.1
Australia	629 000	3.5	449 000	2.7	−28.6
New Zealand	126 000	0.7	107 000	0.6	−15.1
Japan	572 000	3.2	440 000	2.6	−23.1
Total Australasia and Japan	1 327 000	7.4	996 000	6.0	−24.9
Total OECD Countries	**15 523 000**	**86.2**	**14 482 000**	**86.9**	**−6.7**
Yugoslavia	64 000	0.4	38 200	0.2	−40.3
Other European countries	438 000	2.4	383 400	2.3	−12.5
Latin America	187 000	1.0	197 000	1.2	5.3
Asia-Oceania	1 167 000	6.5	984 500	5.9	−15.6
Africa	562 000	3.1	513 200	3.1	−8.7
Origin country undetermined	74 000	0.4	63 400	0.4	−14.3
Total non-OECD Countries	**2 492 000**	**13.8**	**2 179 700**	**13.1**	**−12.5**
TOTAL	**18 015 000**	**100.0**	**16 661 700**	**100.0**	**−7.5**

UNITED KINGDOM

NIGHTS SPENT BY FOREIGN TOURISTS IN TOURIST ACCOMMODATION[1]

(by country of residence)

	1990	Relative share	1991	Relative share	% Variation over 1990
Austria	1 702 000	0.9	1 370 000	0.8	−19.5
Belgium	2 280 000	1.2	2 754 000	1.5	20.8
Denmark	2 184 000	1.1	1 700 000	0.9	−22.2
Finland	983 000	0.5	808 000	0.4	−17.8
France	16 993 000	8.7	14 872 000	8.2	−12.5
Germany	17 394 000	8.9	18 958 000	10.5	9.0
Greece	1 946 000	1.0	1 425 000	0.8	−26.8
Iceland	315 000	0.2	286 000	0.2	−9.2
Ireland	11 433 000	5.8	10 165 000	5.6	−11.1
Italy	8 371 000	4.3	9 001 000	5.0	7.5
Luxembourg	172 000	0.1	123 000	0.1	−28.5
Netherlands	5 517 000	2.8	6 083 000	3.4	10.3
Norway	1 698 000	0.9	1 934 000	1.1	13.9
Portugal	1 269 000	0.6	1 442 000	0.8	13.6
Spain[2]	8 626 000	4.4	9 441 000	5.2	9.4
Sweden	3 167 000	1.6	3 611 000	2.0	14.0
Switzerland	4 257 000	2.2	4 346 000	2.4	2.1
Turkey	1 594 000	0.8	1 546 000	0.9	−3.0
United Kingdom	..	..	..	..	..
Other OECD-Europe	..	..	..	..	..
Total Europe	89 901 000	45.8	89 865 000	49.7	−0.0
Canada	9 352 000	4.8	7 355 000	4.1	−21.4
United States	28 621 000	14.6	24 146 000	13.4	−15.6
Total North America	37 973 000	19.3	31 501 000	17.4	−17.0
Australia	14 257 000	7.3	11 571 000	6.4	−18.8
New Zealand	3 222 000	1.6	3 507 000	1.9	8.8
Japan	3 954 000	2.0	4 041 000	2.2	2.2
Total Australasia and Japan	21 433 000	10.9	19 119 000	10.6	−10.8
Total OECD Countries	**149 307 000**	**76.0**	**140 485 000**	**77.7**	**−5.9**
Yugoslavia	1 678 000	0.9	703 000	0.4	−58.1
Other European countries	7 033 000	3.6	6 597 000	3.6	−6.2
Latin America	2 237 000	1.1	2 506 000	1.4	12.0
Asia-Oceania	21 436 000	10.9	18 182 000	10.1	−15.2
Africa	12 462 000	6.3	10 355 000	5.7	−16.9
Origin country undetermined	2 229 000	1.1	2 000 000	1.1	−10.3
Total non-OECD Countries	**47 075 000**	**24.0**	**40 343 000**	**22.3**	**−14.3**
TOTAL	**196 382 000**	**100.0**	**180 828 000**	**100.0**	**−7.9**

1. Estimates of total number of nights spent in all forms of accommodation, including stays with friends and relatives. Excluding: visitors in transit, visits of merchant seamen, airline personnel and military on duty.
2. Spain includes Canary Islands.

UNITED STATES

ARRIVALS OF FOREIGN TOURISTS AT FRONTIERS

(by country of residence)

	1990	Relative share	1991	Relative share	% Variation over 1990
Austria	107 000	0.3	121 000	0.3	13.1
Belgium	138 000	0.3	149 099	0.3	8.0
Denmark	97 000	0.2	95 399	0.2	−1.7
Finland	103 386	0.3	93 151	0.2	−9.9
France	716 000	1.8	770 230	1.8	7.6
Germany	1 203 000	3.0	1 430 193	3.3	18.9
Greece	53 611	0.1	49 429	0.1	−7.8
Iceland	13 753	0.0	15 183	0.0	10.4
Ireland	99 000	0.3	101 980	0.2	3.0
Italy	396 000	1.0	478 853	1.1	20.9
Luxembourg	10 540	0.0	11 910	0.0	13.0
Netherlands	284 000	0.7	316 609	0.7	11.5
Norway	104 000	0.3	93 691	0.2	−9.9
Portugal	34 881	0.1	36 206	0.1	3.8
Spain	243 000	0.6	291 646	0.7	20.0
Sweden	282 000	0.7	260 424	0.6	−7.7
Switzerland	294 000	0.7	304 541	0.7	3.6
Turkey	31 070	0.1	32 064	0.1	3.2
United Kingdom	2 244 000	5.7	2 495 354	5.8	11.2
Other OECD-Europe	..		..		..
Total Europe	6 454 241	16.3	7 146 962	16.7	10.7
Canada	17 269 000	43.6	18 926 613	44.3	9.6
United States	..		..		..
Total North America	17 269 000	43.6	18 926 613	44.3	9.6
Australia	466 000	1.2	470 595	1.1	1.0
New Zealand	174 000	0.4	145 306	0.3	−16.5
Japan	3 231 000	8.2	3 319 934	7.8	2.8
Total Australasia and Japan	3 871 000	9.8	3 935 835	9.2	1.7
Total OECD Countries	**27 594 241**	**69.7**	**30 009 410**	**70.2**	**8.8**
Yugoslavia	29 184	0.1	27 637	0.1	−5.3
Other European countries	199 000	0.5	208 719	0.5	4.9
Czechoslovakia	15 873	0.0	17 651	0.0	11.2
Hungary	19 719	0.0	20 311	0.0	3.0
Poland	60 765	0.2	51 650	0.1	−15.0
Rumania	15 615	0.0	12 664	0.0	−18.9
USSR	81 000	0.2	100 233	0.2	23.7
Latin America [1]	10 093 673	25.5	10 720 700	25.1	6.2
Argentina	185 000	0.5	280 504	0.7	51.6
Brazil	398 000	1.0	459 384	1.1	15.4
Chile	69 000	0.2	88 673	0.2	28.5
Colombia	155 000	0.4	160 755	0.4	3.7
Mexico	7 217 116	18.2	7 640 752	17.9	5.9
Venezuela	264 000	0.7	310 735	0.7	17.7
Asia-Oceania	1 128 064	2.8	1 258 818	2.9	11.6
China	305 198	0.8	344 263	0.8	12.8
Hong Kong	163 000	0.4	178 381	0.4	9.4
India	110 000	0.3	109 557	0.3	−0.4
Israel	162 000	0.4	169 912	0.4	4.9
Republic of Korea	211 000	0.5	278 182	0.7	31.8
Philippines	98 000	0.2	103 463	0.2	5.6
Saudi Arabia	48 298	0.1	51 148	0.1	5.9
Singapore	53 610	0.1	57 309	0.1	6.9
Taiwan	305 000	0.8	..	..	..
Africa	137 229	0.3	138 101	0.3	0.6
South Africa	38 535	0.1	40 924	0.1	6.2
Origin country undetermined [2]	403 424	1.0	386 137	0.9	−4.3
Total non-OECD Countries	**11 990 574**	**30.3**	**12 740 112**	**29.8**	**6.3**
TOTAL	**39 584 815**	**100.0**	**42 749 522**	**100.0**	**8.0**

1. Latin America includes Central America, Carribean, South America and Mexico.
2. Origin country undetermined includes Middle East only.

MAIN SALES OUTLETS OF OECD PUBLICATIONS
PRINCIPAUX POINTS DE VENTE DES PUBLICATIONS DE L'OCDE

ARGENTINA – ARGENTINE
Carlos Hirsch S.R.L.
Galería Güemes, Florida 165, 4° Piso
1333 Buenos Aires   Tel. (1) 331.1787 y 331.2391
Telefax: (1) 331.1787

AUSTRALIA – AUSTRALIE
D.A. Information Services
648 Whitehorse Road, P.O.B 163
Mitcham, Victoria 3132   Tel. (03) 873.4411
Telefax: (03) 873.5679

AUSTRIA – AUTRICHE
Gerold & Co.
Graben 31
Wien I   Tel. (0222) 533.50.14

BELGIUM – BELGIQUE
Jean De Lannoy
Avenue du Roi 202
B-1060 Bruxelles   Tel. (02) 538.51.69/538.08.41
Telefax: (02) 538.08.41

CANADA
Renouf Publishing Company Ltd.
1294 Algoma Road
Ottawa, ON K1B 3W8   Tel. (613) 741.4333
Telefax: (613) 741.5439
Stores:
61 Sparks Street
Ottawa, ON K1P 5R1   Tel. (613) 238.8985
211 Yonge Street
Toronto, ON M5B 1M4   Tel. (416) 363.3171
Les Éditions La Liberté Inc.
3020 Chemin Sainte-Foy
Sainte-Foy, PQ G1X 3V6   Tel. (418) 658.3763
Telefax: (418) 658.3763

Federal Publications
165 University Avenue
Toronto, ON M5H 3B8   Tel. (416) 581.1552
Telefax: (416) 581.1743

Les Publications Fédérales
1185 Avenue de l'Université
Montréal, PQ H3B 3A7   Tel. (514) 954.1633
Telefax : (514) 954.1633

CHINA – CHINE
China National Publications Import
Export Corporation (CNPIEC)
16 Gongti E. Road, Chaoyang District
P.O. Box 88 or 50
Beijing 100704 PR   Tel. (01) 506.6688
Telefax: (01) 506.3101

DENMARK – DANEMARK
Munksgaard Export and Subscription Service
35, Nørre Søgade, P.O. Box 2148
DK-1016 København K   Tel. (33) 12.85.70
Telefax: (33) 12.93.87

FINLAND – FINLANDE
Akateeminen Kirjakauppa
Keskuskatu 1, P.O. Box 128
00100 Helsinki   Tel. (358 0) 12141
Telefax: (358 0) 121.4441

FRANCE
OECD/OCDE
Mail Orders/Commandes par correspondance:
2, rue André-Pascal
75775 Paris Cedex 16   Tel. (33-1) 45.24.82.00
Telefax: (33-1) 45.24.81.76   or (33-1) 45.24.85.00
Telex: 640048 OCDE

OECD Bookshop/Librairie de l'OCDE :
33, rue Octave-Feuillet
75016 Paris   Tel. (33-1) 45.24.81.67
(33-1) 45.24.81.81

Documentation Française
29, quai Voltaire
75007 Paris   Tel. 40.15.70.00
Gibert Jeune (Droit-Économie)
6, place Saint-Michel
75006 Paris   Tel. 43.25.91.19
Librairie du Commerce International
10, avenue d'Iéna
75016 Paris   Tel. 40.73.34.60
Librairie Dunod
Université Paris-Dauphine
Place du Maréchal de Lattre de Tassigny
75016 Paris   Tel. 47.27.18.56
Librairie Lavoisier
11, rue Lavoisier
75008 Paris   Tel. 42.65.39.95
Librairie L.G.D.J. - Montchrestien
20, rue Soufflot
75005 Paris   Tel. 46.33.89.85
Librairie des Sciences Politiques
30, rue Saint-Guillaume
75007 Paris   Tel. 45.48.36.02
P.U.F.
49, boulevard Saint-Michel
75005 Paris   Tel. 43.25.83.40
Librairie de l'Université
12a, rue Nazareth
13100 Aix-en-Provence   Tel. (16) 42.26.18.08
Documentation Française
165, rue Garibaldi
69003 Lyon   Tel. (16) 78.63.32.23
Librairie Decitre
29, place Bellecour
69002 Lyon   Tel. (16) 72.40.54.54

GERMANY – ALLEMAGNE
OECD Publications and Information Centre
August-Bebel-Allee 6
D-W 5300 Bonn 2   Tel. (0228) 959.120
Telefax: (0228) 959.12.17

GREECE – GRÈCE
Librairie Kauffmann
Mavrokordatou 9
106 78 Athens   Tel. 322.21.60
Telefax: 363.39.67

HONG-KONG
Swindon Book Co. Ltd.
13–15 Lock Road
Kowloon, Hong Kong   Tel. 366.80.31
Telefax: 739.49.75

HUNGARY – HONGRIE
Euro Info Service
kázmér u.45
1121 Budapest   Tel. (1) 182.00.44
Telefax : (1) 182.00.44

ICELAND – ISLANDE
Mál Mog Menning
Laugavegi 18, Pósthólf 392
121 Reykjavik   Tel. 162.35.23

INDIA – INDE
Oxford Book and Stationery Co.
Scindia House
New Delhi 110001   Tel.(11) 331.5896/5308
Telefax: (11) 332.5993
17 Park Street
Calcutta 700016   Tel. 240832

INDONESIA – INDONÉSIE
Pdii-Lipi
P.O. Box 269/JKSMG/88
Jakarta 12790   Tel. 583467
Telex: 62 875

IRELAND – IRLANDE
TDC Publishers – Library Suppliers
12 North Frederick Street
Dublin 1   Tel. 74.48.35/74.96.77
Telefax: 74.84.16

ISRAEL
Electronic Publications only
Publications électroniques seulement
Sophist Systems Ltd.
71 Allenby Street
Tel-Aviv 65134   Tel. 3-29.00.21
Telefax: 3-29.92.39

ITALY – ITALIE
Libreria Commissionaria Sansoni
Via Duca di Calabria 1/1
50125 Firenze   Tel. (055) 64.54.15
Telefax: (055) 64.12.57
Via Bartolini 29
20155 Milano   Tel. (02) 36.50.83
Editrice e Libreria Herder
Piazza Montecitorio 120
00186 Roma   Tel. 679.46.28
Telefax: 678.47.51
Libreria Hoepli
Via Hoepli 5
20121 Milano   Tel. (02) 86.54.46
Telefax: (02) 805.28.86
Libreria Scientifica
Dott. Lucio de Biasio 'Aeiou'
Via Coronelli, 6
20146 Milano   Tel. (02) 48.95.45.52
Telefax: (02) 48.95.45.48

JAPAN – JAPON
OECD Publications and Information Centre
Landic Akasaka Building
2-3-4 Akasaka, Minato-ku
Tokyo 107   Tel. (81.3) 3586.2016
Telefax: (81.3) 3584.7929

KOREA – CORÉE
Kyobo Book Centre Co. Ltd.
P.O. Box 1658, Kwang Hwa Moon
Seoul   Tel. 730.78.91
Telefax: 735.00.30

MALAYSIA – MALAISIE
Co-operative Bookshop Ltd.
University of Malaya
P.O. Box 1127, Jalan Pantai Baru
59700 Kuala Lumpur
Malaysia   Tel. 756.5000/756.5425
Telefax: 757.3661

MEXICO – MEXIQUE
Revistas y Periodicos Internacionales S.A. de C.V.
Florencia 57 - 1004
Mexico, D.F. 06600   Tel. 207.81.00
Telefax : 208.39.79

NETHERLANDS – PAYS-BAS
SDU Uitgeverij
Christoffel Plantijnstraat 2
Postbus 20014
2500 EA's-Gravenhage   Tel. (070 3) 78.99.11
Voor bestellingen: Tel. (070 3) 78.98.80
Telefax: (070 3) 47.63.51

**NEW ZEALAND
NOUVELLE-ZÉLANDE**
Legislation Services
P.O. Box 12418
Thorndon, Wellington   Tel. (04) 496.5652
Telefax: (04) 496.5698

NORWAY – NORVÈGE
Narvesen Info Center – NIC
Bertrand Narvesens vei 2
P.O. Box 6125 Etterstad
0602 Oslo 6   Tel. (02) 57.33.00
             Telefax: (02) 68.19.01

PAKISTAN
Mirza Book Agency
65 Shahrah Quaid-E-Azam
Lahore 54000   Tel. (42) 353.601
             Telefax: (42) 231.730

PHILIPPINE – PHILIPPINES
International Book Center
5th Floor, Filipinas Life Bldg.
Ayala Avenue
Metro Manila   Tel. 81.96.76
            Telex 23312 RHP PH

PORTUGAL
Livraria Portugal
Rua do Carmo 70-74
Apart. 2681
1117 Lisboa Codex   Tel.: (01) 347.49.82/3/4/5
            Telefax: (01) 347.02.64

SINGAPORE – SINGAPOUR
Information Publications Pte. Ltd.
41, Kallang Pudding, No. 04-03
Singapore 1334   Tel. 741.5166
            Telefax: 742.9356

SPAIN – ESPAGNE
Mundi-Prensa Libros S.A.
Castelló 37, Apartado 1223
Madrid 28001   Tel. (91) 431.33.99
            Telefax: (91) 575.39.98

Libreria Internacional AEDOS
Consejo de Ciento 391
08009 – Barcelona   Tel. (93) 488.34.92
            Telefax: (93) 487.76.59
Llibreria de la Generalitat
Palau Moja
Rambla dels Estudis, 118
08002 – Barcelona
     (Subscripcions) Tel. (93) 318.80.12
     (Publicacions) Tel. (93) 302.67.23
            Telefax: (93) 412.18.54

SRI LANKA
Centre for Policy Research
c/o Colombo Agencies Ltd.
No. 300-304, Galle Road
Colombo 3   Tel. (1) 574240, 573551-2
         Telefax: (1) 575394, 510711

SWEDEN – SUÈDE
Fritzes Fackboksföretaget
Box 16356
Regeringsgatan 12
103 27 Stockholm   Tel. (08) 690.90.90
           Telefax: (08) 20.50.21

Subscription Agency-Agence d'abonnements
Wennergren-Williams AB
P.O. Box 1305
171 25 Solna   Tél. (08) 705.97.50
         Téléfax : (08) 27.00.71

SWITZERLAND – SUISSE
Maditec S.A. (Books and Periodicals - Livres
et périodiques)
Chemin des Palettes 4
Case postale 2066
1020 Renens 1   Tel. (021) 635.08.65
         Telefax: (021) 635.07.80

Librairie Payot S.A.
4, place Pépinet
1003 Lausanne   Tel. (021) 341.33.48
         Telefax: (021) 341.33.45

Librairie Unilivres
6, rue de Candolle
1205 Genève   Tel. (022) 320.26.23
         Telefax: (022) 329.73.18

Subscription Agency - Agence d'abonnement
Dynapresse Marketing S.A.
38 avenue Vibert
1227 Carouge   Tel.: (022) 308.07.89
        Telefax : (022) 308.07.99

See also – Voir aussi :
OECD Publications and Information Centre
August-Bebel-Allee 6
D-W 5300 Bonn 2 (Germany) Tel. (0228) 959.120
        Telefax: (0228) 959.12.17

TAIWAN – FORMOSE
Good Faith Worldwide Int'l. Co. Ltd.
9th Floor, No. 118, Sec. 2
Chung Hsiao E. Road
Taipei   Tel. (02) 391.7396/391.7397
        Telefax: (02) 394.9176

THAILAND – THAÏLANDE
Suksit Siam Co. Ltd.
113, 115 Fuang Nakhon Rd.
Opp. Wat Rajbopith
Bangkok 10200   Tel. (662) 251.1630
        Telefax: (662) 236.7783

TURKEY – TURQUIE
Kültür Yayinlari Is-Türk Ltd. Sti.
Atatürk Bulvari No. 191/Kat 13
Kavaklidere/Ankara   Tel. 428.11.40 Ext. 2458
Dolmabahce Cad. No. 29
Besiktas/Istanbul   Tel. 260.71.88
        Telex: 43482B

UNITED KINGDOM – ROYAUME-UNI
HMSO
Gen. enquiries   Tel. (071) 873 0011
Postal orders only:
P.O. Box 276, London SW8 5DT
Personal Callers HMSO Bookshop
49 High Holborn, London WC1V 6HB
        Telefax: (071) 873 8200
Branches at: Belfast, Birmingham, Bristol, Edin-
burgh, Manchester

UNITED STATES – ÉTATS-UNIS
OECD Publications and Information Centre
2001 L Street N.W., Suite 700
Washington, D.C. 20036-4910 Tel. (202) 785.6323
        Telefax: (202) 785.0350

VENEZUELA
Libreria del Este
Avda F. Miranda 52, Aptdo. 60337
Edificio Galipán
Caracas 106   Tel. 951.1705/951.2307/951.1297
        Telegram: Libreste Caracas

Subscription to OECD periodicals may also be
placed through main subscription agencies.

Les abonnements aux publications périodiques de
l'OCDE peuvent être souscrits auprès des
principales agences d'abonnement.

Orders and inquiries from countries where Distribu-
tors have not yet been appointed should be sent to:
OECD Publications Service, 2 rue André-Pascal,
75775 Paris Cedex 16, France.

Les commandes provenant de pays où l'OCDE n'a
pas encore désigné de distributeur devraient être
adressées à : OCDE, Service des Publications,
2, rue André-Pascal, 75775 Paris Cedex 16, France.

02-1993

OECD PUBLICATIONS, 2 rue André-Pascal, 75775 PARIS CEDEX 16
PRINTED IN FRANCE
(78 93 01 1) ISBN 92-64-13829-3 - No. 46427 1993
ISSN 0256-7598